Under the Banner of Heaven

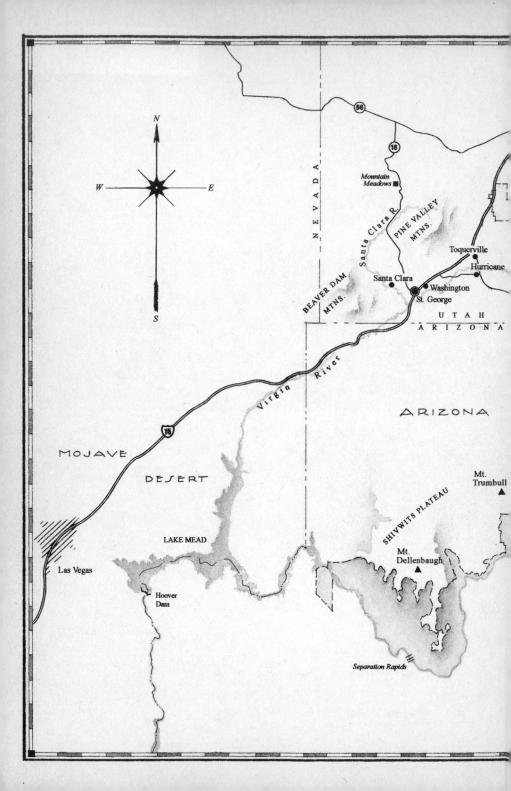

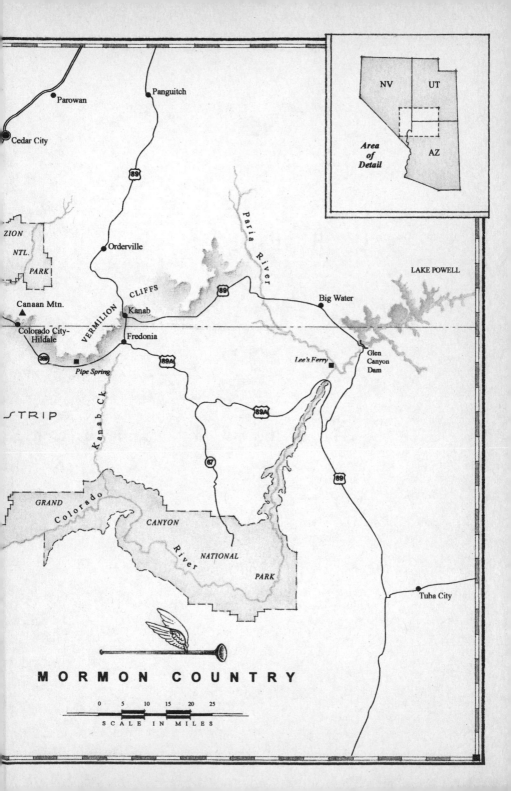

NV   UT

*Area
of
Detail*

AZ

Parowan

Panguitch

Cedar City

89

ZION

NTL.

PARK

Orderville

Paria River

LAKE POWELL

Canaan Mtn.

VERMILION   CLIFFS

Kanab

89

Big Water

Colorado City-
Hildale

Fredonia

Pipe Spring

89B

89A

Kanab Ck.

Lee's Ferry

Glen
Canyon
Dam

STRIP

89A

Colorado

GRAND

67

CANYON

River

NATIONAL

89

PARK

Tuba City

MORMON COUNTRY

0   5   10   15   20   25

S C A L E   I N   M I L E S

Under the

JON KRAKAUER

DOUBLEDAY

Banner of Heaven

A STORY OF VIOLENT FAITH

NEW YORK   LONDON   TORONTO   SYDNEY   AUCKLAND

PUBLISHED BY DOUBLEDAY
a division of Random House, Inc.

DOUBLEDAY and the portrayal of an anchor with a
dolphin are registered trademarks of Random House, Inc.

Book design by Caroline Cunningham
Endpaper map by Katsura & Co.
Interior maps by Jeffrey L. Ward

Library of Congress Cataloging-in-Publication Data

Krakauer, Jon.
Under the banner of heaven : a story of violent faith / Jon Krakauer.—1st ed.
p.   cm.
Includes bibliographical references and index.
1. Mormon fundamentalism.   I. Title.

BX8680.M54K73 2003
289.3'3—dc21
2003043824

ISBN 0-385-50951-0

Grateful acknowledgment is made to the following for
permission to reprint previously published material:

KENNETH ANDERSON: Excerpts from the articles "The Magic of the Great Salt Lake" by
Kenneth Anderson, published in the *Times Literary Supplement,* March 24, 1995; and "A Pecu-
liar People: The Mystical and Pragmatic Appeal of Mormonism" by Kenneth Anderson, pub-
lished in the *Los Angeles Times,* November 28, 1999. Reprinted by permission of Kenneth
Anderson.
BRANT & HOCHMAN LITERARY AGENTS, INC.: Excerpts from *Mormon Country* by
Wallace Stegner (New York: Penguin, 1992). Copyright © 1942, 1970 by Wallace Stegner.
Reprinted by permission of Brant & Hochman Literary Agents, Inc.
THE FREE PRESS: Excerpts from *Feet of Clay: Saints, Sinners, and Madmen: A Study of Gurus*
by Anthony Storr. Reprinted with the permission of The Free Press, a division of Simon &
Schuster. Copyright © 1996 by Anthony Storr.

copyright information continued on page 359

PRINTED IN THE UNITED STATES OF AMERICA

October 2003
First Edition
1 2 3 4 5 6 7 8 9 10

For Linda

We believe in honesty, morality, and purity; but when they enact tyrannical laws, forbidding us the free exercise of our religion, we cannot submit. God is greater than the United States, and when the Government conflicts with heaven, we will be ranged under the banner of heaven and against the Government.... Polygamy is a divine institution. It has been handed down direct from God. The United States cannot abolish it. No nation on earth can prevent it, nor all the nations of the earth combined, . . . I defy the United States; I will obey God.

JOHN TAYLOR (ON JANUARY 4, 1880),
PRESIDENT, PROPHET, SEER, AND REVELATOR,
CHURCH OF JESUS CHRIST OF LATTER-DAY SAINTS

No Western nation is as religion-soaked as ours, where nine out of ten of us love God and are loved by him in return. That mutual passion centers our society and demands some understanding, if our doom-eager society is to be understood at all.

HAROLD BLOOM,
THE AMERICAN RELIGION

Almost everyone in Utah County has heard of the Lafferty boys. That's mostly a function of the lurid murders, of course, but the Lafferty surname had a certain prominence in the county even before Brenda and Erica Lafferty were killed. Watson Lafferty, the patriarch of the clan, was a chiropractor who ran a thriving practice out of his home in downtown Provo's historic quarter. He and his wife, Claudine, had six boys and two girls, in whom they instilled an unusually strong work ethic and intense devotion to the Mormon Church. The entire family was admired for its industriousness and probity.

Allen—the youngest of the Lafferty children, now in his midforties—works as a tile setter, a trade he has plied since he was a teenager. In the summer of 1984 he was living with his twenty-four-year-old wife and baby daughter in American Fork, a sleepy, white-bread suburb alongside the freeway that runs from Provo to Salt Lake City. Brenda, his spouse, was a onetime beauty queen recognized around town from her tenure as the anchor of a newsmagazine program on channel 11, the local PBS affiliate. Although she had abandoned her nascent broadcasting career to marry Allen and start a family, Brenda had lost none of the exuberance that had endeared her to television viewers. Warm and outgoing, she'd made a lasting impression.

On the morning of July 24, 1984, Allen left their small duplex

apartment before the sun was up and drove eighty miles up the interstate to work at a construction site east of Ogden. During his lunch
break he phoned Brenda, who chatted with him for a minute before putting their fifteen-month-old daughter, Erica, on the line. Erica gurgled
a few words of baby talk; then Brenda told her husband everything was
fine and said good-bye.

Allen arrived home around eight that evening, tired from the long
workday. He walked up to the front door and was surprised to find it
locked; they almost never locked their doors. He used his key to enter,
and then was surprised again by the baseball game blaring from the television in the living room. Neither he nor Brenda liked baseball—they
never watched it. After he'd turned off the TV, the apartment seemed
preternaturally quiet to him, as though nobody was home. Allen figured
Brenda had taken the baby and gone out. "I turned to go and see if
maybe she was at the neighbors'," he explained later, "and I noticed
some blood near the door on a light switch." And then he saw Brenda in
the kitchen, sprawled on the floor in a lake of blood.

Upon calling Brenda's name and getting no reply, he knelt beside
her and put his hand on her shoulder. "I touched her," he said, "and her
body felt cool. . . . There was blood on her face and pretty much everywhere." Allen reached for the kitchen phone, which was resting on the
floor next to his wife, and dialed 911 before he realized there was no dial
tone. The cord had been yanked from the wall. As he walked to their
bedroom to try the extension in there, he glanced into the baby's room
and saw Erica slumped over in her crib in an odd position, motionless.
She was wearing nothing but a diaper, which was soaked with blood, as
were the blankets surrounding her.

Allen hurried to the master bedroom only to find the phone in there
out of order, as well, so he went next door to a neighbor's apartment,
where he was finally able to call for help. He described the carnage to the
911 dispatcher, then called his mother.

While he waited for the police to show up, Allen returned to his
apartment. "I went to Brenda and I prayed," he said. "And then as I
stood, I surveyed the situation a little more, and realized that there had
been a grim struggle." For the first time he noticed that the blood wasn't

confined to the kitchen: it smeared the living room walls, the floor, the doors, the curtains. It was obvious to him who was responsible. He'd known the moment he'd first seen Brenda on the kitchen floor.

The cops took Allen down to the American Fork police station and grilled him throughout the night. They assumed he was the murderer; the husband usually is. By and by, however, Allen convinced them that the prime suspect was actually the oldest of his five brothers, Ron Lafferty. Ron had just returned to Utah County after spending most of the previous three months traveling around the West with another Lafferty brother, Dan. An APB went out for Ron's car, a pale green 1974 Impala station wagon with Utah plates.

The slayings appeared to be ritualistic, which drew uncommon attention from the news media and put the public on edge. By the next evening the Lafferty killings led news broadcasts across the state. On Thursday, July 26, a headline on the front page of the *Salt Lake Tribune* announced,

WIDESPREAD SEARCH UNDER WAY
FOR AMERICAN FORK MURDER SUSPECT
By Mike Gorrell, Tribune Staff Writer
And Ann Shields, Tribune Correspondent

AMERICAN FORK—Lawmen in Utah and surrounding states searched Wednesday for a former Highland, Utah County, city councilman and religious fundamentalist charged with the Tuesday murders of his sister-in-law and her 15-month-old baby.

Ronald Watson Lafferty, 42, no address available, was charged with two counts of capital homicide in the deaths of Brenda Wright Lafferty, 24, and her daughter, Erica Lane. . . .

American Fork police have not established a motive for the killings and have refused to comment on rumors that the suspect, an excommunicated member of the Church of Jesus Christ of Latter-day Saints, was involved with either polygamist or fundamentalist religious sects and that those ties may have contributed to the killings. . . .

Neighbors expressed disbelief that "this sort of thing" could happen in their area.

"The whole town's in shock that such a thing could happen in a nice quiet community like American Fork. People who said they had never locked their doors said they were going to now," said one neighbor who asked not to be identified.

Ken Beck, a bishop in the American Fork LDS ward which Allen and Brenda Lafferty attended, said they were "a nice ordinary couple," active in church affairs.

Immediately below this story, also on the front page, was an accompanying piece:

NEIGHBORS RECALL CHANGES IN MURDER SUSPECT, 42
Special to The Tribune

AMERICAN FORK—A determined man who evolved from an active Mormon and conservative Republican to a strict constitutionalist and excommunicated fundamentalist is how neighbors remember Ronald Watson Lafferty. . . .

Mr. Lafferty served on Highland's first City Council when the small northern Utah County town was incorporated in 1977. At the time, Mr. Lafferty successfully led a drive to outlaw beer sales in the town's only grocery store—where travelers to American Fork Canyon still can't buy beer.

"Two years ago, he looked clean, all-American, even in the mornings after milking the family cow," said a neighbor who resides in an acre-lot subdivision filled with children, horses, goats, chickens and large garden plots where Mr. Lafferty once lived.

Last year he and his wife of several years divorced. Mr. Lafferty has not been seen in the neighborhood for a year.

Shortly after Christmas, Mrs. Diana Lafferty, described as "a pillar of the Mormon ward," took the couple's six children out of state.

Neighbors said the divorce stemmed from differences of opinion on religion and politics.

"He talked about standing up for what was right—no matter the consequences," said a neighbor.

Friends said Mr. Lafferty's political beliefs changed as well—or perhaps evolved—from conservative Republican to strict fundamentalism. During the 12 years he lived in Highland, he came to believe in a return to the gold standard, strict constitutionalism and obedience only to "righteous laws," said a neighbor.

"He had a fervent desire to save the Constitution—and the country," said a long-time friend. "It became a religious obsession."

Detectives interviewed as many of Allen's siblings as they could locate, as well as his mother and various friends. As the front page of Saturday's *Tribune* revealed, the cops were beginning to piece together a motive for the brutal acts:

TWO MURDERS A RELIGIOUS REVELATION?
3 CHARGED IN SLASHING OF MOTHER AND INFANT
By Ann Shields
Tribune Correspondent

AMERICAN FORK—Two more men Friday were charged with first-degree murder in connection with the July 24 slaying of an American Fork woman and her 15-month-old daughter as police disclosed that the killings may have been part of a religious "revelation."

Charged Friday with capital homicide were Dan Lafferty, age unavailable, Salem, a former candidate for Utah County sheriff and the victim's brother-in-law, and Richard M. Knapp, 24, formerly of Wichita, Kan.

Dan Lafferty's brother, Ronald Lafferty, 42, Highland, Utah County, was charged Wednesday with two counts of first-degree murder. . . .

Police Chief Randy Johnson . . . revealed Friday that the investigation into the murders has caused police to believe ". . . that Ron had a handwritten revelation which told him to commit this crime. If this document does exist it is a vital piece of evidence and we would like to see it." He asked anyone with information regarding the document to contact the American Fork Police Department or the FBI. . . .

Chief Johnson said the men are believed to be armed and should be considered dangerous, particularly to law enforcement officials. . . .

Neighbors and friends of the suspects and victims noted that Ron Lafferty apparently was affiliated or had founded a polygamist or fundamentalist religious sect, causing speculation that the crimes may have resulted from a religious argument in the family.

On July 30, Ron's run-down Impala was spotted parked in front of a house in Cheyenne, Wyoming. When they raided the home, police didn't find the Lafferty brothers, but they did arrest Richard "Ricky" Knapp and Chip Carnes, two drifters who had been traveling around the West with the Laffertys since early summer. Information provided by Knapp and Carnes led authorities to Reno, Nevada, where, on August 7, the police arrested Ron and Dan as they stood in line for the buffet at the Circus Circus casino.

From jail, before their trial, the brothers launched an unpersuasive media campaign protesting their innocence. Ron insisted that the charges against them were false and that the Mormon Church, which "controlled everything in Utah," would prevent his brother and him from receiving a fair trial. Although he confessed to believing in the righteousness of "plural marriage," Ron said he had never practiced polygamy or belonged to an extremist sect. He then professed to love the Mormon Church, while at the same time warning that the current LDS leadership had strayed from the sacred doctrines of the religion's founding prophet, Joseph Smith.

Four days later Dan Lafferty issued a written statement to the media in which he declared that he and Ron were "not guilty of any of the crimes for which we have been accused," adding that "the time is at hand when the true criminals will be made known."

On December 29, five days before their trial was scheduled to begin in Provo, Lieutenant Jerry Scott, the commander of the Utah County Jail, took Dan from his cell to ask him some questions. When Dan returned, he found his older brother suspended by his neck from a towel rack in an adjacent cell, unconscious and no longer breathing; Ron had used a T-shirt to hang himself. "I pushed the intercom button and told them they better get down there," Dan says. Lieutenant Scott arrived immediately but could detect no pulse in Ron. Although Scott and two other deputies administered mouth-to-mouth resuscitation and CPR, they were unable to revive him. By the time paramedics showed up, said Scott, the inmate "appeared dead."

Despite the fact that Ron had stopped breathing for an estimated fifteen minutes, the paramedics eventually managed to get his heart beating again, and he was placed on a respirator in the intensive care unit of the Utah Valley Regional Medical Center. After remaining comatose for two days, he regained consciousness—an astonishing recovery that Dan attributes to divine intervention. Although the brothers were slated to be tried together three days after Ron emerged from his coma, Judge J. Robert Bullock ordered that Dan should be tried alone, as scheduled, allowing Ron time to recover and undergo extensive psychiatric evaluation to determine if he'd suffered brain damage.

The court appointed two attorneys to represent Dan, but he insisted on defending himself, relegating them to advisory roles. Five days after the trial began, the jury went into deliberation, and nine hours later found Dan guilty of two counts of first-degree murder. During the subsequent session to determine whether Dan should be put to death for his crimes, Dan assured the jurors, "If I was in your situation, I would impose the death penalty," and promised not to appeal if they arrived at such a sentence.

"The judge freaked out when I said that," Dan later explained. "He thought I was expressing a death wish, and warned the jury that they couldn't vote to execute me just because I had a death wish. But I just wanted them to feel free to follow their conscience. I didn't want them to worry or feel guilty about giving me a death sentence, if that's what they thought I deserved. I was willing to take a life for God, so it seemed to me that I should also be willing to give my own life for God. If God wanted me to be executed, I was fine with that."

Ten jurors voted for death, but two others refused to go along with the majority. Because unanimity was required to impose a capital sentence, Dan's life was spared. According to the jury foreman, one of the jurors who balked at executing Dan was a woman whom he had manipulated through "eye-contact, smiles, and other charismatic, non verbal attachments and psycho-sexual seduction," causing her to ignore both the evidence and the instructions provided by the judge. The foreman, aghast that Dan had thereby avoided a death sentence, was furious.

Dan says that he, too, "was a little disappointed that I wasn't executed, in a strange sense."

Addressing the convicted prisoner with undisguised scorn, Judge Bullock reminded Dan that it was "man's law, which you disdain, that saved your life." Then, his disgust getting the better of him, he added, "In my twelve years as a judge, I have never presided over a trial of such a cruel, heinous, pointless and senseless a crime as the murders of Brenda and Erica Lafferty. Nor have I seen an accused who had so little remorse or feeling." This admonishment came from the same hardened judge who, in 1976, had presided over the notorious, history-making trial of Gary Mark Gilmore for the unprovoked murders of two young Mormons.* After telling the 1985 court that the jury had been unable to agree on a sentence of death, Judge Bullock turned to Dan and said, "I mean to see that every minute of [your] life is spent behind the bars of the Utah State Prison and I so order." He sentenced Dan to two life terms.

Ron's trial began almost four months later, in April 1985, after a battery of psychiatrists and psychologists had determined that he was mentally competent. His court-appointed attorneys hoped to get the murder charges reduced to manslaughter by arguing that Ron was suffering from mental illness when he and Dan murdered Brenda Lafferty and her baby, but Ron refused to allow them to mount such a defense.

---

* The first convict to be executed in the United States in more than a decade, Gary Gilmore came to symbolize America's renewed embracing of capital punishment in the 1970s. His story has been memorably told by his brother, Mikal Gilmore, in *Shot in the Heart,* and by Norman Mailer in his Pulitzer Prize–winning work *The Executioner's Song.* The Gilmore and Lafferty trials happened to share a number of protagonists in addition to Judge J. Robert Bullock: one of Gary Gilmore's court-appointed lawyers was Mike Esplin, who was later assigned to represent Ron and Dan Lafferty in their murder trials. And Utah County Attorney Noall T. Wootton prosecuted Gilmore as well as both Lafferty brothers.

"It seems it would be an admission of guilt," he told Judge Bullock. "I'm not prepared to do that."

Ron was convicted of first-degree murder, and on this occasion the jury did not balk at imposing capital punishment. They sentenced him to die, either by lethal injection or four bullets through the heart at close range. Ron chose the latter.

On January 15, 1985, immediately after Judge Bullock decreed that the remainder of Dan Lafferty's life would unfold in captivity, he was taken to the state prison at Point of the Mountain, near Draper, Utah, where a corrections officer cut his hair and sheared off his whiskers. That was nearly seventeen years ago, and Dan hasn't shaved or cut his hair since. His beard, wrapped with rubber bands into a stiff gray cable, now descends to his belly. His hair has gone white and fans across the back of his orange prison jumpsuit. Although he is fifty-four years old and crow's-feet furrow the corners of his eyes, there is something unmistakably boyish about his countenance. His skin is so pale it seems translucent.

A crude tattoo of a spider web radiates from Dan's left elbow, wrapping the crook of his arm in a jagged indigo lattice. His wrists are bound in handcuffs, and his shackled ankles are chained to a steel ring embedded in the concrete floor. On his otherwise bare feet are cheap rubber flip-flops. A large man, he cheerfully refers to the prison's maximum-security unit as "my monastery."

Every morning a wake-up alarm echoes through the halls of the unit at 6:30, followed by a head count. The door to his cell remains locked twenty hours a day. Even when it isn't locked, Dan says, "I'm almost always in my cell. The only time I leave is to shower or serve food—I have a job serving meals. But I don't really associate with people that much. I try not to leave my cell more often than I absolutely have to. There are so many assholes in here. They get you caught up in their little dramas, and you end up having to fuck somebody up. And the next thing you know your privileges are taken away. I've got too much to lose. I'm in a really comfortable situation right now. I've got a really good cellie, and I don't want to lose him."

That "cellie," or cell mate, is Mark Hofmann, a once-devout Mormon who lost his faith while serving as a missionary in England and secretly became an atheist, although he continued to present himself as an exemplary Latter-day Saint when he returned to Utah. Soon thereafter, Hofmann discovered that he had a special talent for forgery. He began to churn out bogus historical documents, brilliantly rendered, which fetched large sums from collectors. In October 1985, upon concluding that investigators were about to discover that several old Mormon documents he'd sold were fakes, he detonated a series of pipe bombs to divert detectives from his trail, killing two guiltless fellow Saints in the process.* Many of Hofmann's forgeries were intended to discredit Joseph Smith and the sacred history of Mormonism; more than four hundred of these fraudulent artifacts were purchased by the LDS Church (which believed they were authentic), then squirreled away in a vault to keep them from the public eye.

Although Hofmann now expresses contempt for religion in general and Mormonism in particular, his atheism doesn't seem to be an issue in his friendship with Dan Lafferty—despite the fact that Dan remains, by his own proud characterization, a religious zealot. "My beliefs are irrelevant to my cellie," Dan confirms. "We're special brothers all the same. We're bound by the heart."

Prior to Dan's conviction, and for more than a decade afterward, he steadfastly maintained that he was innocent of the murders of Brenda and Erica Lafferty. When he was arrested in Reno in August 1984, he told the arresting officers, "You think I have committed a crime of homicide, but I have not." He still insists that he is innocent of any crime but, paradoxically, does not deny that he killed Brenda and Erica. When asked to explain how both these apparently contradictory statements can be true, he says, "I was doing God's will, which is not a crime."

Lafferty isn't reticent about describing exactly what happened on July 24, 1984. He says that shortly after noon, he, Ron, and the two drifters who had been traveling with them, Ricky Knapp and Chip Carnes, drove to the apartment of his youngest brother, Allen, in Amer-

---

* Mark Hofmann's criminal activities have been deftly recounted in *A Gathering of Saints,* by Robert Lindsey, and *Salamander,* by Linda Sillitoe and Allen Roberts.

ican Fork, twenty minutes down the interstate from where he is now imprisoned. Inside the brick duplex he found his fifteen-month-old niece, Erica, standing in her crib, smiling up at him. "I spoke to her for a minute," Lafferty recalls. "I told her, 'I'm not sure what this is all about, but apparently it's God's will that you leave this world; perhaps we can talk about it later.' " And then he ended her life with a ten-inch boning knife.

After dispatching Erica, he calmly walked into the kitchen and used the same knife to kill the baby's mother. Now, seventeen years after committing these two murders, he insists, very convincingly, that he has never felt any regret for the deed, or shame.

Like his older brother, Ron, Dan Lafferty was brought up as a pious Mormon. "I've always been interested in God and the Kingdom of God," he says. "It's been the center of my focus since I was a young child." And he is certain God intended for him to kill Brenda and Erica Lafferty: "It was like someone had taken me by the hand that day and led me comfortably through everything that happened. Ron had received a revelation from God that these lives were to be taken. I was the one who was supposed to do it. And if God wants something to be done, it will be done. You don't want to offend Him by refusing to do His work."

These murders are shocking for a host of reasons, but no aspect of the crimes is more disturbing than Lafferty's complete and determined absence of remorse. How could an apparently sane, avowedly pious man kill a blameless woman and her baby so viciously, without the barest flicker of emotion? Whence did he derive the moral justification? What filled him with such certitude? Any attempt to answer such questions must plumb those murky sectors of the heart and head that prompt most of us to believe in God—and compel an impassioned few, predictably, to carry that irrational belief to its logical end.

There is a dark side to religious devotion that is too often ignored or denied. As a means of motivating people to be cruel or inhumane—as a means of inciting evil, to borrow the vocabulary of the devout—there may be no more potent force than religion. When the subject of religiously inspired bloodshed comes up, many Americans immediately think of Islamic fundamentalism, which is to be expected in the wake of the September 11 attacks on New York and Washington. But men have been committing heinous acts in the name of God ever since mankind began believing in deities, and extremists exist within all religions. Muhammad is not the only prophet whose words have been used to sanction barbarism; history has not lacked for Christians, Jews, Hindus, Sikhs, and even Buddhists who have been motivated by scripture to butcher innocents. Plenty of these religious extremists have been home-grown, corn-fed Americans.

Faith-based violence was present long before Osama bin Laden, and it will be with us long after his demise. Religious zealots like bin Laden, David Koresh, Jim Jones, Shoko Asahara,* and Dan Lafferty are common to every age, just as zealots of other stripes are. In any human endeavor, some fraction of its practitioners will be motivated to pursue that activity with such concentrated focus and unalloyed passion that it will consume them utterly. One has to look no further than individuals who feel compelled to devote their lives to becoming concert pianists, say, or climbing Mount Everest. For some, the province of the extreme holds an allure that's irresistible. And a certain percentage of such fanatics will inevitably fixate on matters of the spirit.

The zealot may be outwardly motivated by the anticipation of a great reward at the other end—wealth, fame, eternal salvation—but the real recompense is probably the obsession itself. This is no less true for the religious fanatic than for the fanatical pianist or fanatical mountain climber. As a result of his (or her) infatuation, existence overflows with purpose. Ambiguity vanishes from the fanatic's worldview; a narcissistic sense of self-assurance displaces all doubt. A delicious rage quickens his pulse, fueled by the sins and shortcomings of lesser mortals, who are

---

* Asahara is the charismatic "Holy Pope" and "Venerated Master" of Aum Shinrikyo, the Japanese sect that carried out a deadly 1995 attack in the Tokyo subways using sarin nerve gas. The theological tenets of Aum Shinrikyo (which means "Supreme Truth") are drawn from Buddhism, Christianity, and Hinduism. At the time of the subway attack, the sect's worldwide membership was estimated to be as high as forty thousand, although it has now dropped to perhaps one thousand. According to terrorism expert Kyle B. Olson, Asahara's followers can still "be seen in Aum-owned houses wearing bizarre electric headsets, supposedly designed to synchronize their brain waves with the cult's leader," who is currently incarcerated in Japan.

soiling the world wherever he looks. His perspective narrows until the last remnants of proportion are shed from his life. Through immoderation, he experiences something akin to rapture.

Although the far territory of the extreme can exert an intoxicating pull on susceptible individuals of all bents, extremism seems to be especially prevalent among those inclined by temperament or upbringing toward religious pursuits. Faith is the very antithesis of reason, injudiciousness a crucial component of spiritual devotion. And when religious fanaticism supplants ratiocination, all bets are suddenly off. Anything can happen. Absolutely anything. Common sense is no match for the voice of God—as the actions of Dan Lafferty vividly attest.

It is the aim of this book to cast some light on Lafferty and his ilk. If trying to understand such people is a daunting exercise, it also seems a useful one—for what it may tell us about the roots of brutality, perhaps, but even more for what might be learned about the nature of faith.

© 2003 Jeffrey L. Ward

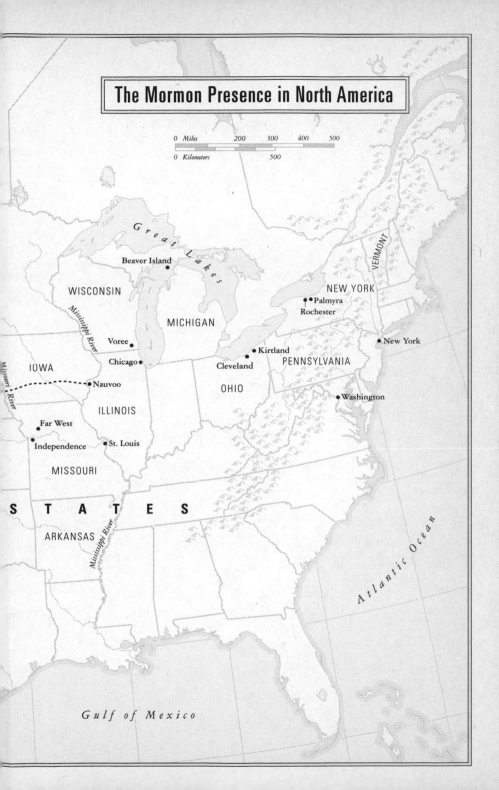

The Mormon Presence in North America

0 Miles   200   300   400   500

0 Kilometers   500

Great Lakes

Beaver Island

WISCONSIN

NEW YORK

VERMONT

Palmyra
Rochester

MICHIGAN

Mississippi River

Voree

New York

Chicago

Kirtland

IOWA

Cleveland

PENNSYLVANIA

Missouri River

Nauvoo

OHIO

Washington

ILLINOIS

Far West

Independence

St. Louis

MISSOURI

S T A T E S

ARKANSAS

Mississippi River

Atlantic Ocean

Gulf of Mexico

PART I

The schisms that shattered Mormonism time and again, more critical than inroads from without, only attest its strength. They were signs of the seriousness with which converts and dissenters took their salvation, ready to stake their souls on points of doctrine which a later, less Biblical generation could treat with indifference.

WILLIAM MULDER AND A. RUSSELL MORTENSEN,
AMONG THE MORMONS

ONE

THE CITY OF THE SAINTS

For thou art an holy people unto the Lord thy God, and the Lord hath chosen thee to be a peculiar people unto himself, above all the nations that are upon the earth.

DEUTERONOMY 14:2

And it shall come to pass that I, the Lord God, will send one mighty and strong, holding the scepter of power in his hand, clothed with light for a covering, whose mouth shall utter words, eternal words; while his bowels shall be a fountain of truth, to set in order the house of God.

THE DOCTRINE AND COVENANTS, SECTION 85
REVEALED TO JOSEPH SMITH ON NOVEMBER 27, 1832

Balanced atop the highest spire of the Salt Lake Temple, gleaming in the Utah sun, a statue of the angel Moroni stands watch over downtown Salt Lake City with his golden trumpet raised. This massive granite edifice is the spiritual and temporal nexus of the Church of Jesus Christ of Latter-day Saints (LDS), which presents itself as the world's only true religion. Temple Square is to Mormons what the Vatican is to Catholics, or the Kaaba in Mecca is to Muslims. At last count there were more than eleven million Saints the world over, and Mormonism is the fastest-growing faith in the Western Hemisphere. At present in the United States there are more Mormons than Presbyterians or Episcopalians. On the planet as a whole, there are now more Mormons than Jews. Mormonism is considered in some sober academic circles to be well on its way to becoming a major world religion—the first such faith to emerge since Islam.

Next door to the temple, the 325 voices of the Mormon Tabernacle Choir swell to fill the tabernacle's vast interior with the robust, haunting chords of "Battle Hymn of the Republic," the ensemble's trademark song: "Mine eyes have seen the glory of the coming of the Lord . . ."

To much of the world, this choir and its impeccably rendered harmonies are emblematic of the Mormons as a people: chaste, optimistic, outgoing, dutiful. When Dan Lafferty quotes Mormon scripture to justify murder, the juxtaposition is so incongruous as to seem surreal.

The affairs of Mormondom are directed by a cadre of elderly white males in dark suits who carry out their holy duties from a twenty-six-story office tower beside Temple Square.* To a man, the LDS leadership adamantly insists that Lafferty should under no circumstances be considered a Mormon. The faith that moved Lafferty to slay his niece and sister-in-law is a brand of religion known as Mormon Fundamentalism; LDS Church authorities bristle visibly when Mormons and Mormon Fundamentalists are even mentioned in the same breath. As Gordon B. Hinckley, the then-eighty-eight-year-old LDS president and prophet, emphasized during a 1998 television interview on *Larry King Live,* "They have no connection with us whatever. They don't belong to the church. There are actually no *Mormon* Fundamentalists."

---

* Control of the LDS Church resides in the hands of fifteen men. At the top of the hierarchical pyramid is the "President, Prophet, Seer, and Revelator," who is believed to be God's direct mouthpiece on earth. The LDS president appoints two trusted apostles to serve as his first counselor and second counselor; collectively these three men function as the First Presidency. Immediately below the First Presidency is the Quorum of the Twelve Apostles, and, together, these fifteen men (they are always men; women are excluded from positions of authority in the Mormon Church) hold sway over the institution and its membership with absolute power. All fifteen men serve for life. At the time of the president's death, the Quorum of the Twelve appoints as new president the apostle from their ranks who has served the longest; hence the exceedingly advanced age of most Mormon presidents.

Nevertheless, Mormons and those who call themselves Mormon Fundamentalists (or FLDS) believe in the same holy texts and the same sacred history. Both believe that Joseph Smith, who founded Mormonism in 1830, played a vital role in God's plan for mankind; both LDS and FLDS consider him to be a prophet comparable in stature to Moses and Isaiah. Mormons and Mormon Fundamentalists are each convinced that God regards them, and them alone, as his favored children: "a peculiar treasure unto me above all people." But if both proudly refer to themselves as the Lord's chosen, they diverge on one especially inflammatory point of religious doctrine: unlike their present-day Mormon compatriots, Mormon Fundamentalists passionately believe that Saints have a divine obligation to take multiple wives. Followers of the FLDS faith engage in polygamy, they explain, as a matter of religious duty.

There are more than thirty thousand FLDS polygamists living in Canada, Mexico, and throughout the American West. Some experts estimate there may be as many as one hundred thousand. Even this larger number amounts to less than 1 percent of the membership in the LDS Church worldwide, but all the same, leaders of the mainstream church are extremely discomfited by these legions of polygamous brethren. Mormon authorities treat the fundamentalists as they would a crazy uncle—they try to keep the "polygs" hidden in the attic, safely out of sight, but the fundamentalists always seem to be sneaking out to appear in public at inopportune moments to create unsavory scenes, embarrassing the entire LDS clan.

The LDS Church happens to be exceedingly prickly about its short, uncommonly rich history—and no aspect of that history makes the church more defensive than "plural marriage." The LDS leadership has worked very hard to persuade both the modern church membership and the American public that polygamy was a quaint, long-abandoned idiosyncrasy practiced by a mere handful of nineteenth-century Mormons. The religious literature handed out by the earnest young missionaries in Temple Square makes no mention of the fact that Joseph Smith—still the religion's focal personage—married at least thirty-three women, and probably as many as forty-eight. Nor does it mention that the youngest of these wives was just fourteen years old when Joseph explained to her that God had commanded that she marry him or face eternal damnation.

Polygamy was, in fact, one of the most sacred credos of Joseph's church—a tenet important enough to be canonized for the ages as Section 132 of *The Doctrine and Covenants,* one of Mormonism's primary scriptural texts.* The revered prophet described plural marriage as part of "the most holy and important doctrine ever revealed to man on earth" and taught that a man needed at least three wives to attain the "fullness of exaltation" in the afterlife. He warned that God had explicitly commanded that "all those who have this law revealed unto them must obey the same . . . and if ye abide not that covenant, then are ye damned; for no one can reject this covenant and be permitted to enter into my glory."

Joseph was murdered in Illinois by a mob of Mormon haters in 1844. Brigham Young assumed leadership of the church and led the Saints to the barren wilds of the Great Basin, where in short order they established a remarkable empire and unabashedly embraced the covenant of "spiritual wifery." This both titillated and shocked the sensibilities of Victorian-era Americans, who tended to regard polygamy as a brutish practice on a par with slavery.† In 1856, recognizing the strength of the anti-polygamy vote, Republican candidate John C. Frémont ran for president on a platform that pledged to "prohibit in the territories those twin relics of barbarism—Polygamy and Slavery." Frémont lost the election, but a year later the man who did win, President James Buchanan, sent the U.S. Army to invade Utah, dismantle Brigham Young's theocracy, and eradicate polygamy.

The so-called Utah War, however, neither removed Brigham from power nor ended the doctrine of plural marriage, to the annoyance and bafflement of a whole series of American presidents. An escalating sequence of judicial and legislative challenges to polygamy ensued, culmi-

---

* Mormons esteem three books of scripture above all others: *The Book of Mormon, The Doctrine and Covenants* (often referred to simply as *D & C*), and *The Pearl of Great Price.*

† It's likely that in the nineteenth century, polygamy was actually abhorrent to many more Americans than slavery was. The latter, after all, had a multitude of proponents in numerous states, whereas it was hard to find many advocates for the former outside Utah Territory.

nating in the Edmunds-Tucker Act of 1887, which disincorporated the LDS Church and forfeited to the federal government all church property worth more than $50,000. With their feet held fast to the fire, the Saints ultimately had no choice but to renounce polygamy. But even as LDS leaders publicly claimed, in 1890, to have relinquished the practice, they quietly dispatched bands of Mormons to establish polygamous colonies in Mexico and Canada, and some of the highest-ranking LDS authorities secretly continued to take multiple wives and perform plural marriages well into the twentieth century.

Although LDS leaders were initially loath to abandon plural marriage, eventually they adopted a more pragmatic approach to American politics, emphatically rejected the practice, and actually began urging government agencies to prosecute polygamists. It was this single change in ecclesiastical policy, more than anything else, that transformed the LDS Church into its astonishingly successful present-day iteration. Having jettisoned polygamy, Mormons gradually ceased to be regarded as a crackpot sect. The LDS Church acquired the trappings of a conventional faith so successfully that it is now widely considered to be the quintessential American religion.

Mormon Fundamentalists, however, believe that acceptance into the American mainstream came at way too high a price. They contend that the Mormon leaders made an unforgivable compromise by capitulating to the U.S. government on polygamy over a century ago. They insist that the church sold them out—that the LDS leadership abandoned one of the religion's most crucial theological tenets for the sake of political expediency. These present-day polygamists therefore consider themselves to be the keepers of the flame—the only true and righteous Mormons. In forsaking Section 132—the sacred principle of plural marriage—the LDS Church has gone badly astray, they warn. Fundamentalist prophets bellow from their pulpits that the modern church has become "the wickedest whore of all the earth."

Mormon Fundamentalists probably cite Section 132 of *The Doctrine and Covenants* more than any other piece of LDS scripture. Their second-most-popular citation is likely Section 85, in which it was revealed to Joseph that "I, the Lord God, will send one mighty and strong . . . to set in order the house of God." Many fundamentalists are convinced that the one mighty and strong is already here on earth among them, "holding the scepter of power in his hand," and that very soon now he will lead the Mormon Church back onto the right path and restore Joseph's "most holy and important doctrine."

T W O

SHORT CREEK

Extreme and bizarre religious ideas are so commonplace in American history that it is difficult to speak of them as fringe at all. To speak of a fringe implies a mainstream, but in terms of numbers, perhaps the largest component of the religious spectrum in contemporary America remains what it has been since colonial times: a fundamentalist evangelicalism with powerful millenarian strands. The doomsday theme has never been far from the center of American religious thought. The nation has always had believers who responded to this threat by a determination to flee from the wrath to come, to separate themselves from the City of Destruction, even if that meant putting themselves at odds with the law and with their communities or families. . . . We can throughout American history find select and separatist groups who looked to a prophetic individual claiming divine revelation, in a setting that repudiated conventional assumptions about property, family life, and sexuality. They were marginal groups, peculiar people, people set apart from the world: the Shakers and the Ephrata community, the communes of Oneida and Amana, the followers of Joseph Smith and Brigham Young.

PHILIP JENKINS,
MYSTICS AND MESSIAHS

Snaking diagonally across the top of Arizona, the Grand Canyon is a stupendous, 277-mile rent in the planet's hide that functions as a formidable natural barrier, effectively cutting off the northwestern corner from the rest of the state. This isolated wedge of backcountry—almost as big as New Jersey, yet traversed by a single paved highway—is known as the Arizona Strip, and it has one of the lowest population densities in the forty-eight conterminous states.

There is, however, one relatively large municipality here. Colorado City, home to some nine thousand souls, is more than five times as populous as any other town in the district. Motorists driving west on Highway 389 across the parched barrens of the Uinkaret Plateau are apt to be surprised when, twenty-eight miles past Fredonia (population 1,036, the second-largest town on the Strip), Colorado City suddenly materializes in the middle of nowhere: a sprawl of small businesses and unusually large homes squatting beneath a towering escarpment of vermilion sandstone called Canaan Mountain. All but a handful of the town's residents are Mormon Fundamentalists. They live in this patch of desert in the hope of being left alone to follow the sacred principle of plural marriage without interference from government authorities or the LDS Church.

Straddling the Utah-Arizona border, Colorado City is home to at least three Mormon Fundamentalist sects, including the world's largest: the Fundamentalist Church of Jesus Christ of Latter Day Saints. More commonly known as the United Effort Plan, or UEP, it requires its members live in strict accordance with the commandments of a frail, ninety-two-year-old tax accountant–turned–prophet named Rulon T. Jeffs.* "Uncle Rulon," as he is known to his followers, traces his divinely ordained leadership in an unbroken chain that leads directly back to Joseph Smith himself. Although his feeble bearing would seem to make him poorly cast for the role, the residents of Colorado City believe that

---

* The part of town lying on the Arizona side of the line is officially called Colorado City, and the portion on the Utah side is officially named Hildale, although old-timers ignore both appellations, preferring to call it Short Creek, which was the town's name until 1962, when it was legally incorporated and renamed. The United Effort Plan is the legal name of the financial trust that owns all the church's assets, including virtually all the land in town.

Uncle Rulon is the "one mighty and strong" whose coming was prophesied by Joseph in 1832.

"A lot of people here are convinced Uncle Rulon is going to live forever," says DeLoy Bateman, a forty-eight-year-old science teacher at Colorado City High School. Not only was DeLoy born and raised in this faith, but his forebears were some of the religion's most illustrious figures: his great-grandfather and great-great-grandfather were among the thirteen founding members of the Mormon Fundamentalist Church, and his adoptive grandfather, LeRoy Johnson, was the prophet who immediately preceded Uncle Rulon as the leader of Colorado City. At the moment, DeLoy is driving his thirdhand Chevy van on a dirt road on the outskirts of town. One of his two wives and eight of his seventeen children are riding in the back. Suddenly he hits the brakes, and the van lurches to a stop on the shoulder. "Now there's an interesting sight," DeLoy declares, sizing up the wreckage of a television satellite dish behind some sagebrush off the side of the road. "Looks like somebody had to get rid of their television. Hauled it out of town and dumped it."

Members of the religion, he explains, are forbidden to watch television or read magazines or newspapers. The temptations of the outside world loom large, however, and some members of the faith inevitably succumb. "As soon as you ban something," DeLoy observes, "you make it incredibly attractive. People will sneak into St. George or Cedar City and buy themselves a dish, put it up where it can't easily be seen, and secretly watch TV during every free moment. Then one Sunday Uncle Rulon will give one of his sermons about the evils of television. He'll announce that he knows *exactly* who has one, and warn that everyone who does is putting their eternal souls in serious jeopardy.

"Every time he does that, a bunch of satellite dishes immediately get dumped in the desert, like this one here. For two or three years afterward there won't be any televisions in town, but then, gradually, the dishes start secretly going up again, until the next crackdown. People try to do the right thing, but they're only human."

As the TV prohibition suggests, life in Colorado City under Rulon Jeffs bears more than a passing resemblance to life in Kabul under the Taliban. Uncle Rulon's word carries the weight of law. The mayor and every other city employee answers to him, as do the entire police force and the superintendent of public schools. Even animals are subject to his whim. Two years ago a Rottweiler killed a child in town. An edict went out that dogs would no longer be allowed within the city limits. A posse of young men was dispatched to round up all the canines, after which the unsuspecting pets were taken into a dry wash and shot.

Uncle Rulon has married an estimated seventy-five women with whom he has fathered at least sixty-five children; several of his wives were given to him in marriage when they were fourteen or fifteen and he was in his eighties. His sermons frequently stress the need for total submission. "I want to tell you that the greatest freedom you can enjoy is in obedience," he has preached. "Perfect obedience produces perfect faith." Like most FLDS prophets, his teachings rely heavily on fiery screeds penned in the nineteenth century by Joseph Smith and Brigham Young. Uncle Rulon likes to remind his followers of Brigham's warning that for those who commit such unspeakable sins as homosexuality, or having sexual intercourse with a member of the African race, "the penalty, under the law of God, is death on the spot. This will always be so."

Polygamy is illegal in both Utah and Arizona. To avoid prosecution, typically men in Colorado City will legally marry only the first of their wives; subsequent wives, although "spiritually married" to their husband by Uncle Rulon, thus remain single mothers in the eyes of the state. This has the added benefit of allowing the enormous families in town to qualify for welfare and other forms of public assistance. Despite the fact that Uncle Rulon and his followers regard the governments of Arizona, Utah, and the United States as Satanic forces out to destroy the UEP, their polygamous community receives more than $6 million a year in public funds.

More than $4 million of government largesse flows each year into the Colorado City public school district—which, according to the *Phoenix New Times,* "is operated primarily for the financial benefit of the FLDS Church and for the personal enrichment of FLDS school district leaders." Reporter John Dougherty determined that school administrators have "plundered the district's treasury by running up thousands of dollars in personal expenses on district credit cards, purchasing expensive vehicles for their personal use and engaging in extensive travel. The spending spree culminated in December [2000], when the district purchased a $220,000 Cessna 210 airplane to facilitate trips by district personnel to cities across Arizona."

Colorado City has received $1.9 million from the U.S. Department of Housing and Urban Development to pave its streets, improve the fire department, and upgrade the water system. Immediately south of the city limits, the federal government built a $2.8 million airport that serves almost no one beyond the fundamentalist community. Thirty-three percent of the town's residents receive food stamps—compared to the state average of 4.7 percent. Currently the residents of Colorado City receive eight dollars in government services for every dollar they pay in taxes; by comparison, residents in the rest of Mohave County, Arizona, receive just over a dollar in services per tax dollar paid.

"Uncle Rulon justifies all that assistance from the wicked government by explaining that really the money is coming from the Lord," says DeLoy Bateman. "We're taught that it's the Lord's way of manipulating the system to take care of his chosen people." Fundamentalists call defrauding the government "bleeding the beast" and regard it as a virtuous act.

Uncle Rulon and his followers believe that the earth is seven thousand years old and that men have never walked on the moon; film clips showing Apollo astronauts on the lunar surface are part of an elaborate hoax foisted on the world by the American government, they say. In addition to the edict against watching television or reading newspapers, residents of Colorado City are forbidden to have any contact with people outside the UEP—including family members who have left the religion. DeLoy, as it happens, is one such apostate.

DeLoy and his immense family live in a correspondingly immense house—at sixteen thousand square feet, it is more than five times as large as a typical three-bedroom home—which he built with his own hands in the middle of town. DeLoy's brother David lives in a similarly large home just a few yards away, on the other side of a six-foot fence. "My brother over the fence there," says DeLoy, gesturing with his chin, "him and I are just as close as any two people on the planet. Our father was disabled when we were small children, so David and I raised each other. But now he isn't allowed to talk to me, because I'm no longer in the religion. If his wife catches him having a conversation with me, she'll take all the children, and Uncle Rulon will marry her to some other man within hours. And David will be what the locals call a 'eunuch': a man who is allowed to remain in the religion but who has had his family taken from him—like what was supposed to happen to me when I left the Work."

DeLoy used to be a respected member of the religion. He has never touched a drop of alcohol or coffee, never smoked a cigarette, never uttered a profane word. He was unwavering in his obedience and made a point to keep his head down. Then, in 1996, relatives of his second wife began spreading scurrilous rumors about him. Somebody shared these rumors with the prophet, and the upshot, DeLoy laments, was that "Uncle Rulon called me into his office and made all kinds of accusations against me."

The prophet, DeLoy says, "was extremely angry—so angry he was actually vibrating, and spittle was flying out of his mouth as he spoke. The normal procedure when the prophet confronts you like that is to basically say, 'I'm sorry I've done this to displease thee. What would thou have me do?' But this time I couldn't bring myself to do it. I just couldn't say it. There was simply no truth in what he had accused me of doing.

"So I leaned over until my face was within inches of his, and then—real calmly, in a soft voice—I said, 'Uncle Rulon, everything you have said is a lie, an absolute lie.' And he just sat back in his chair in total shock. This was not something anyone had ever done."

Upon arriving home DeLoy considered the enormity of what had just occurred: "Uncle Rulon spoke to God on a continual basis. All his wisdom and knowledge supposedly came straight from the Lord. But in a matter of moments it had become apparent to me that this man wasn't really communicating with God, or he would have known that what he accused me of was a lie. Right then and there I decided to leave the Work, even though I knew it would mean the end of my life as I knew it."

When DeLoy failed to show up for the weekly priesthood meeting on the following Sunday, within twenty-four hours Uncle Rulon dispatched someone to DeLoy's house to take away his wives and children. According to UEP dogma, wives do not belong to their husbands, nor do children belong to their parents; all are property of the priesthood and may be claimed at any time. Uncle Rulon decreed that DeLoy's wives and progeny were to be given to another, worthier man immediately.

But both of DeLoy's wives declined to leave him. Uncle Rulon was flabbergasted. "The priesthood means far more than family or anything else," explains DeLoy. "For my wives to defy Uncle Rulon and stick with me, even though I was going straight to hell—that was unheard of." De-Loy's spouses, and all his children except the three oldest, thus became apostates, too.

In Colorado City, the faithful are taught that apostates are more wicked than Gentiles, or even mainline Mormons.* In a sermon preached on July 16, 2000, Bishop Warren Jeffs (Uncle Rulon's son and heir apparent) emphasized that an apostate "is the most dark person on earth." Apostates, he explained, have "turned traitor on the priesthood and their own existence, and they are led about by their master: Lucifer. . . . Apostates are literally tools of the devil."

When DeLoy apostatized, relatives who remained in the religion were forbidden to speak to him, his wives, or his apostate children ever again. And although DeLoy had built and paid for his home, the UEP owns all the land within the city limits, including the lot on which De-Loy's house was built. Uncle Rulon and the UEP have filed a legal action to take possession of DeLoy's house and are currently trying to evict him from Colorado City.

It is no accident that Colorado City is a long way from anywhere. Short Creek, as the town was then known, was settled in the 1920s by a half dozen fundamentalist families wanting to live where they would be free to follow Joseph Smith's Most Holy Principle without outside interference. The UEP, failed to appreciate the extent to which polygamy has periodically stirred public passions, however.

---

* In the unique lexicon shared by Mormons and Mormon Fundamentalists, all those who have never subscribed to the teachings of Joseph Smith are known as Gentiles (e.g., among Mormons, even Jews are referred to as Gentiles). Those who were once devout but have left the faith are apostates. Nonpracticing Saints are "Jack Mormons."

By the early 1950s the population of Short Creek had grown to more than four hundred. This so alarmed government officials and the LDS leadership in Salt Lake City that Arizona governor Howard Pyle, with church encouragement and financial backing, concocted an elaborate plan to raid the town and stamp out polygamy.* On July 26, 1953— eight months before DeLoy Bateman was born—some one hundred state police officers, forty county deputies, and dozens of troops from the Arizona National Guard drove into Short Creek in the predawn darkness and arrested 122 polygamous men and women, including DeLoy's father. The 263 children from these families were declared wards of the state, bussed four hundred miles to Kingman, Arizona, and placed in foster care.

In a carefully worded, multipage statement defending the raid, Governor Pyle called it a "momentous police action against insurrection within [Arizona's] own borders." He explained,

> The leaders of this mass violation of so many of our laws have boasted directly to Mohave county officers that their operations have grown so great that the State of Arizona was powerless to interfere.
>
> They have been shielded, as you know, by the geographic circumstances of Arizona's northernmost territory . . . the region beyond the Grand Canyon that is best known as "The Strip."
>
> This is a land of high plateaus, dense forests, great breaks and gorges, rolling arid lands, and intense color . . . a land squeezed between the even higher plateaus of Utah and the Grand Canyon of Arizona.
>
> The community of Short Creek is 400 miles by the shortest road from the Mohave county seat of Kingman. . . .
>
> Massive cliffs rearing north of Short Creek's little central street provide a natural rock barrier to the north. To the east and west are the sweeping expanses of dry and almost barren plateaus before the forests begin. To the south there is the Grand Canyon.

---

* Governor Pyle said about the raid, "We didn't make a single move that we didn't clear with the Council of Twelve"—the Quorum of the Twelve Apostles, which runs the LDS Church. "They were one thousand percent cooperative, a hundred percent behind it."

It is in this most isolated of all Arizona communities that this foulest of conspiracies has flourished and expanded in a terrifying geometric progression. Here has been a community entirely dedicated to the warped philosophy that a small handful of greedy and licentious men should have the right and the power to control the destiny of every human soul in the community.

Here is a community—many of the women, sadly, right along with the men—unalterably dedicated to the wicked theory that every maturing girl child should be forced into the bondage of multiple wifehood with men of all ages for the sole purpose of producing more children to be reared to become more chattels of this totally lawless enterprise.

One day after the raid, the *Deseret News*, a daily newspaper owned by the LDS Church, editorialized in support of the action: "Utah and Arizona owe a debt of gratitude to Arizona's Howard Pyle . . . we hope the unfortunate activities at Short Creek will be cleaned up once and for all."

The raid made national headlines; it was even reported on the front page of the *New York Times*, with the same prominence given to a story announcing the armistice ending the Korean War. But to the dismay of the LDS leadership, most of the press presented the polygamists in a favorable light. Photographs of crying children being torn from their mothers' arms generated sympathy throughout the nation for the fundamentalists, who protested that they were upstanding, law-abiding Mormons simply trying to exercise their constitutionally protected freedoms.

The raid was widely perceived as religious persecution by overly zealous government agencies, and it sparked a great outcry in support of the polygamists. The *Arizona Republic*, for example, criticized the action as "a misuse of public funds." In 1954, Governor Pyle was voted out of office, thanks largely to the raid and the egg it left on his face. The arrests and subsequent trials cost taxpayers $600,000, yet by 1956 all the polygamists who had been arrested were out of jail and reunited with their families in Short Creek. Members of the UEP unapologetically resumed living the Principle as taught by Joseph Smith, and the

population of the town continued to more than double each decade—
a consequence of the community's giant families and astronomical
birth rate.

Paradoxically, the Short Creek raid proved to be a huge boon to the
FLDS Church. Thanks to the backlash that followed the raid, for most of
the next half century fundamentalists were able to practice polygamy
throughout the Intermountain West with little state interference—until May 1998, when a battered and bruised teenage girl dialed 911 from
a pay phone at a truck stop in northern Utah.

The girl reported to the police that immediately after her sixteenth
birthday, her father, a businessman named John Kingston, had pulled
her out of high school and forced her to become the fifteenth wife of his
brother, David Kingston—the girl's thirty-two-year-old uncle. Both
Kingston brothers are among fifteen hundred members of the so-called
Kingston Clan, a Mormon Fundamentalist sect based in Salt Lake
County, officially known as the Latter Day Church of Christ, led by patriarch Paul Kingston, a lawyer who is married to at least twenty-five
women and has sired some two hundred offspring.

Twice the girl tried to run away from David, but she was caught
each time. After the second escape, she sought refuge with her mother—
who promptly turned the girl over to her father. John Kingston then
drove her to a remote ranch near the Utah-Idaho border that the
Kingstons used as a "reeducation camp" for wayward wives and disobedient children. He took the girl into a barn, pulled his belt off, and used
it to whip her savagely across the buttocks, thighs, and lower back, in-
flicting hideous injuries. The girl later told a judge that before the beating began, her father warned her that "he was going to give me ten licks
for every wrongdoing."

After whipping his daughter, John Kingston departed, at which
point the girl fled from the ranch and limped five miles along a dirt road
until she reached a gas station, where she called the police. Both John
and David Kingston were arrested and subsequently convicted in highly
publicized trials. John found guilty of child abuse and locked up in
the county jail for twenty-eight weeks; David was sentenced to ten years
in prison for incest and unlawful sexual conduct. And Mormon Funda-

mentalists all over the West immediately found themselves uncomfortably back in the public eye.

But if the Kingston convictions made the fundamentalists in Colorado City edgy, they became considerably more nervous in April 2000 when another Utah polygamist, Thomas Arthur Green, was charged with bigamy and first-degree felony rape of a child. The Kingston trial, although front-page news in Utah, didn't make a big splash elsewhere. The state's prosecution of Green turned into a public spectacle, largely of Green's own creation, and his plural marriages were featured in every major media outlet from Seattle to Miami.

Fifty-four-year-old Tom Green is a fat, bearded man with a receding hairline, thirty-two children, and five wives (he has married at least ten different women all told, but the other five have left him). The oldest of his current wives is twenty-two years younger than he is; the youngest is twenty-nine years younger. Home for the gigantic Green family has long been a collection of decrepit trailers plunked down on ten acres of desert in Juab County's desolate Snake Valley, way out toward the Nevada line, a hundred miles from the nearest paved road. Green has modestly christened this little kingdom Greenhaven.

Unlike most polygamists, who conscientiously avoid outside scrutiny, Green has an insatiable thirst for publicity. He and his wives have opened their lives to numerous print journalists and have eagerly appeared on such television shows as *Judge Judy, Jerry Springer, Queen Latifah, Sally Jessy Rafael,* and *Dateline NBC.* They decided to seek this media attention, Green explained in a public statement, after he woke up one morning and "heard a voice say to me, 'Don't hide your light under a bushel, but let your light so shine before men so that they will see your good words and glorify your Father in Heaven.' I told my wives what I had heard and that I understood from it that God wanted us to be an example that plural marriage can work. . . . We are not ashamed of our beliefs, and we are certainly not ashamed of our family. . . . We just want people to realize that polygamists are not a threat, we are not fanatics, we are not criminals."

Unfortunately for Tom Green, Juab County attorney David O. Leavitt—the younger brother of Utah governor Mike Leavitt—happened to turn on his television one night in 1999 to see Green boasting of his young wives on *Dateline NBC*. Although Leavitt had long known about Green's polygamous colony out in the west desert, until he saw Green holding forth in prime time, he'd had no intention of prosecuting him. As a child Leavitt had had friends who were the offspring of polygamists, and his own great-grandfather had married a plurality of wives. In 1993, when Leavitt was fresh out of law school and working as a public defender, he'd even defended a polygamist, and won, by arguing that the religious freedom guaranteed in the U.S. Constitution overruled state laws criminalizing plural marriage.

But then Leavitt saw Green bragging on national television that he had married all of his current wives when they were mere girls. One of them was only thirteen when he, at age thirty-seven, got her pregnant. According to Utah statute, when an adult male has sex with a thirteen-year-old child, a first-degree felony has been committed. "Tom Green at first blush appeared to be someone that no one should bother," Leavitt explained to reporter Pauline Arrillaga of the Associated Press in November 2000. "But this is a man who has taken thirteen- and fourteen-year-old children, deprived them of any education, married them, impregnated them, required the state to pay the bill, and has raped a thirteen-year-old girl." Five months after the *Dateline* show aired, Leavitt filed charges against Green, who was supporting his oversize family by drawing welfare checks.

Investigators from the Utah attorney general's office have documented that between 1989 and 1999, Tom Green and his dependents received more than $647,000 in state and federal assistance, including $203,000 in food stamps and nearly $300,000 in medical and dental expenses. These same investigators estimate that had they been granted complete access to pertinent government files as far back as 1985, when Green began his polygamous lifestyle, they would have been able to show that Green received well over $1 million in welfare.

Linda Kunz Green, now twenty-eight, was thirteen when she married Tom Green. She insists that he has done nothing wrong, that she is no victim. She says that she enjoys being a plural wife and points out that getting married to Green was her idea. Leavitt counters that Linda is simply a victim of what psychologists call the Stockholm syndrome, in which hostages sympathize with, and later defend, their captors. "The ability to choose is an ability that Linda Green never had," Leavitt argues.

At the time Linda Kunz married Green, her mother, Beth Cooke, was also married to Green, although Cooke has since left him. (Seven of the ten women Green has married, and all of his current wives, were the children of his other wives when he married them; he has made a habit of marrying his stepdaughters, all of whom were sixteen or younger when he brought them into his matrimonial bed.) Cooke was raised in Short Creek, the product of a polygamous family. In 1953, when she was nine years old, she watched Mohave County sheriff's deputies arrest her father and thirty other men in the Short Creek raid. Three years later, at the age of twelve, Cooke was married off to her stepfather, Warren "Elmer" Johnson, the brother of Prophet LeRoy Johnson. Cooke became one of seven women married to Elmer.

In 1984, after Elmer Johnson had died and the husband who succeeded him had departed, Cooke and her two daughters were introduced to Green at a Sunday school meeting. "I paid particular attention to him," Cooke told freelance journalist Carolyn Campbell, "because my friend said she had met Tom Green and he was the ugliest man she had ever met." Cooke, who is four years older than Green, thought otherwise. She found him handsome, as well as highly intelligent. She was impressed with the way he took charge of the meeting. He asked her out on a date, during which he announced that he was going to marry her—a prophecy that was fulfilled in short order. The newlyweds honeymooned in Bountiful, Canada, a colony of UEP polygamists in southeastern British Columbia.

By 1985 Cooke couldn't help noticing that her thirteen-year-old daughter, Linda Kunz, was "showing feelings" toward Green. Linda liked to sit in her stepfather's lap and would "hang on to him for the longest time." She talked about him constantly, and eventually asked Cooke if she could marry Green. Cooke consented, and in January 1986, Linda married Tom Green in Los Molinos, Mexico, a polygamous outpost on the Baja Peninsula. "I was happy for my daughter because she was happy and it was what she wanted," Cooke said afterward. "I was happy to share her with a man I loved very dearly and thought was a very special person." Linda Kunz Green was pregnant with Green's child before her fourteenth birthday.

Even though Beth Cooke left Green, she defends her daughter's marriage to him. "Fifteen years later," she said in a 2001 interview with journalist Campbell, "I feel that time has proven it was a good decision. . . . They are prosecuting Tom based on nineteenth-century morals. Now, who cares who sleeps with who? They are all consenting adults. Right now, there are lesbians, homosexuals and single people living together all the time. There are married people living with others who they are not married to."

David Leavitt doesn't consider Green's plural marriages a matter of religious freedom or a harmless sexual relationship between consenting adults. Leavitt views Green as a pedophile, plain and simple. "He preyed on little girls who, from the cradle, knew no other life but polygamy," Leavitt told Holly Mullen, a reporter for the Salt Lake Tribune, in August 2002. "He robbed them of their childhood. When I looked at this picture I realized it was about five women, all of them given in marriage by their mothers, all of them raised by their fathers to marry as children. They are victims of pedophiles, and they are victims of the state of Utah, which turned its back on polygamy for sixty years."

Leavitt's case proved convincing in court. In August 2001, Green was convicted of four counts of bigamy and one charge of criminal non-support of his family. He was sentenced to five years in prison and ordered to pay $78,868 in restitution.

A year later, Leavitt put Green on trial again, for the additional—and considerably more serious—charge of having sex with Linda Kunz when she was thirteen, a crime that could have put him in prison for life. This time around, however, Green got lucky: although he was found guilty of first-degree felony child rape, the judge gave him the minimum sentence, five years to life, to be served concurrently with his previous five-year sentence for bigamy.

The relatively soft punishment riled many Utahans. Two days after

Green was sentenced, an editorial in the *Spectrum*—the daily paper of St. George, Utah, an LDS stronghold less than forty miles from Colorado City—opined,

> Taxpayers and—most importantly—children lost during Tuesday's sentencing hearing for now-infamous polygamist Tom Green. . . .
>
> In some polygamist relationships, particularly those involving young girls, there is a bit of brainwashing that goes on both before and after the illegal "marriages." Girls are led to believe that such a relationship is one way to salvation. Then, they typically are taken as wives by men twice their ages.
>
> Without the context of spiritual marriage, there would be no debate that these are acts of pedophilia. . . .
>
> A man committed what amounts to statutory rape of a 13-year-old girl and, basically, won't serve any time for it.

David Leavitt was also dismayed by Green's lenient sentence. "People in the state of Utah," he proclaimed, "simply do not understand, and have not understood for fifty years, the devastating effect that the practice of polygamy has on young girls in our society." But Leavitt went on to say that a change in how polygamy was regarded by Utahans had begun: "The ball is rolling. Time will demonstrate that this society will understand that the practice of polygamy is abusive to children, is abusive to women, is abusive to society."

Leavitt prevailed against Green in court, and he won plaudits from the LDS Church and establishment editorial writers. But like Arizona governor Howard Pyle, who was voted out of office for masterminding the Short Creek raid of 1953, Leavitt discovered that his anti-polygamy crusade was not popular with the people. In November 2002, the voters of Juab County responded to the conviction of Tom Green by giving the boot to prosecutor David Leavitt.

Ever since the conviction of the Kingstons—even before Tom Green was first charged with bigamy—Mormon Fundamentalists have received support from the American Civil Liberties Union and gay-rights activists in advancing their claims of religious persecution. It has been an especially curious, and uncomfortable, coalition: FLDS doctrine proclaims that sodomy and homosexuality are egregious crimes against God and nature, punishable by death—yet gays and polygamists have joined forces to keep the government out of the bedroom. This partnership is made even more incongruous by the fact that on the other side of the issue, radical feminists have allied themselves with the resolutely antifeminist LDS Church to lobby for aggressive prosecution of polygamists.*

As they have been forced out of the shadows into the probing glare of the news media, polygamists continue to insist that they are simply trying to live in accordance with their deeply held, constitutionally protected beliefs. "What goes on in our homes here is nobody's business," asserts Sam Roundy, Colorado City's polygamous police chief. "We're not infringing on anybody. Don't we have the right to practice our religion?"

But polygamy is a crime in all fifty states, as well as in Canada, and police officers are sworn to uphold the law. This point became problematic for Chief Roundy on February 6, 2002, when Ruth Stubbs—the third wife of one of his police officers—fled Colorado City with her two children and appeared on the evening news in Phoenix, complaining that she had been beaten by her husband, Rodney Holm, and that polygamy is intrinsically abusive.

* In 1993, LDS Apostle Boyd K. Packer (currently second in line to become president and prophet of the Mormons) pronounced that the church faces three major threats: "the gay-lesbian movement, the feminist movement, and the ever-present challenge from the so-called scholars or intellectuals." Over the years, the Mormon leadership has made numerous pronouncements about the "dangers" of the feminist movement and has excommunicated several outspoken feminists. But perhaps the greatest rift between Mormon general authorities and advocates for women's rights occurred when the LDS Church actively and very effectively mobilized Mormons to vote as a bloc against ratification of the Equal Rights Amendment (despite the fact that a poll published in the church-owned *Deseret News* in 1974 showed that 63 percent of Utahans approved of the ERA). Most political analysts believe that had the LDS Church not taken such an aggressive position against the ERA, it would have been easily ratified by the required thirty-eight states, and would now be part of the U.S. Constitution.

Ruth, nineteen when she left Holm and visibly pregnant with her third child, had been pulled out of school following the sixth grade. Immediately after her sixteenth birthday, she was summoned to a meeting with Uncle Rulon and his son Warren Jeffs, who informed her that in twenty-four hours she would be marrying Officer Holm—a handsome, taciturn man who was exactly twice as old as she was. Ruth had wanted to marry someone else, a boy much closer to her own age. When she balked at becoming Holm's plural wife and asked for some time to consider her options, her older sister Suzie Stubbs—one of the two women already married to the police officer—called Ruth "an asshole for doing that to Rod." Suzie leaned hard on Ruth to become Holm's third wife, until Ruth finally caved in and married him.

"They told me who to marry," Ruth asserted after she escaped from Colorado City. "I think women should have the right to say 'yes' or 'no'—to have the right to say what's going on in their lives." Not only had Holm broken the law by marrying three women, he had committed statutory rape—a felony in both Utah and Arizona—by having sexual intercourse with Ruth when she was sixteen.

To date, the Colorado City police department has not disciplined Officer Holm, who is acting like the aggrieved party in this dispute. Assisted by UEP attorneys, Rodney Holm is presently trying to obtain legal custody of Ruth's children so they can be "raised with FLDS values," in the company of his other eighteen kids.

In October 2002, the Utah attorney general's office charged Holm with felony bigamy and three counts of unlawful sex for his relationship with Ruth. The state's case against Rodney Holm is crippled, however, by a rather significant impediment: in November 2002, Ruth Stubbs disappeared after submitting a signed, handwritten note to the court stating that she did not want Holm to "go to jail!" and refusing to testify against him. As an editorial in the St. George daily *Spectrum* noted, "This turn in an already odd case shows how complicated it is to prosecute the members of the Fundamentalist Church of Jesus Christ of Latter Day Saints who engage in unlawful activities."

Before she vanished, Ruth Stubbs was living in the Phoenix home of her aunt Pennie Peterson, who ran away from Colorado City herself at the age of fourteen, when the prophet commanded her to become the fifth wife of a forty-eight-year-old man. Sixteen years later, Peterson remains very bitter about the UEP's polygamous culture. "Polygamists say they are being attacked because of their religion," she told the *Salt Lake Tribune,* "but where in the Constitution does it say that it's OK to molest and impregnate young girls?"

The mayor of Colorado City, Dan Barlow, considers apostates like Pennie Petersen to be both misinformed and motivated by revenge, and views the prosecution of Rodney Holm as government harassment of an unorthodox but honorable religious minority. To Barlow, the Holm case is disturbingly reminiscent of the 1953 raid on Short Creek. "They're coming after us again," he complains, "and they're even using the same language."

But there is a documented pattern of sexual abuse in Colorado City that severely undermines Mayor Barlow's attempt to frame the issue as one of religious persecution. In April 2002, for instance, the mayor's own son and namesake, Dan Barlow Jr., was charged with molesting five of his daughters over a period of many years. The town closed ranks around him, and his father, the mayor, went before the court and pleaded for leniency. In the end, four of the daughters refused to testify against Barlow. He got off with a suspended sentence after agreeing to sign a statement that said, "I made a mistake. I want to make it right. I am so sorry. I want to be a good person. I have raised a good family, been a good father. I love them all, a fatherly love."

"Nobody who knows anything about this religion is surprised Dan didn't go to jail," says Debbie Palmer, a former member of the Canadian branch of the religion, barely able to contain her disgust. "Do you have any idea what kind of pressure those poor Barlow girls must have been under not to testify against their father, the mayor's son? I'm sure the prophet told them that if they said one word, they were going straight to hell. When I was abused by prominent members of the religion, that's what I was told, every time."

Folks in Colorado City pay little heed to such blasphemous talk from the likes of Palmer. They're convinced that Satan, along with nefarious Gentiles and apostates who've fallen under his influence, are wholly to blame for the town's problems. "Satan has been jealous of God since day one," a young, bright-eyed, very devoted member of the priesthood explains after first looking nervously up and down the dry bed of Short Creek, then looking up and down the wash once more, to make sure nobody is around to see him talking to a Gentile writer. "Satan wants to rule. He doesn't want God to rule, so he tricks weak people into apostatizing and going over to the other side." This young man, along with most of the other residents of Colorado City, believes that in very short order the world will be thoroughly cleansed of Satan's minions—apostates, mainline Mormons, and Gentile writers alike—because the prophet has told him so many times in the past few years.

In the late 1990s, as the new millennium approached, Uncle Rulon assured his followers that they would soon be "lifted up" to the Celestial Kingdom, while "pestilence, hail, famine, and earthquake" would sweep the wicked (i.e., everyone else) from the face of the earth. Fearing that single women would be left behind to perish in the apocalypse because they had not yet been given the opportunity to live the Principle, the prophet married off a spate of teenage girls to older, already married men. Ruth Stubbs was one such bride. When the year 2000 came and went without the arrival of Armageddon, or anyone being lifted up, Uncle Rulon explained to his followers that they were to blame, because they hadn't been sufficiently obedient. Contrite, the residents of Colorado City promised to live more righteously.

"Predicting the end of the world is a win-win situation for Uncle Rulon," apostate DeLoy Bateman observes. "You can always just blame it on the iniquities of the people if it doesn't happen, and then use that as a club to hold over their heads and control them in the future."

Bountiful and Environs

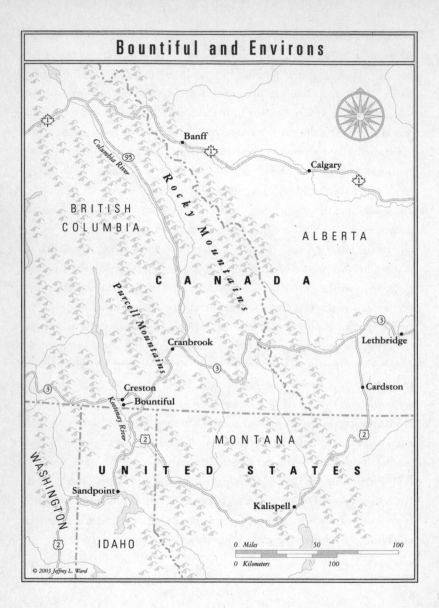

Banff

Calgary

Columbia River

BRITISH
COLUMBIA

Rocky Mountains

ALBERTA

C A N A D A

Purcell Mountains

Cranbrook

Lethbridge

Creston

Cardston

Bountiful

Kootenay River

MONTANA

WASHINGTON

U N I T E D   S T A T E S

Sandpoint

Kalispell

IDAHO

0 Miles   50   100

0 Kilometers   100

© 2003 Jeffrey L. Ward

THREE

BOUNTIFUL

*The essential principle of Mormonism is not polygamy at all, but the
ambition of an ecclesiastical hierarchy to wield sovereignty; to rule the
souls and lives of its subjects with absolute authority, unrestrained by
any civil power.*

SALT LAKE TRIBUNE,
FEBRUARY 15, 1885

Nine hundred miles north of Colorado City, just over the Canadian border, the Purcell Mountains rise steeply from the wide, green bottom-
lands of the Kootenay River. Here, a few miles outside Creston, British
Columbia, a cluster of houses and farms stands amid the hayfields, hard
beneath the precipitous, thickly forested slopes of Mount Thompson.
This bucolic-looking settlement is known as Bountiful. Although its
rain-soaked surroundings are a far cry from the desiccated landscape of
Colorado City, the two places are inextricably linked. Bountiful is home
to some seven hundred Mormon Fundamentalists who belong to the
UEP and answer unconditionally to Prophet Rulon Jeffs. Girls from
Bountiful are regularly sent south across the international border to be
married to men in Colorado City, and even greater numbers of girls from
Colorado City are brought north to marry Bountiful men.

Debbie Oler Blackmore Ralston Palmer spent most of her life in
Bountiful. In 1957, when she was two years old, her father, Dalmon

Oler, moved his family to the Creston Valley in order to join a fundamentalist group that had settled there a few years earlier. It was led by a handsome, charismatic man named Ray Blackmore who had allied the group with the UEP polygamists in Short Creek/Colorado City under Prophet LeRoy Johnson.

Like many Canadian Mormons, Ray Blackmore was descended from Utah polygamists who had been sent north of the border to continue the doctrine of plural marriage when the LDS Church was forced to renounce polygamy in the United States. By the time Debbie moved to Bountiful, families headed by Eldon Palmer and Sam Ralston* had already joined the Blackmore clan and were openly practicing plural marriage.

Upon arriving in Bountiful, Debbie's father wasted no time in acquiring his own plurality of wives, eventually marrying six women and fathering forty-five children, of whom Debbie was the oldest. In an attempt to keep track of so many offspring, her father resorted to giving all the kids born in any given year a name beginning with the same letter. "We called them the A's or the T's or the J's or whatever," he explained on Canadian television. Nineteen seventy-six, for example, was the era of the J's: between June and October of that year, Oler's wives gave birth to Jared, Jeanette, Julia, and Jennifer.

Dalmon Oler acquired his second wife, Memory Blackmore, just a year after arriving in Bountiful. She was the oldest daughter of Ray Blackmore, and her marriage to Debbie's dad gave Debbie her first inkling that plural marriage wasn't always as wonderful as she had been told. "Mother Mem" was insecure and terribly jealous, and she beat Debbie when her birth mother wasn't present. When Debbie was six, her birth mother died, and Mem grew even more violent in her treatment of Debbie, who, even as a young girl, was proving to be intelligent and willful and disinclined to defer blindly to authority. Debbie tended to ask questions and to think for herself—qualities not regarded as attributes in the Fundamentalist Church.

Until 1986, when Rulon Jeffs assumed leadership of the UEP, the

---

* Not his real name.

prophet was LeRoy Johnson, a plainspoken farmer known to his followers as "Uncle Roy." Many of Johnson's sermons were variations on the
theme "The path to heaven is through total obedience." Today, Uncle
Roy's legacy is visible throughout Bountiful, where the community
motto—"Keep Sweet, No Matter What"—is posted on walls and refrig-
erator doors in every home.

Mormonism is a patriarchal religion, rooted firmly in the traditions
of the Old Testament. Dissent isn't tolerated. Questioning the edicts of
religious authorities is viewed as a subversive act that undermines faith.
As the eminent LDS first counselor N. Eldon Tanner famously declared
in the official church magazine, *Ensign,* in August 1979, "When the
prophet speaks, the debate is over." Men, and only men, are admitted to
the priesthood and given positions of ecclesiastical authority, including
that of prophet. And only prophets may receive the revelations that determine how the faithful are to conduct their lives, right down to the design of the sacred undergarments individuals are supposed to wear at all
times. All of this holds true in both the mainstream LDS Church and in
the Fundamentalist Church, although the fundamentalists take these
rigid notions—of obedience, of control, of distinct and unbending roles
for men and women—to a much greater extreme. The primary responsibility of women in FLDS communities (even more than in the mainline
Mormon culture) is to serve their husbands, conceive as many babies as
possible, and raise those children to become obedient members of the religion. More than a few women born into the FLDS Church have found
this to be problematic. Debbie Palmer is one of them.

Tracing a mazelike series of lines with her index finger, Debbie attempts to demystify an incredibly complicated schematic diagram that
at first glance appears to map out the intricacies of some massive engineering project—a nuclear power plant, perhaps. Upon closer examination, the diagram turns out to be her family tree.

When Debbie was fourteen, she felt "impressed by the Lord" to
marry Ray Blackmore, the community leader. Debbie asked her father to
share her divine impression with Prophet LeRoy Johnson, who would
periodically travel to Bountiful from Short Creek to perform various
religious duties. Because Debbie was lithe and beautiful, Uncle Roy

approved of the match. A year later the prophet returned to Canada and married her to the ailing fifty-seven-year-old Blackmore. As his sixth wife, Debbie became a stepmother to Blackmore's thirty-one kids, most of whom were older than she was. And because he happened to be the father of Debbie's own stepmother, Mem, she unwittingly became a stepmother to her stepmother, and thus a stepgrandmother to herself.

Following Ray Blackmore's death in 1974, Debbie's father, Dalmon Oler, became the leader of Bountiful. He held that position until 1985, when Ray's scheming twenty-nine-year-old son, Winston Blackmore, successfully forced him from power, ruined him financially, and very adroitly maneuvered to assume leadership of Bountiful himself. Relying on charm, coercion, and a network of spies that the KGB would have envied, Winston consolidated his power over the ensuing years. He is presently the presiding bishop of the church's Canadian branch, superintendent of the Bountiful schools (which are funded by the taxpayers of British Columbia), editor of the community newspaper, and manager of all the community's significant business interests.* The control he exerts over the lives of his followers is staggering. Winston has also fathered approximately a hundred children, at last count, with more than thirty wives. He answers to nobody but God and the prophet in Colorado City.

After Winston pushed Debbie's father out of the way, she and Winston became bitter enemies, but they remained tightly bound by a mind-boggling web of family connections. Although Debbie is just a year older than Winston, she is his stepmother. Her oldest daughter is his half sister. Debbie's actual sister became the first of Winston's numerous wives.

One of Debbie's stepchildren is Alaire Blackmore, seven years older than Debbie, who had been adopted by Ray Blackmore at birth. When Alaire was eighteen, she was married to Ray, her own adoptive father. Alaire was thus a cowife to Debbie as well as Debbie's stepdaughter. After Ray died, Alaire was married to Debbie's father; when Winston assumed power she was taken from Debbie's dad and married to Winston—who was her own brother by adoption. Although these rela-

---

* It was in fact Winston who christened the community Bountiful. Until he took control, it was called Lister.

tionships are almost impossible to make sense of without a flow chart, such convoluted permutations are simply business as usual in Bountiful and other polygamist societies.

For all their fecundity, Mormon Fundamentalists are strangely squeamish about sex. Boys and girls are forbidden to date, or even flirt, before marriage. Sex education consists of teaching children that the human body is a shameful vessel that should be veiled from the eyes of others at all times. "We were told to treat each other like snakes," explains one of Debbie's sons. Women and girls are required to wear long dresses, even while swimming. Boys and men wear long pants and long-sleeved shirts. Both genders must wear sacred long underwear beneath their clothing at all times, even on sweltering summer days. According to the Law of Chastity, sexual intercourse is officially forbidden even between husband and wife unless the woman is ovulating.

Gravel crunching beneath its tires, Debbie's car rounds a bend, and the house where she grew up suddenly comes into view, moldering at the edge of a soggy hillside bearded in ferns and evergreen forest. It's been many years since she's been back here. "See where that car is parked off to the side there?" Debbie says, pointing to an old vehicle rusting beneath a graceful canopy of red cedars. "When I was six, that's where Renny Blackmore* took me. Said he was going to teach me how to drive." Instead of giving Debbie a driving lesson, Renny (one of Winston's teenage brothers) sexually assaulted her. "Yechh," she recalls, grimacing. "Thinking about what he did to me in that car still gives me a creepy feeling."

In spite of—or, more likely, precisely because of—the atmosphere of sexual repression in Bountiful, incest and other disturbing behaviors are rampant, although the abuse goes conspicuously unacknowledged. Debbie remembers older boys taking girls as young as four into a big white barn behind the school to play "cows and bulls" among the hay bales. A boy who would grow up to become a prominent member of the church

---

* Not his real name.

leadership raped one of Debbie's friends when he was twelve and the girl was seven. When Debbie was four, she says, Winston's fourteen-year-old brother, Andrew Blackmore,* jammed "a stick up my vagina and left it in there for a while, telling me to lie very still and not to move."

Before Debbie's father died, in 1998, he built a much larger second home just above the modest building where Debbie was raised: a barnlike, white clapboard house with fourteen bathrooms and fifteen bedrooms where some fifty people reside. These days the household is presided over by Memory Blackmore—"Mother Mem"—and her forty-one-year-old son, Jimmy Oler, Debbie's half brother. Neither of them is home at the moment, but a half dozen teenage girls are juggling babies on their hips in the huge downstairs living room; they are the wives of Jimmy and some of the other Bountiful men. Among these girls is a giggling, gap-toothed kid who looks like she belongs in elementary school—but happens to be immensely pregnant.

At the top of the stairs is a long hallway plastered with snapshots of Debbie's extended family. Debbie herself appears in several of the photos. One of them shows her as a smiling teenager in a pink, frilly, ankle-length dress. It was taken at her wedding to Ray Blackmore, when she was only a year older than the pregnant fourteen-year-old downstairs. Debbie's new husband, standing beside her in the picture, is a wizened, gray-haired man, almost four times as old as she is. "I got pregnant soon after that," she says, "but I miscarried the baby. I was told it was because I had violated the Law of Chastity by having sex during my pregnancy. Ray blamed me for it, and made me feel wicked."

This double bind left Debbie reeling. "Ray would almost never talk to me," she says. "He would ignore me for days on end. The only time he paid attention to me was when we had sex. It got so if I didn't have a penis in me I didn't think I was loved. And I was just a child when I was forced to deal with all of this! I was made to feel like a whore, a person with no worth beyond my vagina and my womb. Around town, I became the butt of mean jokes."

Ray Blackmore died of leukemia in 1974, after nineteen-year-old

---

* Not his real name.

Debbie had been married to him for a little over three years and had given birth to his daughter. Soon thereafter Debbie was ordered, against her wishes, to marry Sam Ralston—one of Bountiful's founding patriarchs, a violent, fifty-four-year-old sociopath who already had four wives. After giving birth to two of Ralston's children and enduring years of cruelty at his hands, she became desperate enough to run away to the only refuge she could think of: her father's home.

The next time Prophet LeRoy Johnson—Uncle Roy—was in Canada, however, he commanded Debbie to return to Sam Ralston. "I begged him not to make me do it," she says, "but he told me that when they married me to Sam they did it because they hoped it would encourage him in the priesthood and help him feel better toward my father. I was shocked, realizing for the first time that my marriage to Sam was something the men wanted me to do, not God." Debbie dutifully returned to Ralston, whereupon he told her, she says, "that I was an evil woman and he would make me pay for my wickedness."

Debbie grew depressed, and increasingly self-destructive. Her father became so alarmed by her deteriorating condition that he clandestinely rescued Debbie and her children from Ralston's home, installed them in his own household, and convinced Uncle Roy to "release" her from the marriage. But the failure of her second marriage reinforced the opinion in Bountiful that she was a dull-witted, disobedient nuisance, more trouble to the community than she was worth.

"I began taking pills," she says, "lots of pills: sleeping pills, painkillers, tranquilizers." When Debbie sought solace from her father, he simply quoted scripture, telling her, "You must have a broken heart and a contrite spirit to know God." In 1980, one night not long after this bit of advice, she was weeping and semicomatose from her medications when her father came into her bedroom and began to comfort her. Soon, however, she became dimly aware through the narcotic fog that his ministrations had become something more: he was engaging in sexual intercourse with her. She remained passive and made no effort to stop him. Later, she wondered guiltily if she had somehow encouraged his incestuous attentions.

In the months that followed, Debbie tried to drown herself in the

Goat River, a fast mountain stream that flows past Bountiful, but she failed at that, as well. After she attempted suicide once more, this time with an overdose of sedatives, she was committed to the psychiatric ward of a nearby hospital. While she was recovering, an acquaintance named Michael Palmer* came to visit her in the hospital. Palmer—a thirty-eight-year-old long-haul trucker married to two of Winston Blackmore's sisters—was part of the religion but worked outside of Bountiful. Debbie recalls that during his visit, Palmer "touched me and kissed me. He made me feel beautiful." When she was released from the hospital, though, the community still thought of her as a difficult, uncontrollable woman, and nobody was sure what should be done with her.

Uncle Roy—who was by then ninety-three years old, very ill, and fast fading into senility—came to Canada and asked Debbie if there were any men that she liked. Michael Palmer, she replied. "So the prophet told Michael to marry me," she explains. "I became Michael's third wife. At first life with Michael was wonderful. He held me and helped me throw away my pills. When I had my first baby girl by Michael he was happy and actually played with the baby. He encouraged me to have ideas. I loved him."

The marriage was not without difficulties, however. The two women already married to Michael, Marlene and Michelle Blackmore (who happened to be Debbie's stepdaughters), were intensely jealous of each other, and Debbie's installation in their home as a new "sister wife" only added to their misery. Sharing Michael proved especially difficult for Michelle, his first wife. On the nights when it was Michael's turn to sleep with Debbie, Michelle would listen from the room directly below, alternately crying hysterically and straining to hear sounds of passion that would prove to her that Michael preferred Debbie. "I found Michelle this way one night when Michael and I had just finished making love and I went downstairs to check on the children," says Debbie. "When I saw her, I felt like we were trapped in the middle of a nightmare. I felt violated, but the shame and agony I saw on her face made it impossible for me to even say anything."

---

* Not his real name.

At one point Michelle discovered that Michael had had intercourse with Debbie when she was pregnant—a serious violation of the Law of Chastity. Debbie remembers being confronted afterward by Michelle, "her face black with rage and pain, spitting out her venomous jealousy: 'You are a harlot and a whore, and because you tempted Michael to have sex with you while you are pregnant, he is an adulterer, and my chance to be exalted is gone! I'm going to tell Winston, and you're going to be in big trouble.' " Michelle did, and Debbie was.

In 1986 Uncle Roy died, and Rulon Jeffs became the UEP's new prophet. In the climate of upheaval that followed, there was turmoil in both Bountiful and Colorado City. Because Michael worked outside of the community, among Gentiles, he fell out of favor and was secretly voted out of the priesthood. He was crushed when he learned of his rejection, and the disappointment triggered a latent instability in his personality.

Michael became emotionally withdrawn and angry. He sexually molested one of Debbie's sons, as well as another boy outside of the family. On October 27, 1986, Debbie's daughter Sharon was lying in bed with a high fever. Michael went into her bedroom, Debbie says, "and began wiping her face with a cold cloth. Then he took the nightgown off her thirteen-year-old body and washed first her back, then her breasts. When she asked him to stop he acted like he didn't hear her and kept doing it. He washed her over and over, and then put the nightgown back on her and put her between his legs on the carpet and continued to massage her breasts and scalp."

After blurting out to her mother what Michael had done, Sharon cried uncontrollably for weeks. She told Debbie that she was "terrified she would have to marry Michael, because some of her friends in Colorado City had had to marry their stepfathers after being molested by them."

In December 1987, Winston ordered Sharon—who was his half sister—to move out of Debbie's house and move in with him. When Debbie learned of this, she says, "I went wild. I'd seen him take so many women's children away from them, and I wasn't going to let him take Sharon. I went straight down to Winston's house and confronted him.

He was in bed. I stormed into his bedroom and started screaming that there was no way he was going to get Sharon."

Debbie vividly remembers the reaction this provoked in Winston, who was unaccustomed to having a woman disobey him. "He issued a clear, unmistakable threat," she says. "This cold look came into Winston's eyes and he told me, 'You might want to be careful. . . . I've got at least six boys who will rearrange your face if I just give them the word.' "

Debbie stood her ground. "Sharon will come here and live with you," she vowed, "only over my dead body." And then she walked out and went home.

By this point Winston had moved Michelle and Marlene out of Michael's house and was haranguing Debbie to vacate the premises as well, so that he could take possession of it. "Every single day Winston would come to the door and yell at me," Debbie remembers. "He'd shout, 'You have to leave! You have to leave *NOW!*' But I didn't have anywhere to go. Except my dad's house. And I couldn't go back there. Not after what had happened with him." Mustering her mulish resolve, each time Winston showed up Debbie would let him rant, then silently wait for him to leave. She refused to move out. Her obstinacy enraged him. Alone in Michael's big house with her kids, Debbie thought about women who had summoned the courage to leave Bountiful. On many occasions over the years, Winston, Uncle Roy, and Uncle Rulon had warned that those foolish enough to forsake the religion would be "cast into outer darkness and ground into native element." They would end up walking the streets as whores, selling their bodies to dirty Gentiles, damned until the end of time. Debbie had never doubted that this was exactly what happened to all those who left Bountiful and abandoned the faith.

More and more, however, the behavior of some of her brethren within the religion struck her as anything but righteous. Debbie was finding it increasingly difficult to believe that God made his will known through the commandments of self-proclaimed prophets like the leaders of the UEP. She discovered herself trying to "unravel where God stops and men begin." The prospect of abandoning everything she believed to be true about the world and her place in it was a terrifying intellectual leap to make, she says, "but I knew I must take responsibility for my life and my children, and quit pretending that God ever had anything to do with the pain I was in."

Debbie spent the day of February 7, 1988, cleaning the house with obsessive thoroughness. It was Sunday. She put a turkey in the oven to bake. A strange feeling came over her, like she was walking around in a dream. It was a frigid, foggy day, with snow blanketing the ground, but she didn't notice the cold. "I got the kids all to bed really early," she remembers. "On some level I guess I knew what I was about to do just before I put the kids to bed. I suddenly realized, 'Everything is ready now. The house is perfect.' I chopped a big pile of cedar kindling, put it in a corner cupboard with some fire paper, and put a match to it. Then I went into my bedroom at the other end of the house and shut the door. I got out the photo albums that told the story of my life. I sat on the bed and looked at them for a long time, then put them back on the shelf. And then I sat down to wait.

"I thought about the kids. I tried thinking about leaving Bountiful and moving to Calgary and trying to make it on my own, but it made my head hurt too much. It was a blinding pain—I couldn't think about it. I just stayed in my room with the door shut until I could hear the crackling of the flames. At that point I walked to the bedroom door and opened it without really even being conscious of doing it. Down the long hallway, the kitchen was alive with licking, twisting flames dancing across the ceiling toward me. I knew then that I had to get the children out. As I ran downstairs to wake them, I could feel my heart throbbing in my ears."

After Debbie ushered all the children outside, Winston arrived and drove them all down the hill to his own house. A policeman from Creston came over and asked Debbie how the fire had started. "I was cooking a turkey in the oven," she lied convincingly, "and must have forgotten to turn it off." This seemed to satisfy him, and after a few minutes he left. Debbie found herself alone in Winston's kitchen. After a while she went back out into the raw night and walked up the hill to where her home was burning. "The firemen were there by then," she says, "running all over the place. Suddenly they all came pouring out of the house, yelling that it was at flash point. A second later the whole thing exploded in flames, and all the windows blew out.

"I stood a short distance away in a field, next to a barbwire fence, watching the flames roar against the mountains behind, swaying and shaking uncontrollably. After a while I realized that the men had stopped spraying water on the fire and were leaving, so I turned to leave myself. When I uncurled my fingers from the fence, my hand was damp with blood. I had been holding tightly onto a strand of barbwire and it had cut deep into my hand, but I hadn't felt a thing."

Burning down her house was a desperate act, but it served as the instrument of her emancipation. Not long after the embers had cooled, Debbie loaded her five children and a few garbage bags holding all their worldly belongings into a rust-ravaged car. Then she drove out of Bountiful and steered the vehicle east over the snow-choked Rocky Mountains, determined to create a new life for her family and herself, beyond the grasp of Winston, Uncle Rulon, and the UEP.

FOUR

ELIZABETH AND RUBY

But then I sigh and, with a piece of scripture,
Tell them that God bids us do good for evil;
And thus I clothe my naked villainy
With odd old ends stol'n forth of Holy Writ,
And seem a saint when most I play the devil.

WILLIAM SHAKESPEARE,
RICHARD III

On June 5, 2002, fourteen-year-old Elizabeth Smart was abducted at knifepoint from her Salt Lake City bedroom in the middle of the night while her parents slept in a nearby part of the house. Details of the audacious kidnapping were reported breathlessly and without pause by the news media, leaving much of the country aghast and riveted. When a massive investigation failed to locate Elizabeth or her unidentified abductor by summer's end, people assumed the worst: that she had been subjected to some unspeakable ordeal and murdered. Then, nine months after she disappeared, she turned up alive, surprising almost everyone.

The astonishing reappearance of Elizabeth Smart occurred in the jittery days immediately before the invasion of Iraq. Most Americans, made fretful by the uncertainties of the imminent war, were desperate for some good news and rejoiced with commensurate intensity when the girl was reunited with her family. President George W. Bush took time out from planning the assault on Baghdad to phone Elizabeth's father and convey the nation's collective jubilation over her safe return. Ed Smart, brimming with emotion, called the outcome a miracle. "God lives!" he declared. "The prayers of the world have brought Elizabeth home."

Like so many other Americans, Dan Lafferty found himself spellbound by the Elizabeth Smart saga, monitoring its heartrending convolutions via a small television in his cell at the Utah State Prison. Within hours of the girl's rescue, the media disclosed that her abductor was an excommunicated Mormon. "With that small piece of information," boasts Lafferty, "I immediately guessed that he was probably a fundamentalist, and that Elizabeth was somehow involved in a polygamy situation."

Lafferty was soon proven correct. The man who kidnapped Elizabeth turned out to be a forty-nine-year-old Utahan named Brian David Mitchell. Although he was indeed a Mormon Fundamentalist, he was not affiliated with the Fundamentalist Church of Jesus Christ of Latter Day Saints (the faction that holds sway in Bountiful and Colorado City–Hildale) or any other established sect; he was a so-called independent, of whom there are untold multitudes currently practicing polygamy throughout the western United States, Canada, and Mexico. Thanks to the torrent of publicity generated by his 2001 trial and imprisonment, polygamist Tom Green had been the most widely recognized independent fundamentalist. But that was before Mitchell was arrested for kidnapping Elizabeth Smart and became a fixture in the news.

Mitchell was not born into fundamentalism. He'd spent most of his life as a dutiful Latter-day Saint, and for three years he'd actually worked at the Salt Lake Temple, the epicenter of the establishment church, where he performed in ritual reenactments of sacred history. His wife, Wanda Barzee, was an upstanding Saint, as well, who for a period had played organ at the Mormon Tabernacle. One of Barzee's music teachers described the couple as "the epitome of righteousness, fulfilling every church duty and assignment."

Mitchell's unflagging zeal raised eyebrows even then, however. During his tenure as a temple worker, his job was to act the part of Satan in staged religious dramas. According to the *Salt Lake Tribune*, Mitchell was so convincing in the role that "he made church officials uneasy." Inevitably, his religious ardor brought him in contact with the fundamentalist fringe, which has a ubiquitous, if shadowy, presence up and down the Wasatch Front. By the mid-1990s Mitchell had grown firm in his conviction that the church leaders had erred, ruinously, more than a century before when they'd let the federal government force them to renounce polygamy. He and Barzee embraced Mormon Fundamentalism as passionately as they'd previously embraced mainstream Mormonism, and were officially cast out of the LDS Church.

On Thanksgiving Day 2000, Mitchell announced to Barzee and anyone else who would listen that he had received a revelation in which the Lord commanded him to take seven additional wives. Subsequent divine commandments revealed that Mitchell's name was actually Immanuel David Isaiah, and that he had been placed on earth to serve as a mouthpiece for the Lord during the Last Days. Mitchell stopped shaving and cutting his hair, dressed in billowing robes fashioned after the garb of Old Testament prophets, and gained a reputation throughout the Salt Lake Valley as an eccentric but harmless street preacher. He often introduced himself as "God be with us," and Barzee as "God adorn us."

A year after determining that God wanted him to marry a plurality of women, Mitchell crossed paths with a wealthy Mormon housewife named Lois Smart outside a downtown shopping mall; he told her his name was Immanuel. Smart, who had a soft spot for the destitute—particularly those as pious as Immanuel/Mitchell appeared to be—gave the robed holy man a five-dollar bill and offered him employment doing odd jobs around her lavish Salt Lake City home. Thus, in November 2001, did Mitchell end up working half a day at the Smart residence, helping Lois's husband, Ed Smart, patch their roof and rake leaves in their yard. During the five hours he spent on the $1.1 million property, Mitchell met the Smarts' fourteen-year-old daughter, Elizabeth, and became infatuated with her angelic features and innocent demeanor. He decided that God intended her to be his polygamous wife.

Over the months that followed, Mitchell obsessively stalked Elizabeth, spying on her from the lower slopes of the Wasatch Range, which rises directly above the Smarts' affluent Federal Heights neighborhood. Around two in the morning on June 5, 2002, Mitchell placed a chair beneath a small window that had been left ajar on the first floor, sliced through a flimsy screen, and squeezed through the opening into the Smarts' kitchen. Making his way through the vast, 6,600-square-foot house, he located the upstairs bedroom Elizabeth shared with her nine-year-old sister, Mary Katherine, and woke Elizabeth. Unbeknownst to Mitchell, he also woke Mary Katherine; feigning sleep, the younger girl stole a furtive glimpse at the intruder in the darkness and heard him threaten her sister. After telling Elizabeth to put on some shoes, Mitchell hustled her past the bedroom where the Smart parents were sleeping soundly, and exited the house.

Mitchell marched Elizabeth at knifepoint four miles into the foothills west of her home. Upon reaching a secluded campsite in Dry Creek Canyon, he and Barzee conducted a weird, self-styled wedding ritual to "seal" the girl to Mitchell in "the new and everlasting covenant"—a Mormon euphemism for polygamous marriage. Barzee then demanded that Elizabeth remove her red pajamas. When the girl balked, Barzee explained that if she refused to cooperate, Mitchell would forcibly disrobe her. Faced with this prospect, Elizabeth complied, whereupon Mitchell consummated the marriage by raping his fourteen-year-old bride.

Back in the Smart household, sister Mary Katherine had remained in her bed, too terrified by what she'd witnessed to get up and alert her parents. At least two hours passed before she finally summoned the courage to go to their bedroom and wake them. Horrified and trying to comprehend how his eldest daughter could have been snatched from her own bed, Ed Smart, even before he called the police, phoned the president of his local LDS stake, who in turn mobilized a search party of trusted Saints. Searchers immediately began combing the neighborhood for Elizabeth, but found no sign of her.

For at least two months after her abduction, Elizabeth was held at a series of campsites hidden in a labyrinth of scrub-choked ravines above her home, close enough to hear would-be rescuers calling her name. Sometimes she was kept in a subterranean hollow covered with a lean-to; on other occasions her ankle was chained to a tree. Using his gift for

fundamentalist rhetoric and adroitly manipulating the religious indoctrination Elizabeth had received since she was old enough to talk,
Mitchell cowed the girl into becoming an utterly submissive polygamous concubine—buttressing his powers of theological persuasion with
threats to kill her and her family. Raised to obey figures of Mormon authority unquestioningly, and to believe that LDS doctrine is the law of
God, she would have been particularly susceptible to the dexterous fundamentalist spin Mitchell applied to familiar Mormon scripture. The
white robes Mitchell and Barzee wore, and forced Elizabeth to wear, resembled the sacred robes she had donned with her family when they
entered the Mormon temple. When Mitchell bullied Elizabeth into submitting to his carnal demands, he used the words of Joseph Smith—
words she had been taught were handed down by God Himself—to
phrase those demands. "Being brought up as she was made her especially
vulnerable," says Debbie Palmer, who is intimately acquainted with the
coercive power of fundamentalist culture from her own upbringing in
Bountiful. "Mitchell would never have been able to have such power
over a non-Mormon girl."

Once he'd gained psychological control of Elizabeth, Mitchell felt
sufficiently confident that she wouldn't flee or try to alert the police that
he often took her to public places, albeit with her blond braids covered
in a head scarf and her face hidden behind a burqa-like veil. In September, Mitchell even brought Elizabeth, thus disguised, to a lively, beer-
fueled party in downtown Salt Lake attended by more than a hundred
revelers (most of whom were not particularly pious), where she was photographed by one partygoer but not recognized. On at least one occasion
while Elizabeth was under Mitchell's control, according to one of her un-
cles, for the better part of a day Mitchell left the girl "completely by herself, but she didn't try to run away."

On July 24, acting with customary brazenness, Mitchell attempted
to kidnap a fifteen-year-old cousin of Elizabeth's. Resorting to the same
method he'd used previously, Mitchell placed a chair beneath an open
window, cut through its screen with his knife, and was preparing to
crawl into the girl's home when he inadvertently knocked some framed
pictures onto the floor, creating a racket that woke up the household and

caused him to flee. Because the police were convinced at the time that they already had the prime suspect in custody—another former laborer for the Smarts, Richard Ricci, who had a fishy alibi and a voluminous criminal history going back thirty years—it didn't occur to the cops that the sliced screen and chair left at the scene of this attempted break-in were significant clues. They failed to give serious consideration to the possibility that Elizabeth's abductor might be someone other than Ricci and might still be on the loose, attempting to kidnap other girls.

Late one night in October, Mary Katherine—the younger sister who was the only outside witness to the crime—abruptly told Ed Smart, "Dad, I think I know who it is." She was pretty sure that the person she had seen abducting Elizabeth was the small bearded man who had helped fix the roof—the self-proclaimed prophet who had called himself Immanuel. Smart reported his daughter's belated disclosure to the Salt Lake City police, but because Mary Katherine had waited four months to identify the perpetrator, detectives didn't give it much credence. They nevertheless worked with the Smart family to produce three composite sketches of Immanuel, based on their hazy memories of what he had looked like when he'd worked around their house in November 2001. The Smarts thought the last of these renderings was a reasonable likeness and wanted to go public with it, but the cops refused, arguing that it wasn't accurate enough and would only inundate them with false leads. Besides, they still thought Ricci (who had died in jail on August 27 of a brain hemorrhage) was the culprit.

Frustrated, the Smarts took matters into their own hands. In early February 2003 they held a press conference during which they released the best police sketch to the public. Soon thereafter a woman who saw the composite drawing called to report that it bore a resemblance to her brother, a man of strong religious views named Brian David Mitchell who refered to himself as Immanuel. She sent in a photo of Mitchell, which on February 15 was broadcast on the television show *America's Most Wanted,* along with photos and videotape of Elizabeth and footage of Ed Smart pleading with viewers to help find his daughter.

On March 12, 2003, an alert motorist who had watched the *America's Most Wanted* segment spotted someone who resembled Mitchell in the suburb of Sandy, walking down State Street, a busy, six-lane thoroughfare that is one of the main north-south arterials in Salt Lake County. The Mitchell look-alike was dressed in seedy robes and sandals and was accompanied by a middle-aged woman and a teenage girl, who were similarly attired. The motorist dialed 911.

A pair of police officers, Karen Jones and Troy Rasmussen, pulled up in a squad car and stopped the oddly dressed trio. The man, who had a bushy salt-and-pepper beard and wore flowers in his unkempt hair, gave his name as Peter Marshall and insisted on speaking for the two females, who were wearing sunglasses and cheap gray wigs in an apparent attempt to disguise their identities. When questioned directly, the teenager denied that she was Elizabeth Smart, adamantly maintaining that her name was Augustine Marshall. She said she was eighteen years old and that the man with the beard was her father. She seemed extremely reluctant to say or do anything without his consent.

Officer Jones took the girl aside and questioned her further, but "Augustine" continued to be evasive and uncooperative. When Officer Rasmussen asked her why she was wearing a wig, "she became angry," he told NBC News. "Told me that was personal, none of my business." The cops nevertheless persisted in asking if she was Elizabeth Smart, and after forty-five minutes of grilling the teen finally relented. On the brink of tears, she conceded her true identity with a biblical utterance: "Thou sayest"—Jesus's reply to Pilate when asked if he was king of the Jews.

Even after she had revealed that she was indeed Elizabeth and was sitting in the back of the squad car on her way to be reunited with her father at the police station, she continued to express concern for the well-being of Mitchell and Barzee. "The first question out of her mouth," said Officer Jones, "was 'What's gonna happen to them? Are they going to be OK?' Didn't want them in trouble, didn't want them to be hurt. . . . She started crying and cried all the way to the department."

Many have wondered how Brian David Mitchell managed to exert such power over the girl, and why during the nine months Elizabeth was his captive she apparently made no effort to escape. But Julie Adkison— a young Mormon woman who became acquainted with Mitchell seventeen months before he kidnapped Elizabeth Smart—has no difficulty comprehending how Elizabeth came under his sway. Adkison was twenty years old and selling shoes at Salt Lake City's Fashion Place mall when she met Mitchell, who expressed an avid interest in sandals and began telling her about the intimate chats he regularly had with God. Not long thereafter, Mitchell handed her a written marriage proposal explaining that the Lord wished for her to become his plural wife. Adkison declined the invitation to become betrothed to Mitchell but continued to meet with him; once she sat with him in a city park for more than five hours, mesmerized as he held forth on Mormon theology. She felt strangely drawn to Mitchell, she told *Newsweek* magazine, because "everything he said was stuff I was raised on. . . . I wanted to leave for hours, but I just sat there." Had she been as young and impressionable as Elizabeth Smart, Adkison admitted, "There is no telling what I would have done."

Considering the traumas to which she was subjected as Mitchell's captive, Elizabeth appeared to be recovering with surprising grace after being rescued, according to those close to her. Although Elizabeth's father cautioned that she faced "a long road back," he said that she was faring remarkably well since rejoining her family. David Hamblin, the bishop of the Smarts' LDS ward, pronounced that despite what Mitchell may have done to her, Elizabeth remained "pure before the Lord."

From his prison cell, Dan Lafferty speculates that Elizabeth "will be fine after a couple of months or so." But he regards Elizabeth's tribulations from a perspective not far removed from that of her tormentor— one of a religious zealot with whom, after all, Lafferty has much in common. After averring that he "was happily shocked when I heard that she had been found and that she was alive," Lafferty opines that Elizabeth "has had a very eye-opening experience"—one that will prevent her from ever viewing her life "in the same way as before." Disquietingly, he sees this is as a "blessing," rather than something to mourn.

As for Brian David Mitchell, in the days following his arrest he steadfastly insisted that he had done nothing wrong, arguing that forcing a fourteen-year-old girl into polygamous bondage was not a criminal act because it was a "call from God." Speaking through an attorney, he explained that Elizabeth was "still his wife, and he still loves her and knows that she still loves him."

Dan Lafferty was not the first person to surmise that Mitchell was a Mormon Fundamentalist who kidnapped Elizabeth Smart in order to make her a plural wife. Immediately after she was abducted—nine months before Lafferty made the same speculative leap—a resident of Phoenix, Arizona, named Flora Jessop e-mailed a statement to the media hypothesizing that Elizabeth had been kidnapped by a polygamist. Her conjecture, although based largely on "gut instinct," was rooted in personal experience: Jessop grew up in Colorado City as one of twenty-eight siblings in a polygamous family. When she was fourteen she filed sexual abuse charges against the family patriarch, her fundamentalist father, but the judge presumed she was lying and dismissed the case, after which leaders of the FLDS Church confined her in the home of a relative for two years. A defiant, strong-willed girl, she created so much trouble for her keepers that when she was sixteen church authorities gave her a choice: "They told me I had to either marry this guy they'd picked for me—one of my dad's brother's sons—or be committed to the state mental hospital," says Jessop. She opted for the arranged marriage and then fled both the marriage and Colorado City at the first opportunity. Now thirty-four, she's an antipolygamy activist and has founded an organization called Help the Child Brides.

Jessop is extremely relieved that Elizabeth Smart was discovered alive and thinks the outpouring of support Elizabeth has received is wonderful. But in Jessop's view it underscores the disturbing absence of support for another young victim of polygamy—her sister, Ruby Jessop—whose predicament she first brought to the attention of government officials more than a year before Elizabeth was abducted.

Ruby was fourteen years old when she was observed innocently kissing a boy she fancied in Colorado City. For this unforgivable sin she was immediately forced to marry an older member of her extended family, whom she despised, in a fundamentalist ceremony presided over by Warren Jeffs. Like Elizabeth, Ruby was raped immediately after the wedding ceremony—so brutally that she spent her "wedding night" hemorrhaging copious amounts of blood. Unlike Elizabeth, however, Ruby attempted to flee her coerced marriage, running to the home of a sympathetic brother where she thought she would find refuge. Lured away from her brother's house by false promises, in May 2001 Ruby was allegedly abducted by members of the FLDS Church and brought to the home of her stepfather, Fred Jessop, second councilor to the prophet—the same house where Flora Jessop had been confined seventeen years earlier.

Flora—who fled Colorado City on the day Ruby was born: May 3, 1986—called the county sheriff to report that her sister had been kidnapped. When a sheriff's deputy came to Colorado City to look into the supposed crime, he was told by leaders of the church that the girl was "on vacation"; the deputy accepted this unskeptically and departed. Flora, furious at this apparent dereliction of duty, redoubled her efforts to persuade someone in a position of state authority to take action on behalf of her little sister. A month later, thanks to Flora's agitation, FLDS members were compelled by the Utah Department of Child and Family Services to bring Ruby to nearby St. George and meet with a social worker. Interviewed in the intimidating presence of one of her alleged abductors, Ruby told the social worker that "everything was fine" and was promptly returned to members of the faith. Two years after that, as a sixteen-year-old, she gave birth to a child. Despite Flora's ongoing efforts to rescue her, nobody outside of Colorado City has heard from Ruby since the summer of 2001. She has effectively vanished into the folds of the Fundamentalist Church.

Antipolygamy activist Lorna Craig, a colleague of Flora Jessop's, is baffled and outraged by Utah's indifferent treatment of Ruby—especially when compared to the colossal effort the state mustered to rescue Elizabeth Smart and prosecute her abductors. Craig notes that both Elizabeth and Ruby were fourteen when they were kidnapped, raped, and "kept captive by polygamous fanatics." The main difference in the girls' respective ordeals, she says, is that "Elizabeth was brainwashed for nine months," while Ruby had been brainwashed by polygamous fanatics "since birth." Despite the similarity of their plights, Elizabeth's abusers were jailed and charged with sexual assault, aggravated burglary, and aggravated kidnapping, while Ruby, says Craig, "was returned to her abusers, no real investigation was done, no charges were brought against anyone involved."

The dissimilar outcomes are attributable, in Craig's view, to the fact that Ruby Jessop was born into a polygamous community that has been allowed to break state and federal laws with impunity for many decades. Craig points out that because the mayor, the police, and the judge in Colorado City–Hildale are themselves polygamists who are absolutely obedient to the prophet, there is "nowhere for victims of abuse to turn. . . . I would say that teaching a girl that her salvation depends on her having sexual relations with a married man is inherently destructive." Such relationships, Craig argues bitterly, should be considered "a crime, not a religion."

FIVE

THE SECOND GREAT AWAKENING

The sober preacher trained in the dialectics of the seminary was rare west of the Appalachians. One found instead faith healers and circuit-rider evangelists, who stirred their audiences to paroxysms of religious frenzy. . . .

The revivals by their very excesses deadened a normal antipathy toward religious eccentricity. And these Pentecostal years, which coincided with Joseph Smith's adolescence and early manhood, were the most fertile in America's history for the sprouting of prophets.

FAWN BRODIE,
NO MAN KNOWS MY HISTORY

Shortly after the rescue of Elizabeth Smart and the arrest of Brian David Mitchell, FBI agents discovered a twenty-seven-page booklet Mitchell had written two months before he abducted Elizabeth. Titled "The Book of Immanuel David Isaiah," it purported to be a divine manifesto, as revealed to Immanuel/Mitchell, announcing the inauguration of a new fundamentalist church, the Seven Diamonds Plus One, which would serve as "a brilliant shining diadem of truth." The tract identified Immanuel/Mitchell as the "one . . . mighty and strong," and proclaimed that God had ordained him to lead the new church—the "true and living Church of Jesus Christ of Latter-day Saints in its purified and exalted state." "The Book of Immanuel David Isaiah" also explained that God had transferred the "keys and powers and ordinances of the Holy Priest-hood for the salvation of mankind . . . through a succession of prophets." The booklet traced this divinely ordained lineage from Adam to Noah to Abraham to Moses to Jesus "unto Joseph Smith, Jr. and from Joseph Smith, Jr. unto Immanuel David Isaiah and from Immanuel David Isaiah unto the end of the earth."

To comprehend Brian David Mitchell—or to comprehend Dan Lafferty, or Tom Green, or the polygamous inhabitants of Bountiful and Colorado City—one must first understand the faith these people have in common, a faith that gives shape and purpose to every facet of their lives. And any such understanding must begin with the aforementioned Joseph Smith Jr., the founder of the Church of Jesus Christ of Latter-day Saints. More than a century and a half after his passing, the sheer force of Joseph's personality still holds extraordinary sway over Mormons and Mormon Fundamentalists alike. "I admire Joseph Smith," affirms Dan Lafferty, his eyes burning. "I admire nobody else as much."

Whether one believes that the faith he spawned is the world's only true religion or a preposterous fable, Joseph emerges from the fog of time as one of the most remarkable figures ever to have breathed American air. "Whatever his lapses," Harold Bloom argues in *The American Religion,* "Smith was an authentic religious genius, unique in our national history. . . . In proportion to his importance and his complexity, he remains the least-studied personage, of an undiminished vitality, in our entire national saga."

Joseph was born on December 23, 1805, in the Green Mountains of Vermont. His father, Joseph Smith Sr., was a tenant farmer, perpetually on the lookout for his main chance, who had lost all his money a short while earlier in a failed scheme to export ginseng root to China. Finding himself broke and saddled with a crushing debt, Smith *père* was reduced to scraping out a meager living from a plot of rocky, barely cultivable farmland rented in ignominy from his father-in-law.

New England was then in the midst of an extended economic depression, and penury dogged the Smith family throughout the childhood of Joseph Junior. Constantly searching for better prospects, the family moved five times during the boy's first eleven years before settling in Palmyra, a town of four thousand in western New York be-side the Erie Canal, which at that time was under construction. The canal was the most ambitious engineering venture of that era and had sparked a robust, if temporary, boom in the local economy. Joseph Senior hoped to be a beneficiary of this uptick.

Here is how the Smith clan is described upon their arrival in Palmyra in 1817, in a typically snide article about the budding prophet published in a local newspaper, the *Reflector,* on February 1, 1831, as Joseph's new religion began to make a splash:

> Joseph Smith, Senior, the father of the personage of whom we are now writing, had by misfortune or otherwise been reduced to extreme poverty before he migrated to Western New York. His family was large, consisting of nine or ten children, among whom Joe Junior was the third or fourth in succession. We have never been able to learn that any of the family were ever noted for much else than ignorance and stupid-ity, to which might be added, so far as it may respect the elder branch, a propensity to superstition and a fondness for everything *marvelous.*

The latter characterization refers to the spiritual enthusiasms of the Smith parents—particularly the prophet's mother, Lucy Mack Smith. "Lucy had a vigorous but unschooled mind," observed Fawn Brodie in *No Man Knows My History,* her magnificent, contentious biography of Joseph Smith:

> Lucy especially was devoted to the mysticism so often found among those suddenly released from the domination and discipline of a church. . . . She accepted a highly personalized God to whom she would talk as if He were a member of the family circle. Her religion was intimate and homely, with God a ubiquitous presence invading dreams, provoking miracles, and blighting sinners' fields.

Young Joseph's theological proclivities clearly owed much to Lucy. And just as clearly, both mother and son were hugely influenced by the tenor of the times.

Following the Revolutionary War, the new republic was jarred by a period of ecclesiastical turmoil, during which the established churches were viewed by a large segment of the populace as spiritually bankrupt. The flood of religious experimentation that roiled the United States during the first decades of the nineteenth century, christened the Second Great Awakening, was roughly analogous to the religious upheaval that swept the country in the 1970s (absent the patchouli and LSD). In the early 1800s the ferment was especially strong near the nation's expanding frontiers—including western New York, where the religious fervor flared with such intensity that the area around Palmyra became known as the "burnt-over district."

People imagined the acrid scent of brimstone in the air. The Apocalypse seemed just around the corner. "Never in the history of Western society had the millennium seemed so imminent," the Mormon historian Hyrum L. Andrus has written; "never before had people looked so longingly and hopefully for its advent. It was expected that twenty years or less would see the dawn of that peaceful era." It was in this superheated, anything-goes religious climate that Joseph Smith gave birth to what would become America's most successful homegrown faith.

An earnest, good-natured kid with a low boredom threshold, Joseph Junior had no intention of becoming a debt-plagued farmer like his father, toiling in the dirt year in and year out. His talents called for a much grander arena. Although he received no more than a few years of formal schooling as a boy, by all accounts he possessed a nimble mind and an astonishingly fecund imagination. Like many autodidacts, he was drawn to the Big Questions. He spent long hours reflecting on the nature of the divine, pondering the meaning of life and death, assessing the merits and shortcomings of the myriad competing faiths of the day. Gregarious, athletic, and good-looking, he was a natural raconteur whom both men and women found immensely charming. His enthusiasm was infectious. He could sell a muzzle to a dog.

The line separating religion from superstition can be indistinct, and this was especially true during the theological chaos of the Second Great Awakening, in which Joseph came of age. The future prophet's spiritual curiosity moved him to explore far and wide on both sides of that blurry

line, including an extended foray into the necromantic arts. More specifically, he devoted much time and energy to attempting to divine the
location of buried treasure by means of black magic and crystal gaz-
ing, activities he learned from his father. Several years later he would
renounce his dabbling in the occult, but Joseph's flirtation with folk
magic as a young man had a direct and unmistakable bearing on the religion he would soon usher forth.

Although "money digging," as the custom was known, was illegal,
it was nevertheless a common practice among the hoi polloi of New
England and upstate New York. The woods surrounding Palmyra were
riddled with Indian burial mounds that held ancient bones and artifacts,
some of which were crafted from precious or semiprecious metals. It
therefore comes as no surprise that a boy with Joseph's hyperactive mind
and dreamy nature would hatch schemes to get rich by unearthing the
gold rumored to be buried in the nearby hills and fields.

Joseph's money digging began in earnest a few months shy of his
fourteenth birthday, two years after his family's arrival in Palmyra, when
he heard about the divining talents of a girl named Sally Chase, who
lived near the Smith family farm. Upon learning that she possessed a
magical rock—a "peep stone" or "seer stone"—that allowed her to "see
anything, however hidden from others," Joseph harangued his parents
until they let him pay the girl a visit.

Sally's peep stone turned out to be a small, greenish rock. She placed
it in the bottom of an upturned hat, then instructed Joseph to bury his
face in the hat so as to exclude the light. When he did so, he was treated
to magical visions. One of the things that appeared to him was a pocket-
sized, white-colored stone "a great way off. It became luminous, and
dazzled his eyes, and after a short time it became as intense as the mid-
day sun." He immediately understood that this rock was another peep
stone; the vision also indicated its precise location underground, beneath
a small tree. Joseph located the tree, started digging, and "with some labor and exertion" unearthed the first of at least three peep stones he
would possess in his lifetime.

His career as a "scryer"—that is to say, a diviner, or crystal gazer—
was launched. Soon his necromantic skills were sufficiently in demand

that he was able to command respectable fees to find buried treasure for property owners throughout the region. By 1825, his renown was such that an elderly farmer named Josiah Stowell came from Pennsylvania to meet Joseph, and was so impressed by the encounter that he hired the twenty-year-old to travel with him to the Susquehanna Valley to locate, with his peep stones, a hidden lode of silver rumored to have been mined by the Spaniards centuries earlier. Stowell paid Joseph the generous salary of fourteen dollars a month for his services—more than the monthly wage earned by workers on the Erie Canal—plus room and board.

These and other details of Joseph's money digging were revealed in affidavits and other documents generated by a trial held in March 1826, *People of the State of New York v. Joseph Smith,* in which the young scryer was hauled into court and found guilty of being "a disorderly person and an imposter." Although Joseph had applied himself to scrying with vigor, dedication, and the finest tools of his trade, it seems that he had been unable to find Stowell's silver mine. Nor, in fact, during the previous six years he had worked as a money digger, had he ever managed to unearth any other actual treasure. When this had come to light, a disgruntled client had filed a legal claim accusing Joseph of being a fraud.

The trial, and the raft of bad press it generated, brought his career as a professional diviner to an abrupt halt. He insisted to his numerous critics that he would mend his ways and abandon scrying forever. Only eighteen months later, however, peep stones and black magic would again loom large in Joseph's life. Just down the road from his Palmyra home he would finally discover a trove of buried treasure, and the impact of what he unearthed has been reverberating through the country's religious and political landscape ever since.

One night in the autumn of 1823, when Joseph was seventeen, ethereal light filled his bedroom, followed by the appearance of an angel, who introduced himself as Moroni and explained that he had been sent by God. He had come to tell Joseph of a sacred text inscribed on solid gold plates that had been buried fourteen hundred years earlier under a rock on a nearby hillside. Moroni then conjured a vision in Joseph's mind, show-ing him the exact place the plates were hidden. The angel cautioned the boy, however, that he shouldn't show the plates to anyone, or try to en-rich himself from them, or even attempt to retrieve them yet.

The next morning Joseph walked to the hill that had appeared to him in the vision, quickly located the distinctive rock in question, dug beneath it, and unearthed a box constructed from five flat stones ce-mented together with mortar. Inside the box were the golden plates. In the excitement of the moment, however, he forgot Moroni's admonition that "the time for bringing them forth had not yet arrived." When Joseph tried to remove the plates, they immediately vanished into the ether, and he was hurled violently to the ground. He later confessed that greed had gotten the better of him, adding, "Therefore I was chastened" by the angel.

Moroni was nevertheless willing to give Joseph another chance to prove his worthiness. The angel commanded the boy to return to the same place each year on September 22. Joseph dutifully obeyed, and every September he was visited by Moroni on what would later be named the Hill Cumorah to receive instruction about the golden plates, and what God intended for him to do with them.

On each occasion Joseph left empty-handed, to his great disappoint-ment. During their annual meeting in 1826, though, Moroni gave him reason for renewed hope: the angel announced that if Joseph "would Do right according to the will of God he might obtain [the plates] the 22nt Day of September Next and if not he never would have them." By gaz-ing into his most reliable peep stone, Joseph further learned that in or-der for him to be given the plates, God required that he marry a girl named Emma Hale and bring her along on his next visit to the hill, in September 1827.

Emma was a winsome neighbor of Josiah Stowell's in Pennsylvania whom Joseph had met a year earlier while searching fruitlessly for the silver mine on Stowell's property. During that initial encounter, Emma and Joseph had felt a strong spark of mutual attraction, and he made several trips to the Hale home to ask for her hand in marriage. On each occasion Emma's father, Isaac Hale, strenuously objected, citing Joseph's disreputable past as a money digger. Mr. Hale pointed out to his love-struck daughter that only a few months earlier, young Joe Smith had been convicted of fraud in a court of law.

Joseph grew despondent over Hale's dogged refusal to let Emma marry him, and desperate. September was fast approaching. If he and Emma weren't betrothed by then, Moroni would withhold the golden plates from him forever. Borrowing a horse and sleigh from a fellow scryer, Joseph made one more trip to Pennsylvania, and on January 18, 1827, he persuaded Emma to defy her father, run away with him, and elope.

Eight months later, shortly after midnight on the appointed day, Joseph and Emma went to the Hill Cumorah. After being denied the plates on his previous four visits, this time Joseph left nothing to chance. Carefully adhering to the time-honored rituals of necromancy, the young couple were dressed entirely in black, and had traveled the three miles from the Smith farm to the hill in a black carriage drawn by a black horse. High on the steep west slope of the hill, Joseph again dug beneath the rock in the dark of night, while Emma stood nearby with her back turned to him. He soon unearthed the stone box that he had been prevented from removing four years earlier. This time, however, Moroni allowed him to take temporary possession of its contents.

The box contained a sacred text, "written on golden plates, giving an account of the former inhabitants of this continent," which had been hidden on the hill for fourteen hundred years. Each of the gold pages on which this sacred narrative was inscribed, Joseph reported, was "six inches wide and eight inches long and not quite as thick as common tin. They were filled with engravings in Egyptian characters and bound together in a volume, as the leaves of a book with three rings running through the whole." The stack of metal pages stood about six inches high.

Joseph gathered up the plates and headed home with them. Later, nineteen witnesses would testify that they had actually seen the gold book; as eight of them swore jointly in an affidavit printed in *The Book of Mormon,* Joseph "has shewn unto us the plates . . . which have the appearance of gold; and . . . we did handle with our hands: and we also saw the engravings thereon, all of which has the appearance of ancient work, and of curious workmanship."

Although the text was written in an exotic, long-dead language described as "reformed Egyptian," Moroni had also given Joseph a set of "interpreters": divinely endowed spectacles that would allow the person wearing them to comprehend the strange hieroglyphics. By means of these magic glasses, Joseph began deciphering the document, dictating his translation to a neighbor named Martin Harris, who acted as his scribe. After two months of painstaking work they completed the first 116 pages of translation, at which point the two men took a break, Moroni retrieved the golden plates and magic spectacles, and Joseph reluctantly allowed Harris to borrow the manuscript to show his skeptical, disapproving wife.

Disaster then struck: Harris somehow mislaid all 116 pages. The prevailing view is that his wife was so furious that Harris had gotten involved in such nonsense that she stole the pages and destroyed them. Whatever became of the vanished translation, Joseph was devastated when Harris confessed what had happened. "Oh, my God," Joseph exclaimed. "All is lost!" It looked like his sacred mission had come to a premature end, with nothing at all to show for it.

In September 1828, however, after much praying and contrition on Joseph's part, Moroni returned the plates, and the translation resumed, initially with Emma Smith serving as scribe (later others shared this duty, as well).* But the angel hadn't returned the spectacles along with the plates this time around, so to decipher the Egyptian characters Joseph relied instead on his favorite peep stone: a chocolate-colored, egg-shaped rock that he had discovered twenty-four feet underground, in the company of Sally Chase's father, while digging a well in 1822.

---

* The 116 missing pages have never turned up. Some evidence suggests that prior to his conviction, Mark Hofmann (the forger who is now Dan Lafferty's cell mate at Point of the Mountain) had hatched a scheme to "discover" the long-lost text. Because Hofmann's forgery, taken at face value, would presumably have reflected poorly on Joseph Smith and *The Book of Mormon,* the LDS Church would probably have paid him handsomely for the document, then hidden it in the president's vault with the other potentially embarrassing historical documents that church leaders have thus far managed to keep away from the prying eyes of scholars.

Day after day, utilizing the technique he had learned from Sally, Joseph would place the magic rock in an upturned hat, bury his face in it with the stack of gold plates sitting nearby, and dictate the lines of scripture that appeared to him out of the blackness. He worked at a feverish pace during this second phase of the translation, averaging some thirty-five hundred words a day, and by the end of June 1829 the job was finished.

Joseph took the manuscript to the publisher of the local newspaper, the Palmyra-based *Wayne Sentinel,* and asked him to print and bind five thousand copies of the book—an uncommonly large printing for a self-published volume by an unknown figure, which indicates that Joseph had giddy expectations for how it would be received by the public. He intended to charge $1.25 per copy—not an exorbitant price, by any means, but still about twice as much as most local wage earners made in a day.

The skeptical publisher demanded $3,000 in advance to print the books, much more cash than Joseph could lay his hands on. As was his wont when confronted with an apparently insurmountable hurdle, he sought divine guidance. God announced, in reply, that it was His divine wish that Martin Harris—Joseph's acolyte and scribe—pay the printer's bill. Speaking through Joseph, God told Harris:

> I command thee that thou shalt not covet thine own property, but impart it freely to the printing. . . .

> And misery thou shalt receive, if thou wilt slight these counsels; yea, even the destruction of thyself and property. . . . Pay the printer's debt!

Previously, Harris had usually been putty in Joseph's hands, but his involvement with the translation had already cost him dearly: his wife had grown so exasperated over his obsession with the golden bible that she'd divorced him. Harris thus balked at heeding the commandment when Joseph first presented it to him. In the end, however, a stern directive from God wasn't something Harris was prepared to ignore, so he reluctantly agreed to sell his farm in order to finance the publication.

Nine months after the translation was completed, the 588-page book finally rolled off the presses and went on sale in the printer's brick storefront in downtown Palmyra. Little more than a week after that—on April 6, 1830—Joseph formally incorporated the religion that we know today as the Church of Jesus Christ of Latter-day Saints. The religion's foundation—its sacred touchstone and guiding scripture—was the translation of the gold plates, which bore the title *The Book of Mormon*.

SIX

CUMORAH

The authority that Mormonism promised rested not on the subtlety of its theology. It rested on an appeal to fresh experience—a set of witnessed golden tablets that had been translated into a book whose language sounded biblical. Joseph Smith instinctively knew what all other founders of new American religions in the nineteenth century instinctively knew. Many Americans of that period, in part because of popular enthusiasm for science, were ready to listen to any claim that appealed to something that could be interpreted as empirical evidence.

R. LAURENCE MOORE,
RELIGIOUS OUTSIDERS AND THE MAKING OF AMERICANS

Today, no less than in the nineteenth century, the Hill Cumorah is one of the holiest sites in all of Mormondom, and sooner or later most Latter-day Saints make a pilgrimage here. To a Utah Mormon, accustomed to the eleven-thousand-foot peaks of the Wasatch Front thrusting heavenward like the teeth of God over Temple Square and the City of the Saints, Cumorah's puny dimensions must come as something of a disappointment. A mound of glacial scrapings left behind after the last ice age, it humps up no more than a couple of hundred feet above the surrounding cornfields, and most of Cumorah is shrouded in a gloomy tangle of vegetation.

All the same, this modest drumlin is the highest landform in the

vicinity, and from its crest one can glimpse the office towers of downtown Rochester, twenty miles distant, shimmering through the mid-
summer haze. The summit is adorned with an American flag and an
imposing statue of the angel Moroni. On the slope beneath Moroni's
massive, sandaled feet, the unruly forest has been cleared and a broad
swath of the hillside planted with impeccably groomed bluegrass. Somewhere on this part of Cumorah, 175 years ago, Joseph Smith dug up the
golden plates that launched the Mormon faith.

It's a steamy evening in mid-July, and more than ten thousand
Saints are politely streaming into the meadow at the drumlin's base, on
which rows of plastic seats have been set up to accommodate them. Immediately above the meadow, a multilevel stage, half as big as a football
field, covers the hill's lower apron, surrounded by a steel forest of fifty-
foot light towers. The elaborate stage, the lights, and the Mormon
throngs all materialize here every summer for "The Hill Cumorah
Pageant: America's Witness for Christ," which is due to begin at sunset.

According to promotional materials published by the LDS Church,
the pageant is "America's largest and most spectacular outdoor theatri-
cal event . . . , a magnificent, family-oriented production," replete with
arresting special effects straight out of Hollywood: "volcanoes, fireballs,
and explosions with sound effects from the movie 'Earthquake.' A
prophet is burned at the stake. Lightning strikes the mast of a ship. A
5,000K carbon arc-light 'star' (with FAA clearance) appears at the Na-
tivity scene. Christ appears in the night sky, descends, teaches the people, then ascends into the night sky and disappears." The pageant, which
has been staged here since 1937, is held for seven nights every July, and
draws near-capacity crowds each night. Admission is free.

As dusk settles, the soothing harmonies of the Utah Symphony Or-
chestra and Mormon Tabernacle Choir drift over the field from concert
loudspeakers. Two squads of sheriff's deputies direct traffic into pastures
that have been transformed into vast parking lots. A surging tide of
Saints is now moving from their cars and chartered buses toward the
seats, and as they traverse Highway 21 to reach the meadow beneath Cumorah they are confronted with grim-faced clumps of anti-Mormon
picketers.

The demonstrators, who belong to evangelical Christian denominations, wave hand-lettered placards and shout angrily at the Mormons: "Joseph Smith was a whoremonger!" "There is only one gospel!" *"The Book of Mormon* is a big fairy tale!" "Mormons are NOT Christians!"

Most of the Mormons stroll quietly past the ranting evangelicals, unperturbed, without rising to the bait. "Oh, gosh, we're used to that kind of thing," says Brother Richard, a wide, cheerful man with liver spots and a comb-over, who brags that he has twenty-eight grandchildren. He and his wife drove here in a thirty-seven-foot Pace Arrow from Mesa, Arizona. This is their eighth visit to the pageant.

"Come the judgment, we'll see who winds up in the Celestial Kingdom and who doesn't," Richard muses. "But just between you and me? Them folks waving the signs is the ones that should be worried." As this thought escapes his lips, the glint in his eye momentarily vanishes and his guileless face darkens with pity. "The Lord allows everyone to choose for themselves whether to see the truth or ignore it. You can't force a man to heaven, even though it's for his own good."

The LDS Church produces the Hill Cumorah Pageant at no small expense. Although non-Saints are encouraged to attend, and the church considers the flamboyant shows a powerful tool in its tireless efforts to convert the world, more than 95 percent of the people in attendance belong to the church already. Mostly the pageant functions as a Mormon jamboree, an occasion for members of the tribe to gather at their place of origin and celebrate one another's testimonies of faith.

The pageant has the energy of a Phish concert, but without the drunkenness, outlandish hairdos (Brother Richard's comb-over notwithstanding), or clouds of marijuana smoke. People started arriving hours ago to claim the best seats. While they wait for the show to start, families sprawl on blankets along the edges of the meadow, eating fried chicken and Jell-O salad from plastic coolers. Clean-cut teenagers, shrieking gleefully, toss Frisbees and water balloons in the gloaming. Order, needless to say, prevails. This is a culture that considers obedience to be among the highest virtues.

The sun finally skids behind the horizon in an ozone-enhanced blaze of orange. A scrubbed Mormon "elder," in his early twenties, walks out

and leads the audience in a heartfelt prayer. A few seconds after he fin-
ishes there is a fanfare of trumpets, and lasers pierce the night sky with
shafts of dazzling light. A thrill ripples through the crowd. Great bil-
lows of ersatz fog roll across lower Cumorah. Emerging from the mist,
627 actors march onto stage, costumed as a curious ménage of biblical
figures and pre-Columbian North Americans, some wearing headgear
adorned with towering antlers.

Suddenly a disembodied voice—a stern baritone that sounds like it
could belong to God Himself—thunders from the seventy-five loudspeakers: "This is the true story of a people who were prepared by the
Lord to be ready for the coming of the savior, Jesus Christ. He came to
them in the Americas, but their story began in the Old World, in
Jerusalem . . ." For the next two hours, the rapt audience is treated to a
dramatic reenactment of *The Book of Mormon.*

The narrative inscribed on the golden plates, translated by Joseph Smith
as *The Book of Mormon,* is the history of an ancient Hebrew tribe, headed
by a virtuous man named Lehi. In raising his large brood, Lehi drummed
into the heads of his offspring that the most important thing in life is to
earn God's love, and the one and only way to do that, he explained, is to
obey the Lord's every commandment.

Lehi and his followers abandoned Jerusalem six hundred years before
the birth of Christ, just ahead of the last Babylonian conquest, and
journeyed to North America by boat. In the New World, alas, long-
simmering family jealousies flared. Lehi had always favored his youngest
and most exemplary son, Nephi, so it shouldn't have surprised anybody
when the old man bequeathed leadership of the tribe to him.* But this
infuriated Nephi's miscreant brother Laman, causing the tribe to split
into two rival clans after Lehi's passing: the righteous, fair-skinned
Nephites, led by Nephi, and their bitter adversaries, the Lamanites, as

---

* Even abridged, *The Book of Mormon* is a fantastically complex story that requires no small
effort to digest, and the names of the protagonists do not always lodge easily in the non-
Mormon memory. But an attempt to recall Moroni and Nephi will be rewarded later in this
book, for both these fabled personages figure in the modern saga of Dan Lafferty.

the followers of Laman were known. The Lamanites were "an idle people, full of mischief and subtlety," whose behavior was so annoying to God that He cursed the whole lot of them with dark skin to punish them for their impiety.

Shortly after the resurrection of Christ, according to *The Book of Mormon,* Jesus visited North America to share His new gospel with the Nephites and Lamanites and to persuade the two clans to quit squabbling. Heeding His message, for several hundred years they united amicably as Christians and prospered. But then the Lamanites began to backslide into "unbelief and idolatry." An unbridgeable rift developed between the clans, and they fought each other with escalating violence.

Tensions continued to build, eventually sparking a full-blown war that culminated, around A.D. 400, with a brutal campaign in which the reprobate Lamanites slaughtered all 230,000 of the Nephites (which explains why Columbus encountered no Caucasians when he landed in the New World in 1492). Facing starvation, the handful of Nephite children clinging to life at war's end were forced to cannibalize the flesh of dead family members, but in the end they, too, succumbed. The victorious Lamanites survived to become the ancestors of the modern American Indians, although eventually these "red sons of Israel" lost all memory of both the Nephites and their Judaic heritage.

The leader of the Nephites during their final, doomed battles had been a heroic figure of uncommon wisdom named Mormon; the last Nephite to survive the genocidal wrath of the Lamanites was Mormon's son Moroni, whose account of the Nephites' demise makes up the final chapter of *The Book of Mormon.* This same Moroni would return as an angel fourteen centuries later to deliver the golden plates to Joseph Smith, so that the blood-soaked history of his people could be shared with the world, and thereby effect the salvation of mankind.

The Book of Mormon has been much derided by non-Mormons since before it was even published. Critics point out that the gold plates, which would presumably prove the book's authenticity, were conveniently returned to Moroni after Joseph completed his translation, and they haven't been seen since. Scholars have observed that no archaeological artifacts with links to the supposedly advanced and widespread Nephite civilization have ever been found in North America or anywhere else.

As history, moreover, *The Book of Mormon* is riddled with egregious anachronisms and irreconcilable inconsistencies. For instance, it makes many references to horses and wheeled carts, neither of which existed in the Western Hemisphere during the pre-Columbian era. It inserts such inventions as steel and the seven-day week into ancient history long before such things were in fact invented. Modern DNA analysis has conclusively demonstrated that American Indians are not descendants of any Hebraic race, as the Lamanites were purported to be. Mark Twain famously ridiculed *The Book of Mormon*'s tedious, quasi-biblical prose as "chloroform in print," observing that the phrase "and it came to pass" is used more than two thousand times.

But such criticism and mockery are largely beside the point. All religious belief is a function of nonrational faith. And faith, by its very definition, tends to be impervious to intellectual argument or academic criticism. Polls routinely indicate, moreover, that nine out of ten Americans believe in God—most of us subscribe to one brand of religion or another. Those who would assail *The Book of Mormon* should bear in mind that its veracity is no more dubious than the veracity of the Bible, say, or the Qur'an, or the sacred texts of most other religions. The latter texts simply enjoy the considerable advantage of having made their public debut in the shadowy recesses of the ancient past, and are thus much harder to refute.

In any case, like a movie that is panned by New York critics yet goes on to become a huge blockbuster in the hinterlands, the tremendous popularity of *The Book of Mormon* makes it impossible to dismiss. The sheer quantity of copies in print—at last count over a hundred million—lends the book a certain gravitas, even among cynics. The numbers speak eloquently to the book's power as a sacred symbol and its raw narrative force. The simple truth is, *The Book of Mormon* tells a story that multitudes have found compelling—and continue to find compelling, as the swarms who flock to the Hill Cumorah Pageant every July attest.

In early nineteenth-century America, vestiges of a previous civilization—ruins such as the many Indian burial mounds near Joseph's home—were everywhere. *The Book of Mormon* explained the origins of these ancient tumuli in a way that dovetailed neatly with both Christian scripture and a theory then in wide circulation, which posited that the American Indians were descended from the lost tribes of Israel. Joseph's book worked both as theology and as a literal history of the New World. To an awful lot of people, the story makes perfect sense.

Joseph began winning converts almost immediately after he received the plates from Moroni, well before the book was printed and made public. The excitement conveyed by Martin Harris, Joseph's parents and siblings, and others who swore they had actually "seen and hefted" the "golden bible" convinced their friends and associates to become "Mormonites," as the Latter-day Saints were initially called. When the Mormon Church was formally established in April 1830, it claimed some fifty members. A year later the membership exceeded one thousand, and fresh converts were arriving all the time.

Suitably awed that God had chosen Joseph to receive the gold plates, converts had no trouble believing his assertion that his new religion was "the only true and living church upon the face of the earth" or that *The Book of Mormon* was an essential update to both the Old Testament and the New Testament. They were taught that it was an even newer testament, which provided a more accurate and complete account of sacred history.

Joseph explained that in the first century after the crucifixion of Jesus, the Christian leadership had taken a wrong theological turn and had led the church astray. Calling this blunder the "Great Apostasy," he divulged that virtually all Christian doctrine that had developed thereafter—Catholic and Protestant alike—was a whopping lie. Fortunately, *The Book of Mormon* would set the record straight and restore the true Church of Christ.

There was an appealing simplicity to the book's central message, which framed existence as an unambiguous struggle between good and evil: "There are two churches only; the one is the church of the Lamb of God, and the other is the church of the devil; wherefore, whoso belongeth not to the church of the Lamb of God belongeth to that great church, which is the mother of abominations."

The Book of Mormon appealed, as well, because it was so thoroughly American. Most of its narrative was set on the American continent. In one of the book's most important moments, Jesus Christ pays a special visit to the New World immediately after His resurrection to tell His chosen people—residents of what would become America—the good news. Moroni delivers the golden plates to a quintessentially American prophet—Joseph—who later receives a revelation in which God lets it be known that the Garden of Eden had been located in America. And when it is time for Jesus to return to earth, He assures Joseph, the Son of Man will be making His glorious arrival in that same corner of America.

But perhaps the greatest attraction of Mormonism was the promise that each follower would be granted an extraordinarily intimate relationship with God. Joseph taught and encouraged his adherents to receive personal communiqués straight from the Lord. Divine revelation formed the bedrock of the religion.

God, of course, regularly communicated with Joseph as well his followers. The imparting of heavenly truth began with *The Book of Mormon*, but by no means did it end there. The Lord routinely issued commandments to Joseph, continually revealing sacred principles that needed to be revised or changed outright. Indeed, the notion that each Mormon prophet receives guidance from an ongoing series of revelations was, and remains, one of the religion's crucial tenets. These revelations are compiled in a thin volume titled *The Doctrine and Covenants,* which in some ways has supplanted *The Book of Mormon* as the Latter-day Saints' most consequential scriptural text.

With these revealed scriptures guiding the way, Joseph made his divine mission known: his job was to reinstate the Lord's One True Church and thereby prepare the earth for the Second Coming of Christ, which was surely imminent. Joseph explained to his rapt followers that they were the Lord's Elect—God's own peculiar people, the true sons and daughters of Israel—and every one of them would be called on to play a crucial role in the Last Days before the Millennium drew nigh. They were, Joseph declared, Latter-day Saints.

SEVEN

THE STILL SMALL VOICE

From its inception, the revelatory tradition in Mormonism engendered strife. The doctrine of modern, continuing revelation, begun by Joseph Smith and accepted by most groups claiming descent, leaves social order open to counterclaims that strike at the heart of ecclesiastical order. If one person may speak for God, why may not another? By claiming an ongoing dialogue with divinity, Joseph Smith opened the door to a social force he could barely control.

RICHARD L. SAUNDERS,
"THE FRUIT OF THE BRANCH,"
DIFFERING VISIONS: DISSENTERS IN MORMON HISTORY

Yea, thus saith the still small voice, which whispereth through and pierceth all things, and often times it maketh my bones to quake while it maketh manifest, saying:

And it shall come to pass that I, the Lord God, will send one mighty and strong . . . to set in order the house of God.

THE DOCTRINE AND COVENANTS, SECTION 85

The brick farmhouse stands by itself, surrounded by snow-covered fields in a sparsely populated Utah valley. Mist rises off a nearby river in the eight-degree cold. Inside, a tall, blue-eyed man sits at an uncluttered desk, studying a book through wire-rimmed spectacles. As he bends closer to the page to wrest meaning from the lines of type, winter sunlight streams through a nearby window and glints off the top of his shiny pate, which is ringed with a halo of wispy white hair. The man's name is Robert Crossfield, and the volume that so intensely commands his attention is titled *The Second Book of Commandments*. He wrote and published it himself, under the other name he is known by: the Prophet Onias. Modeled after *The Doctrine and Covenants* (the collected revelations of Joseph Smith), *The Second Book of Commandments* is a compilation of 205 revelations Crossfield/Onias has received from the Lord since 1961.

Crossfield is a Mormon Fundamentalist and a polygamist, but he insists that his belief system amounts to a much kinder, more compassionate brand of faith than the fundamentalism of Rulon Jeffs, Winston Blackmore, or Dan Lafferty—three men with whom he is intimately acquainted. Notably, for instance, Crossfield detests violence. And although he is convinced of the divine righteousness of plural marriage as the principle was revealed to Joseph Smith, he believes it is sinful for a man to coerce a woman to marry him, or even to *ask* a woman to marry him; in every case the woman must choose the man for the marriage to be legitimate.

Born in northern Alberta in 1929, Crossfield is the son of a farmer who went broke trying to homestead on the prairie west of Edmonton. As a nineteen-year-old, Robert came down with tuberculosis and was confined to a sanatorium for nine months. While bedridden, he passed the endless hours by reading whatever the nurses brought around, and one of the books left by his bedside happened to be a copy of *The Book of Mormon*. The young Robert Crossfield, who was not religious, was moved by boredom to open the book and read it.

"In the back of *The Book of Mormon*," says Crossfield, "it promises that if you read it with a sincere heart, and you ask the Lord if it's true, he'll manifest the truth of it unto you by the gift of the Holy Ghost. Well, the Holy Ghost came to me after I finished it and showed me very strongly that this book was true. So I converted myself to the Mormon Church." Crossfield became an active and very pious Saint, was married in the Edmonton LDS Temple, and went to work as an accountant to support his growing family.

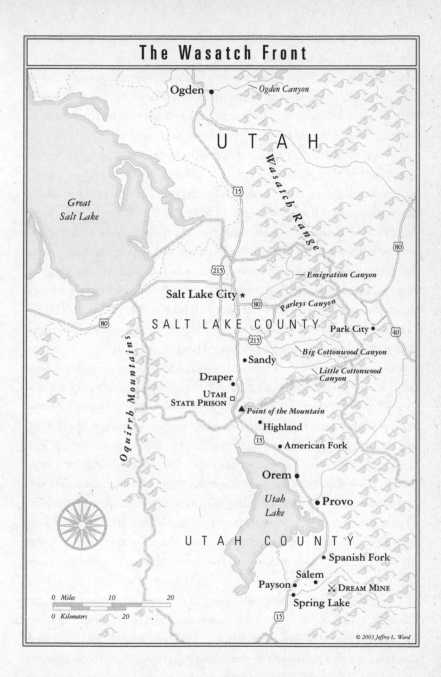

The Wasatch Front

Ogden

Ogden Canyon

U T A H

Wasatch Range

15

*Great
Salt Lake*

215

Emigration Canyon

Salt Lake City ★

80

Parleys Canyon

SALT LAKE COUNTY

Park City

215

40

Big Cottonwood Canyon

Sandy

*Little Cottonwood
Canyon*

Draper

UTAH
STATE PRISON

▲ *Point of the Mountain*

Highland

15

American Fork

Orem

*Utah
Lake*

Provo

UTAH COUNTY

Spanish Fork

Salem

Payson

✕ DREAM MINE

Spring Lake

15

Oquirrh Mountains

80

0 Miles   10   20

0 Kilometers   20

© 2003 Jeffrey L. Ward

Then, in March 1961, while he was toiling over a ledger at McLeod Mercantile in Spruce Grove, Alberta, "the still small voice of the Lord" suddenly came to him, revealing that he had been chosen to serve as God's mouthpiece—that he was a holy prophet of the Lord. And the very first words God uttered to him that day affirmed the correctness of *D & C* 132 and the principle of plural marriage.

A few months after God first spoke to him, Crossfield left Spruce Grove to become office manager of a farmer's cooperative in Creston, British Columbia, a small agricultural town immediately north of the Idaho panhandle. Just down the road from Creston, it turned out, was a flock of fundamentalists allied with the UEP polygamists who lived in what was then called Short Creek, Arizona. Like their brethren in the States at that time, the Creston polygamists followed the teachings of Prophet LeRoy Johnson—the humble, much beloved Uncle Roy. Upon his arrival in Creston, Crossfield heard about the "polygs" in the neighborhood and was curious. He began attending their prayer meetings. Right away they struck him as kindred souls.

Debbie Palmer was six years old when Crossfield appeared in Bountiful. She remembers him as a dour, wraithlike man with a pockmarked face who would show up at her home to have long theological discussions with her father. Crossfield was a mysterious presence, she recalls, who hovered at the fringe of the community: "When I was a young girl, the Prophet Onias—I guess he was still calling himself Robert Crossfield in those days—seemed weird and creepy. My friends and I were terrified we would be forced to marry him as soon as we turned fourteen." Crossfield made a much better impression on Ray Blackmore, Uncle Roy, Debbie's dad, and the other fundamentalist leaders, who admired his forthrightness and integrity and soon invited him to join their community.

God continued to speak to Crossfield throughout his tenure in the Creston Valley, as he immersed himself in fundamentalist doctrine. Most of these revelations closely reiterated the teachings of Uncle Roy, confirming that the leaders of the LDS Church had "cut themselves off from the voice of the Lord" and betrayed some of Joseph Smith's most important tenets—including the sacred principle of plural marriage.

By 1972 Crossfield had received twenty-three significant revelations, which he collected into a single volume titled *The First Book of Commandments,* paid a few thousand dollars to have printed, and distributed to libraries and religious bookstores across Canada and the western United States. But one of these slender tomes happened to find its way into the hands of LDS President Mark E. Peterson in Salt Lake City, "and that was the end of my church membership," Crossfield explains. "Came right from the top. I was excommunicated from the Mormon Church." A tight laugh erupts from deep within his chest. "I loved that church. Still do, in fact. It brought me great joy to attend every Sunday, and I kept going to church long after I was excommunicated. But then they eventually told me I couldn't come anymore."

Rejection by the mainline church was considered a badge of honor by the Creston fundamentalists, who admired Crossfield for his outspoken views—until God began revealing to Crossfield that Uncle Roy and the other UEP leaders had themselves gone astray and were misinterpreting various important points of sacred doctrine. Not to put too fine a point on it, in 1974 God told Crossfield that Crossfield's version of the One True Church was correct and Uncle Roy's version was wrong.

Back in March 1962, just a few months after Crossfield began attending prayer meetings with the polygamists in Creston, God had told him, "I will raise up one mighty and strong among you, having the scepter of justice in his hand, who shall grind in pieces all those who would oppose My work, for the prayer of the righteous shall not go unheeded." This was a direct reference to *D&C* 85, in which God first told Joseph Smith that he would be sending "one mighty and strong" to "set in order the house of God."* Although Crossfield never explicitly claimed in public to be the one mighty and strong, several of his published revelations leave little doubt that, privately at least, he believed he might indeed be "the one."

In a commandment Crossfield received in 1975, God called him by

---

* Over the years, more than twenty fundamentalists—Ron Lafferty, Rulon Jeffs, and Brian David Mitchell (the abductor of Elizabeth Smart) among them—have claimed to be the "one mighty and strong" sent by God to reinstate the doctrine of plural marriage and "set in order" the modern LDS Church.

the name "Onias," revealed that he was the true prophet and rightful
leader of the LDS Church, and explained that Onias had been put on
earth specifically "to set in order My Church."* According to God, Uncle Roy and his lieutenants in the UEP were supposed to take their
marching orders from Crossfield/Onias.

Of course, none of this went over well with Uncle Roy or the other
men who ran the UEP's affairs in Creston and Colorado City. The leader
of the Creston polygamists promptly informed Crossfield/Onias that his
presence was no longer welcome at the Creston prayer meetings, and he
was kicked out of the UEP. Unfazed, Onias moved to Idaho, and then, in
the early 1980s, to a little town outside of Provo, Utah.

The official title of the supreme leader of the LDS Church—today, as in
centuries past—is "President, Prophet, Seer, and Revelator." This is because from its inception, Mormonism was a faith in which religious
truth and ecclesiastical authority were supposed to be derived from a
never-ending string of divine revelations.

In the beginning, Joseph Smith had emphasized the importance of
personal revelation for everyone. Denigrating the established churches
of the day, which were more inclined to filter the word of God through
institutional hierarchies, he instructed Mormons to seek direct "impres-
sions from the Lord," which should guide them in every aspect of their
lives. Quickly, however, Joseph saw a major drawback to such a policy:
if God spoke directly to all Mormons, who was to say that the truths He
revealed to Joseph had greater validity than contradictory truths He
might reveal to somebody else? With everyone receiving revelations, the
prophet stood to lose control of his followers.

---

* In the Old Testament, Onias was a Jewish high priest who lived in Jerusalem two centuries before Christ. Onias gained renown for defying the ruling tyrant, King Antiochus
Epiphanes, and refusing to worship his idols. To punish Onias, the king stripped him of his
priesthood and installed a toady, Menelaus, in his stead. Onias responded by gathering an
army of one thousand men, storming the temple in Jerusalem, and banishing Menelaus, enabling the Jews to worship within its sacred walls once again. Coincidentally (or perhaps
not), Robert Crossfield had an ancestor named William Onias Crossfield, born in Quebec in
1879.

Joseph acted fast to resolve this dilemma by announcing in 1830—the same year the Mormon Church was incorporated—that God had belatedly given him another revelation: "No one shall be appointed to receive commandments and revelations in this church excepting my servant Joseph Smith, Jr." But the genie was already out of the bottle. Joseph had taught and encouraged his Saints to receive personal revelations, and the concept proved to be immensely popular. People liked talking to God directly, one-on-one, without intermediaries. It was one of the most appealing aspects of Joseph's new church.

Thus, even after Joseph told his followers that henceforth they were forbidden to receive divine commandments concerning church doctrine, many of these Saints quietly ignored the edict and continued to heed the voice of God, whether He was talking to them about matters of theology or personal issues. The simple fact was, God's words were always going to carry more weight than Joseph's, and there wasn't much the prophet could do about it. This goes a long way toward explaining why, since 1830, some two hundred schismatic Mormon sects have splintered off from Joseph's original religion; in fact, sects continue to splinter off on an ongoing basis. The UEP communities in Colorado City and Creston are a prime example. The followers of Robert Crossfield, the Prophet Onias, are another—and one of them would turn out to be Dan Lafferty.

An hour down the Interstate from Salt Lake City, the stolid, can-do city of Provo covers the flats between Utah Lake and eleven-thousand-foot Provo Peak. Boasting a population of slightly more than one hundred thousand, it is the seat of Utah County, and home to both the LDS Missionary Training Center—from which thirty thousand young men and women go forth each year to proselytize around the globe—and Brigham Young University (BYU)—Mormondom's flagship institution of higher learning, owned and tightly controlled by the LDS Church.

For a person accustomed to the multiethnic commotion of Los Angeles, Vancouver, New York, or even Denver, walking across the BYU campus can be a jarring experience. One sees no graffiti, not a speck of litter. More than 99 percent of the thirty thousand students are white.

Each of the young Mormons one encounters is astonishingly well groomed and neatly dressed. Beards, tattoos, and pierced ears (or other body parts) are strictly forbidden for men. Immodest attire and more than a single piercing per ear are forbidden among women. Smoking, using profane language, and drinking alcohol or even coffee are likewise banned. Heeding the dictum "Cougars don't cut corners," students keep to the sidewalks as they hurry to make it to class on time; nobody would think of attempting to shave a few precious seconds by treading on the manicured grass. Everyone is cheerful, friendly, and unfailingly polite.

Most non-Mormons think of Salt Lake City as the geographic heart of Mormonism, but in fact half the population of Salt Lake is Gentile, and many Mormons regard that city as a sinful, iniquitous place that's been corrupted by outsiders. To the Saints themselves, the true Mormon heartland is here in Provo and surrounding Utah County—the site of chaste little towns like Highland, American Fork, Orem, Payson, and Salem—where the population is nearly 90 percent LDS. The Sabbath is taken seriously in these parts. Almost all businesses close on Sundays, as do public swimming pools, even on the hottest days of the summer months.

This part of the state is demographically notable in other aspects, as well. The LDS Church forbids abortions, frowns on contraception, and teaches that Mormon couples have a sacred duty to give birth to as many children as they can support—which goes a long way toward explaining why Utah County has the highest birth rate in the United States; it is higher, in fact, than the birth rate in Bangladesh. This also happens to be the most Republican county in the most Republican state in the nation. Not coincidentally, Utah County is a stronghold not only of Mormonism but also Mormon Fundamentalism.

Salem is a farming community twelve miles south of Provo, situated where the orchards and potato fields of the east bench rub up against the high, craggy mountains of the Wasatch Front. This is where Dan Lafferty was born and raised. From miles away, one's eyes are drawn to a gargantuan white structure clinging to the steep hillside immediately above Salem: the legendary Dream Mine, which drew the Prophet Onias to the area in the early 1980s.

The Dream Mine was the lifework of a salt-of-the-earth Mormon named John Hyrum Koyle, who passed away in 1949 at the age of eighty-four. Koyle counted himself among those special Saints who had been blessed with the gift of prophecy. He'd predicted the stock market crash of 1929 to the exact day. He'd prophesied the date World War II would end. He'd foretold of the devastating floods that swept through northern Utah thirty-four years after his death. But his most notable and far-reaching prophecy concerned the Dream Mine.

On the night of August 27, 1894, the angel Moroni—the same Moroni who had given the gold plates to Joseph Smith sixty-seven years earlier—visited Koyle in a dream. Moroni guided Koyle to the top of a nearby mountain, where the ground opened to admit them deep into the earth. There, Moroni led Koyle through nine enormous caverns overflowing with gold. It had been gathered by the Nephites (of *The Book of Mormon*), but all that wealth had made them prideful and covetous, so God had taken it away from them some two thousand years ago and hidden it deep beneath this mountain, along with ancient records documenting the entire history of the Mormons' forebears.

Moroni informed Koyle that the gold would remain hidden inside the mountain until just before the Second Coming of Christ, by which time the world's mightiest civilizations would have crumbled and horrible strife would afflict all of humankind. At that desperate moment, Koyle would unearth the Nephites' gold and use it to provide for the faithful, enabling them to survive the privations of the Last Days. Moroni showed Koyle exactly where he should start digging and assured him the gold would eventually be unearthed there—but not until the Second Coming was imminent.

Koyle filed a mining claim on the hillside east of Salem and started digging on September 17, 1894. At the time, much of the American West was undergoing a boom in mining, so it was relatively easy for Koyle to find financial backers, almost all of them devout Mormons who saw the Dream Mine as a sound spiritual investment, as well as a surefire

way to get rich. Some seven hundred thousand shares of stock were eventually sold. By the mid-1940s a shaft had been excavated thirty-four
hundred feet into the mountain. The fact that no gold had yet been
found didn't particularly worry Koyle or his investors: Moroni had assured him that the riches would be uncovered when the Last Days were
at hand, and not a moment before.

The LDS leadership, though, took a dim view of Koyle's mine. In
the modern church, as in Joseph Smith's day, major revelations were supposed to be channeled through the LDS president, prophet, seer, and
revelator—and nobody else. Church authorities repeatedly proclaimed
that Koyle was a false prophet and warned the faithful not to invest in
the Dream Mine, but many Saints continued to believe in Koyle's vision.
Finally, in 1948, the LDS leadership excommunicated Koyle. Heartbro-
ken and humiliated, he died a year later. Thousands of Koyle's followers,
however, remained convinced that Koyle's prophecy would eventually
come to pass—and remain convinced today. The Prophet Onias is one of
these believers.

Onias first heard about the Dream Mine shortly after he converted to
Mormonism. He bought three hundred shares of stock in the mine, at $3
a share, and later persuaded his mother to buy three hundred shares, as
well. In the late 1970s he began receiving revelations about the mine:
the Lord commanded him to buy land in Salem at the base of the mine
and build a "City of Refuge" there, where the righteous could hunker
down in safety during the Last Days, when all hell broke loose around
them. Onias moved to Utah County and made a $1,500 down payment
on five acres below the mine entrance. Along the way he crossed paths
with Bernard Brady and Kenyon Blackmore, local businessmen and ardent supporters of the Dream Mine who owned expensive homes in an
upscale community immediately adjacent to the mine.

Brady is a fleshy, pink-faced man in his mid-fifties who is easy to
like. A natural salesman, he maintains a relentlessly upbeat demeanor
that only occasionally shows cracks around the edges. Born into a good
Mormon family in Malad City, Idaho (just north of the Utah border), at
the age of nineteen, immediately prior to embarking on a two-year LDS

mission to Switzerland, he had an experience that changed his life: before leaving Malad, he developed a severe allergic reaction to a routine inoculation. "I felt really strange and kind of weak right after they gave me the shots," he recalls. "I had to sit down. They gave me some orange juice and I started feeling better, so I left the doctor's office and went back to work."

But soon after Brady returned to his job filling bags of flour at his family's grain mill, he started feeling woozy, prompting his mother to drive him home. "It was a hot August day," he says, "but I felt this unbelievable chill, like I was going to freeze to death. So she put me on her bed with all these blankets and went in to call the doctor. All of a sudden I stopped breathing. Just quit. Then I noticed that the ceiling was coming closer and closer and closer. It took me a moment to realize that the ceiling wasn't moving—I was. I was floating. I turned and looked down, and saw my body there on the bed below me. But the thing I remember most was this overwhelmingly powerful feeling of peace and well-being and love—that all was well in the world. I'd never felt anything like it. It was absolutely amazing.

"I was just about to hit the ceiling and bust right through it when I started thinking to myself, 'Something isn't right here. I should be breathing.' So I commanded myself to breathe, and as soon as I did that I immediately found myself back down on the bed, inside my body, and my lungs started filling with air. But after I'd exhaled, my breathing didn't automatically continue—it stopped again. So I thought, 'Well, I better do that again.' So I did that about three times, willing myself to breathe each time. And then my body finally took over and I started breathing again involuntarily.

"But when I started breathing, I felt awful again—really sick—where just a few seconds earlier I'd been feeling *so* good, floating around in the room."

Upon regaining consciousness, Brady was rushed to the hospital by his mother. After spending a night there he recovered fully, but his near-death experience made a profound impression that has remained with him, very vividly, ever since. As he floated high above his body in the throes of anaphylactic shock, God ceased to be an abstract concept. He had felt the presence of the Lord firsthand, and he yearned to recapture that overpowering sense of the divine in his Mormon faith.

For several years before he met the Prophet Onias, Brady had been growing increasingly disaffected with the LDS Church. He was discouraged by the lack of religious passion among most of the Mormons he knew. Too many members of the church seemed to him to be merely going through the motions, treating it more as a social organization than as a means for spiritual enlightenment. Then, in the late 1970s, Brady met Kenyon Blackmore and entered into a business partnership with him, selling investments in tax shelters and other financial instruments that promised incredibly high returns to speculators.

"Ken was really intriguing to me," says Brady. "He knew more about Mormonism than anybody I've ever met, yet he said he wasn't a Mormon. After I'd worked with him for six months or so, I sat him down and asked him to level with me: 'How can you know all this stuff and not be a member of the LDS Church?' So he took a deep breath and told me all about fundamentalism." Blackmore turned out to be a Canadian-born polygamist. Although he wasn't directly affiliated with the UEP or any other fundamentalist group, one of his first cousins was Winston Blackmore, who had recently maneuvered to become the leader of the polygamists in Bountiful, British Columbia, with whom Onias had once been friendly. Two of Onias's daughters were in fact married to Winston Blackmore's brothers—Kenyon Blackmore's cousins.

"Ken was my first exposure to Mormon Fundamentalism," Brady continues. "The whole concept sort of blew me away: all these things that Joseph Smith had revealed, but had then been abandoned by the modern Church. I went home and shared what Ken had told me with my wife. She and I both did a lot of questioning about whether it was true or not. We went through an intense period of investigating and fasting and praying. At the end both of us were impressed that the fundamentalist message was basically true. And if it was true, we couldn't ignore it. That was the frame of mind I was in when I first met the Prophet Onias, Bob Crossfield."

Because Brady was a stockholder in the Dream Mine, he was well acquainted with the prophecies of John Koyle, one of which referred to a "lightly complected man with white hair who would come from the North with whom the stockholders would rally and bring remarkable changes in and around the mine." This seemed to predict the arrival of Onias in Salem, impressing Brady. Coincidentally, at the time he met Onias, Onias was in the process of putting together an organization called the School of the Prophets, and he invited Brady to become one of the school's six original counselors.

Modeled on an institution of the same name established by Joseph Smith in 1832, Onias intended his School of the Prophets to be a mechanism for instilling crucial Mormon principles that had been forsaken by the modern LDS Church: plural marriage; the tenet that God and Adam, the first man, were one and the same; and the divinely ordained supremacy of the white race. All of which was customary fundamentalist fare. But there was one aspect of Onias's School of the Prophets that set him apart from the leaders of other polygamist sects: he instructed his followers how to receive divine revelations. Indeed, teaching this sacred art—which had been widely practiced by Mormons in Joseph's day yet all but abandoned by the modern Church—was the school's main thrust. Onias intended to restore the gift of revelation by teaching twentieth-century Saints how to hear the "still small voice" of God, which, as Joseph explained in Section 85 of *The Doctrine and Covenants,* "whispereth through and pierceth all things, and often times it maketh my bones to quake."

Brady, energized by Onias's ideas, set out to recruit worthy candidates for the school. One of them turned out to be a fellow named Watson Lafferty Jr. "He was a real quality individual," Brady asserts. "And Watson said he had five brothers who were just like him. So I met them, and the whole Lafferty family was outstanding. They all had real strong convictions, but especially Watson's older brother Dan. He would go out of his way to help others much more than most people would. And Dan was unique in the strength of his desire to do what was meaningful, to do what was right. A white lie here and there—to most people that wouldn't be a big thing. But to Dan it would be unthinkable."

Brady pauses, and a look of overwhelming regret darkens his face. For a moment he looks like he's going to burst into tears. He recovers his composure, with visible effort, then, in a faltering voice, continues: "So I introduced Dan Lafferty to Bob Crossfield. Looking back on it now, it's unfortunate that I was the catalyst who brought Bob and the Laffertys together. But it happened."

EIGHT

THE PEACE MAKER

In an age in which economists take for granted that people equate well-being with consumption, increasing numbers of people seem willing to trade certain freedoms and material comforts for a sense of immutable order and the rapture of faith.

EUGENE LINDEN,
THE FUTURE IN PLAIN SIGHT

Dan Lafferty grew up with his five brothers and two sisters on a four-acre farm just west of Salem, Utah. Their father, Watson Lafferty Sr., had served as a barber on an aircraft carrier in World War II; following the war he enrolled in chiropractic college on the G.I. Bill. Upon completion of his training, he opened a combination chiropractic practice–barbershop–beauty salon in a spare room in his home, and settled down to raise his family to be exemplary Latter-day Saints.

Watson Lafferty spent a lot of time thinking about God. He also spent a lot of time thinking about the government, and the relationship the former should properly have with the latter. He was highly impressed with the ideas of Ezra Taft Benson—the prominent Mormon apostle, Red-baiter, and John Birch Society supporter who in 1961 announced that there was an "insidious infiltration of communist agents and sympathizers into almost every segment of American

Life."* Even in archconservative, ultra-Mormon Utah County, the hard rightward lean of Watson's political views, as well as his extreme piety, caused the Lafferty patriarch to stand out.

Dan characterizes his dad as "strong-willed," a "very individual in-dividual," and "strict about a lot of things." In fact, Watson Lafferty was a formidable disciplinarian who did not hesitate to beat the living tar out of his children or his wife, Claudine, to enforce his rules. Commonly, the children were present to witness the punishment when Watson hit Claudine—a reserved, submissive wife whom Dan describes as "a good woman and an excellent mother." The children were also present when Watson clubbed the family dog to death with a baseball bat.

Among Watson Lafferty's more strongly held beliefs was a deep dis-trust of conventional medicine. When Dan's oldest sister, Colleen, came down with acute appendicitis as a young girl, their father was adamant that she be treated at home with prayer and homeopathic remedies. Only after her appendix burst and death was imminent did he grudg-ingly take Colleen to the hospital. Watson ultimately died himself in 1983 after refusing medical treatment for advanced diabetes.

Despite the fact that Watson was a violent bully, Dan loved his fa-ther intensely and admired him. To this day Dan considers him a superb role model. "I was blessed to be raised in a very special and happy fam-ily," Dan insists. "We never wanted for anything. My parents truly loved and cared for each other." Dan recalls that his dad often took his mom out dancing, and "it wasn't unusual to hear my father ask my mother if he had told her lately that he loved her." Once when Dan was attending the Provo temple with his family—with everyone dressed in white tem-ple garments, and the women and men sitting on opposite sides of the hall—he remembers his father leaning over to ask him, sotto voce, "if I had ever seen anyone as beautiful as my mother" as she sat with the other women across the room. In the celestial glow of the temple's sacred chambers, Dan remembers vividly, his mother looked "angelic and radiant."

---

* Benson, who served as secretary of agriculture under President Eisenhower, eventually be-came president and prophet of the entire LDS Church, holding that position from 1985 un-til his death in 1994.

According to Dan, his parents placed "their family at the very center of their life, along with the LDS Church." The Laffertys belonged to
a congregation in the nearby community of Spring Lake, says Dan, and
worshiped at "the perfect picture-postcard church, by a lake, with just a
few houses around. It was in that lake where I learned to swim and fish,
and in the winter we had ice-skating parties with family and friends."
Young Dan was a model Latter-day Saint, virtuous and compliant,
"zooming down the highway to heaven," as he puts it. "I was a hundred-
and-ten-percenter. I sang in the choir. I always paid my tithing; in fact,
I always paid a little extra, just to make sure I made it into the highest
kingdom of glory."

Although Dan's father adhered rigidly to Mormon doctrine, he
could not be called a fundamentalist. "I don't think the word *polygamy*
was ever mentioned while I was growing up," says Dan. "It never even
crossed my mind. The first time I ever had a conversation with anyone
about polygamy, it was about a group of missionaries in France who were
excommunicated after they studied Section 132 together and decided
polygamy was a principle that should be practiced. I can still remember
thinking to myself, 'How could anyone sacrifice their membership in
the church over that old, discontinued principle?' "

After high school Dan went on a two-year mission to Scotland,
where he met Matilda Loomis, a divorced mother of two young girls,
who made a powerful impression on him. Six years after returning from
his mission, Dan bumped into Matilda by chance at a missionary reunion. "I was getting kind of old by then," Dan says, "and my father and
older brother, Ron, had been getting on me to get married. I had met a
lot of lovely girls previously, but whenever I prayed about whether I
should marry them, I realized none of them was the right one. So then I
ran into Matilda at this reunion, and I thought, Well, I should probably
pray about marrying her, too, before she goes back to Scotland, just in
case that's what God has in mind for me. And this time I was quite surprised to get a positive answer to my prayers. So I told Matilda that we
should get married.

"I thought it was going to be really awkward trying to explain that
God intended her to be my wife, and I was worried how she would react.

So I was kind of thrown off when she answered, 'Yeah, I know.' I said, What do you mean, 'I know'? She explained that God had told her to come to America just for that reason, to get married. She said that she was expecting me to ask her." Within three months Dan and Matilda were sealed as husband and wife in the Provo temple and moved to California, with Matilda's kids in tow, so that Dan could enroll in the Los Angeles College of Chiropractic.

One Sunday near the end of their five years in California, Dan and Matilda happened to hear a member of their local LDS ward give a talk about plural marriage. "During the talk this guy said, 'Okay, let's see a show of hands from everybody who comes from a polygamous background,' " Dan recalls. "And there were only like four people who didn't raise their hands in the whole congregation. That really got my attention. I decided to learn everything I could about polygamy."

When Dan completed his chiropractic training he moved his family back to Utah County, and there he embarked on an energetic investigation of the polygamous history of the Latter-day Saints. Nosing around in the special collections of the Brigham Young University library one afternoon, he came across a fifty-one-page typescript of a nineteenth-century tract in praise of plural marriage: *An Extract, From a Manuscript Entitled "The Peace Maker," or the Doctrines of the Millennium: Being a Treatise on Religion and Jurisprudence. Or a New System of Religion and Politicks.* It had been written by a mysterious figure named Udney Hay Jacob. The booklet's title page indicated that it had been published in 1842 in Nauvoo, Illinois, and that the printer was none other than Joseph Smith himself.

The Peace Maker offered an elaborate biblical rationale for polygamy, which it proposed as a cure for the myriad ills that plagued monogamous relationships and, by extension, all of humankind. Part of that cure was making sure that women remained properly subservient, as God intended. According to the tract,

> The government of the wife is therefore placed in the husband by the
> law of God; for he is the head. I suffer not a woman saith the Lord to
> teach, or to usurp authority over a man, but to be in subjection. . . .

A right understanding of this matter and a correct law properly executed would restore this nation to peace and order; and man to his true dignity, authority and government of the earthly creation. It would soon rectify the domestic circle and establish a proper head over the families of the earth, together with the knowledge and restitution of the whole penal law of God, and be the means of driving Satan, yea of driving Satan from the human mind. . . .

Gentlemen, the ladies laugh at your pretended authority. They, many of them, hiss at the idea of your being the lords of the creation. . . . Nothing is further from the minds of our wives in general, than the idea of submitting to their husbands in all things, and of reverencing their husbands. They will boldly ridicule the idea of calling them sincerely in their hearts lords and masters. But God has positively required this of them. . . .

Here, the wife is pronounced the husband's property, as much so as his manservant, his maidservant, his ox, or his horse. . . .

It is evident that by [abandoning the sacred principle of plural marriage], an endless catalogue of crime has been created that otherwise could never have existed; and that does exist at this moment in these States. Husbands forsake their wives, and often brutally abuse them. Fathers forsake their children; young maidens are seduced and abandoned by the deceiver; wives are poisoned and put to death by their husbands; husbands are murdered by their wives; new born babes are cruelly murdered to hide the false shame created by the false, and wicked, and tyrannical law against polygamy. . . .

While on the other hand polygamy regulated by the law of God as illustrated in this book could not possibly produce one crime; neither could it injure any human being. The stupidity of modern Christian nations upon this subject is horribly astonishing. . . .

The question is not now to be debated whether these things are so: neither is it a question of much importance who wrote this book! But the question, the momentous question is: will you now restore the law of God on this important subject, and keep it? Remember that the law of God is given by inspiration of the Holy Ghost. Speak not a word against it at your peril.

Because Joseph Smith was listed on the title page as the printer of *The Peace Maker,* because the treatise precisely reflected many of his teachings—and because it concluded with the cryptic declaration that it was not "a question of much importance who wrote this book!"—scholars and others have long speculated that Joseph was the author. Determining who wrote *The Peace Maker* was important to Dan Lafferty. "I really wanted to know if this was Joseph Smith's writing," he says. "So I studied, and prayed, and after a period of time the Lord gave me enough knowledge to become quite satisfied that Joseph Smith wrote it. . . . I don't know for sure that it's Joseph Smith, but I'll be surprised if it wasn't."

The fact that *The Peace Maker* was apparently the work of the prophet made Dan especially receptive to the ideas expounded in its pages. With all the zeal one would expect from a "hundred-and-ten-percenter," he wasted no time in applying the book's fundamentalist strictures to his household, which had by then grown to include Matilda, her two daughters from a previous marriage, and four children she and Dan had conceived together.

Under the new rules, Matilda was no longer allowed to drive, handle money, or talk to anyone outside the family when Dan wasn't present, and she had to wear a dress at all times. The children were pulled out of school and forbidden to play with their friends. Dan decreed that the family was to receive no outside medical care; he began treating them himself by means of prayer, fasting, and herbal remedies. In July 1983, when their fifth child was born, a son, Dan delivered the baby at home and circumcised the boy himself.

They began raising much of their own food, scavenging the rest from Dumpsters behind grocery stores, where stale, unsold bread and overripe produce were regularly discarded. Dan turned off the gas and electricity. No publications of any kind were allowed in the home, except LDS books and magazines. Dan even got rid of all their watches and clocks, believing they should "keep time by the spirit." When Matilda disobeyed Dan, he spanked her.

Spank was the verb Dan used. According to Matilda, the blows he delivered felt more like "thumps." And when he thumped her, he often did it in front of Dan's mother, his brothers, and all their children. Afterward, he warned Matilda that if she continued to disobey, she would be forced out of the marriage without her children—who, according to the principles elucidated in *The Peace Maker,* were the father's property.

Dan also announced that he intended to engage in spiritual wifery at the earliest opportunity. And the first woman he proposed taking as a plural wife was Matilda's oldest daughter—his own stepdaughter.

"I had come to a place there was no choices," Matilda later testified in court. "I could either go and leave my kids, or stay and accept it." She elected to stay.

Matilda said that the first years of their marriage had been "extremely happy and hopeful. . . . And then it just disintegrated. . . . I would dream of him dying so I could get out." By then, she said, her life had become "a hellish situation."

PART II

The earnest cadres of bureaucrats who today direct the Mormon Church's growth across the world . . . are the spiritual descendants of those deeply disciplined Mormon pioneers. The Mormon Church, then and now, is founded upon complete obedience to hierarchical Church authority, and to the surety of revelation from above. . . .

The doctrine of obedience sounds inimical to American individualism and alien to Protestantism generally, and it is. Yet the American frontier where Mormonism grew up has always been riven by contradictory attitudes toward individualism. It could be deadly in a place where cooperation, and indeed absolute obedience of the kind Mormons then and now understand, might offer the only means to survive. Survival was often collective or not at all, a lesson not lost on Mormons of later generations. Though the contemporary image of Mormons may be one of conservative rectitude, hopelessly middle-class and lower-middle-brow, tinged with both the Church's nineteenth-century polygamous past and its refusal until the 1970s to give up official racism, the institutional preoccupation of the Church from its moment of inception has been with sheer survival.

KENNETH ANDERSON
"THE MAGIC OF THE GREAT SALT LAKE,"
TIMES LITERARY SUPPLEMENT, MARCH 24, 1995

It is almost impossible to write fiction about the Mormons, for the reasons that Mormon institutions and Mormon society are so peculiar that they call for constant explanation.

WALLACE STEGNER,
MORMON COUNTRY

NINE

HAUN'S MILL

Bearing persecution became the distinctive badge of membership in the church; it was the test of faith and of one's chosenness. By the end of their stay in Missouri, Mormons had accumulated a long list of trials to commemorate. . . .

Opposition gives value to struggle and inculcates self-confidence. . . . It is difficult to imagine a successful Mormon Church without suffering, without the encouragement of it, without the memory of it. Persecution arguably was the only possible force that would have allowed the infant church to prosper.

R. LAURENCE MOORE,
RELIGIOUS OUTSIDERS AND THE MAKING OF AMERICANS

When Mormonism made its debut, Joseph Smith's embryonic religion was not welcomed with open arms by everyone. The very first review of *The Book of Mormon,* published in the Rochester *Daily Advertiser* on April 2, 1830—four days before Joseph's church was even legally incorporated—typified reaction to the new faith among many in western New York. The review began, *"The Book of Mormon* has been placed in our hands. A viler imposition was never practiced. It is an evidence of fraud, blasphemy, and credulity, shocking both to Christians and moralists."

Joseph's widespread reputation as a charlatan, along with a rash of malicious rumors about his "gold Bible," had fueled animosity throughout the Palmyra region. In December 1830 Joseph received a revelation in which God, noting the hostility in the New York air, commanded him to move his flock to Ohio. So the Latter-day Saints packed up and resettled just east of present-day Cleveland, in a town called Kirtland.

In Ohio the Mormons found their neighbors to be relatively hospitable, but in the summer of 1831 the Lord revealed to Joseph that Kirtland was merely a way station, and that the Missouri frontier was in fact "the land which I have appointed and consecrated for the gathering of the Saints." God explained that northwestern Missouri was among the earth's holiest places: the Garden of Eden had not been located in the Middle East, as many believed, but rather in Jackson County, Missouri, near what, by the nineteenth century, had become the city of Independence. And it was here, too, that Christ would make His triumphant return before the century was out. Heeding the Lord's words, Joseph instructed his followers to assemble in Jackson County and start building a New Jerusalem there. Saints began pouring into northwestern Missouri, and continued arriving in ever-greater numbers through 1838.

The people who already lived in Jackson County were not happy about the monumental influx. The Mormon immigrants for the most part hailed from the northeastern states and favored the abolition of slavery; Missourians tended to have southern roots—many of them actually owned slaves—and were deeply suspicious of the Mormons' abolitionist leanings. But what alienated the residents of Jackson County most was the impenetrable clannishness of the Mormons and their arrogant sense of entitlement: the Saints insisted they were God's chosen people and had been granted a divine right to claim northwestern Missouri as their Zion.

Everything the Mormons did seemed to heighten the Missourians' apprehension. The Saints used church funds to purchase large tracts of land in Jackson County. They engaged in commerce exclusively with other Saints whenever possible, undermining local businesses. They voted in a uniform bloc, in strict accordance with Joseph's directives, and as their numbers increased they threatened to dominate regional politics. Reflecting a common fear among Missourians, a letter pub-

The Mormon Presence in 19th-Century Missouri and Illinois

© 2003 Jeffrey L. Ward

lished in 1833 in a Fayette newspaper warned, "The day is not far distant . . . when the sheriff, the justices, and the county judges will be
Mormons."

Mormons were eager to embrace any Gentiles who cared to convert,
but the Saints had little interest in associating with Missourians who remained too ignorant or obstinate to grasp God's plan for mankind.
Joseph preached something he called "free agency"; everyone was free to
choose whether to be on the side of the Lord or the side of wickedness; it
was an entirely personal decision—but woe to those who decided wrong.
If you knowingly chose to shun the God of Joseph and the Saints, you
were utterly undeserving of sympathy or mercy.

This polarizing mind-set—"If you're not with us, you're against
us"—was underscored by a revelation Joseph received in 1831, in which
God commanded the Saints to "assemble yourselves together to rejoice
upon the land of Missouri, which is the land of your inheritance, which is
now the land of your enemies." When Missourians became aware of this
commandment, they regarded it as an open declaration of war—an impression that seemed to be confirmed by an article published in a Mormon newspaper promising that the Saints would "literally tread upon the
ashes of the wicked after they are destroyed from off the face of the earth."

In the 1830s northwestern Missouri was still untamed country inhabited by rough, strong-willed characters. Jackson County residents
initially responded to the perceived Mormon threat by holding town
meetings, passing anti-Mormon resolutions, and demanding that civil
authorities take some kind of action. When such gestures failed to stem
the tide of Saints, however, the citizens of Independence took matters
into their own hands.

In July 1833 an armed mob of five hundred Missourians tarred and
feathered two Latter-day Saints and destroyed a printing office because
an LDS newspaper had published an article deemed overly sympathetic
to the antislavery viewpoint. Three days later the same mob rounded up
nine Mormon leaders and, under the threat of death, forced them to sign
an oath promising to leave Jackson County within a year. That autumn,
thugs razed ten homes, killed one Saint, and stoned numerous others.

Then, one cold November night, vigilantes systematically terrorized every Mormon settlement in the region. After savagely beating the men, they drove twelve hundred Saints from their homes, forcing them to run for their lives into the frigid darkness. Most of them fled north across the Missouri River, never to return to Jackson County.

Joseph deplored violence, and for the better part of five years he forbade the Mormons to retaliate, even though the attacks against them continued. But by the summer and fall of 1838, the tension between Gentiles and the ten thousand Saints who were by then in Missouri reached critical mass.

In 1836 the Missouri legislature, hoping to relocate the Saints in an out-of-the-way place that would forestall bloodshed, had designated sparsely populated Caldwell County as a zone of Mormon settlement, prompting most of the Saints in Missouri to move there from adjacent, less-welcoming counties. By 1838 the Mormons had purchased some 250,000 acres in Caldwell County from the federal government and built a thriving town they christened Far West.

At first the exodus to Caldwell County seemed to defuse the tension between Mormons and Gentiles. But in the summer of 1838 trouble erupted in neighboring Daviess County, where Mormons had spilled over the county line and begun establishing large new settlements. August 6 was Election Day in Missouri. That morning after the polls opened in Gallatin, the Daviess county seat, a Whig candidate for the state legislature, William Peniston, climbed on top of a barrel and bellowed to the rabble that Mormons were "horse thieves, liars, counterfeiters, and dupes." Hoping to prevent the thirty or so Mormons present from casting their ballots, another Missourian then loudly opined that Mormons should no more have the right to vote "than the niggers."

The incendiary rhetoric provoked a drunk Missourian to beat up a diminutive Mormon shoemaker named Samuel Brown. When other Mormons came to Brown's aid, a vicious brawl broke out. Wielding clubs, rocks, whips, and knives, the badly outnumbered Saints managed to overcome the Missourians and drive them off, leaving dozens of their foes severely wounded. But it was a Pyrrhic victory. The enraged citizens of Gallatin vowed to pay the Mormons back in kind.

Over the next two months, Missourians launched a campaign of harassment and violence against the Mormon residents of Daviess County, forcing most of them from their homes. Finally, on October 14 in Far West, Joseph assembled several hundred of his followers in the town square and urged them to fight back. Seething, the prophet declared:

> We are an injured people. From county to county we have been driven by unscrupulous mobs eager to seize the land we have cleared and improved with such love and toil. We have appealed to magistrates, judges, the Governor, and even the President of the United States, but there has been no redress for us. . . .
>
> If the people will let us alone, we will preach the gospel in peace. But if they come on us to molest us, we will establish our religion by the sword. We will trample down our enemies and make it one gore of blood from the Rocky Mountains to the Atlantic Ocean. I will be to this generation a second Mohammed, whose motto in treating for peace was "the Alcoran [Qur'an] or the Sword." So shall it eventually be with us—"Joseph Smith or the Sword!"*

It was an impassioned speech, and the Mormons responded. Venting years of pent-up anger, they began raiding Gentile towns and plundering food, livestock, and valuables, burning approximately fifty non-Mormon homes in the process.

---

* Joseph was not the only person to draw parallels between the founding prophets of Mormonism and Islam. Most such comparisons were made by Gentile critics intending to denigrate the Saints and their faith, but certain undeniable similarities were also noted by those sympathetic to Joseph's church. Among these admirers was Sir Richard F. Burton, the famous nineteenth-century libertine and adventurer who had extensive firsthand knowledge of Islamic cultures. Upon visiting Salt Lake City soon after the Mormons arrived there, Burton observed that Mormonism, "like El Islam," claimed to be "a restoration by revelation of the pure and primaeval religion of the world." In 1904 the esteemed German scholar Eduard Meyer spent a year in Utah studying the Saints, which moved him to predict, "As Arabia was to be the inheritance of the Muslims, so was America to become the inheritance of the Mormons." And in 1932, after acknowledging in a book called *Revelation in Mormonism* that "similarities between Islam and Mormonism have been misunderstood and exaggerated," George Arbaugh nevertheless went on to assert, "Mormonism is one of the most boldly innovating developments in the history of religions. Its aggressive theocratic claims, political aspirations, and use of force, make it akin to Islam."

Outraged, Missourians retaliated with counterattacks, destroying several Mormon cabins. Eleven days after Joseph's forceful call to arms, a skirmish resulted in the death of three Saints and one Gentile. Making matters even worse, the carnage from this fight was wildly exaggerated in an inflammatory letter to Missouri governor Lilburn Boggs, wherein it was falsely reported that the Saints had slaughtered fifty Missourians. Upon reading this, Boggs—who had won the 1836 gubernatorial election on an anti-Mormon platform—issued a now-infamous order to the top-ranked general of the Missouri Militia: "The Mormons must be treated as enemies, and must be exterminated, or driven from the state, if necessary for the public peace. Their outrages are beyond all description."

Days later, three companies of the Missouri Militia, commanded by Colonel Thomas Jennings, launched a surprise attack on a Mormon settlement known as Haun's Mill. Late in the afternoon of October 30, 1838, as the sun "hung low and red in a beautiful Indian summer sky," some twenty-five Mormon families working in the fields were surprised to see 240 troops appear suddenly from the surrounding woods, aim their muskets, and fire in unison at the Saints.

The commander of the Mormons, realizing that his lightly armed community had no chance against such an overwhelming force, immediately waved his hat and yelled out his desire to surrender. The Missourians ignored his pleas for mercy and kept shooting, inciting panic among the Saints. Many of the Mormons scattered into nearby thickets, but three boys and fifteen men sought refuge inside the settlement's blacksmith shop. There were wide, unchinked gaps between the logs that formed the walls, and shooting the Mormons through these gaps was no more difficult for the Missourians than plinking hogs in a pen. As more and more Saints were killed, the Missourians walked right up to the shop, poked the barrels of their guns between the logs, and fired at the heap of groaning bodies from point-blank range.

When the Missourians detected no further movement inside, they entered and found a ten-year-old boy, Sardius Smith, cowering under the bellows. The youth begged for his life, but a Missourian named William Reynolds put a gun to the boy's head. Sardius's younger brother, who was shot through the hip but survived by feigning death beneath the corpses, later reported that one of the Gentiles begged Reynolds not to shoot Sardius, on account of his youth, at which point Reynolds responded by explaining that Mormon children needed to be exterminated because "nits will make lice." And then he dispassionately blasted the top of the boy's skull off.

All told, eighteen Saints were slaughtered in and around the blacksmith shop. The event became known as the Haun's Mill Massacre, and was stamped into the Latter-day Saints' collective memory. More than 160 years later, Mormons still speak of it with indignation and undiminished rage.

Joseph Smith was sixteen miles away when the carnage occurred at Haun's Mill, supervising the defense of Far West, which was being surrounded by ten thousand Missouri troops. He learned of the calamity the night after it happened, and sank into a black depression. Over the months since the discord had escalated into increasingly bloody clashes, Joseph had waffled between aggressively fighting back and seeking a peaceful end to the conflict through compromise. After the massacre at Haun's Mill, the prophet seemed to suddenly recognize that if he engaged in a full-blown war with the Gentiles, he and his followers would be annihilated.

Immediately upon having this epiphany, Joseph dispatched five Mormons to meet with the Gentiles and "beg like a dog for peace." The general of the Missouri Militia informed them that there was only one way for the Saints to avert imminent eradication: without delay, they would have to deliver Joseph and six other Mormon leaders to face charges of treason; provide monetary compensation to the Missourians for property that had been plundered and destroyed; surrender all Mormon weapons; and then abandon the state of Missouri altogether.

The conditions were unreasonably harsh, yet Joseph had no real choice but to accept them. Addressing the faithful in Far West, he put on a brave face and announced, "I shall offer myself up as a sacrifice to save your lives and save the Church. Be of good cheer, my brethren. Pray earnestly to the Lord to deliver your leaders from their enemies. I bless you all in the name of Christ."

The Saints surrendered on November 1. Joseph, his brother Hyrum, and five other Mormon leaders were taken into custody by the Missourians, hastily court-martialed, and found guilty of treason—a capital crime. Missouri general Alexander Doniphan was ordered, "Sir: You will take Joseph Smith and the other prisoners into the public square of Far West, and shoot them at 9 o'clock tomorrow morning."

But Doniphan was an uncommonly principled man, and he balked at carrying out the order. Joseph and his cohorts were American citizens, and Doniphan knew it was illegal for the military to court-martial and summarily execute civilians. Indicating that he refused to participate in such a travesty of justice, General Doniphan wrote a note to his commanding officer that read, "It is cold-blooded murder. I will not obey your order . . . ; and if you execute those men, I will hold you responsible before an earthly tribunal, so help me God!"

Thanks to Doniphan's brave refusal, the execution of the Mormons was called off, and Joseph's life was spared for the time being. The Saints, however, were forced to accede to all the other conditions of their surrender, and once they had been disarmed they became easy prey for Missourians bent on revenge. Their possessions were plundered, their cabins torn down and burned for firewood, their livestock shot for amusement. Mormon men were indiscriminately beaten; rapes of women and girls were reported. And on top of everything else, they were told that they had just a few months—until the spring of 1839—to leave the state.

It proved to be a difficult winter for the Saints. As the faithful endured famine and crippling cold, anticipating their forced departure from Missouri, Joseph remained locked up along with nine other Mormon leaders indicted for treason and murder. The prophet, unrepentant, penned an angry screed from jail, warning, "The murders at Haun's Mill, the exterminating order of Governor Boggs, and the one-sided rascally proceedings of the Legislature, have damned the State of Missouri to all eternity."

As the winter wore on, the tide of public opinion began to turn in the Saints' favor. Details of the Haun's Mill Massacre were reported in various Missouri newspapers, prompting calls for an investigation. Arti-

cles sympathetic to the Mormons were published throughout the region.
The ongoing incarceration of Joseph and his brethren became a growing
embarrassment to Governor Boggs, the legislature, and local officials,
who were increasingly reluctant to bring the accused to trial lest the
Saints win an acquittal.

To save face, the sheriff responsible for guarding the jailed Mormons
was encouraged by those in power to accept an $800 bribe, get drunk,
and conveniently fall asleep, thereby allowing the prisoners to escape.
On April 16, 1839, Joseph and his nine cell mates slipped away into the
night and fled cross-country to rejoin their fellow Saints, most of whom
had by then completed their exodus from Missouri and were safely across
the Illinois state line.

TEN

NAUVOO

If our theory of revelation-value were to affirm that any book, to possess it, must have been composed automatically or not by the free caprice of the writer, or that it must exhibit no scientific and historic errors and express no local or personal passions, the Bible would probably fare ill at our hands. But if, on the other hand, our theory should allow that a book may well be a revelation in spite of errors and passions and deliberate human composition, if only it be a true record of the inner experiences of great-souled persons wrestling with their fate, then the verdict would be much more favorable.

WILLIAM JAMES,
THE VARIETIES OF RELIGIOUS EXPERIENCE

Laid out across a limestone flat beside the mud-brown flow of the Mississippi River, Nauvoo is a small, tidy town with little on its surface to distinguish it from hundreds of other small, tidy towns that freckle the American heartland. A month after breaking out of jail in Missouri, however, Joseph Smith surveyed the shore along this majestic bend in the river and resolved that the Kingdom of God's capital city would be erected precisely here, in Hancock County, Illinois.

A low-lying promontory on the river's east bank, the site was a patch of malarial swamp "so wet," as Joseph himself described it, "that it was with the utmost difficulty that a footman could get through, and totally impossible for [ox] teams." But the place had a couple of mitigating attributes: it was all but uninhabited, and the owner was willing to sell acreage to the Saints on credit. A deal was struck, construction commenced with characteristic Mormon industriousness, and within five years more than fifteen thousand of the Lord's Elect were living in and around Nauvoo—ten times its current population—making it the second-largest municipality in Illinois. From nothing, the Saints created a city that rivaled Chicago.

Unlike Chicago, moreover, Nauvoo was no mere city; it was a theocratic principality, with Joseph at its head, possessing sovereign rights and powers unique not only in Illinois but in the entire nation. These special rights were granted in a highly unusual charter passed without fanfare by the Illinois General Assembly in December 1840—a time when the state was eager to attract hardworking settlers who would contribute to the economy and sympathy for the Mormons was running high because of their expulsion from Missouri.

As an unintended consequence, Illinois set Joseph up as de facto emperor of his own autonomous city-state. He had himself officially anointed "King, Priest, and Ruler over Israel on Earth." He commanded a well-armed and rigorously disciplined militia, the Nauvoo Legion, which boasted nearly half as many men as the entire American Army at the time, and then, eager for still more military power, he petitioned the U.S. Congress for authorization to establish a one-hundred-thousand-man fighting force under his personal control.

Congress thought better of granting this latter request, but Joseph was on a roll nevertheless. Which probably came as no surprise to the prophet, because he believed that his was the Lord's One True Church and he was being guided by the hand of God. Secure in this knowledge, and eager to extend his influence to the whole country, in January 1844 Joseph announced his candidacy for president of the United States.*

Although historians are in unanimous agreement that Joseph "had a snowball's chance in hell" of winning the November election, as the

---

* Joseph's opponents were the Whig candidate Henry Clay, Democrat James K. Polk, and James G. Birney of the Liberty party. In an extremely close election, Polk emerged as the winner with a 48.1 percent plurality, defeating Clay by a scant 38,367 votes.

Jacksonian scholar Robert Remini phrased it, it is not clear whether Joseph himself shared this view. Already, after all, he'd accomplished much more than anyone could have imagined when he'd incorporated his peculiar new church in Palmyra fourteen years earlier. Joseph took the presidential campaign quite seriously, in any case, dispatching 586 of his most capable and persuasive missionaries—including ten members of the Quorum of the Twelve Apostles—to all twenty-six states and Wisconsin Territory in order to drum up support for his run at the nation's highest office.

An argument can be made that Joseph ran for president because he had come to believe that it was the only way his Saints were ever going to gain state protection from the terrible persecutions they had been subjected to wherever they had attempted to live. Having tried repeatedly, and failed on each occasion, to persuade elected officials that the government had both a moral and a legal obligation to protect the Mormons from the violent mobs that wanted to eradicate them, Joseph may have decided that his only recourse was to occupy the White House himself.

Joseph venerated the U.S. Constitution as a divinely inspired document. For years he had complained that political leaders were disregarding their sworn duty to safeguard the Mormons' constitutionally guaranteed freedom to worship without being subjected to harassment, and worse, at the hands of the religious majority. Yet in both word and deed, Joseph repeatedly demonstrated that he himself had little respect for the religious views of non-Mormons, and was unlikely to respect the constitutional rights of other faiths if he somehow won the presidency and were running the show.

The Mormons did not transform Nauvoo into a bustling hub of enterprise and godliness without first enduring serious setbacks. In 1839 and 1840, before the swamps were drained, epidemics of malaria and cholera swept through the settlement, killing hundreds of Saints, including the prophet's own father and one of his brothers. And the Missouri hostilities continued to plague Joseph and his followers long after they had been driven from that state.

Although Joseph had managed to escape from jail, criminal charges against him were still pending in Missouri. Considered a fugitive from justice, he was under constant threat of being extradited to stand trial. There was a bounty on his head. Sheriffs from Missouri came to Illinois on at least two occasions bearing writs for Joseph's arrest. In May 1841 a sheriff's posse managed to surprise the prophet outside of Nauvoo, arrested him, and had almost hauled him across the border into Missouri before Joseph managed to finagle his release with a writ of habeas corpus. It was a very close scrape, and the harassment provoked Joseph's ire. During a public speech soon after his 1841 arrest, he vented his anger by prophesying that retired governor of Missouri Lilburn Boggs—the Saints' despised nemesis—would "die by violent hands within one year."

On the evening of May 6, 1842, Boggs was reading a newspaper in the study of his Independence home when a gunman lurking outside shot him four times through a window. Two balls hit Boggs in the neck; the other two pierced his skull and lodged in the left lobe of his brain. Everyone assumed that he would die, and Boggs's demise was reported in newspapers across the country. Most of these papers speculated that the assassin had been a Mormon bent on fulfilling Joseph Smith's prophecy.

The handgun used to shoot the ex-governor was discovered outside Boggs's study, where it had been tossed into a puddle. An investigation quickly determined that the pistol had recently been stolen from a local store. The storekeeper told the sheriff, "I thought the niggers had taken it, but that hired man of Ward's—the one who used to work with the stallion—he came in to look at it just before it turned up missing!" The "hired man of Ward's" was an accomplished horseman from Nauvoo named Orrin Porter Rockwell. He had arrived in Independence a couple of months earlier, then quietly slipped out of town immediately after Boggs was shot.

As it turned out, the reports of Boggs's death were premature. Somehow he recovered from his severe brain injuries. The papers were right about the would-be killer, though: Rockwell was almost certainly the would-be assassin, and he was a Mormon. Afraid of nothing, and fiercely devoted to the prophet, Rockwell was already becoming legendary for his willingness to spill the blood of those who had wronged the church, thereby giving them an opportunity to atone for their sins—a career that would become his life's work and inspire admiring Mormons to christen him the "Destroying Angel" and the "Mormon Samson."

Although Joseph may not have ordered Rockwell to shoot Boggs, it was commonly understood by the faithful that it was a Saint's sacred duty to assist in the fulfilling of prophecies when the opportunity arose. Once Boggs's death had been foretold by the prophet, nobody needed to tell Porter Rockwell what to do. Few inhabitants of Missouri (and perhaps even fewer Saints up the river in Nauvoo) doubted that the attempted assassination was the work of Mormondom's Destroying Angel, but Rockwell had no difficulty eluding arrest. Neither he nor any other Saint was ever brought to justice for the deed.

Life in Nauvoo, meanwhile, continued apace. The city of the Saints was booming. There on the banks of the great American river, the Mormons seemed to have at last found a secure foothold from which to spread Joseph's religion far and wide. He and his followers had come an impressively long way in the seventeen years since Moroni had entrusted Joseph with the gold plates. And new converts to the Mormon Church were arriving in Nauvoo in ever greater throngs, many now coming from as far afield as England and Scandinavia.

The Second Great Awakening had been crawling with impassioned, silver-tongued prophets who roamed the land hawking upstart creeds. Almost all of these novel faiths provided reassuring answers to the mysteries of life and death, and promised converts that they would be rewarded for their devotion by spending the hereafter on easy street. But almost none of the new churches managed to establish an enduring body of followers. Most are now long forgotten. So why did Joseph's new religion triumph when so many of his competitors vanished with scarcely a trace? To be sure, there were numerous reasons why so many people found Mormonism so appealing. Probably none, however, was more salient than the colossal force of Joseph's personality.

Charisma is a quality that's hard to define and even harder to explain, but Joseph was flush with it. The term is derived from the Greek

kharis, meaning "graced" or "a special gift of God," and the Latin word
charisms, defined as "gift of the holy spirit." Its meaning has evolved
through the centuries and is now seldom associated with sanctity, but
Joseph's brand of charisma seems to have been true to the original definition. He was imbued with that exceedingly rare magnetism possessed
by history's most celebrated religious leaders—an extraordinary spiritual power that always seems to be wrapped in both great mystery and
great danger. More than a century and a half after his death, Joseph's personal incandescence has lost little of its intensity. One can still see it
blazing in the eyes of his Saints.

In any religion there is a tendency for the devout to reinvent their
founding prophet as an idealized deity, obscuring and protecting him
behind an impenetrable armor of myth. Mormons are certainly no different from the faithful of other sects in this regard, and they have done
their best to airbrush every blemish from the portraits of Joseph they
display to the world. But unlike Moses, Jesus, Muhammad, and Buddha, Joseph was a modern prophet who lived in the brightly lit age of
the affidavit and the printing press. Because many who felt the pull of
his immense charm left a written record of their observations, his im-
perfect humanity has not been so readily erased from the historical
record.

The fact that he remains accessible to us as a real person, warts and
all, makes it easier to feel empathy for Joseph, and sympathy. It also
allows fascinating insights into what makes a religious genius tick.*
According to Fawn Brodie, Joseph's biographer, the prophet had an arresting physical presence:

> He was big, powerful, and by ordinary standards very handsome, ex-
> cept for his nose, which was aquiline and prominent. His large blue
> eyes were fringed by fantastically long lashes which made his gaze
> seem veiled and slightly mysterious. . . . When he was speaking with

---

* "Religious genius" is a wonderfully apt characterization that originated with William
James, who introduced it, generically, in the first of the lectures collected in *Varieties of Reli-
gious Experience.* It was borrowed by Harold Bloom some ninety years later, in his book *The
American Religion,* as the perfect way to describe Joseph Smith.

intense feeling the blood drained from his face, leaving a frightening, almost luminous pallor. . . . He was no ordinary man.

When Joseph addressed a crowd, he had a knack for making each individual feel as though he or she were being spoken to personally by the prophet. He seemed to sense each Saint's spiritual needs—the entire congregation's innermost hopes and pains and hungers—and then deliver a sermon that resonated in perfect pitch with every person's private longing. Here is how Juanita Leavitt Brooks, an eminent Mormon historian, described the first time a convert named John D. Lee heard the prophet preach in Missouri in 1838*:

> Lee had come prepared to be impressed, but the reality exceeded his expectations. He thought Joseph Smith carried an air of majesty that made him seem taller than his six feet as he faced the audience, and more handsome and commanding than an ordinary man. Attracting every eye and holding every heart by the sheer magnetism of his personality, he played upon the congregation as though it were a musical instrument responsive to his slightest touch.

Fawn Brodie was struck by accounts of Joseph's "magnificent self-assurance":

> Increased success had served to intensify his boldness and exuberance. The zest for living that he radiated never failed to inspire his own people with a sense of the richness of life. They followed him slavishly and devotedly, if only to warm themselves in the glow of his presence.
>
> They built for him, preached for him, and made unbelievable sacrifices to carry out his orders, not only because they were convinced that he was God's prophet but also because they loved him as a man. They were as elated when he won a wrestling match as they were awed when he dictated a new revelation. They retold tales of his generosity and tenderness, marveling that he fed so many of the poor in Nauvoo

---

* Lee would become infamous in 1857, after the Saints had emigrated to Utah, for his role in the Mountain Meadows massacre.

at his table without stint, and that he entertained friend and enemy
alike. He was a genial host, warmhearted and friendly to all comers,
and fiercely loyal to his friends.

Arguing that the popularity of the Mormon Church was primarily a
function of Joseph's singular charisma, Brodie insists that *The Book of
Mormon* "lives today because of the prophet, not he because of the book."
Perhaps. But the allure of the new theology he introduced should not be
discounted. Joseph's inspired reworking of the traditional Christian narrative had much to do with his religion's rapid growth.

To believers, of course, Mormon doctrine is the incontrovertible
word of God. That word was nevertheless delivered via a very human
instrument—Joseph Smith—who possessed uncanny theological in-
stincts. Mormonism appeared in the right place, at the right time, to
exploit a ripe niche that had opened in the nation's ever-shifting spiritual ecology. Many Americans were dissatisfied with the calcified religions of the Old World. Joseph preached a fresh message that was
exactly what a great number of people were eager to hear. He took measure of the public's collective yearning and intuitively shaped his ideas
to fit the precise dimensions of that inchoate desire.

Joseph had convincing answers to the thorniest existential questions—answers that were both explicit and comforting. He offered a
crystal-clear notion of right and wrong, an unambiguous definition of
good and evil. And although his perspective was absolutist and unyielding, it presented a kinder, gentler alternative to Calvinism, which had
been the ecclesiastical status quo in the early years of the American republic. Calvinists taught that mankind was by nature evil, and was
watched over by a wrathful God bent on making humans atone for
Adam's original sin. They warned that the fires of hell were real. Suffering, they preached, was good for you.

In Joseph's more optimistic cosmology, God's chosen people—the
Mormons—were inherently virtuous (albeit surrounded by wickedness)
and didn't need to atone for anything. Making money was a righteous
pursuit: the Lord smiled on the rich, as well as those who aspired to be-

come rich. And anyone who elected to obey church authorities, receive the testimony of Jesus, and follow a few simple rules could work his way up the ladder until, in the afterlife, he became a full-fledged god—the ruler of his very own world. "Joseph was no hair-shirt prophet," Fawn Brodie observed.

> He believed in the good life, with a moderate self-indulgence in food and drink, occasional sport, and good entertainment. And that he succeeded in enjoying himself to the hilt detracted not at all from the semi-deification with which his own people enshrouded him. Any protests of impropriety dissolved before his personal charm. "Man is that he might have joy" had been one of his first significant pronouncements in the *Book of Mormon,* and from that belief he had never deviated. He was gregarious, expansive, and genuinely fond of people. And it is no accident that his theology in the end discarded all traces of Calvinism and became an ingenious blend of supernaturalism and materialism, which promised in heaven a continuation of all earthly pleasures—work, wealth, sex, and power.

Joseph's budding religion was both a reflection of the era's Jacksonian ideals and a reactionary retreat from them. On the one hand, Joseph was a champion of the common man and a thorn in the side of the ruling elite. But on the other, he was deeply suspicious of the confusing babble of ideas sweeping the country, and was made nervous by the fickleness of democratic governance. His church was an attempt to erect a wall against modernity's abundance of freedom, its unbridled celebration of the individual. Mormonism's strictures and soothing assurances—its veneration of *order*—beckoned as a refuge from the complexity and manifold uncertainties of nineteenth-century America.

Joseph's fresh take on Christianity excited his followers. Converts were energized by his groundbreaking doctrines—and the innovations didn't stop: Mormons could watch their church taking form before their very eyes, in all sorts of novel and fantastic ways. By the mid-1840s, when Nauvoo was in full flower, Joseph had received 133 divine commandments that were weighty enough to be recorded for eternity in *The Doctrine and Covenants,* reflecting a significant evolution in Mormon theology. In several important regards, the religion practiced in Nauvoo was quite different from the religion practiced in Palmyra when the church was initially incorporated. And none of these changes had greater repercussions than the commandment Joseph recorded on July 12, 1843—canonized in *D&C* as Section 132—which very nearly shattered the church, brought about Joseph's death at the hands of a lynch mob, and has been reverberating through American society ever since. It was in *D&C* 132 that God revealed the "new and everlasting covenant" of plural marriage, a custom more commonly known to non-Mormons as polygamy.

ELEVEN

THE PRINCIPLE

It was in Kirtland . . . that Joseph began to tamper delicately with one of the most basic mores in Occidental society. He looked upon that society with singular detachment that can come only to a man satisfied with his own ultimate authority and possessed by a longing to remold the world closer to his heart's desire. Nothing was so sacred that it could not be recast into a new utility or a new beauty.

Monogamy seemed to him—as it has seemed to many men who have not ceased to love their wives, but who have grown weary of connubial exclusiveness—an intolerably circumscribed way of life. "Whenever I see a pretty woman," he once said to a friend, "I have to pray for grace." But Joseph was no careless libertine who could be content with clandestine mistresses. There was too much of the Puritan in him, and he could not rest until he had redefined the nature of sin and erected a stupendous theological edifice to support his new theories on marriage.

FAWN BRODIE,
NO MAN KNOWS MY HISTORY

In the early 1980s, when Dan Lafferty came across a copy of *The Peace Maker* in the library of Brigham Young University, he quickly became convinced that it had been written by Joseph Smith, using the pen name of Udney Hay Jacob. The booklet had been printed in Nauvoo in 1842, by the prophet's own press. But Dan Lafferty is probably wrong about its authorship. Udney Hay Jacob was no apparition; his was not a nom de plume. He actually existed, and most scholars believe that Jacob, not Joseph Smith, wrote *The Peace Maker.* But most of those same scholars also acknowledge that the treatise would never have been published by the church printing office, with Joseph's name on the title page, had the prophet not wholly endorsed it. If he wasn't the author of *The Peace Maker,* Joseph was almost certainly responsible for the booklet's conception and publication.

Joseph had been considering polygamy, and its place in the cosmological order, at least since the church was founded, but he was reluctant to broach this delicate subject with his Saints, lest they recoil in shock. By the time the Mormons were established in Nauvoo, he thought they might finally be ready to "receive the principle," and he seems to have published *The Peace Maker* as a trial balloon. According to John D. Lee, who was living in Nauvoo when the booklet appeared, "Joseph, the Prophet, set a man by the name Sidney Hay Jacobs [sic], to select from the Old Bible such scriptures as pertained to polygamy, or celestial marriage; and to write it in pamphlet form, and to advocate that doctrine. This he did as a feeler among the people, to pave the way for celestial marriage."*

Unfortunately, the feeler did not produce the desired response. *The Peace Maker* created an uproar, prompting Joseph to claim, disingenuously, that it had been published "without my knowledge," adding, "Had I been apprised of it, I should not have printed it." The outcry over the booklet forced the prophet to issue strong public denunciations of polygamy, which was awkward because he had, in fact, been secretly engaging in spiritual wifery at least since 1833, and there is compelling circumstantial evidence that he began the practice even earlier.

One of the first women rumored to have been intimate with Joseph outside his marriage to Emma was Marinda Nancy Johnson, whom he met in 1831, shortly after the Saints moved from Palmyra to Kirtland, Ohio. Marinda's mother, who suffered from chronic rheumatism that had

---

* "Celestial marriage," "spiritual wifery," and "plural marriage" are among the terms Joseph Smith coined as euphemisms for polygamy.

paralyzed one of her arms, was among the crowds of curious Ohioans who came to see the Mormon Prophet with their own eyes. Accompanying the ailing woman was her husband, Benjamin, and a skeptical Methodist preacher who demanded of Joseph, "Here is Mrs. Johnson with a lame arm; has God given any power to men now on earth to cure her?"

Taking hold of Mrs. Johnson's incapacitated hand, Joseph declared, "Woman, in the name of the Lord Jesus Christ, I command thee to be whole!"

According to a credible witness, "Mrs. Johnson at once lifted [her arm] up with ease." Both Mr. and Mrs. Johnson were so moved by this miracle that they converted on the spot to Mormonism and invited the prophet to meet their fifteen children, including fifteen-year-old Marinda.

When she learned that her parents had come under the sway of Joseph Smith, Marinda later told a journalist, she initially felt "indignation and shame" that they had been duped by such a "ridiculous fake." But that was before she met Joseph herself, and was exposed to the direct radiance of his charm. Later, upon encountering him for the first time, she reported, the prophet

> looked her full in the eye. With the greatest feeling of shame ever experienced, she felt her very soul laid bare before this man as she realized her thoughts concerning him. He smiled and her anger melted as snow before the sunshine. She knew he was what he claimed to be and never doubted him thereafter.

In the summer of 1831 the Johnson family took Joseph and Emma Smith into their home as boarders, and soon thereafter the prophet purportedly bedded young Marinda. Unfortunately, the liaison apparently did not go unnoticed, and a gang of indignant Ohioans—including a number of Mormons—resolved to castrate Joseph so that he would be disinclined to commit such acts of depravity in the future.

According to Luke Johnson, Marinda's older brother, on March 24, 1832, "a mob of forty or fifty" came to the Johnson house, forced their way into Joseph's room

in the middle of the night, and Carnot Mason dragged Joseph out of
bed by the hair of the head; he was then seized by as many as could get
hold of him and taken about forty rods from the house, stretched on a
board, and tantalized in the most insulting and brutal manner; they
tore off the night clothes that he had on, for the purpose of emasculating him, and had Dr. Dennison there to perform the operation; but
when the Dr. saw the Prophet stripped and stretched on the plank, his
heart failed him and he refused to operate.

Having lost the nerve to follow through with their castration plans, the
mob severely beat Joseph, covered his naked body with tar, plastered
him with feathers from a down pillow, and then abandoned him in the
woods.

Despite this harrowingly close call, Joseph remained perpetually
and hopelessly smitten by the comeliest female members of his flock.
Among them was a nubile resident of Kirtland named Fanny Alger, who
was introduced to Joseph in 1830, after her parents became some of the
earliest converts to the church. By the winter of 1833, when Fanny was
sixteen, she had moved into the Smith household as a domestic servant
and had grown very close to both Smiths, particularly Emma. According
to a Mormon named Ann Eliza Webb Young, Fanny was "a very pretty,
pleasing young girl," and Mrs. Smith "was extremely fond of her; no
own mother could be more devoted, and their affection for each other
was a constant object of remark, so absorbing and genuine did it seem."

Joseph, however, was also extremely fond of young Fanny, and he
took her as his plural wife in February or March 1833; she may well have
been the second woman, after Emma, whom he formally married. He
tried to keep the relationship secret, but Emma eventually discovered
Joseph and Fanny flagrante delicto, and by the fall of 1835 had thrown
the girl out of their house.

Neither Emma's tears nor her rage were enough to make Joseph
monogamous, however; nor were the prevailing mores of the day. He
kept falling rapturously in love with women not his wife. And because
that rapture was so wholly consuming, and felt so good, it struck him as
impossible that God might possibly frown on such a thing. Joseph

wasn't by nature reflective or deliberative. He conducted his life impulsively, acting according to instinct and emotion. The Lord, it seemed to him, must surely have intended man to know the love of more than one wife or He wouldn't have made the prospect so enticing. In the Old Testament, moreover, Joseph found ample proof that this was indeed God's intent, wherein the polygamous customs of Abraham and Jacob—the patriarchs from whom the Mormons were directly descended—were recounted without reproach or shame.

Joseph continued to take plural wives throughout the 1830s in Ohio and Missouri, and he married with even greater frequency in Nauvoo in the early 1840s, but he did whatever was necessary, including bald-faced lying, to conceal his polygamous behavior—not only from censorious non-Mormons but from all but a select few of his own followers, as well. As the prophet explained to his innermost circle in 1832, "he had inquired of the Lord concerning the principle of plurality of wives, and he received for answer that the principle of taking more wives than one is a true principle, but the time had not yet come for it to be practiced." More correctly, the time had not yet come for the practice to be made public.

So Joseph kept the fact of his multiple wives a secret and bided his time until the proper moment for revealing the sacred principle arrived. He did not have similar qualms about revealing other divine commandments, however. In Nauvoo the prophet entered a phase of feverish doctrinal creativity, resulting in the church's most innovative theological developments.

During this period, for instance, Joseph revealed the principle of vicarious baptism for the dead, whereby living Saints could be baptized in proxy for deceased ancestors—giving departed generations an opportunity to experience salvation through the One True Church, even if the departed had passed away long before Joseph introduced Mormonism to the world. It was also in Nauvoo that he introduced the elaborate rituals of the temple endowment ceremony, and revealed not only that God had once been a man, but—even more astonishing—that every man has the capacity to become a god.

And then, on July 12, 1843, he formally codified the divine commandment revealing the sacred importance of plural marriage. Unlike the other revelations of this period, it was kept secret and wasn't acknowledged until 1852, a full eight years after the prophet's death.

This burst of theological inspiration coincided with an extended eruption of libidinous energy. Between 1840 and 1844 God instructed the prophet to marry some forty women. Most were shocked and revolted when Joseph revealed what the Lord had in mind for them. Several were still pubescent girls, such as fourteen-year-old Helen Mar Kimball. Although she acquiesced when the prophet explained that God had commanded her to become his plural wife—and that she would be permitted twenty-four hours to comply—Helen later confided to a friend, "I was young, and they deceived me, by saying the salvation of our whole family depended on it."

Joseph married Helen Mar Kimball in Nauvoo in May 1843. Earlier that same month, young Lucy Walker was also wed to the prophet after being similarly coerced. Her father had been among those shot during the Haun's Mill Massacre (although he was one of the lucky few who managed to survive the carnage inside the blacksmith shop). In January 1842 Lucy's mother died of malaria, a plague that was rife in Nauvoo's swamps. Joseph responded to this tragedy by sending Lucy's grief-stricken father on a two-year mission to the eastern states to heal his broken heart; in their father's absence, the prophet then "adopted" Lucy and most of her siblings. According to Lucy's autobiography, while she was living in the prophet's home, "President Joseph Smith sought an interview with me, and said, 'I have a message for you, I have been commanded of God to take another wife, and you are the woman.' My astonishment knew no bounds."

When the horrified girl balked at his proposal, Joseph explained to Lucy that if she refused she would face eternal damnation. "I have no flattering words to offer," he said. "It is a command of God to you. I will give you until to-morrow to decide this matter. If you reject this message the gate will be closed forever against you."

Lucy reacted with both anger and despair: "This aroused every drop of scotch in my veins. For a few moments I stood fearless before him, and looked him in the eye. I felt at this moment that I was called to place myself upon the altar a living sacrifice . . . this was too much, the thought was unbearable." Courageously, she replied to the prophet that unless she, personally, received a revelation straight from God that He wanted her to wed the prophet, she wouldn't do it. At which point, she wrote, Joseph stood before her with "the most beautiful expression of countenance, and said, 'God Almighty bless you, You shall have a manifestation of the will of God concerning you; a testimony that you can never deny.' "

According to Lucy's memoirs,

It was near dawn after another sleepless night when my room was lighted up by a heavenly influence. To me it was, in comparison, like the brilliant sun bursting through the darkest cloud. My soul was filled with a calm, sweet peace that I never knew. Supreme happiness took possession of me, and I received a powerful and irresistible testimony of the truth of plural marriage, Which has been like an anchor to the soul through all the trials of life. I felt that I must go out into the morning air and gave vent to the Joy and gratitude that filled my soul. As I descended the stairs, Prest. Smith opened the door below; took me by the hand and said: "Thank God, you have the testimony. I too, have prayed." He led me to a chair, placed his hands upon my head, and blessed me with Every blessing my heart could possibly desire.

Lucy Walker was married to the prophet on May 1, 1843, a day after turning seventeen.

It beggars the imagination to consider how Joseph managed to maintain relationships with forty spouses. Not even this profusion of wives, however, managed to sate his appetite. According to Sarah Pratt, the wife of Mormon apostle Orson Pratt,

the prophet Joseph used to frequent houses of ill-fame. Mrs. White, a very pretty and attractive woman, once confessed to me that she made a business of it to be hospitable to the captains of the Mississippi steamboats. She told me that Joseph had made her acquaintance very

soon after his arrival in Nauvoo, and that he had visited her dozens of
times.

Nauvoo was a closely woven, self-absorbed community that generated a
robust flow of gossip. Try as he might, it was impossible for Joseph to
conceal so much illicit activity from his followers. Time and again public allegations would be made against the prophet, but he was extremely
adept at portraying his accusers as instruments of Satan out to defame
not only him, a persecuted innocent, but all of Mormondom. Joseph repeatedly managed to sweep unsavory charges under the rug before ir-
reparable damage could be inflicted—a talent he shared, of course, with
many successful religious and political leaders through the ages.

Throughout this period of frenzied coupling, Joseph adamantly denied that he endorsed plural marriage, let alone engaged in the practice
himself. "When the facts are proved, truth and innocence will prevail at
last," he asserted in a speech given to the citizens of Nauvoo in May
1844. "What a thing it is for a man to be accused of committing adultery, and having seven wives, when I can find only one. I am the same
man, and as innocent as I was fourteen years ago; and I can prove them
all perjurers."

His denials had always gotten him off the hook before, but his re-
peated success at wiggling out of tight situations incubated a dangerous hubris, which in turn increased his sexual recklessness—and it all
caught up to him shortly after he delivered the speech quoted above. In
the spring of 1844 a scandal of Monica Lewinsky–like proportions exploded in Nauvoo, and this time, finally, the conflagration was too big
and too hot to be extinguished by the prophet's charm.

TWELVE

CARTHAGE

When Smith led his followers into Nauvoo, one may argue that Smith had done all he needed to do. His followers had memories of persecution to nurture. They had created distinct forms of worship organized around an unusual concept of priesthood and had gathered a community. Smith entered Nauvoo with a political welcome and a generous city charter that allowed Mormons a considerable amount of autonomy. Yet, precisely at that point, he embarked on a course of new departures, introduced in politically maladroit ways, that threatened to destroy everything he had created.

R. LAURENCE MOORE,
RELIGIOUS OUTSIDERS AND THE MAKING OF AMERICANS

Despite Joseph Smith's many forceful denials, by 1844 several members of the prophet's inner circle had been told the truth about his spiritual wifery, and some had been shown the secret revelation of July 12, 1843, concerning the doctrine of celestial marriage; a few were even practicing polygamy themselves. But not everyone who had been let in on the secret approved of the doctrine. Foremost among those who objected was his original wife, Emma Smith. She had been married to Joseph since 1827, still loved him, and, at the age of thirty-nine, had no desire to share her husband with dewy juveniles less than half her age. Joseph had promised to be faithful to Emma when he'd made his wedding vows, and she expected him to keep that promise.

Outspoken by nature, Emma despised polygamy and did not hesitate to make her views known to the prophet. At one point she even threatened to take a plural husband if he didn't give up his plural wives, prompting Joseph, on June 23, 1843, to complain to his secretary that Emma was "disposed to be revenged on him for some things. She thought that if he would indulge himself she would too."

Emma harangued Joseph so relentlessly about his philandering that the original intent of the revelation canonized as Section 132 seems to have been simply to persuade Emma to shut up and accept his plural wives—while at the same time compelling her to refrain from indulging in any extracurricular sex herself. Indeed, on the morning of July 12, just before Joseph recorded the notorious revelation for posterity, his brother Hyrum explicitly urged the prophet, "If you will write the revelation on celestial marriage, I will take and read it to Emma, and I believe I can convince her of its truth, and you will hereafter have peace."

A very dubious Joseph replied, "You do not know Emma as well as I do."

But Hyrum persisted: "The doctrine is so plain, I can convince any reasonable man or woman of its truth, purity or heavenly origin." Thus persuaded, Joseph agreed to commit to paper the revelation that became Section 132. Not coincidentally, it repeatedly mentions Emma by name. For example, in the revelation's fifty-fourth verse God warns,

> And I command mine handmaid, Emma Smith, to abide and cleave unto my servant Joseph, and to none else. But if she will not abide this commandment she shall be destroyed, saith the Lord; for I am the Lord thy God, and will destroy her if she abide not in my law.

The meat of the matter—the part of the commandment that gives men license to marry a plurality of wives—occurs just before the conclusion of the revelation, when the Lord tells Joseph,

If any man espouse a virgin, and desire to espouse another . . . , then he is justified; he cannot commit adultery for they are given unto him. . . .

And if he have ten virgins given unto him by this law, he cannot commit adultery, for they belong to him, and they are given unto him; therefore he is justified. . . .

But if one or either of the ten virgins, after she is espoused, shall be with another man, she has committed adultery, and shall be destroyed; for they are given unto him to multiply and replenish the earth, according to my commandment.

After Joseph had finished dictating the revelation to his secretary, Hyrum delivered the ten-page document to Emma.* Unfortunately for Joseph, it did not have the desired effect. When Emma read it, she became apoplectic. Hyrum reported that "he had never received a more severe talking to in his life," and "that Emma was very bitter and full of resentment and anger." She proclaimed that she "did not believe a word" of the revelation and remained steadfast in her refusal to accept Joseph's marriages to other women. Which didn't deter the prophet from taking more wives; but he made no further effort to win Emma's consent.

Emma sought solace from her friend William Law, who, although also a close friend of Joseph's, was sympathetic to Emma's plight. A longtime member of the church, Law possessed incorruptible integrity and had served as the prophet's trusted second counselor for more than two years. In January 1844 Law encountered Joseph on the streets of

---

* William Clayton, Joseph's loyal personal secretary, declared in a letter twenty-eight years later, "I did write the revelation on Celestial marriage given through the Prophet Joseph Smith on the 12th day of July 1843. When the revelation was written there was no one present except the prophet Joseph, his brother Hyrum and myself. It was written in the small office upstairs in the rear of the brick store which stood on the banks of the Mississippi River. It took some three hours to write it. Joseph dictated sentence by sentence and I wrote it as he dictated. After the whole was written Joseph requested me to read it slowly and carefully which I did, and he then pronounced it correct."

Nauvoo and begged him to renounce the detestable polygamy revelation. According to Law's son Richard, his father put his arms around the neck of the prophet and "was pleading with him to withdraw the doctrine of plural marriage . . . with tears streaming from his eyes. The prophet was also in tears, but he informed [Law] that he could not withdraw the doctrine, for God had commanded him to teach it, and condemnation would come upon him if he was not obedient to the commandment."

Law's abhorrence of polygamy, to say nothing of the emotional support he provided Emma, severely strained his relationship with Joseph. Their friendship was finally severed altogether when Joseph "endeavored to seduce" Law's wife, Jane, by making "the most indecent and wicked proposals" to her. Incensed and disgusted, in April 1844 William Law demanded that the prophet publicly acknowledge his wicked behavior and "cease from his abominations."

Joseph responded by having Law excommunicated; Law's reaction to this insult was to declare that Joseph was a "fallen prophet" and then, on May 12, to establish an institution he called the Reformed Mormon Church, which did not sanction polygamy. According to Fawn Brodie,

> Law had courage, tenacity, and a strange, misguided idealism. Although he was surrounded chiefly by men who believed Joseph to be a base imposter, he clung to the hope that that he could effect a reformation in the church. To this end he set up a church of his own, with himself as president, following faithfully the organization of the main body.
>
> This in itself would not have been serious, for Joseph had seen rival prophets spring out of the grass at his feet before and they had come to naught. Usually they tried to imitate him, giving out revelations that sounded stale and flat beside his own. But Law was cut to a different pattern. Actually he was on the road to complete and ugly disillusionment, but he was walking backward away from the church, looking eagerly for something in the landscape to which he could cling, grasping at every tree and hedgerow.

His desperate desire to reform the church made him far more formidable than if he had set out to damn the prophet and all his works.

Law was also made formidable by dint of being rich, which allowed him to buy his own printing press. On June 7, 1844, the first and only edition of a newspaper called the *Nauvoo Expositor* emerged from the new press. Law printed one thousand copies. The lead editorial exclaimed, "We are earnestly seeking to explode the vicious principle of Joseph Smith, and those who practice the same abominations and whoredoms." The four-page broadsheet railed against Joseph's disdain for the separation of church and state, his usurpation of political power, and his shady financial dealings, but the paper's primary objective was to expose the secret doctrine of polygamy. The editors promised that in the coming days, "several affidavits will be published, to substantiate the facts alleged."

Most of Nauvoo's residents reacted to the publication with anger—directed not at Joseph, to whom they remained devoted, but at the paper and its owners. The prophet was nevertheless worried that the *Expositor* put his control of the church in dire peril, so he called an emergency meeting of the Nauvoo city council. Warning that the paper threatened to "destroy the peace of the city" and was a "public nuisance," Joseph, acting in his capacity as mayor, ordered the city marshal to "destroy the printing press from whence issues the *Nauvoo Expositor* . . . and burn all the *Expositors* and libelous handbills found in said establishment."

On the evening of June 10, more than two hundred armed members of the Nauvoo Legion—led by Hyrum Smith and Apostle John Taylor, under orders from the legion's commander, Lieutenant General Joseph Smith—broke down the front door of the *Expositor* offices with a sledgehammer, smashed the press, scattered the type, and then burned the wreckage "to ashes, while the multitude made the air ring with their hideous yells." The publishers of the *Expositor* sought redress from the local courts, charging the prophet and his henchmen with a variety of crimes. The problem was, Joseph controlled the courts, along with every other branch of government in Nauvoo. To nobody's surprise, all those involved in the destruction of the press were completely exonerated, including the prophet. William Law, fearing for his life, had by this time fled Nauvoo. His Reformed Mormon Church withered and ultimately disappeared.

Joseph, it seemed, had prevailed yet again over his adversaries. He'd badly miscalculated how non-Mormons in Hancock County would react to these shenanigans, however. Relatively few people outside of Nauvoo knew much at that point about Joseph's doctrine of polygamy, but bad blood between the Saints and the Gentiles who lived around them had been building for at least two years. Although Joseph and his followers had been welcomed by the citizens of Illinois when they'd first arrived, the same attitude of divine entitlement that had turned Missourians against the Mormons gradually antagonized the residents of Hancock County as well.

The county was named after John Hancock, the first person to sign the Declaration of Independence, a committed populist with pronounced contempt for those in positions of authority who abused their power. In the spirit of their county's namesake, non-Mormons were especially alarmed by Joseph's penchant for theocratic governance, as well as his apparent disregard for every article of the United States Constitution except those that assured Mormons the freedom to worship as they saw fit.

Joseph often asserted his belief in the ideal of democracy and in the essential value of the protections codified in the Constitution. But he also believed that democracy and constitutional restraint were rendered moot in his own case, because he had been singled out by the Lord to be His messenger. God spoke through him. Upon Joseph's divine installation as ruler of the world, there would be no further need for democracy because God, for all intents and purposes, would be in charge. Surely, Joseph believed, the American people would understand this once they were given an opportunity to hear his message—the righteousness and undeniable truth of the Mormon faith.

But Joseph's avowed intent to replace the elected government of the United States with a "government of God" was poorly received by the Gentile residents of Hancock County, who didn't fancy becoming subjects of King Joseph Smith. Joseph's non-Mormon neighbors were distressed by the way the Saints voted as a uniform bloc in lockstep with the prophet's instructions, using that leverage to exert inordinate influence in the state government. Freedom of the press, moreover, was taken no less seriously in Hancock County than in the rest of Jacksonian America. When Joseph ordered the destruction of the *Nauvoo Expositor,* it confirmed a growing fear among non-Mormons that he was a megalomaniacal tyrant who posed a clear and present danger to the peace and stability of the region.

The obliteration of the *Expositor* had the county's Gentile residents literally up in arms. An editorial published in the nearby town of Warsaw howled, "War and extermination is inevitable! CITIZENS ARISE, ONE AND ALL!!! Can you *stand* by, and suffer such INFERNAL DEVILS! To ROB men of their property rights, without avenging them? We have no time for comment! Everyman will make his own. LET IT BE WITH POWDER AND BALL!"

The air over Hancock County crackled with hostility. Anticipating imminent retaliation from the Gentiles, on June 18 Joseph declared martial law and mobilized his Mormon army—the five-thousand-man Nauvoo Legion. Fearing the outbreak of civil war, Illinois's governor, Thomas Ford—a fair-minded leader who was not unsympathetic to the Mormons—responded by demanding that Joseph and Hyrum Smith, John Taylor, and others responsible for destroying the press surrender to face charges in Carthage, the Hancock County seat. Governor Ford promised that if the prophet turned himself in, he would personally guarantee Joseph's safety. But, Ford cautioned, "If you, by refusing to submit, make it necessary to call out the militia, I have great fears that your city will be destroyed, and your people many of them exterminated. You know the excitement of the public mind. Do not tempt it too far."

Joseph replied to Ford, saying he worried that if he and his cohorts were to turn themselves over to non-Mormon authorities, they would be taken "from place to place, from court to court, across creeks and prairies, till some bloodthirsty villain could find his opportunity to shoot us." Instead of surrendering, in the middle of the night on June 23,

Joseph and his brother Hyrum were rowed across the Mississippi by their fearsome bodyguard, Porter Rockwell, where they fled into the wilds of Iowa, intending to make a break for the Rocky Mountains.

A day later, though, while Joseph and Hyrum waited for the delivery of horses to carry them west, Joseph received an impassioned letter from Emma urging him to return to Nauvoo. The messenger who delivered the letter told the prophet that many of the Saints believed he had abandoned them out of cowardice: "You always said if the church would stick to you, you would stick to the church; now trouble comes and you are the first to run."

Shamed, Joseph returned to Illinois to face prosecution, fearing the worst. "I am going like a lamb to the slaughter," he warned those who rowed him back across the river.

Joseph and eleven others who were charged with destroying the press surrendered on June 24. As they traveled the twenty-five miles from Nauvoo to Carthage, the roads were lined with Illinois militiamen and other Gentiles who heckled the prophet lustily: "God damn you, Old Joe, we've got you now!"

"Clear the way and let us see old Joe, the prophet of God. He's seen the last of Nauvoo. We'll use him up and kill all the damn Mormons!"

In Carthage, the streets were jammed with armed, inebriated, poorly disciplined members of numerous local militias, all screaming for the prophet's head. Governor Ford, determined to protect Joseph and give him a fair trial, ordered all the militiamen in town to disband except for a single company of Carthage Greys, who were assigned to guard the jail and safeguard the prisoners.

Ten of the Mormons in custody posted bail and were allowed to go free, but Joseph and Hyrum, who had been charged with treason in addition to the less serious crimes charged to the other defendants, were incarcerated in the Carthage jail, a two-story structure with yard-thick walls built from red limestone cut from a local quarry. There were just six rooms in the entire building: two locked cells for holding prisoners, plus four rooms (one of which was a cramped attic garret) that served as living quarters for the jailer, his wife, and their seven children.

Initially the prophet and his brother were held in the downstairs debtors' cell, which was well lit and reasonably comfortable. The jailer, George Stigall, was not Mormon, but he was a decent man, and he worried that this downstairs cell, with its large, ground-level windows, might provide insufficient protection from the enraged men outside who wished to harm his prisoners. So the jailer permitted them to bide their time upstairs in his own bedroom, and friendly visitors were given unrestricted access to the Smith brothers. By this means, two guns were smuggled in to them—a six-shot pepperbox revolver and a single-shot pistol.

Late on the afternoon of June 27, while Joseph and Hyrum were being visited in their quarters by Apostles John Taylor and Willard Richards, approximately 125 militiamen from the virulently anti-Mormon town of Warsaw assembled outside the jail in the damp summer heat. Earlier, in deference to the governor's orders, these Warsaw Dragoons had left Carthage, but they hadn't gone far. They disguised themselves by rubbing gunpowder on their faces and at day's end came storming back into town.

Just seven members of the Carthage Greys were on guard when the Dragoons appeared outside the jail and charged the front entrance. The Greys fired their muskets directly into the mob, but as part of a prearranged plan the guards had loaded their weapons with blanks, so none of the Dragoons was harmed. After discharging their ersatz fusillade, the guards stepped aside, allowing the hate-crazed mob to burst through the front door, firing their guns indiscriminately as they entered; two of their balls came within inches of hitting the jailer's wife.

The militiamen swarmed upstairs and tried to force their way into the bedroom where the prisoners were quartered. Joseph and Hyrum brandished their smuggled weapons while Taylor and Richards each grabbed a walking stick, positioned themselves on either side of the doorway, and began whacking furiously at the mob's muskets as the barrels were poked through the partially opened door.

Two bullets ripped through the door panel; the second one smashed into Hyrum's neck, severing his spinal cord, and he dropped to the floor, dead, where four more balls immediately struck his body. Joseph responded by reaching around the doorjamb and blindly firing all six rounds of his revolver, wounding at least one of the Warsaw Dragoons.

The attackers had succeeded in forcing the door open, however, and a lethal rain of bullets now sprayed into the room. Taylor, in desperation, attempted to jump out of an open window but was shot first in the left thigh and then in the chest; although the latter bullet struck a watch in his vest pocket and therefore wasn't lethal, the impact knocked the wind out of him and sent him sprawling onto the floor. Frantically trying to escape the flying bullets, he crawled under a bed, where another ball tore into his forearm and yet another hit his pelvis, "cutting away a piece of flesh from his left hip as large as a man's hand."

Seeing no alternative, Joseph also tried to spring from the window, but as he crouched above the sill in silhouette, two shots from inside the room pierced his back and a third bullet, fired from a musket on the ground outside, exploded into his chest. Uttering a plaintive "Oh Lord, my God!" he pitched forward out of the window. The prophet dropped twenty feet, slammed into the earth with a dull thud, and lay motionless, twisted on his left side. A second lieutenant in the Carthage Greys who witnessed Joseph's fall reported that as soon as he hit the ground, he was "shot several times and a bayonet run through him." After a few moments, another militiaman cautiously approached the body, prodded it, and announced to the crowd that Joe Smith was dead.

Willard Richards, meanwhile, emerged tentatively from behind the door, unharmed except for slight wounds where a ball had grazed his throat and earlobe. When the Dragoons had initially forced their way into the room, Richards was standing on the hinge side of the doorway, and as the door flew open he was inadvertently squeezed between it and the wall. He remained there, standing unnoticed behind the door, until the shooting stopped. After determining that all the militiamen had departed, he left his hiding place and walked to the window. On the ground below he saw "a hundred men near [Joseph's] body, and more coming round the corner of the jail."

Then Richards noticed John Taylor lying on the floor, awash in his own blood but still breathing. Taylor's watch, struck by the bullet that would otherwise have ended his life, had stopped at sixteen minutes and twenty-six seconds past five o'clock on June 27, 1844. Mormons the world over have committed this time and date to memory, marking the death of their great and beloved prophet. Joseph Smith was thirty-eight years old.

Defying the odds, Taylor survived the grave injuries he sustained in the Carthage jail and later became the church's third president and prophet, succeeding Brigham Young in 1877. Nine years after that, Taylor would receive a notorious, furiously disputed revelation in which God would affirm to him the righteousness of the principle of plural marriage—a revelation that would ultimately give birth to the modern fundamentalist movement, lead to the settlement of Short Creek, and transform the life of Dan Lafferty.

THIRTEEN

THE LAFFERTY BOYS

It should be obvious to any man who is not one himself that the land is overrun with messiahs. . . . It should be a matter of common observation that this clamour of voices represents the really vigorous wing of American religious life. Here is religion in action, and religion actively in the making. . . . The truth is, of course, that the land is simply teeming with faith—that marked credulity that accompanies periods of great religious awakening and seems to be with us a permanent state of mind. By no stretch of the vocabulary could our age be called an age of doubt; it is rather an age of incredible faith.

CHARLES W. FERGUSON,
THE CONFUSION OF TONGUES

After Dan Lafferty read *The Peace Maker* and resolved to start living the principle of plural marriage, he announced to his wife, Matilda, that he intended to wed her oldest daughter—his stepdaughter. At the last minute, however, he abandoned that plan and instead married a Romanian immigrant named Ann Randak, who took care of some of Robert Redford's horses on a ranch up Spanish Fork Canyon, in the mountains east of the Dream Mine. Ann and Dan had met when he'd borrowed a horse from her to ride in a local parade. She wasn't LDS, says Dan, "but she was open to new experiences. Becoming my plural wife was her idea." Ann, he adds, "was a lovely girl. I called her my gypsy bride."

Living according to the strictures laid down in *The Peace Maker* felt good to Dan—it felt *right,* as though this really was the way God intended men and women to live. Inspired, Dan sought out other texts about Mormonism as it was practiced in the early years of the church.

It didn't take him long to discover that polygamy wasn't the only divine principle the modern LDS Church had abandoned in its eagerness to be accepted by American society. Dan learned that in the nineteenth century, both Joseph Smith and Brigham Young had preached about the righteousness of a sacred doctrine known as "blood atonement": certain grievous acts committed against Mormons, as Brigham explained it, could be rectified only if the "sinners have their blood spilt upon the ground." And Dan learned that Joseph had taught that the laws of God take precedence over the laws of men.

Legal theory was a subject of particular interest to Dan. His curiosity had first been aroused when he was training to be a chiropractor in California, following a run-in he had with state and county authorities. At the time, he supported his family primarily by running a small sandwich business out of their home. Dan, Matilda, and the oldest kids would get out of bed before dawn every morning in order to make and wrap stacks of "all-natural" vegetarian sandwiches, which Dan would then sell to other chiropractic students during the lunch hour.

"It was a very profitable little hustle," Dan says proudly. "Or it was until the Board of Health closed me down for not following regulations. They claimed I needed a license, and that I wasn't paying the required taxes." Just before he was put out of business, Matilda had given birth to a baby boy. Money was tight. Losing their main source of income was problematic. It also proved to be a pivotal event in Dan's passage to fundamentalism.

"After they shut me down," Dan recalls, "I didn't know quite what to do. It didn't seem right to me that the government would penalize me just for being ambitious and trying to support my family—that they would actually force me to go on welfare instead of simply letting me run my little business. It seemed so stupid—the worst kind of government intrusion. In *The Book of Mormon,* Moroni talks about how all of us have an obligation to make sure we have a good and just government, and when I read that, it really got me going. It made me realize that I needed to start getting involved in political issues. And I saw that when it comes right down to it, you can't really separate political issues from religious issues. They're all tied up together."

Upon completing his chiropractic training and returning to Utah, Dan went to work as a chiropractor for his father. By then the Lafferty parents had sold their farm and bought a house in the old part of downtown Provo; Dan's father ran his practice out of a basement office in this home. In 1981, shortly after Dan started working for Watson Sr., the LDS Church sent both of the elder Laffertys abroad on a two-year mission, at which point Dan and his younger brother Mark (who had graduated the Los Angeles College of Chiropractic six months after Dan), agreed to take over the practice in their father's absence.

Dan and Mark had always enjoyed each other's company. "As children," says Dan, "we were inseparable." Every morning and evening of their childhood they sat together across a milk pail to milk the family cow. They spent their summer vacations practically joined at the hip, "playing in the barns, jumping in the hay, throwing the football, playing in our tree hut," he recalls. "It's funny to remember how hard it was to stop playing even long enough to get a drink or take a pee. Nothing tasted so good as cold water from the faucet that filled the watering trough, and nothing felt so good as taking a pee when the pressure got so bad we had to stop playing because you couldn't hold it any longer." When their younger brothers—Tim, Watson Jr., and Allen—were old enough, the smaller boys eagerly joined in Dan and Mark's escapades. Then, says Dan, "we'd all line up along the fence, oldest to youngest, and have a group pee. The little guys loved to do what Mark and I did, especially lining up to pee on a fence."

When Dan and Mark started working together in their father's office, the special closeness they had shared in their youth was rekindled. During breaks between patients they engaged in heartfelt discussions about everything that was most important to them—and increasingly what seemed most important concerned religious doctrine and its power to remedy the insidious evils inflicted by the government on its citizens. Regarding the timing of these heart-to-heart talks, Dan reports, "I began to observe a fascinating phenomenon." Dan and Mark were usually so busy seeing patients that often several days would pass between their religious-political discourses. But on those days when they would unexpectedly have gaps in the schedule in which to talk at length, says Dan, "rather mysteriously, my younger brothers would show up, unannounced. And we would have some very, very valuable time discussing issues." These impromptu get-togethers happened often enough, says Dan, "that it seemed like it had to be more than just a coincidence." Five of the six Lafferty brothers—Dan, Mark, Watson, Tim, and Allen—were usually present for these ad hoc conferences; the only brother who failed to attend was Ron, the eldest of the Lafferty offspring, who was six years older than Dan, and had always acted less like a sibling than a father figure to his brothers.

Dan usually led the discussions, which inevitably described how the government had far exceeded its constitutionally mandated reach and was dangerously out of control. Buttressing his arguments by quoting scripture from *The Book of Mormon,* he patiently explained to his brothers that the government had no right to require American citizens to obtain any kind of license, or pay taxes, or submit to the oppressive burden of a Social Security number. "I had come to realize," Dan says, "that a license was simply an agreement with the government to let them have control of your life. And I decided I didn't want them to have control of my life. . . . I already had a basic right to enjoy all of the basic activities of a human being, without their permission."

Although Dan had not yet allied himself with any established fundamentalist church or prophet, his self-directed studies had transformed him into a de facto Mormon Fundamentalist—and an exceedingly ardent one. The impetus for most fundamentalist movements—whether Mormon, Catholic, Evangelical Christian, Muslim, or Jewish—is a yearning to return to the mythical order and perfection of the original church. Dan Lafferty was moved by this same desire.

The more he studied historical Mormon documents, the more certain Dan became that the LDS Church had blundered off course around 1890, when then-president and prophet Wilford Woodruff was coerced into doing away with the doctrine of plural marriage by the godless government in Washington, D.C. The modern LDS Church, Dan had become convinced, was an elaborate fraud.

Like fundamentalists in other faiths, he was intent on adhering unfailingly to God's "true" commandments, as determined by a rigorously literal interpretation of his church's earliest and most sacred texts. And he was no less intent on adhering to the "true" commandments of his country's earliest and most sacred texts, as well. To Dan, such documents as the *Book of Mormon, The Peace Maker,* the United States Constitution, and the Declaration of Independence are all of a piece: they are holy scriptures that provide a direct link to the Almighty. The authority that flows from their divinely inspired sentences is absolute and immutable. And it is the duty of righteous men and women to conduct their lives according to a stringently literal reading of those sentences.

For people like Dan who view existence through the narrow lens of literalism, the language in certain select documents is assumed to possess extraordinary power. Such language is to be taken assiduously at face value, according to a single incontrovertible interpretation that makes no allowance for nuance, ambiguity, or situational contingencies. As Vincent Crapanzano observes in his book *Serving the Word,* Dan Lafferty's brand of literalism

> encourages a closed, usually (though not necessarily) politically conservative view of the world: one with a stop-time notion of history and a we-and-they approach to people, in which *we* are possessed of truth, virtue, and goodness and *they* of falsehood, depravity, and evil. It looks askance at figurative language, which, so long as its symbols and metaphors are vital, can open—promiscuously in the eyes of the strict literalist—the world and its imaginative possibilities.

For his part, Dan scoffs at this sort of pointy-headed exegesis. "I was just on a quest," he insists. "A quest to find the truth."

After seeking guidance through prayer and receiving confirmation that he was acting in accordance with the Lord's wishes, Dan sent his driver's license back to the state of Utah, revoked his marriage license, and returned his Social Security card. He ignored posted speed limits, which he believed were illegal, and simply drove "wisely and carefully" instead. And he quit paying taxes of any kind—including the sales tax when he shopped in local stores, which provoked frequent confrontations with cashiers.

Energized by the self-evident righteousness of his crusade, in the summer of 1982 Dan declared himself a candidate for sheriff of Utah County and embarked on a lively political campaign, speaking at public forums, writing letters to the Provo newspaper, doing radio interviews, and riding in small-town parades. He promised, if elected, to enforce the laws according to a scrupulously literal interpretation of the U.S. Constitution. As he explained, "My motive in running was to restore the primacy of Common Law juries, and to restore the fundamentals of the Constitution."

On October 4, 1982, Dan was driving home after meeting with another candidate for sheriff (the American Fork police chief, with whom Dan had hoped to engage in a public debate), when he was stopped on Interstate 15 by a Utah state trooper for speeding and not having a vehicle inspection sticker. "I had already had some confrontations with the officer who pulled me over," Dan allows. "He knew I would be driving home from this debate meeting, and he had set a trap for me. They wanted to get a felony against me so I couldn't run for office, and they swarmed me on the freeway. I had just published an important article in the paper—a very important article—which had really unnerved a lot of people, about how the powers of government were being improperly used through improper warrants of arrest—how it was unconstitutional to stop a person on the freeway and arrest them.

"When the officer pulled me over, he told me he had read my article—'I've got it right here in my car,' he said. So I told him, 'Well, if you've read the article, you understand why you can't arrest me right now. If you want to arrest me, go get a warrant from a judge, bring it to my home, and I'll conform to the proper procedures.' " Dan had by now locked the car doors and rolled up all the windows, leaving only a one-inch gap at the top of the driver's window, which, he says, "I figured was narrow enough to keep a hand from reaching in and grabbing me, but would allow me to talk to the officer."

The trooper wasn't amused. He ordered Dan out of the car. "When I refused to get out," says Dan, "the cop did something I hadn't anticipated: he grabbed the top of the window with both hands and pulled hard, pulling the window out of its tracks, and then he tried to reach in and grab me. So I said, 'Well, I gotta go now! See you later!' and took off."

The state troopers gave chase and apprehended Dan a short while later. He was charged with five crimes (including second-degree felony escape, third-degree felony assault by a prisoner, and evading an officer) and locked up in the county jail. At his justice court trial, Dan served as his own attorney and attempted to mount a defense based on several arcane points of constitutional law. The judge repeatedly pointed out, however, that justice courts in Utah are not empowered to hear constitutional matters, which infuriated Dan. He was further angered when the judge overruled his objection to the makeup of the four-woman jury (Dan argued that he was entitled to have at least one male on the jury).

When Dan ignored the judge's instructions and continued to argue his case on constitutional grounds, the exasperated judge declared him in contempt of court—at which point Dan's brothers and several other supporters staged a riot in the courtroom, shouting that they were placing the judge, prosecutor, and court clerk under "citizen's arrest." In the middle of this melee, Dan stood up and loudly admonished the judge, "In the name of Christ, do justice or be struck down!"

In the end, the theatrics didn't do anything to help his case. Dan was sent to the state prison for a forty-five-day psychiatric evaluation, then transferred to the county jail to serve a thirty-day sentence.

His stay behind bars only hardened his resolve. As a matter of principle, he stopped paying the property taxes on his father's home and business. His father's property, Dan explains, was "owned free and clear. By paying property taxes, you are basically telling the government that they're the ones who really own the property, because you give them the right to take it from you if you don't pay your taxes. And I was willing to force a standoff to determine who actually owned that property."

When that inevitable standoff occurred, Dan did not prevail. The Utah County assessor notified him that the county was taking possession of the Lafferty home for nonpayment of taxes, as well as seizing all of Watson Lafferty's office equipment. At which point Dan politely informed the assessor's office "that I intended to defend myself against any invasion of my constitutional God-given rights."

Dan's four younger brothers fully supported him in his ongoing battles with the state. But when Dan's father—who was still out of the country on his LDS mission—learned that his home and business equipment were about to be auctioned off for nonpayment of taxes, he was furious. Watson Sr. called Dan from abroad to express his profound displeasure, and to accuse Dan of "hypnotizing" his brothers; the Lafferty patriarch even suggested that Dan was trying to hypnotize him and Claudine from afar, over the telephone line.

Watson managed to save his home from the auction block by cutting short his mission and rushing back to Provo with Claudine, but he remained furious at Dan. Although his father's wrath saddened Dan, it did not dissuade him from his crusade.

During the last months of 1982 through early 1983, that crusade became more overtly religious, and Dan's four younger brothers became increasingly infected with his fundamentalist zeal. The Lafferty boys started meeting on a more regular basis to discuss the merits of polygamy and other principles advocated in *The Peace Maker*. When three of Dan's brothers attempted to impose these principles in their own homes, however, their wives refused and began to complain to Dianna—the wife of Ron, the eldest Lafferty brother—about the disturbing changes in their husbands' personalities.

FOURTEEN

BRENDA

{Fundamentalist movements} are embattled forms of spirituality, which have emerged as a response to a perceived crisis. They are engaged in a conflict with enemies whose secularist policies and beliefs seem inimical to religion itself. Fundamentalists do not regard this battle as a conventional political struggle, but experience it as a cosmic war between the forces of good and evil. They fear annihilation, and try to fortify their beleaguered identity by means of a selective retrieval of certain doctrines and practices of the past. To avoid contamination, they often withdraw from mainstream society to create a counterculture; yet fundamentalists are not impractical dreamers. They have absorbed the pragmatic rationalism of modernity, and, under the guidance of their charismatic leaders, they refine these "fundamentals" so as to create an ideology that provides the faithful with a plan of action. Eventually they fight back and attempt to resacralize an increasingly skeptical world.

KAREN ARMSTRONG,
THE BATTLE FOR GOD

Ron and Dianna Lafferty lived with their six kids in Highland, a small, prosperous, semirural community tucked against the foot of the Wasatch Range, just north of American Fork, midway between Provo and Salt Lake City. In 1982, Ron was a Highland city councilman and a stalwart of the local LDS congregation, where he had been appointed first counselor to the bishop and was a leader of youth activities.* By all accounts he was a wonderful father to his six children, and he and Dianna had an uncommonly solid marriage—a relationship envied by most of their acquaintances. "I remember a marriage that was so happy for sixteen and a half years," says a close friend of Dianna's named Penelope Weiss. "The first thing my daughter said when I told her about what happened, you know, with Dan and Ron and all, she said, 'That can't be true!' She said, 'All of us young girls wanted a marriage just like Ron and Dianna's marriage.' "

Ron's apparent contentment, however, masked troubles that had been churning just beneath the surface since childhood. Although his father's violent outbursts scarred all the Lafferty children to some degree, Ron—who had an especially close relationship with his perpetually downtrodden mother—seems to have suffered the greatest emotional damage. According to Richard Wootton, a psychologist who has examined Ron extensively over his nineteen years in prison, Ron remembers "seeing his mother hit by his father and being so mad that he wished he could have been big enough to have kicked his father's ass. . . . I think that stayed with him. And it became a pattern by which he kind of handled difficult, mistrustful situations."

Ron's anguish wasn't apparent to outsiders. As a child, he had been popular with other kids in the community and brought home decent, if unspectacular grades. He was also an outstanding athlete who starred on his high school football team and was captain of the wrestling squad. Throughout adolescence and young adulthood he appeared to thrive. As was expected of high achievers in the Mormon faith, after graduating from high school and completing a stint in the army, he went on a two-year mission for the church, eager to spread the gospel so that others might experience the incomparable joy of being a Latter-day Saint.

---

* Each LDS congregation (called a "ward") is headed by a bishop—a lay member, always male—who must be approved by the First Presidency and the Quorum of the Twelve Apostles, the topmost peak of the hierarchy that runs the world church from Salt Lake City. The bishop in turn appoints two counselors, who together function as a three-man bishopric that closely oversees everything within their ward.

There is nothing easy about being a Mormon missionary. Missionaries must pay their own way, and they are required to go wherever in the world the church decides they are needed. In Ron's case, after four weeks of indoctrination at the Missionary Training Center in Provo, he was called upon to save souls in Georgia and Florida. As an obedient Saint, he had already pledged not to drink, smoke, take illegal drugs, ingest caffeine, masturbate, or engage in premarital sex.* As a missionary, he was now also forbidden to read anything but LDS literature or listen to any music not produced by the church. Movies, television, newspapers, and magazines were strictly off-limits. He was permitted to write letters home just once per week, and he could phone his family only on Christmas and Mother's Day.

Ron dutifully followed these rules, for the most part, but he had a rebellious streak that emerged from time to time. Perhaps not surprisingly, given the warped relationship he had with his father, figures of authority provoked a complicated emotional response in Ron. Part of him was desperately eager to please his superiors, while another part raged inwardly against anyone who held power over him. Every now and then Ron felt compelled to let his keepers know that they didn't own him.

In those days, missionaries were required to wear hats. According to Dr. Wootton, who is Mormon, Ron "refused to wear a hat. In the summertime when it was hot and muggy in Florida, as it is, they were supposed to wear coats. He wouldn't wear a coat. He made a statement at one time that he 'wasn't down there to make a fashion statement.' He 'was down there to convert people and fulfill a mission.' "

Every morning Ron would roll out of bed at 6:00 A.M., don black slacks, a crisply pressed white shirt, and an ugly clip-on tie, and then study scripture for two or three hours before hitting the streets to troll for prospective converts. Like all LDS missionaries, to accomplish the latter he had to endure insults, threats of physical violence, flying spit,

---

* All Mormons are supposed to adhere to these strictures, most of which can be traced to a Draconian, late-twentieth-century interpretation of a confusing revelation Joseph Smith received in 1833—commonly known as the "Word of Wisdom" and canonized as Section 89 of *The Doctrine and Covenants*—in which the Lord commanded his Saints to abstain from "strong drink" and certain other vices.

and callous rejection; typically he would have a door slammed in his face forty or fifty times a day. Ron, however, turned out to be astonishingly good at this line of work. Nothing fazed him. The incessant rain of ridicule and dismissal glanced off him as though he had a Teflon hide.

Ron *knew* the LDS Church was God's One True Church, and he was determined to share this glorious fact with as many people as he could. Typically, an especially dedicated missionary might convert no more than three or four people a year—and feel justly satisfied for this accomplishment.* Ron, in marked contrast, had baptized more than fifty people into the LDS Church by the time his two-year mission was over.

While saving souls in Florida, Ron met a sweet young nursing student, fell in love, and married her at the conclusion of his mission. He then took his new wife, Dianna, to Utah, so they could live near his parents and siblings. Ron landed a good job operating heavy equipment for a construction company owned by a fellow Mormon, and settled down to raise a family of faithful Saints.

Comfortably reestablished in Utah County, Ron functioned as the emotional anchor for the greater Lafferty clan. His younger brothers and sisters had looked up to him for counseling and emotional support since they were small children; he had tended to be the one who mediated family disagreements. One of Ron's siblings affectionately characterized him as "a mother-hen type," and he relished the role. For the two decades after he returned from his mission, he made certain he was available whenever his mother or his brothers and sisters needed him.

By mid-1982 it was apparent to Dianna that several of Ron's siblings were in acute need of some brotherly guidance. In August of that year she became aware that four of the other five Lafferty wives were being made miserable by the fundamentalist strictures that Dan had been urging his brothers to adopt, so Dianna pleaded with Ron to have a talk with Dan and his other brothers to "straighten them out." Ron agreed to pay them a visit.

One evening when his five brothers were meeting at their parents' Provo home to discuss religion and politics, Ron stopped by to join in

---

* In recent years the annual average has been slightly more than two conversions per missionary.

the discourse—the first time he had ever attended one of these gatherings. His brothers welcomed him warmly, even when he began to read from an essay published by the LDS Church warning of the evils of fundamentalism and admonishing all Saints to obey the teachings of the church's president and prophet, Spencer W. Kimball. As the evening progressed, Ron asked increasingly pointed questions about Dan's new beliefs, and he tried as hard as he could to persuade his younger brothers that Dan's nutty ideas were putting their eternal souls in grave jeopardy.

"Ron was embarrassed by me," Dan remembers. "He was a devout Saint, and he said I was an embarrassment to the Mormon Church. He told me, 'There's no place in this church for extremes!' "

Conceding nothing, Dan fired back, "Well, how about extremely good? All I'm trying to do is be extremely good!" Dan argued with great passion that the LDS Church had taken a wrong turn when it had abandoned polygamy, and that the only way to put it back on a true course was to adopt the sacred tenets advanced in *The Peace Maker.* Ron tried to refute Dan's arguments, point by point, by quoting scripture from the Bible and *The Book of Mormon.* Dan countered with points of his own drawn from the same texts, as well as from the Constitution. "Ron wasn't at that meeting too awfully long," as Dan remembers it, "before he stopped trying to convince us we were wrong. 'What you guys are doing is right,' he admitted. 'It's everyone else who is wrong.' " In the space of a few hours, Dan had converted Ron from a dutiful Saint into a fire-breathing Mormon Fundamentalist. Dianna told her friend Penelope Weiss that when Ron returned home late that night, "A totally different man walked in the door."

Having adopted their defiant worldview, Ron became a regular attendee at his brothers' meetings. He threw away his driver's license and removed the license plates from his vehicle. And then he quit his job—which greatly heightened Dianna's concern, because the family was already balanced tenuously on the edge of financial ruin. Ron was in the latter stages of what was, for him, a large construction project: a four-unit apartment complex he had financed with a bank loan and was building himself, after hours, as a business investment. Up until this time, after working all day at his "real" job, he'd been devoting most evenings to building the fourplex and spending the remainder of his nights constructing a "dream house" in Highland for his own family. His two after-hours construction projects were straining their cash flow to the limit and beyond.

Compounding their woes, the economy throughout the Rocky Mountain region had just plunged into an abysmal recession. Ron and Dianna failed to make their loan payments. There wasn't enough money for groceries or clothes for the kids. Ron began to succumb to the stress. "It was a really bad recession," Weiss remembers. "Ron was going to lose everything. In fact, the papers were already made up for the bank to take away their home, which he had worked so hard on for so many years."

It was during this crisis that Dianna, on behalf of her sisters-in-law, asked Ron to visit with his brothers and straighten them out. "Ron was really vulnerable right then," Weiss explains. "Dianna told me at the time that Ron was so upset he would regularly just break down and cry. She'd tell him, 'Ron, don't worry about it; we can start over. We did it once, we'll do it again.' But he'd just look at her and say, 'We've sacrificed too much. I can't bear losing it all.'

"And just then Dan came along," Weiss declares with anguish in her voice. Dan's religious ideas included a message that Ron found particularly comforting during that difficult period. "Dan convinced Ron that God didn't want us to have material things, that it was good to lose everything. Dan told him that he had a higher calling. That God intended for Ron to be a missionary for the things Dan was teaching. And Ron really believed it—all of it. In fact, he even quit his job. Dan said it was all going to be okay, because he—Ron—was going to be called as the next president and prophet of the LDS Church, that Dan would be made his first counselor, and that the four other Lafferty boys would be made second counselors."

Very soon after Ron was converted to Dan's brand of fundamentalism, he instructed Dianna to begin following the onerous rules set forth in *The Peace Maker.* "I went over to their house one day," Weiss remembers, "and Dianna was shaking and shaking a gallon jug full of cream. I asked her, 'What in the world are you doing?' She said, 'Ron wants me to make our own butter from now on.'

"This was just one little example of how Ron expected her to live. Basically he expected her to be his slave. And it was such a complete reversal from the way he'd been. Before Dan brainwashed him, Ron had treated Dianna like a queen. He was just one of the nicest men I've ever known. But when this happened, he became one of the meanest men I've ever known.

"Dianna could see right away that the changes in Ron were a really bad thing, and I've never seen a woman work harder at trying to save a man. She would stay up most of the night trying to talk sense into him. In the hope of bringing him around and saving him, she tried to remain on his good side by going along with some of his crazy demands. But she was only willing to go so far, and then she'd have to say, 'No, Ron, this just isn't right.' "

As Ron became more controlling and more extreme, Dianna slowly lost hope that she could change Ron back into the loving father and considerate husband she'd known previously. He began to talk with growing enthusiasm about polygamy, which made her sick to even contemplate. When Ron announced that he intended to marry off their teenage daughters as plural wives, Dianna reached her breaking point. Desperate, she turned for help to Weiss and other close friends, to leaders of her LDS ward, and especially to Brenda Lafferty—who was married to Allen, the youngest of the six Lafferty brothers.

After Dan persuaded his brothers to adopt his fundamentalist beliefs, all their wives acquiesced and submitted, to one degree or another, to the humiliations decreed in *The Peace Maker*—all their wives, that is, except one: Brenda Wright Lafferty. Intelligent, articulate, and assertive, "Brenda stood up to those Lafferty boys," says her mother, LaRae Wright. "She was probably the youngest of the wives, but she was the strong one. She told the other wives to stand up for their rights and to think for themselves. And she set an example by refusing to go along with Allen's demands. She told him in no uncertain terms that she didn't want him doing things with his brothers. And the brothers blamed her for that, for keeping their family apart. The Lafferty boys didn't like Brenda, because she got in their way."

Brenda was the second oldest of seven children raised by LaRae, a schoolteacher, and Jim Wright, an agronomist. Born in Logan, Utah, Brenda moved with her family to Ithaca, New York, when she was just a year old, in order for her father to obtain his doctorate at Cornell University. Jim and LaRae pined for the wide-open country of the Rocky Mountain West, but upstate New York was not without appeal, and there was a major attraction just up the road from Ithaca: Palmyra, the birthplace of their LDS faith. As soon as he received his Ph.D., however, Jim moved his family back to the West—to Twin Falls, Idaho, an agricultural town forty miles north of the Utah state line, where Brenda enjoyed a storybook childhood.

"She was outgoing, full of life, and had a lot of personality," says her older sister, Betty Wright McEntire. "Brenda was just real fun. We were best friends." Popular, active in school government, and a member of the drill team, Brenda was an ambitious student who excelled at almost everything she tried. She was also beautiful, in the wholesome, all-American farm-girl idiom: in 1980 she was first runner-up in the Miss Twin Falls Pageant.

After graduating from high school with honors, Brenda enrolled at the University of Idaho, where she was elected president of her sorority. "But," says her mother, "that wasn't the kind of life she wanted to lead, so she came back home to Twin Falls and went to the College of Southern Idaho for two years, then transferred to Brigham Young University." While attending BYU, Brenda joined a "young adult ward"—an LDS student congregation—where she met Allen Lafferty. "Allen wasn't a student, but for some reason he started attending that student ward in Provo," LaRae explains. "He had a lot of charisma, they hit it off, and they just started going together."

"When Brenda started going out with Allen, I was out of the country, on a mission in Argentina," her sister Betty says. "But she wrote to me every week, and I could tell she was pretty serious about this guy. She'd dated a lot of boys before, but she never got stuck on any one person. Allen was different. He was a returned missionary, and the Laffertys were the picture-perfect LDS family. Everybody in Provo seemed to know them. Plus, Allen is a charmer—all the Lafferty boys have this ability to charm the socks off you. They have this look in their eyes. And Brenda fell for it. Even from Argentina it was obvious she was really in love with Allen." On April 22, 1982, Allen and Brenda were sealed for time and eternity as husband and wife in the Salt Lake City temple. She was twenty-one years old.

At BYU, where Brenda majored in communications, she anchored a television newsmagazine program on KBYU—the local PBS affiliate broadcast throughout Utah on channel 11. According to Betty, "Her ambition was to become an anchorwoman like Michelle King.* We were brought up to be very independent. Our parents taught us that we were given certain talents and we needed to pursue them—that we shouldn't go through life relying on others when we had all these abilities.

"Then Brenda got married, and Allen didn't want her to work, so she kind of put her broadcasting career on the shelf temporarily, and took a lower-profile job at Castleton's, one of the nicer stores at the Orem Mall, just to get insurance and help support the family. But Allen started pressuring her to quit that job, too, because he wanted her to be a traditional, subservient wife. He wanted her to be totally reliant on him."

According to LaRae, "Brenda really wanted a career in broadcast journalism. We found out later, after the fact, that she had been offered a job at BYU, teaching in the communications department. Allen wouldn't let her take it, though, so she became a housewife. It's clear from her journals that within about two months after marrying Allen, she realized she had made a mistake. But then she got pregnant with Erica."

"When Allen first became part of our family," says Betty, "there was this instant attachment. We all liked him. He was like a wonderful big brother to us. At the time, we had no idea that there was all this other stuff going on in his family. Then we started to notice how fanatical they all were."

---

* Currently the popular co-anchor of the evening news on KUTV, Salt Lake City's CBS affiliate, Michelle King graduated from the BYU communications department just two years before Brenda did.

Betty remembers visiting Brenda and Allen one night when her sister was pregnant with Erica: "Brenda wanted to go out and get something to eat, but Allen wouldn't patronize any restaurant that stayed open on Sundays. So we drove around from place to place, and Allen would make us sit in the car while he went in to find out if they were open on Sundays. Each place was, so he wouldn't let us eat there. After a while, Brenda and I got so frustrated we just asked him to take us home.

"Allen had a very successful tile business, but he insisted on always being paid in cash. He didn't believe in having a checking account, because he didn't want the IRS to be able to trace his income. He didn't want to have a Social Security card. None of this came out until after they got married.

"We started noticing that Allen was always trying to get around the law. When it came time to pay taxes that first year after they got married, Allen told Brenda that he wasn't going to pay them. She said, 'Oh yes, we are! That's what you do. You honor the law!' When Allen refused, she had our dad help her prepare the taxes for them. I remember when the car registration came due, Allen wouldn't let Brenda go get it registered. She told him, 'Yes I am, because I don't want to get a ticket!' They had a big fight about it. We just weren't raised like that. So she always made sure to do the things they were supposed to: she paid the taxes, renewed the licenses, those kinds of things. She resisted Allen as much as she could.

"But then the baby got sick and he wouldn't let Brenda take Erica to the doctor. And it just kept getting worse and worse."

Allen's father, Watson Lafferty Sr., had long been afflicted with diabetes, which he refused to treat with insulin. In late 1983, after he and Claudine had returned from their mission and were again living in the family home in Provo, Watson's diabetes took a sharp turn for the worse. His sons continued to refuse medical treatment for him, however. Their herbal and homeopathic remedies failed to alleviate the illness, and he died. "The whole family seemed evil to Brenda by then," says Betty. "Then and there she could tell something really bad was going on with them."

Life was growing more horrific for Dianna Lafferty, too. Her home in

Highland was just a few minutes away from the small apartment where Allen, Brenda, and their baby were living in American Fork. Overwhelmed and desperate, Dianna turned to Brenda for help. Although Brenda held stubbornly to her belief that she could turn Allen around, she was convinced that Ron was too far gone, and that he would never abandon his fanatical ideas. Both Ron and Dan had been excommunicated from the LDS Church. Ron no longer had a job. He was increasingly abusive to Dianna, and talked with ever greater fervor about taking plural wives. Brenda urged Dianna to divorce Ron, for her children's sake and her own.

Leaving Ron was all but unthinkable for Dianna. As she later explained to the Utah County prosecutor, she had six children, hadn't graduated from college, had never held a job, and possessed no marketable skills. "I can't even type," she confessed in despair. But at her core she knew Brenda was right: leaving Ron was imperative. Relying on Brenda, close friends, and members of the Highland LDS ward, Dianna summoned enough courage to initiate divorce proceedings.

The divorce was finalized in the autumn of 1983. Around Thanksgiving Dianna packed up the kids and moved to Florida, putting as much space as she could between her and the Lafferty boys. Even though he'd had every opportunity to see it coming, the departure of his wife and children came as a stunning blow to Ron. Despondent at the prospect of Christmas without them, he planned to spend the holidays far from Utah, where he was reminded of his missing family everywhere he turned. Ron decided to visit a colony of polygamists near Woodburn, Oregon, headed by a charismatic figure named John W. Bryant.

Before landing in Woodburn (a farm town just north of Salem, the Oregon state capital), Bryant had established polygamist settlements in Utah, California, and Nevada. Like so many other renegade prophets, he had on occasion asserted that he was the "one mighty and strong" but he differed from his fundamentalist brethren in some unusual aspects. Bryant was a libertine by temperament, and his teachings emphasized experimentation with drugs and group sex—homosexual as well as heterosexual—proclivities seldom acknowledged by other Mormon Fundamentalists.

Such scandalous behavior was completely new to Ron, who was both enthralled and taken aback by what he saw during his extended visit to Bryant's commune. When one of the prophet's wives let Ron know she found him attractive, Ron was extremely tempted to hop into bed with her, but he worried that doing so might make Bryant jealous and angry, so he left and returned to Utah.

Ron arrived back in the Provo area just after Bernard Brady had introduced Dan to Prophet Onias, the Canadian fundamentalist. Dan in turn introduced Onias to Ron and the other Lafferty brothers, and very soon thereafter, Ron, Dan, Mark, Watson, and Tim Lafferty were inducted into Onias's School of the Prophets. Allen, the youngest sibling, was eager to participate as well, but Brenda put her foot down. "She refused to let Allen join," LaRae Wright confirms.

Although standing up to Allen meant standing up to the entire Lafferty clan, Brenda did not shy away from such confrontations. Not only was she quite willing to argue theology with the Lafferty brothers, she possessed an impressive command of LDS scripture that allowed her to more than hold her own when debating fundamentalist doctrine with Ron and Dan. They came to despise her for defying them and for her influence over Allen, whom they considered "pussy-whipped."

When Ron's father was dying of diabetes, Ron had called a family meeting to discuss the funeral and other details. Allen brought Brenda to the meeting, which made Ron furious. He called her a bitch and worse, and berated her with such unrestrained spleen that Brenda finally left in tears. But she did not remain intimidated very long.

"Brenda was the only one of the Lafferty wives who was educated," Betty points out. "And her education was what they were afraid of. Because Brenda was confident in her beliefs, and her sense of right and wrong, and she wasn't about to let anyone take that away from her. She felt it was her duty to defend the other women. She was their only hope." Reflecting on the load her little sister had shouldered, Betty pauses before continuing: "At that point she was still just twenty-three years old.

To be that young, and to be surrounded by all these older people who were supposed to be more mature than she was—yet she was the one who they turned to." Betty pauses again. "My sister was an amazing woman."

Although Brenda managed to keep Allen from joining Onias's School of the Prophets, she could not prevent him from associating with Dan and his other brothers. "But she tried to keep a watchful eye on him," says Betty. "Around this time my little sister, Sharon, and I went to visit Brenda and Allen. While we were there, Brenda made sure that whenever Allen went anywhere, either Sharon or I went with him. Then when we'd get home she'd question us about where he went, and who he talked to. At the time I thought that was kind of weird. Now I see that she was just trying to keep tabs on how much he was talking to his brothers."

FIFTEEN

THE ONE MIGHTY AND STRONG

As a religious city-state under tight control, Nauvoo was a haven where the followers of Joseph Smith had their most important choices—what they should do to serve God—made for them . . . , and their identity as God's chosen people was assured through him. . . .

As is common in such situations, the threat of evil was projected onto others. . . . Hence, at Nauvoo the innocent children of God realized their identity through their struggle against the evil followers of Satan, who dominated American society everywhere except in the city of the Saints.

The problem, of course, with this kind of dichotomous myth is that, for the people who hold it, guilt and innocence become matters of belief, not evidence.

JOHN E. HALLWAS AND ROGER D. LAUNIUS,
CULTURES IN CONFLICT

When the Utah businessman and Dream Mine supporter Bernard Brady brought Prophet Onias and the Lafferty brothers (minus Allen) together one crisp fall evening near the end of 1983, it seemed to all who were present to be an especially auspicious union. There was an instant feeling of kinship and shared values, and the men talked excitedly until "the wee hours of the morning," according to Onias. Giddy with their sense of divinely empowered mission, everyone at the gathering was convinced that, collectively, they were destined to alter the course of human history.

"Five of the six brothers," Onias said, "became extremely enthusiastic when they realized that we had just been given a commandment by the Lord to send three sections of *The Book of Onias* to all the stake and ward authorities."* He was referring to a revelation he'd received on November 26 of that year, in which God had commanded Onias to "prepare pamphlets to send out to the presidents of stakes and bishops of wards of My church"—the LDS Church—so that those who had committed fornication against Him would "be warned." The pamphlet consisted of excerpts from Onias's collected revelations, cautioning the entire LDS leadership—from the president and putative prophet in Salt Lake City down to the bishop of every ward across North America—that God was extremely unhappy with the way they'd been running His One True Church.

God was especially steamed, Onias explained, that modern Mormon leaders were blatantly defying some of the most sacred doctrines He had revealed to Joseph Smith in the nineteenth century. Most egregiously, the men at the helm of the church continued to sanction and zealously enforce the government's criminalization of plural marriage. And only slightly less disturbing, from Onias's perspective, was the blasphemy perpetrated by LDS President Spencer W. Kimball in 1978 when he decreed that black-skinned men should be admitted into the Mormon priesthood—a historic, earth-shaking turnabout in church policy widely applauded by those outside the church. God had revealed to Onias, however, that blacks were subhuman "beasts of the field, which were the most intelligent of all animals that were created, for they did walk upright as a man doeth and had the power of speech."†

---

* *The Book of Onias* is an alternative title for *The Second Book of Commandments;* they are the same book. The LDS Church is organized into "stakes" of approximately three thousand members, which are the rough equivalent of archdioceses in the Catholic Church, and "wards," which are the neighborhood congregations within each stake. Typically each stake is made up of between five and twelve wards.

† In the LDS faith, all males deemed worthy are inducted into the "priesthood" at the age of twelve, which entails the assignment of specific responsibilities and privileges, as well as conferring inestimable status within the church. Before 1978, blacks were denied admission into the priesthood—a major affront that helps explain why there are relatively few Mormons of African descent. Women of all races continue to be barred from the priesthood.

According to the pamphlet, God had given Onias an earful about blacks being ordained as LDS priests:

Behold I say unto you, at no time have I given a commandment unto My church, nor shall I . . . that the children of Ham, even the Negro race and all its peoples, should receive My holy Priesthood. . . .

And have I not spoken to My servant Joseph Smith, even your head, that none of this race could or would be ordained to My holy Priesthood until the seed of Abel shall rise above the seed of Cain? . . .

For Satan was the founder of this black race, for he came to Cain after God had taken away his power to procreate the children of righteousness, and showed him how he could place his seed into animals, and the seed of animals into other animals, for he did corrupt the seed of the earth in this manner, hoping to thwart the works of God.

And for this reason the earth was destroyed by the flood, to destroy from the face of the earth these abominations which Cain created, for he had corrupted all flesh. . . .

For Satan has infiltrated My church, and seeketh to become its head.

But those who have heeded him shall shortly be exposed by their folly, for [neither] My name nor My church shall be mocked longer, for it shall shortly be cleansed and purged and tried in the fire, that all those who profess to know Me, and know Me not, will be exposed.

The pamphlet further warned that God had dispatched Onias to "cleanse My house of its filthiness" and put the institutions of Mormondom back on the road to righteousness. God had revealed,

I shall endow [Onias] with My Spirit, and the wicked he shall expose, and they shall not stand, and they shall gnash their teeth in anger, and their anger shall eat them up.

For I am the Lord God Almighty, and My words shall not be mocked. . . .

And what a great noise and commotion they shall make when they fall. . . .

And My servant [Onias] who is held in derision, I shall place in
him My Spirit, and he shall be as a fire that devoureth; and the words
that he shall write and speak shall expose many and cause many to fall,
for they repent not.

By sending this pamphlet to the leaders of the LDS Church, Onias intended to give them the opportunity to make a choice: confess their errors and turn over control of the church to the Lord's chosen prophet, the
"one mighty and strong," or face God's wrath. To a detached observer
this seems like an act of astonishing naïveté and hubris on Onias's part,
but the pamphlet's text resonated with tremendous power for the Lafferty brothers. It had the ring of long-denied truth. They believed they
had found, in Onias, a crucial ally in their struggle to restore the church
of Joseph Smith to righteousness and prepare the earth for the Second
Coming of Christ.

Onias was no less enamored of the Laffertys, and what they could do
to advance his ambitions for the School of the Prophets. Applying the
full brunt of their prodigious energy, the Lafferty brothers dived head-
long into the tedious chore of printing, folding, and collating more than
fifteen thousand of Onias's pamphlets, then addressing and mailing
them to LDS leaders around the country. "It was like a miracle to us,"
Onias says, "for what would have taken us several months to accomplish
in our spare time, they were able to accomplish in two weeks working
day and night."

By early 1984 the newly established School of the Prophets was
meeting on a weekly basis, usually at the Provo home of the Laffertys'
mother, Claudine, upstairs from the family chiropractic clinic. Thanks
to the enthusiasm of the five brothers, the school got off to a flying start.
Onias appreciated the Laffertys' pivotal role in his school's successful
launch. The Laffertys, it seemed to him, were heaven-sent.

Onias soon got confirmation that in fact they were. On January 8, he
received a revelation in which God explained that before the Lafferty
boys were even born, He had singled them out "to be an elect people, for
they are the true blood of Israel and the chosen seed." Six weeks later,
Onias received another revelation in which God commanded him to ap-

point Ron Lafferty bishop of the school's Provo chapter, which he gladly did. All the younger brothers, including Dan, clearly looked up to Ron—as indeed they had their entire lives. When Ron assumed the bishop's responsibilities, everyone in the School of the Prophets approved.

Ron's promotion to a position of authority lifted his morale at a moment when such a boost was sorely needed, because the prior months had delivered an avalanche of setbacks and disappointments. As Ron recorded in a journal entry,

> The events of the past year have caused me to do a great deal of research and scripture study and spend a great deal of time on my knees in prayer. I have been stripped of all my material wealth, my family has divorced me and moved to Florida, I have been unjustly excommunicated from the church that I love so dearly.

Ron no longer had a job or a regular paycheck. He was regarded as a pariah by his church and community. Because the home he'd so painstakingly built with his own hands had been taken from him, he was reduced to living out of his 1974 Impala station wagon—the only asset of any value still in his possession. And yet he claimed in his journal to be grateful for such humiliations, saying, "These experiences have caused me to establish a personal relationship with my Father in Heaven and He has revealed to me, at least in part, the outcome of all these trials."

Though Ron claimed to enjoy wearing a hair shirt, however, his actions suggested otherwise. The departure of his wife and their six children to a distant corner of the nation gnawed at him day and night. Over time his hurt was transformed into an implacable rage, and most of that anger was directed at the three individuals who, in his estimation, bore responsibility for Dianna's decision to abandon him: Richard Stowe, Chloe Low, and Brenda Lafferty.

Stowe, a pharmacist by trade and a neighbor of Ron and Dianna's, was president of the LDS Highland Stake. He directed the stake's High Council Court, which had tried Ron in August 1983 and subsequently excommunicated him. Much worse, in Ron's view, Stowe had offered crucial financial assistance to Dianna, via the church, which had allowed her to survive while the divorce was being finalized; and Stowe had also provided a great deal of counseling and emotional succor.

Chloe Low had been an uncommonly close friend to both Ron and Dianna for a dozen years. Her husband, Stewart Low, was the bishop of Ron and Dianna's LDS ward, and had handpicked Ron to be his first counselor in the bishopric. Chloe had long admired the Lafferty family, and she went to Dan for chiropractic treatment when her back gave her trouble. As Ron and Dianna's marriage began to fall apart, Chloe offered unstinting support to both of them, but when Ron's behavior grew increasingly monstrous, she came down firmly on Dianna's side of the fence. Once, when Ron was making life particularly unbearable for Dianna, Chloe invited her and her children to stay in the Low home for four days; on another occasion Chloe took them in for ten days. After the execution of the divorce, Chloe had been there to help Dianna and her kids pack up the shards of their broken lives and move to Florida. As Ron saw it, without Chloe Low's advocacy and assistance, Dianna would never have had the wherewithal to leave.

The greatest portion of Ron's long-simmering wrath, however, was reserved for Brenda Wright Lafferty—Allen's smart, beautiful, headstrong wife—whom Ron regarded as being instrumental in persuading Dianna to abandon him.

Rejected by his wife, scorned by his community, Ron poured himself completely into the School of the Prophets. It became his family, his life, his world. Much of Ron's time with the school was occupied by expediting the shipping of the pamphlets to LDS leaders, urging them to abandon their ungodly path. But the school's main thrust, as Onias had conceived it, was to teach the faithful how to receive and interpret revelations from God, and as the winter of 1984 edged toward spring, Ron began receiving this instruction in earnest.

On February 24, Ron became the first of Onias's students to take delivery of a commandment from the Almighty. Sitting at a computer he'd borrowed from Bernard Brady, Ron closed his eyes and waited until he felt the spirit of the Lord cause a finger to depress a key, and then another, and another. By and by, a message from God inched across the screen: Ron's inaugural revelation. He received a second revelation on February 25, and a third on the 27th.

Upon witnessing his brother receiving revelations from God, Dan was spellbound, and excited. "I never received any revelations when we were in the School of the Prophets," he explains. "Everyone else in the school did, and I've received revelations since then, so now I understand the phenomenon, but I didn't at that time. So I was fascinated. I'd ask, 'What is it like?!' Ron said it was hard to describe, but I remember once he said, 'It's like a blanket falls over you, and you can feel the Lord's thoughts, and you write them down.' One revelation came to him a single word at a time, and he didn't even know if it was coherent until he was done receiving it, and then went back and read it. But they didn't always come that way. Sometimes he'd receive whole phrases at a time."

The revelation Ron received on February 27 was in fact a message from the Lord to Ron's wife, with Ron simply serving as the conduit. In this commandment God reiterated that the earth would soon be destroyed, and He warned Dianna:

Thou are a chosen daughter but My wrath is kindled against thee because of thy rebelliousness against thy husband, and I command thee to repent. Have I not said that it is not good for a man to be alone? I will not suffer My servant Ron to be alone much longer for even now I am preparing someone to take thy place. Nevertheless if thou wilst speedily repent I will greatly bless thee and thy children, otherwise I will remove thee from thy place for I will not suffer that thy children should suffer longer because of thy disobedience. I have heard the prayers of My son Ron and I know his desires, and it is only because of his desires that I have spared thee till now.

Harken unto My word for the time is short. I am Alpha and Omega even the beginning and the end and surely I will fulfill all My promises unto My servant Ron. Even so Amen.

According to psychiatrist C. Jess Groesbeck, who examined Ron after the murders, as Ron began to understand that Dianna really was going to take their children and leave forever, it slowly "becomes clear that this man is losing the most important thing he's ever lost in his life. . . . I can't stress enough how deep this loss was. . . . He feels low, worthless. And his anger and aggression are almost unbounded. . . . He compensates by creating a new but unreal view of himself and the world. He develops an inflated God-like self-image in an effort to avoid the pain and deny the truth of what he really is."

Buttressing Dr. Groesbeck's assessment, on March 13 the still small voice of the Lord spoke to Ron once again, revealing,

And the thing that ye have thought concerning the One Mighty and Strong is correct, for have I not said that in these the last days I will reveal all things unto the children of men? For was not Moses the One Mighty and Strong, and was not Jesus the One Mighty and Strong, and was not My servant Onias the One Mighty and Strong, and art thou not One Mighty and Strong, and will I not yet call others Mighty and Strong to set in order My church and My kingdom? For it was never meant that there should be only one One Mighty and Strong, for there are many, and they who have thought otherwise have erred.

In Dr. Groesbeck's learned opinion, this revelation was a delusional artifact, as were all Ron's revelations, spawned by depression and his deeply entrenched narcissism, with no basis whatsoever in reality. Which is, of course, what nonbelievers typically say about people who have religious visions and revelations: that they're crazy. The devout individuals on the receiving end of such visions, however, generally beg to differ, and Ron is one of them.

Ron *knows* that the commandments he'd received were no mere figment of his imagination. The Lord spoke to him. And he wasn't about to believe the words of some faithless, pencil-neck shrink over the voice of the Almighty. That, after all, would really be crazy.

Before actually carrying out the murders of Brenda and Erica Lafferty, Ron hadn't done anything that was terribly outlandish, or unique, according to the cultural norms of Utah County. Ron's revelations can be viewed, in one sense, simply as a time-honored response to a major life crisis—a response exhibited by many a religious fanatic before him. In *Feet of Clay,* a study of self-proclaimed prophets, English psychiatrist Anthony Storr points out that such gurus often receive momentous revelations and profound insights immediately following

> a period of mental distress or physical illness, in which the guru has been fruitlessly searching for an answer to his own emotional problems. This change is likely to take place in the subject's thirties or forties, and may warrant the diagnosis of mid-life crisis. Sometimes the revelatory answer comes gradually; at other times, a new insight strikes like a thunderbolt. . . . The distress of chaos followed by the establishment of a new order is a typical course of events which takes place in all creative activity, whether in the arts or the sciences. This *Eureka* pattern is also characteristic of religious revelation and the delusional systems of people we label insane.*

Prompted by Onias's instruction, throughout February and March Ron received approximately twenty revelations. Some he recorded on Brady's computer on the spot, as they came to him; more often he kept the revelations in his head for a while before committing them to print, in order to mull them over and better understand them.

The most disturbing of Ron's revelations occurred in late March, and he recorded it by hand, on a sheet of yellow legal paper:

> Thus Saith the lord unto My servants the Prophets. It is My will and commandment that ye remove the following individuals in order that My work might go forward. For they have truly become obstacles in My path and I will not allow My work to be stopped. First thy brother's wife Brenda and her baby, then Chloe Low, then Richard Stowe. And it is My will that they be removed in rapid succession and

---

* Reprinted with the permission of The Free Press, a division of Simon & Schuster Adult Publishing Group, from *Feet of Clay: Saints, Sinners, and Madmen: A Study of Gurus* by Anthony Storr. Copyright © 1996 by Anthony Storr.

that an example be made of them in order that others might see the fate of those who fight against the true Saints of God. And it is My will that this matter be taken care of as soon as possible and I will prepare a way for My instrument to be delivered and instructions be given unto My servant Todd.* And it is My will that he show great care in his duties for I have raised him up and prepared him for this important work and is he not like unto My servant Porter Rockwell[?]† And great blessings await him if he will do My Will, for I am the Lord thy God and have control over all things. Be still and know that I am with thee. Even so Amen.

Upon receiving this revelation, before sharing it with others in the School of the Prophets, Ron showed it to Dan. "Ron was a little bit frightened by the things he was receiving," says Dan. "I told him, 'Well, I can see why you're concerned, as well you should be. . . . All I can say is make sure it's from God. You don't want to act on commandments that are not from God, but at the same time you don't want to offend God by refusing to do his work.'"

Over the days that followed, both Ron and Dan pondered the removal revelation intensely. During this period Ron had yet another revelation, in which he was told that he was "the mouth of God" and Dan

---

* Todd was Michael Todd Jeffory Judd, a beefy, fair-haired hitchhiker whom Watson Lafferty had happened to pick up one afternoon. Todd was hungry, so Watson brought him to Claudine Lafferty's home for a meal, where he met some of the other Lafferty brothers and was invited to attend meetings of the School of the Prophets. Todd stayed at Claudine's for two weeks, then, around the time Ron received this revelation, traveled to Arizona with Watson for three additional weeks to work for him on a construction project. Todd and Watson began to quarrel, however, and one day Watson returned to the apartment they were sharing to discover that Todd had stolen all of his belongings and disappeared, ending his association with the Lafferty clan and the School of the Prophets before he could be called upon to "remove" the named individuals.

† Orrin Porter Rockwell, the "Destroying Angel," who, in 1842, attempted to assassinate Governor Lilburn Boggs of Missouri, Joseph Smith's nemesis. Rockwell, who served as the personal bodyguard to both Joseph Smith and Brigham Young, was celebrated by nineteenth-century Mormons for killing scores of men deemed enemies of the LDS Church with his .44-caliber Colt revolver. A popular, long-established restaurant in Utah County, called Porter's Place, is named after him.

was "the arm of God." The brothers interpreted this to mean that Dan was to do the actual killing.

Seeking further guidance, they considered a passage near the beginning of *The Book of Mormon* in which Nephi—the obedient, highly principled prophet "who had great desires to know the mysteries of God"—is commanded by the Lord to cut off the head of Laban of Jerusalem—a scheming, filthy-rich sheep magnate who turns up in the pages of both *The Book of Mormon* and the Old Testament.

Nephi at first resists the commandment: "I said in my heart, never at any time have I shed the blood of man, and I shrunk and would that I might not slay him."

But then God speaks to Nephi again: "Behold the Lord slayeth the wicked to bring forth His righteous purposes: It is better that one man should perish, than that a nation should dwindle and perish in unbelief."

Thus reassured, Nephi says in *The Book of Mormon,* "I did obey the voice of the Spirit, and took Laban by the hair of the head, and I smote off his head with his own sword."*

Thanks to a revelation Ron had received back on February 28, the story of Nephi slaying Laban was imbued with special significance for Dan. In this revelation, God had commanded:

> Thus saith the Lord unto My servant Dan. . . . Thou art like unto Nephi of old for never since the beginning of time have I had a more obedient son. And for this I will greatly bless thee and multiply thy seed, for have I not said if ye do what I say I am bound[?] Continue in My word for I have great responsibility and great blessings in store for thee. That is all for now. Even so Amen.

This revelation had a tremendous impact on Dan: after God had declared that he was like Nephi, according to Mark Lafferty, Dan "was willing to do anything that the Lord commanded him."

---

* According to several accounts, when Joseph Smith dug up *The Book of Mormon* on the Hill Cumorah in 1827, he found Laban's sword in the ancient stone box that held the golden plates.

. . .

In the fundamentalist worldview, a sharp dividing line runs through all of creation, demarcating good from evil, and everybody falls on one side of that line or the other. After much praying, Ron and Dan decided that the four individuals God had commanded them to remove must, a priori, be wicked—they were "children of perdition," as Dan phrased it— and therefore deserved to be murdered. Having determined that the so-called removal revelation was true and valid, the Lafferty brothers further concluded that "it would be wise to act on the things it suggested."

Whenever a member of the School of the Prophets received a revelation, it was standard procedure for the commandment to be presented to the other members for evaluation. On March 22, just before the school's weekly meeting at Claudine Lafferty's home, Ron took Bernard Brady into a side room and handed him the removal revelation. "He asked me to look it over," says Brady, "and then he left the room. As I read it, my hands began to shake. I got cold all over. I couldn't believe what I was reading." When Ron returned a few minutes later, Brady told him, "This scares me to death. I don't want to have anything to do with anything like that. I think it is wrong." When the meeting commenced a few minutes later, neither Ron nor Brady said anything to the other members about the revelation.

Ron had brought to that meeting a woman named Becky, whom he'd recently taken as a spiritual wife without benefit of a license or civil ceremony. The couple then went to Wichita, Kansas, for a honeymoon, so Ron wasn't present when the school met the next time, on March 29; nor was Dan. Watson showed up with a pearl-handled straight razor, however, which he asked the somewhat puzzled members to "dedicate as a religious instrument for destroying the wicked, like the sword of Laban."

"Of course we refused," says Onias, who did not yet know about the removal revelation. Watson was angered by this rebuff, Onias remembers, and "left the meeting with a bad spirit."

Tensions between Onias and some of the Lafferty brothers—primarily Watson, Ron, and Dan—had been building for several weeks. Soon after he had been appointed bishop of the school, Ron had begun to openly challenge Onias's authority. Onias noticed a distinct change in Ron's personality, "from an extremely kind gentleman to a man full of hate and anger. In his position as bishop, he started to dictate to everyone, and would get angry if they didn't do what he said." When Onias urged all members of the school to seek gainful employment in order to fund the construction of a "City of Refuge" below the Dream Mine, which was one of the school's priorities, Ron angrily criticized him, arguing that there was no need for anybody to get a job, because surely God would provide the school with sufficient wealth, through miraculous means, to complete their work.

In one of Ron's revelations, God had, in fact, instructed him to send his brother Mark to Nevada to wager on a horse race to raise funds for the City of Refuge. With the Lord letting Mark know which mount to bet on, it seemed that they couldn't lose. But they did. Afterward, Onias couldn't resist telling the brothers, "I told you so," causing relations between Ron and the prophet to deteriorate even further.

Around Thanksgiving of 1983, when Ron had gone to Oregon to visit John Bryant's polygamist commune, he had been introduced to some new sensual experiences, including intoxicants. As part of their religious rituals, Bryant's group administered wine as a sacrament, and Ron partook with the others. Having been raised in a household that was strictly abstemious, this was his first experience with alcohol, and he found it quite agreeable. It gave him a nice, mellow feeling that "heightened his sense of the spirit." Thereafter Ron described wine as "the gift of God."

Thus introduced to the pleasures of "strong drink" (as alcoholic beverages are negatively characterized in Section 89 of *The Doctrine and Covenants*), when Ron returned to Utah he insisted that the School of Prophets substitute wine for the juice or water they ordinarily served as a sacrament at the beginning of each meeting. This was another direct challenge to Onias's authority, and it provoked a dramatic confrontation during the meeting of March 9. On that occasion Ron continued to gulp down glasses of wine after the sacrament was offered, and was soon stinking drunk. He began to mock Onias, who had refused the wine and taken water instead. According to Onias, Ron "kept ridiculing me, saying that I was too old and slow and it was about time I was released. He did this very sarcastically and said that the Lafferty brothers should take over. He was supported by Dan and Watson."

It was in this atmosphere of growing rancor that Ron's removal revelation was put before the school for evaluation. During the meeting of April 5, he showed a copy of it to all the members and asked them to confirm its validity. The nine men who were present that evening earnestly discussed the revelation, then held a vote to determine its legitimacy as a divine commandment. "Ron, Dan, and Watson were in favor of accepting it as a valid revelation," says Bernard Brady. "Everybody else said, 'No way! Don't even consider it! Forget the whole thing!' At which point Ron, Dan, and Watson became really angry, got up, and walked out of the meeting, ending their association with the school."

The disagreement among the school's members that evening underscores the conundrum that inevitably confronts any prophet who encourages his acolytes to engage in dialogue with God: sooner or later, God is apt to command an acolyte to disobey the prophet. And to true believers—to zealots like Ron and Dan Lafferty—the word of God will trump the word of a mere prophet like Onias every time.

Worried that Ron might actually attempt to carry out the removal revelation and murder the four named individuals, Brady formally registered his concern in an affidavit, which he signed and had notarized on April 9:

State of Utah

ss.

County of Utah

AFFIDAVIT

KNOW ALL MEN BY THESE PRESENTS, that I, Bernard Brady, a Free and Natural Citizen of the United States of America, do hereby depose and say that I have reason to believe and fear that lives of the following ten people are in jeopardy: Robert Crossfield; Bernard Brady; David Olsen; David Coronado; Tim Lafferty; Mark Lafferty; Brenda

Lafferty; Brenda Lafferty's baby daughter; Chloe Low; and Richard Stowe.

I, Bernard Brady, do further depose and say that it is my belief that this jeopardy results from the thoughts, beliefs, attitudes, understanding, and potential actions of the following four individuals: Ron Lafferty; Dan Lafferty; Watson Lafferty; and Todd (last name unknown).

Brady's concern was genuine and acute, but he didn't alert the police; nor did any other members of the School of the Prophets. Brady merely filed the affidavit in a desk drawer in his home, so that if Ron did kill anyone, Brady could prove that he was blameless.

Neither did any of the school members—despite their alarm upon learning of the removal revelation—see fit to alert any of the people designated for removal. Later that month, however, Dan took it upon himself to inform his youngest brother, Allen, with whom he had always been especially close, that God had commanded the ritual murder of Brenda and their baby girl, Erica, and that Ron and Dan intended to see that the commandment was carried out.

Allen expressed shock, then asked, "Why? Particularly why Erica, being an innocent child? Why would she be involved?"

At which point Ron angrily cut in, "Because she would grow up to be a bitch, just like her mother!"

Dan earnestly asked Allen what he thought of Ron's revelation. Allen replied that because he, personally, hadn't received any such revelation from God, he couldn't accept it; he said he would defend his wife and child with his life. But Allen never bothered to tell Brenda of his brothers' declared intent to murder her and their baby.

Betty McEntire, Brenda's older sister, hasn't been able to reconcile the fact that Allen withheld this information. "If he had told Brenda about Ron's revelation," Betty insists, "she would have been out of there in a minute, and she'd still be alive today. But Brenda didn't know anything about it. I can't understand why none of the people who did know about it never warned her. Especially Allen. It was like he was starting to succumb to his brothers.

"Brenda loved Allen, and he showed over and over again that he wasn't worthy of her love. Your duty, as a husband, is to protect your wife and child, and he let them down. I think Allen learned about the revelation way back in April, yet he said nothing. I can't comprehend that. I can't forgive him for that. All these years later, I'm still terribly angry. That he betrayed her love. That he had the very best, and he just threw it away."

In May 1984, Ron and Dan left Utah in Ron's dilapidated Impala wagon and began an extended sojourn across most of the American West and into Canada, stopping along the way to call on various fundamentalist communities. Nobody in the School of the Prophets heard from Dan or Ron through all of June and most of July. "I felt a little better with them out of the area," says Bernard Brady, "because they weren't going to be around to commit any murders. It seemed like the direction things were going, nobody had anything to worry about."

But early on the morning of July 25, the phone rang as Brady was getting ready to go to work. "It was Tim Lafferty," says Brady, his voice breaking as he remembers the moment. "He said . . . um . . . he said, 'Bernard, I've got some bad news. They carried out the revelation. Ron and Dan. They killed some people yesterday.' " Brady covers his face with his hands, then continues. "My legs buckled. I collapsed. I couldn't believe what I was hearing."

SIXTEEN

REMOVAL

Mere anarchy is loosed upon the world,
The blood-dimmed tide is loosed, and everywhere
The ceremony of innocence is drowned;
The best lack all conviction, while the worst
Are full of passionate intensity.

Surely some revelation is at hand;
Surely the Second Coming is at hand.
The Second Coming! Hardly are those words out
When a vast image out of Spiritus Mundi
Troubles my sight: somewhere in the sands of the desert
A shape with lion body and the head of a man,
A gaze blank and pitiless as the sun,
Is moving its slow thighs, while all about it
*Reel shadows of the indignant desert birds.**

WILLIAM BUTLER YEATS,
"THE SECOND COMING"

* Reprinted with permission of Scribner, an imprint of Simon & Schuster Adult Publishing Group, from *The Collected Works of W. B. Yeats, Volume 1: The Poems, Revised,* edited by Richard J. Finneran. Copyright © 1924 by the Macmillan Company; copyright renewed © 1952 by Bertha Georgie Yeats.

Even though Brenda was unaware of the removal revelation, she had plenty of other reasons to fear all the Laffertys, including Allen. And fear them she did, but that didn't deter her from standing up to the brothers on behalf of Dianna and the other wives.

When Brenda disobeyed Allen, or her assertiveness embarrassed him in front of his brothers, he was apt to berate her with uncontrollable fury. Other times he vented his anger by beating her. One night toward the end of winter in 1984, Betty Wright McEntire was awakened after midnight by a frantic phone call from Brenda. "She told me to meet her at a McDonald's halfway between Salt Lake and American Fork, where she and Allen lived," Betty remembers. "I asked what was wrong, and she goes, 'I just need to talk to you.' So I got out of bed and drove down there.

"When I got to the McDonald's she told me, 'I'm leaving him.' I said, 'What?! I had no idea things were that bad.' She said, 'Well, I've been secretly saving some money, and I'm going to go live with Grandpa and Grandma in Montana. I'll get a job there and take care of the baby on my own.' "

But immediately after this meeting with her sister, Brenda changed her mind and stayed with Allen, which raises the question, Why? Especially after she had been so resolute in urging Dianna Lafferty to leave Ron. "How come Brenda didn't split? Because she loved Allen," Betty explains, "and she wasn't one to quit. He was the father of her baby girl. She wanted it to work. She really thought she could save him from his brothers. She was a very determined woman."

Betty makes a painful confession, however. When Brenda confided to her at McDonald's under the cruel fluorescent glare that she was leaving Allen, Betty reflexively admonished, "But you can't! You're married now. If things are bad, you just need to work them out!" At the time, Betty says, she didn't have "a clue that he was beating her, and I didn't know any of the stuff about the School of the Prophets; we only learned about it after her death, when we read her journals. My mom and dad were always there for her, but she didn't tell us what was really going on. Because if there was any way my dad would have known, he would have driven down and taken her and the baby back to Idaho, where they would have been safe, no question."

One Sunday morning about two months after Brenda met Betty in the middle of the night at McDonald's, LaRae Wright, the women's mother, says she received a very disturbing phone call from Brenda: "She was in a panic. She said, 'Things aren't going well with Allen. Can I come home?' We said, 'Of course!' Well, then we didn't hear back from her, so I called her that evening and she said, 'We've worked things out.' So she didn't come to Idaho, after all. I don't know what was going on, but she never came home."

By then, Ron and Dan were long gone from Provo and Utah County, driving around the West in Ron's Impala wagon on their impromptu pilgrimage to polygamist communities. "We traveled up into Canada, down through the western U.S., and across the Midwest," Dan recalls. "As I look back at it now, it was an important trip for me because I got to know my brother for the first time, really. Until then, I never knew Ron all that well. He's six years older than me. We were never that close as kids. We all looked up to him, and I wanted to be close to him, but we just didn't have the opportunity."

Day after day, taking turns at the wheel, Ron and Dan rolled across the continent in the old Chevrolet. At times they would drive for hours without speaking, simply gazing up at the massive thunderheads that boiled forty thousand feet into the afternoon sky, transforming the plains into a vast, shifting checkerboard of shadow and dazzling sunlight. More often the brothers talked, and when they did it was with passionate intensity. Usually the topic of conversation was the removal revelation.

In the revelation's second sentence, God had told Ron, "It is My will and commandment that ye remove the following individuals in order that My work might go forward." Brenda and Erica Lafferty, Chloe Low, and Richard Stowe needed to be killed, God said, because "they have truly become obstacles in My path and I will not allow My work to be

stopped." Understanding "My work" to mean building the City of
Refuge, Ron began to tell Dan of "a great slaughter that was to take
place" before the construction could commence.

Sitting in a small cinder-block room deep in the bowels of the
maximum-security unit at Point of the Mountain, Dan tilts his head
back and gazes blankly at the ceiling, letting details from that eventful
summer bubble back up into his consciousness. The road trip stretched
into weeks, then months, and as the length of the trip increased, Dan remembers, "I noticed my brother getting more and more agitated—it
seemed like he was becoming more bloodthirsty, really. He started saying things like, 'It's gonna happen soon.' And eventually he began to focus on a particular date that the removals should be carried out. After a
while he said, 'I think the twenty-fourth of July is when it's going to
happen.'

"As I observed Ron going through these changes—and the things
he was saying were really freaking me out—all I could do was pray. I
asked God, 'Look, you know I will do whatever you want me to do.
Should I stay with my brother and carry this thing out? Or should I separate from him and have nothing more to do with this?' But the answer
I got was to stay with Ron."

A few times during their trip, Ron and Dan decided to separate for a
week or two. At one point Ron hopped a freight train east, while Dan
took the Impala and kept to a different itinerary. Dan arrived at their rendezvous site in Wichita, Kansas, in mid-June, several days before Ron.
While he waited for his brother to show up, he got a job as a day laborer
through the local employment office, tearing down an old bank. During
his brief tenure on this project, Dan met a twenty-four-year-old named
Ricky Knapp who was wielding a shovel on the same demolition crew.

According to Dan, he and Knapp "became good friends. He had just
gotten out of jail, and we had some good conversations. And I really liked
him." After his release, Knapp had found himself without a roof over his
head, so Dan invited Knapp to stay with him in the back of the Impala,
and Knapp accepted. When Ron arrived in Wichita soon thereafter,
Knapp decided to join the brothers for the remainder of their road trip.

Knapp had an associate who was a small-time marijuana farmer.

One afternoon before they left Wichita, Knapp took Dan to a field outside of town where this farmer had thrown away the "shake" from his
most recent harvest—the leaves and stems discarded after the resinous
buds had been trimmed and packaged for sale. Knapp and Dan filled a
grocery bag with this poor-grade weed and stashed it in the Impala. It
was foul stuff, Dan recalls, "but you could get a low-level buzz after
smoking four or five big joints."

This wasn't the first time Dan had smoked marijuana; he had actually
been introduced to it fifteen years earlier. Ironically, it was the "Word of
Wisdom"—Section 89 of *The Doctrine and Covenants,* famously prohibiting
Mormons from using tobacco and "strong drink"—that had first aroused
Dan's curiosity about pot. Specifically, his interest was piqued by verse 10
of the revelation, which reads, "Verily I say unto you, all wholesome herbs
God hath ordained for the constitution, nature, and use of man."

Dan had occasion to satisfy his curiosity in 1969 when he returned
from his mission and took a construction job in Colorado Springs, Colorado. Among the folks he worked with, he says, were "a lot of people who
smoked pot . . . and although I wouldn't try it myself, I was observant and
analytical of them and their practices, and I asked a lot of questions, which
soon gave me the impression that there was some big lie being perpetu-
ated about this stuff." Eventually a girl he had a crush on in Colorado convinced him to sample some high-potency dope, he remembers: "I was
launched into my first orbit into the expanded universe inside my head."

Dan smoked pot a few more times during that period of his young
adulthood, but he worried that he was committing a sin, and when he
moved from Colorado back to Utah County he "repented and became a
hundred and ten percent Mormon again."* Dan didn't smoke any more

---

* Interestingly, in 1915 Utah became the first state in the Union to criminalize marijuana.
The impetus for the ban came from the LDS Church, which was concerned about increasing
marijuana use among its members. Latter-day Saints, it turns out, were way ahead of the
curve when it came to smoking dope, thanks to polygamists who'd developed a taste for
cannabis in Mexico, where some six thousand of them had fled by the early years of the twentieth century to escape federal prosecution. In the summer of 1912, the Mexican Revolution
flared through northern Mexico, and the escalating violence compelled most of these expa-
triate polygamists to return to Utah, where they introduced marijuana into the broader Mormon culture, alarming the LDS general authorities.

marijuana until he met Ricky Knapp in the summer of 1984, at which point, he says, "I felt I was having my heart and mind opened to something much more mysterious and serious than I had ever imagined." As he reflected on the various references to herbs in Joseph's published revelations, Dan became convinced that the prophet "must have come across some of the mind-expanding herbs."

Unlike Dan, Ron had never tried marijuana before Ricky Knapp entered their lives, but after hooking up with Dan and Knapp in Wichita, Ron was easily persuaded to smoke some of Knapp's low-grade cannabis. According to Dan, Ron thereby "got to feel what a mild high was like, and to experience the munchies. It was probably rather fortuitous [that the marijuana was so weak] because he was a little fearful at first, and later on, when we got good stuff to smoke, he tended to get pretty paranoid." Paranoid or not, Ron quickly adopted Dan's view that marijuana enhanced one's "spiritual enlightenment."

When Dan became reacquainted with marijuana through his association with Knapp, he says that because he was no longer under the thumb of the LDS Church, "for the first time I was able to get high with a clear conscience, and perhaps that is why, rather than just experiencing 'the gladdening of the heart,' I began to experience the 'enlivening of the soul.' I began to have what I would call wonderful spiritual insights." Getting baked, Dan observed, was "much like becoming a child and being introduced into a whole new world. . . . I've concluded that the scripture which says, 'Unless you become like a little child, you can't see the Kingdom of Heaven' is another secret reference to getting high; as is also the mysterious account of Moses seeing God through the burning bush."*

---

* After Dan and Ron were arrested, Dan made a statement from jail in praise of "spirit herbs," which was widely publicized. "Because of that statement," Dan says, "many people have wondered if I was on drugs or drunk when I did the killings, but neither was the case. I had smoked some good bud with my third wife about a week earlier . . . and I drank a beer Alex Joseph bought me the day I left his compound in Big Water on about July 22"; but that, he insists, was the full extent to which he used intoxicants during the period leading up to the murders.

After their contretemps with the School of the Prophets in April 1984 but before leaving Utah on their road trip, Ron and Dan had paid a visit to the directors of the Dream Mine in order to discuss the City of Refuge they intended to build near the mine entrance. This was their second visit to the directors: a couple of months earlier, Dan had offered to donate the labor of all six Lafferty brothers to help extract the gold everybody knew was close at hand, in order to finance the City of Refuge, but the managers of the mine had politely declined the offer. This time, Ron and Dan dispensed with all niceties and flat-out demanded that the directors turn over management of the mine to them; if they refused, Ron warned, the directors "would feel the hand of the Lord." Ignoring the threat of divine retribution, the mine managers declined this offer as well, albeit less politely this time around.

Despite being rebuffed in their efforts to take control of the Dream Mine and being expelled from the School of the Prophets, Ron and Dan remained excited about building the City of Refuge on Onias's property below the mine. Toward this end, during their road trip they sought out a number of preeminent polygamists across the West and attempted to enlist their support for the project—among them John W. Bryant, the self-proclaimed prophet Ron had visited the previous December. After leaving Wichita at the beginning of July, Ron, Dan, and Ricky Knapp steered the Impala west, aiming for Bryant's commune amid the tall fir trees and lush berry farms of Oregon's Willamette Valley.

Upon their arrival there, Ron electrified Bryant's followers with an impromptu sermon about the City of Refuge and the role it would play during the Last Days. According to one of these postulants, Laurene Grant, Ron "just had so much to love. Everyone picked up on it. Everyone just started to bubble." Grant, a mother of four children, was also impressed with Dan, who used his chiropractic skills to treat members of the commune. She compared Dan to Christ, saying, "He was just so gentle and so loving."

By the time the Laffertys bid farewell to Bryant's group and the damp charms of the Pacific Northwest, Dan had taken Grant as his third wife. The newlyweds and her two youngest children drove away together in Grant's car, while Ron, her two older sons, and Knapp departed in the Impala. They agreed to meet in two weeks, at the Confederated States of the Exiled Nation of Israel—the Utah compound of Alex Joseph, one of America's best-known polygamists. Joseph, six or seven of his wives, and their many children lived in Big Water, a faded desert settlement near the southwestern end of Lake Powell, the second-largest reservoir in the nation.* Big Water happened to be not terribly far from Colorado City, the stronghold of Uncle Roy's Fundamentalist Church of Jesus Christ of Latter Day Saints—the most populous polygamist sect in the nation.

Ron, Ricky Knapp, and Grant's older boys drove south on Interstate 5 into California. While they were making a bathroom stop at a rest area outside of Sacramento, the youngsters struck up a conversation with a twenty-three-year-old drifter and petty thief from New Mexico named Chip Carnes. The brakes had failed on his run-down car, and after the boys introduced him to Ron, Ron offered to help Carnes get the vehicle to a repair shop in Sacramento.

Strapping a spare tire to the rear bumper of the Impala, Ron instructed Carnes to drive with the nose of his car pushed tight against the tire, so that Ron could use the Impala's brakes to slow Carnes's vehicle when they needed to come to a stop. By this sketchy but ultimately effective method they got the brakeless machine to a mechanic's shop in Sacramento. As it turned out, though, Carnes didn't have enough money to get the old beater repaired. So he sold the car to the mechanic on the spot, contributed the modest proceeds to the Impala's gasoline fund, and

---

* Joseph, a former police officer from Modesto, California, was raised in the Greek Orthodox faith and converted to Mormonism in 1965. Excommunicated four years later when he began taking plural wives, he founded a sect called the Church of Jesus Christ in Solemn Assembly. (All told, Joseph married at least twenty-one women.) His self-deprecating wit, idiosyncratic theological views, and insatiable appetite for publicity made him a darling of the international news media. In 1983, shortly before the Laffertys visited him, Joseph successfully ran for mayor of Big Water on a Libertarian platform, promising that he would turn the town into a tax-free sanctuary; thereafter he boasted that he was the only polygamist elected to public office in the United States (he was also commander of the Lake Powell Coast Guard Auxiliary). Late in life he came to believe that Jesus had been a visionary seaman and was crucified by the Romans after He discovered the secret of transoceanic navigation. A prodigious smoker, Joseph died in 1998 of colon cancer at the age of sixty-two.

climbed into the green station wagon with Ron, Knapp, and Grant's kids, all bound for southern Utah to hook up with Dan and his latest wife.

Dan and Laurene Grant got to Big Water first. By this point, after approximately a week of marriage, the newlyweds were no longer getting along so well, prompting Grant to ask Dan for a "writ of divorcement." Dan complied, and then, even before Ron showed up, he stuck out his thumb and hitchhiked back to Utah County, leaving Grant at Alex Joseph's place to await the arrival of Ron and her two oldest children.

Ron and his four passengers rolled up in the Impala just after Dan left. They stayed in Big Water only overnight, but while they were there Ron shared his removal revelation with Alex Joseph. According to Chip Carnes, who was eavesdropping, "They were discussing Ron coming back to Utah and collecting up his guns and going on a shooting spree." Joseph, Carnes recalled, tried to talk Ron out of it.

Dan, meanwhile, had gone to see his second wife, Ann Randak, in Spanish Fork Canyon. After spending a day and a night with her, on July 23 Dan kissed her good-bye and went to Orem to visit his original wife, Matilda, and their children; it was the first birthday of his youngest child, a son. Dan had scarcely seen the boy in the months since he was born—and although he didn't realize it at the time, he would never see him again after this encounter.

Dan's visit with Matilda and his kids was brief: that afternoon he bid them farewell and went to his mother's home in Provo to meet Ron, who had driven there after leaving Big Water. Ron, Dan, Knapp, and Carnes spent the rest of the day at Claudine Lafferty's house doing laundry and tuning up the Impala's engine. They also discussed their plans for the following day.

The next day, July 24, was Pioneer Day.* Earlier, Dan, Knapp, and Carnes had talked about driving up the freeway to Salt Lake City to watch the parade and participate in the celebrations. But at some point on Monday, July 23, according to Dan, "God spoke to Ron and told him

---

* Commemorating the Mormons' arrival in the Salt Lake Valley on July 24, 1847, after their exodus from Nauvoo, Pioneer Day is perhaps the Saints' most important holiday, marked throughout Utah by parades, public speeches, and fireworks that make the festivities of the Fourth of July pale by comparison.

we needed to go somewhere else instead. He told Ron that the next day was 'The Day.' "

On Monday evening, the four men sat at Claudine Lafferty's dining room table while Ron and Dan conferred about the removal revelation. As the brothers talked, Claudine sat on a nearby sofa, knitting. Although she listened intently to their conversation, she said nothing. According to Carnes's testimony in court,

> Ron was discussing things from the Bible. He was talking about a revelation that he had received. In that revelation he . . . claimed that he was told that he had to eliminate some people. I heard the name Brenda mentioned once, and I heard something about a baby mentioned once.

As they hashed out the finer points of the revelation, Dan wondered whether it was really necessary to cut the throats of the four individuals slated for removal, as Ron had been instructed in one of his revelations. "He asked Ron how come he couldn't just go in and shoot them," Carnes said. "Ron replied that it was the Lord's command that they—that their throats be slashed."

Betty Wright McEntire heard all of this for the first time when, twelve years later, she listened to Carnes testify from the witness stand of the Fourth District Court in Provo. And when she learned that Claudine Lafferty had been sitting right there, quietly listening as her two oldest sons discussed the imminent murder of her daughter-in-law and baby granddaughter, Betty was stunned. "How could someone hear what they were planning and not do anything to warn Brenda?" she asks. "I just can't understand it."

July 19 had been Brenda Lafferty's twenty-fourth birthday. Betty had volunteered to drive down to American Fork and take care of baby Erica so that Brenda and Allen could go out for a night on the town. Betty was really looking forward to seeing both Brenda and Erica. The baby, now almost fifteen months old, had just started to say her first intelligible words.

Allen and Brenda "went up to Salt Lake for dinner," Betty says. "I was so excited for her to come home, because I was about to get married and I wanted to show her pictures of the wedding dress I had picked out, and to talk about wedding stuff. But when they got home from dinner it was obvious she and Allen had had a fight. I could tell she had been crying. I was really disappointed, but I knew that I should leave. I had given her a music box for her birthday. I remember she wound it up and put it on the TV stand, and we listened to it for a minute, then I kissed the baby good-bye and left. That was the last time I ever saw my sister."

On the morning of the July 24, Pioneer Day, Dan got up, prayed, and felt prompted by the Lord to saw the barrel and stock off a 12-gauge, pump-action shotgun that he had been storing at his mother's house. While he used a hacksaw to cut down the weapon in Claudine's garage, Ron, Ricky Knapp, and Chip Carnes loaded their belongings into the Impala. Among the items they placed in the car were a .30-30 Winchester and a .270 deer rifle. As they were lashing some items onto the vehicle's roof, a troubled Carnes told Ron, "I don't see any reason for anybody to kill any baby."

Ron replied that Erica was a "child of perdition" and therefore needed to be removed. In any case, Ron added, not only had God specifically named the baby in His commandment, but after Brenda was killed, the baby wouldn't have a mother, so it would in fact be a blessing if Erica were removed along with her mom.

When the station wagon was loaded, the four men climbed in, with Dan at the wheel, and drove over to Mark Lafferty's farm to pick up another weapon, a 20-gauge shotgun, which Dan had loaned to Mark a few years earlier. Mark handed the gun to Ron, and as he did so he asked, skeptically, "What are you going to do with that?"

"I'm going hunting," Ron said.

Knowing that no game was in season, Mark countered, "What are you going to hunt?"

"Any fucking thing," Ron answered, "that gets in my way."

Ron, Dan, Knapp, and Carnes then drove off in the Impala to shoot the guns at a nearby gravel quarry; Ron wanted to "sight them in," which involved shooting at cans and then adjusting each weapon's sights to ensure its accuracy at a given distance. When they got to the quarry and started firing, however, they discovered that they'd brought the wrong ammunition for the deer rifle: it had a .270-caliber bore, but the only shells they had were .243 caliber, too small to be fired in that particular weapon. They decided to go back to Mark's house and see if he knew where Ron's .243-caliber rifle was.

When they got to Mark's, Carnes recalls, "Ron hollered out the window and asked if he had the .243. Mark replied and said, 'No, I think it's at Allen's house.' "

Around 1:30 in the afternoon, Dan eased the Impala into Allen's driveway in front of the brick duplex he and Brenda rented on a quiet street in American Fork, twenty minutes up the freeway from Provo. Ron stepped out of the car and went to the door alone. The foot-long section of gun barrel that Dan had sawed off the shotgun earlier in the day, which Ron now intended to use as a club, was hidden up his right sleeve. A ten-inch boning knife, as sharp as a scalpel, was tucked into his left boot.

Ron opened the screen door and "knocked loudly, for a long time," says Dan. "I knew he was anticipating taking the lives of Erica and Brenda right then and there. So I was out there in the car, praying: 'I hope this is what you intended, God, because if it ain't, you better do something right now!' And then nothing happened. No one answered the door. After a few minutes Ron turned around and came back to the car, quite puzzled, and kind of shrugged his shoulders. I had a real happy feeling then, because I thought the whole thing had just been a test of faith—like when God tested Abraham—and Ron had just passed the test. I thought, 'Oh thank you, God!' And then I started the car and drove away.

"Ron was sitting in the passenger's seat looking kind of befuddled. He was the one who kind of always told the rest of us where we were going, what to do next. I had driven about a block and a half away from the house when I was suddenly overcome by a weird feeling. It was like this thing I once saw on the TV news: a guy was about to get on an airplane, but when he got to the door he turned around and walked away. And then the plane crashed. They interviewed the guy and asked him why he hadn't gotten on the plane. 'I can't explain it,' he told them. 'I just felt like I shouldn't.' Well, that's what it was like for me as I drove away from Allen's. I had this strong feeling that I should turn the car around, so I did, and I knew I was going back to the apartment—although I didn't know why, because nobody was home. The other guys in the car all asked me, 'What are you doing?' I said, 'I'm going back to Allen's, but I don't understand why.'

"A number of things went through my mind. By this point in time I'd had enough spiritual experiences, things that I considered miraculous, that I believed I was going back for a purpose. I thought, Well, maybe Ron wasn't supposed to do it. Maybe I'm going back because I'll be the one who is supposed to take care of this business for the Lord. I wasn't sure, but I just had a real comfortable feeling about what I was doing. At this point it was like someone had taken me by the hand, and was just leading me comfortably along.

"Ron asked me if I was sure about what I was doing. He said he didn't want me to do anything that he was unwilling to do himself. But I explained that I felt good about it. It felt right."

Dan pulled into Allen's driveway again, walked up to the door, and knocked. This time, after only two or three knocks, Brenda opened it. Dan asked if Allen was home. She replied that he was at work. Dan asked if she knew whether the .243 deer rifle was in the apartment somewhere. Brenda said she was sure it wasn't there. Then Dan asked if he could use the phone. Losing her patience, she said, "No. You cannot come in and use the phone." Dan protested that he only wanted to make a very brief call, but Brenda was apparently becoming increasingly suspicious and continued to refuse him entry.

At this point, Dan recalls, "I was kind of silently talking to God, and I asked, 'What do I do now?' It felt comfortable to push past her and enter the house, so that's what I did."

According to Chip Carnes, as soon as Dan forced his way into the apartment, the door slammed behind him, and "I heard what sounded like somebody hitting the floor. . . . And then I heard a vase break."

When Dan pushed his way inside, he says, "I think it kind of un-nerved Brenda. She made a very interesting comment, rather prophetic. She said, 'I knew you were going to do something that nobody could stop.' Then she started apologizing for a whole bunch of stuff—for in-fluencing Ron's wife, stuff like that. Then I thought to myself, 'You are a bitch.' And I felt impressed to wrestle her to the ground. I crossed her arms, threw her onto her stomach, and sat on top of her, holding her wrists from behind."

Outside the apartment, Carnes, Knapp, and Ron were still waiting in the Impala. Carnes turned to Knapp and said, "It's getting kind of noisy in there."

"You're right," Knapp replied, then said to Ron, "Maybe you ought to go help." At which point Ron got out of the car and went to the door.

When he tried to enter, though, Dan had Brenda pinned on the floor against the door, so Ron "had to push his way in," according to Carnes. "But as soon as Ron got inside the house, I heard Brenda saying, 'I knew it was going to come to this.' And then I heard Ron calling her a bitch and a liar, and I heard what sounded like a pretty good fight, things breaking. And I heard Brenda screaming, 'Don't hurt my baby! Please don't hurt my baby!' And Ron was still going on calling her a bitch and a liar. And she was saying she wouldn't lie anymore. And he just kept on beating her. You could hear a beating going on.

"And then I heard a baby crying, 'Mommy! Mommy! Mommy!' And then after that everything just kind of got quiet."

When Ron forced his way inside, says Dan, "He shut the door be-hind him and he asked, 'What are you doing?' I said, 'Well, I feel like I'm fulfilling the revelation now.' I was trying to whisper, because I didn't want Brenda to hear things that would make her uncomfortable. Then Ron said, 'How are you going to do it?' So I asked him to give me a minute to pray about it. And I kind of said to myself, 'What am I sup-posed to do, Lord?' Then I felt impressed that I was supposed to use a knife. That I was supposed to cut their throats. Ron asked, 'What knife are you going to use?' I had a knife on my belt, and Ron had a butcher knife in his boot. I told him, 'That butcher knife you purchased.' At which time he took the knife out of his boot and set it on the floor where I could reach it. Then he tried to knock Brenda unconscious with his fist.

"He hit her in the face, over and over again, until blood started to splatter on the wall, but he hurt his hand so he had to quit hitting her. By that point enough blood had splattered that I lost my grip on Brenda and she stood up. Ron moved around to block her from leaving. Her face looked pretty bad where he had been hitting her. She was pretty freaked out. She said to me, 'Hold me, please. Just hold me.' I could tell she was just doing it in an attempt to get sympathy. Ron told her, 'Yeah, well, I wish I had someone to hold me, too, you fucking bitch. But because of you, I don't have a wife anymore.'

"That shut her up for a minute. So then she said, 'I'll do anything you want.' And Ron said, 'Okay, sit in the corner.' She leaned against the wall and started to slide down into the corner when Ron turned to me and said, 'Let's get out of here.' I could tell he was very frightened. I told him, 'You leave if you need to. I'll take care of what I feel I'm being led to do, then I'll be ready to go.' At that point Brenda must have realized what I was talking about, because she bolted past Ron and tried to leave. He didn't do anything to try and stop her. I had to jump around him and grab her from behind. She'd made it as far as the kitchen by that point, and was trying to reach the sliding glass doors out back. She'd gotten hold of the drapes, at which point I grabbed her by the hair and pulled her back, popping a number of the clips off the top of the drape. When I finally got my hands on her she fainted, and I just laid her down on the linoleum floor.

"Unlike my older brother," Dan says, "I didn't really have bad feelings toward Brenda or Erica. I was just doing God's will. Seeing Brenda lying there in the middle of the kitchen floor, I prayed about what to do next. I told Ron, 'Get me something to tie around her neck so she won't regain consciousness.' Because I was feeling now like I was supposed to take the child's life first. Ron went and cut the cord off the vacuum cleaner and brought it to me. And then another fascinating thing took place: as he attempted to put the cord around her neck, some unseen force pushed him away from her. He turned and looked at me and says, 'Did you see that?!'

"I said, 'Yes, I did. Apparently this is not for you to do. Give me the cord.' I wrapped it around her neck twice and tied it very tightly in a double overhand knot."

After Brenda had made her final desperate attempt to flee and then passed out on the kitchen floor, Ricky Knapp and Chip Carnes, still outside in the car, heard nothing more from inside the duplex. The silence scared Carnes, who told Knapp to get in the driver's seat and then commanded, "Let's get out of here."

Knapp started the car and backed out of the driveway, but then lost his nerve. "I can't leave them," he told Carnes. He parked the Impala on the street in front of the apartment and waited, while Carnes slouched out of sight in the backseat.

After tying the vacuum cord around Brenda's neck, Dan says, "I went into the front room and picked up the knife, then I walked down the hall, being led by the spirit, because I didn't know the layout of the house, or which room was the baby's. The first door I opened was where the baby was. She was standing there in the corner of her crib. I walked in. I closed the door behind me for privacy. I think the baby thought I was her father, because I had a beard, and Allen had a beard at that time. And we have identical voices.

"I spoke to her for a minute. I told her, 'I'm not sure what this is all about, but apparently it's God's will that you leave this world; perhaps we can talk about it later.' And then I set my hand on her head, put the knife under her chin like this, and I just . . ." Pausing in his monologue, Lafferty uses his manacled hands to matter-of-factly demonstrate how he pulled the razor-sharp butcher's knife so forcefully across Erica's neck that he very nearly decapitated her; afterward, all that held the baby's head to her tiny body were a few thin shreds of skin and tendon.

"I closed my eyes," he continues, "so I didn't see what I was doing. I didn't hear anything." Lafferty shares the details of Erica's murder in a preternaturally serene voice, as if he were recounting a trip to a hardware store. "Then I walked down the hall into the bathroom and washed the blood off the knife. I didn't feel anything. At the time, I didn't even know if I had really killed Erica. Not until later, when they showed me the pictures of the crime scene. . . . I'm pretty sure she didn't suffer.

Maybe I believe that just to make myself feel better—I don't know. But hopefully the knife was so sharp she didn't feel any pain.

"Anyway, I washed the knife off. And when the knife was clean I walked into the kitchen and stood over Brenda. Straddling her, I untied the cord and took it off her neck. I grabbed her by the hair, placed the knife against the side of her neck, and drew it across her throat. Again I closed my eyes, so I didn't actually see anything. But this time I could hear the blade cut through the trachea, and feel it hit the bone of her spinal column. Then I walked back into the bathroom and washed off the knife a second time, turned to Ron, and said, 'Okay, we can leave now.' "

Ron and Dan walked out the back door and returned to the car. When Knapp and Carnes saw the brothers' blood-soaked clothing, Dan says, "they kind of freaked out." Carnes, especially, started to come apart.

Frightened by the overpowering smell of blood in the car, Carnes grabbed Dan's shirt and demanded, hysterically, "You need to get rid of that smelly thing!"

"When he said that," Dan remembers, "I thought to myself, Hey, it's not even over yet. Why should I change my clothes now? We still have two other residences to visit." But Dan obliged Carnes, all the same. As the Impala pulled away from the apartment, Dan removed his bloody shirt, borrowed a clean shirt from Carnes, and put it on.

Ron, too, was extremely agitated, but Dan remained calm and un-ruffled: "I was completely comfortable that things had happened the way God intended them to happen. Ron was very shaken and very weak. He kept talking about the smell of blood on his hands. I put my hand on his shoulder and tried to comfort him."

As they drove, Ron seemed to regain some of his composure. Guiding the Impala through the thick July heat, taking care not to exceed the speed limit, he knew exactly where he was going: Highland, the next town to the north, where he and Dianna and their children used to live—and where Chloe Low still lived.

Four months earlier God had instructed Ron,

It is My will and commandment that ye remove the following indi-viduals in order that My work might go forward. . . . First thy

brother's wife Brenda and her baby, then Chloe Low, then Richard
Stowe. And it is My will that they be removed in rapid succession.

With the murders of Brenda and Erica, the first half of the revelation had
been fulfilled. As they drove the short distance to Low's home, Ron and
Dan talked about how they would carry out the rest of it. Following the
commandment as closely as possible, they intended to first remove Low,
then Stowe, executing them "in rapid succession" before the day was
out. Although the brothers agreed that killing Low should "be easy, because she was a small woman," Ron confessed to Dan, "I'm afraid I don't
have the energy if we have to take the life of Chloe Low."

    "You're worrying about things you shouldn't worry about," Dan as-
sured him. "I'll take care of that, just like I've taken care of this. Because
it's the Lord's business."

PART III

The best fruits of religious experience are the best things that history has to show. . . . The highest flights of charity, devotion, trust, patience, bravery to which the wings of human nature have spread themselves have been flown for religious ideals.

WILLIAM JAMES, THE VARIETIES OF RELIGIOUS EXPERIENCE

One is often told that it is a very wrong thing to attack religion, because religion makes men virtuous. So I am told; I have not noticed it. . . .

You find as you look around the world that every single bit of progress in humane feeling, every improvement in the criminal law, every step toward the diminution of war, every step toward better treatment of the colored races, or every mitigation of slavery, every moral progress that there has been in the world, has been consistently opposed by the organized churches of the world. . . .

My own view on religion is that of Lucretius. I regard it as a disease born of fear and as a source of untold misery to the human race. I cannot, however, deny that it has made some contributions to civilization. It helped in early days to fix the calendar, and it caused Egyptian priests to chronicle eclipses with such care that in time they became able to predict them. These two services I am prepared to acknowledge, but I do not know of any others.

BERTRAND RUSSELL, WHY I AM NOT A CHRISTIAN, AND
OTHER ESSAYS ON RELIGION AND RELATED SUBJECTS

SEVENTEEN

EXODUS

They went in bitterness and in hope. The persecutions, the massacres, the martyrdom of the prophet, the bloody flux and the black canker and desolate graves, had cemented them into a unit, and every successive wagon train for many years was like new flight out of Egypt. The Old Testament parallel was like a bugle in the brain; some of them probably even hoped for a pursuing Pharaoh and a dividing of waters. They had found their strength: Mormonism in exodus was a herd, like a herd of buffalo, and its strength was the herd strength and the cunning of the tough old bulls who ran the show. Brigham Young was no seer and revelator, but a practical leader, an organizer and colonizer of very great stature.

WALLACE STEGNER,
MORMON COUNTRY

As dawn began to brighten the eastern sky, Porter Rockwell—the Destroying Angel, Joseph Smith's staunch bodyguard and enforcer—hurtled toward Nauvoo at full gallop, seething with rage. It was June 28, 1844. Twelve hours earlier the Mormon prophet had been shot dead in the Carthage jail by a band of Illinois militiamen, despite Governor Thomas Ford's personal promise that Joseph would be protected from harm. When Rockwell reached Nauvoo, he shouted the grim news as he rode through the streets of the waking city: "Joseph is killed—they have killed him! Goddamn them! They have killed him!"

The Saints reacted to Joseph's death with woe and staggering grief, vowing through their tears to exact revenge. First, however, they had to address a more pressing concern: the survival of Mormonism. The ten thousand mourners filing through Joseph's mansion to pay their respects and view his corpse despaired over who among the living would be able to lead the church through the months of critical peril that loomed. As distinguished historian D. Michael Quinn noted in his book *The Mormon Hierarchy: Origins of Power,* "Institutionally, Mormonism faced a dilemma of paramount consequence at Smith's death in June 1844: Can the church survive without the founding prophet? Like the removal of a keystone from an arch, would the entire structure collapse?"

Joseph had neglected to provide his followers with a clear mechanism for determining his successor. Indeed, over the years he had hinted at various conflicting criteria for the transfer of power. The result, owing to his untimely demise, was a leadership vacuum that several would-be prophets scrambled to fill. Among the leading claimants were:

- Joseph's eldest son, Joseph Smith III, who was only eleven years old when his father was killed and whom the prophet probably intended to be his successor when the boy became an adult.
- Joseph's younger brother Samuel H. Smith.
- Sidney Rigdon, the influential theologian whom Joseph had picked as his vice-presidential running mate in his 1844 campaign for the United States presidency—despite the fact that Rigdon, who suffered from "nervous spasms and swoonings," was emotionally erratic and unreliable.
- Brigham Young, the stalwart, ambitious president of the church's Quorum of the Twelve Apostles.

The contenders fell into two camps: those bitterly opposed to polygamy, who saw Joseph's death as an opportunity to eradicate the practice before it gained traction, and those who had already taken plural wives and regarded polygamy as a divinely ordained principle that must be sustained. Joseph had first come forward with his covert revelation sanctioning celestial marriage scarcely a year before his martyrdom—and even after he'd documented the revelation in writing, only a select group of his most trusted cronies had been let in on the secret. During the bleak, chaotic days that followed Joseph's murder, 95 percent of Mormons still had no clue that their prophet had married more than one wife and had declared plural marriage to be one of the most crucial keys to gaining entry to the Kingdom of Heaven.

Emma Smith, Samuel Smith, Sidney Rigdon, William Law, and others who despised polygamy—committed Mormons who were convinced that it would be the ruin of their church—desperately wanted to install a successor to Joseph who would revoke the doctrine before it took hold. On July 13 Emma warned that if the next leader of the Mormons "is not a man she approves of she will do the church all the injury she can."

Apostles John Taylor, Willard Richards, Brigham Young, and their brethren in the pro-polygamy camp wanted just as desperately to install a prophet who would uphold the doctrine, lest the plural wives these men had covertly married be branded as whores.

The succession crisis was further complicated by the fact that ten members of the Quorum of the Twelve Apostles, including Brigham Young, were roaming far afield during the spring of 1844, having been dispatched across the nation by Joseph to drum up support for his bid to become president of the United States. Young, who was in Massachusetts when Joseph was shot, didn't learn about the prophet's death until nineteen days after the fact. Crushed by the news, Brigham initially despaired that without Joseph, the Mormon Church would surely disintegrate. "My head felt so distressed," he lamented, "[I] thought it would crack." As soon as they heard of the assassination, Brigham and the rest of the apostles rushed back to Nauvoo with the utmost haste.

The anti-polygamy camp maneuvered furiously to have one of their own confirmed as prophet before the full Quorum of the Twelve Apostles had a chance to return to Nauvoo from various distant corners of the republic. Young Joseph Smith III had the most legitimate claim to the throne, but because he had not yet even reached puberty, the anti-polygamists focused their energies on giving the job to the departed prophet's younger brother, Samuel H. Smith, instead. On July 30, however, just as it was looking as if he had the job locked up, Samuel abruptly died. Compelling circumstantial evidence suggests that he succumbed from poison administered by Hosea Stout, the chief of the Nauvoo police, who was loyal to Brigham Young and the other polygamists.

Following Samuel Smith's suspect death, Sidney Rigdon—another anti-polygamist—launched a frantic last-ditch effort to grab Joseph's mantle before Brigham and the other apostles arrived back in Nauvoo. Hurriedly securing the support of others in the anti-polygamy faction, he successfully maneuvered to have himself appointed "guardian" of the church, although the appointment wouldn't be official until it could be confirmed by a vote at a special churchwide gathering scheduled for August 8. It appeared to be a fait accompli—until Brigham Young and the rest of the apostles suddenly showed up on the night of August 6, just in time to put the brakes on the anti-polygamists' scheme to install Rigdon as Joseph's replacement.

On the morning of August 8, 1844, the faithful of Nauvoo assembled to hear Rigdon and Young each explain why he should be the new Mormon leader. Rigdon argued his case for ninety minutes, with passion, but failed to persuade his fellow Saints that he was God's clear choice for the job. Then it was Brigham's turn to address the crowd, and an astonishing thing was said to have occurred, leaving no doubt about who would be the next prophet.

"Brigham Young arose and roared like a young lion," recalled John D. Lee, "imitating the style and voice of Joseph, the Prophet. Many of the brethren declared that they saw the mantle of Joseph fall upon him. I myself, at the time, imagined that I saw and heard a strong resemblance to the Prophet in him, and felt that he was the man to lead us." Numerous Saints who witnessed Brigham's address (and even greater numbers who didn't) swore that he underwent an incredible transfiguration as he spoke, temporarily assuming the voice, the appearance, and even the physical stature of Joseph, who was a considerably taller man. After such a performance, Brigham had no trouble convincing most of those present that he should be their next leader, and thus did he become the Mormons' second president, prophet, seer, and revelator.

It is interesting to speculate about what would have happened had

Brigham's return to Nauvoo been delayed thirty-six hours, which might have allowed Rigdon to commandeer the helm of the church. One can safely assume that Mormon culture (to say nothing of the culture of the American West) would be vastly different today. In all likelihood the Mormons would never have settled the Great Basin, and LDS polygamy would have died in the cradle. As Rigdon's own son John observed, the Latter-day Saints "made no mistake in placing Brigham Young at the head of the church. . . . If Sidney Rigdon had been chosen to take that position the church would have tottered and fallen."

Like Joseph Smith, Brigham Young had been born poor in rural New England, where the brouhaha of the Second Great Awakening made a lasting imprint on his consciousness. He was baptized into the Mormon Church in 1832, at the age of thirty-one, and quickly became one of Joseph's most loyal lieutenants.

Brigham's devotion to the founding prophet was deep and unswerving. He believed wholeheartedly in even Joseph's most extreme theological tenets—he may well have believed in them with greater conviction than Joseph himself did. Brigham was, however, Joseph's opposite in almost every imaginable way.

Joseph was tall, athletic, and handsome; Brigham was short and thick (at his heaviest, he weighed more than 250 pounds), with small, porcine eyes. Joseph was emotional, charismatic, an impulsive dreamer and incorrigible charmer; Brigham was steady, dependable, and pragmatic to a fault, a brilliant organizer who thought things through and paid attention to the details. Joseph craved the adoration of his followers; Brigham didn't ask the Saints to love him—he demanded only their respect and unconditional obedience. Joseph conversed constantly with God, and in his lifetime received 135 revelations that were canonized in *The Doctrine and Covenants,* as well as many dozens more that were never published; Brigham had only a single canonized revelation, *D&C* 136, which, characteristically, had nothing to do with sacred mysteries: it simply specified how the Mormons should organize their wagon trains for their migration to Utah.

To be sure, nobody ever called Brigham a religious genius, but when the Mormons faced imminent extermination in the wake of Joseph's martyrdom, religious genius wasn't what they needed. Instead, they required discipline and firm, decisive leadership, which is what Brigham ably provided. George Bernard Shaw praised him as "the American Moses." He was the right man at the right time.

In May 1845, nine men were indicted for the murders of Joseph and Hyrum Smith, seven of whom were brought to trial in Carthage. Among the defendants in *People v. Levi Williams,* as the case was designated, were some of western Illinois's leading personages, including a colonel, a major, and two captains in the Carthage Greys; an Illinois state senator; and the editor of the Warsaw newspaper. Given the virulent anti-Mormon feelings throughout Hancock County, bringing the guilty to justice wasn't going to be easy. Adding to the likelihood that no convictions would be forthcoming, both John Taylor and Willard Richards—the Mormon apostles who'd witnessed the murders—announced that they refused to appear in court, fearing (with good reason) that if they came anywhere near Carthage, they would immediately be killed.

The trial was held, regardless. On May 30, to nobody's astonishment, all nine defendants were found not guilty. Although the Mormons expected this verdict, they were nevertheless infuriated by it. An editorial in the Nauvoo paper declared, "The murderers can rest assured that their case, independent of earthly tribunals, will be tried by the Supreme Judge of the universe, who has said vengeance is mine and I will repay."

A month later, on the first anniversary of Joseph Smith's death, Brigham spoke bitterly of the trial verdict and proclaimed that "it belongs to God and his people to avenge the blood [of His] servants." Toward this end, he instructed church authorities to issue a formal "Oath of Vengeance," which was immediately made part of the temple endowment ceremony, one of the church's most sacred rituals.

The oath required Mormons to pledge, "I will pray, and never cease to pray, and never cease to importune high heaven to avenge the blood of the Prophets on this nation, and I will teach this to my children, and my children's children unto the third and fourth generations." This solemn vow to take vengeance was recited by every Latter-day Saint who participated in the standard temple ritual until it was removed from the endowment ceremony in 1927, after the oath was leaked to the non-Mormon press, sparking an outcry from politicians and the Gentile public that it was treasonous.

In the months following Joseph's murder, most residents of Nauvoo didn't need any prodding to seek revenge against Gentiles. Ever since the assassination, non-Mormons had stepped up their violent campaign to drive the Saints from Hancock County. Emboldened by the acquittal of Joseph's killers, throughout the summer of 1845 anti-Mormon vigilantes led by Levi Williams (the primary defendant in the murder trial) roamed the county setting fire to Mormon homes and farms. By September 15, 1845, forty-four Mormon residences had been burned to the ground.

On September 16, Porter Rockwell was on his way to help a Mormon family salvage possessions from the ruins of one such incinerated home when he chanced upon Lieutenant Frank Worrell of the Carthage Greys—the same man who had been in charge of guarding the jail on the evening Joseph was murdered. Worrell had commanded the militiamen who'd conspired to fire blank cartridges at the approaching mob and had then stepped aside so the vigilantes could assassinate the prophet without impediment. When Rockwell encountered Worrell on that September afternoon, the latter was on horseback, chasing a local sheriff who'd had the temerity to express sympathy for the Mormons. As Worrell galloped after the terrified sheriff, Rockwell fired a rifle ball into Worrell's gut. The victim "jumped four feet in the air," said a witness to the shooting, "and rolled away from his horse dead."

The killing of Worrell significantly worsened relations between the Saints and their adversaries. A few days later, a band of Mormons captured a youthful Gentile man named McBracking, whom they suspected of burning Mormon homes. McBracking begged for his life, but the Saints weren't in a forgiving mood. They castrated him, cut his throat, sliced off one of his ears, and shot him two or three times. As Joseph had preached three years earlier, some sins were so heinous that the only way the guilty party could atone for them was to "spill his blood upon the ground, and let the smoke thereof ascend up to God."

By now passions were at flash point on both sides of the conflict. Posses of enraged Mormons and Gentiles ranged back and forth across the county in a rampage of arson and plunder, burning more than two hundred homes. Worried that Hancock County was again on the brink of full-blown civil war, Governor Thomas Ford dispatched four hundred troops to Nauvoo, along with a committee of respected dignitaries (including renowned statesman Stephen A. Douglas) who were implored to negotiate a lasting solution to the hostilities.

It had become clear to Brigham that there was no future for the Saints anywhere near Hancock County. On September 24 he sent a letter to Governor Ford's blue-ribbon committee saying that in return for a cease-fire from the Gentiles, the Mormons would promise to vacate not only Illinois but the whole of the United States: they would depart the following spring, as soon as the prairie grass along their intended route west was high enough to provide forage for their beasts of burden. The Gentiles agreed to the deal on the first of October, giving the Saints a window of relative peace in which to build wagons and stockpile supplies in preparation for their mass evacuation.

For the Saints' next homeland, Brigham Young wanted to find a place that was both a long way from civilization and would seem repugnant to Gentile settlers, so that his people might live free from persecution. After considering Oregon, California, and Canada's Vancouver Island, he and his counselors decided the Saints would make their final stand amid the sparsely inhabited deserts of the Great Basin, which at the time belonged to Mexico.

The Saints didn't intend to abandon the City of Joseph until the weather warmed, but when news arrived that a warrant had been issued for Brigham's arrest on charges of harboring counterfeiters, an earlier departure suddenly seemed like a good idea.* On February 4, 1846, the first

---

* Nauvoo had long been a notorious haven for printers of bogus money, thanks to a highly unusual provision in the city charter granting the town leaders extraordinary powers of habeas corpus. This much-abused clause permitted Brigham, and Joseph before him, to provide legal immunity to individuals charged with crimes beyond the city limits. And like the residents of present-day Colorado City who see nothing wrong with "bleeding the beast" by committing welfare fraud, neither Brigham nor Joseph believed that the counterfeiters in

platoon of Mormon emigrants boarded flatboats at the Nauvoo dock, rowed west across the dark, near-freezing waters of the Mississippi River, and clambered uncertainly onto the Iowa shore, which was still in the iron grip of winter. The great exodus was launched.

Disillusioned by Joseph's murder, as well as by disturbing rumors of clandestine debaucheries practiced by their leaders, hundreds of Mormons had split away from the church in the preceding months.* But the overwhelming majority loaded up whatever possessions would fit into their wagons, abandoned the rest to their enemies, and followed Brigham into the wilderness. By May of that year more than six thou-

---

their midst were criminals in the eyes of the Lord; they were, to the contrary, helping advance the Kingdom of God every time they bilked a Gentile with their fraudulent greenbacks, and thus deserved to be protected from arrest.

* After Sidney Rigdon's ambition to replace Joseph Smith was quashed by Brigham Young's ascendancy, Rigdon and a few hundred followers established a church of their own in Pittsburgh, Pennsylvania, but it quickly dwindled to nothing. Apostle Lyman Wright broke away with numerous unhappy Mormons to form another short-lived church in Texas. And a charismatic charlatan and onetime Baptist named James Jesse Strang drew seven hundred disenchanted Saints away from Brigham's church—including Joseph's mother, his lone surviving brother, two of his sisters, and Martin Harris, the man who'd mortgaged his farm to pay for publication of *The Book of Mormon*. Strang attracted this following by pronouncing that an angel had visited him at the exact moment of the prophet's murder and anointed him Joseph's successor. Fifteen months later, Strang claimed to have discovered an ancient text titled the *Book of the Law of the Lord*, inscribed on a set of brass folios he called the Plates of Laban, which he found near Voree, Wisconsin, buried on a hillside; according to Strang, this document had originally been part of the set of gold plates unearthed by Joseph in 1827 that yielded *The Book of Mormon*. Impressed by these plates, the "Strangites" joined their prophet in establishing a colony on Beaver Island, off the northwest coast of Michigan's lower peninsula, where Strang had himself crowned "King James 1 of the Kingdom of God on Earth," began taking plural wives, and ruled with absolute power. It was to be a brief reign, however: in 1856 a gang of disgruntled Beaver Island denizens ambushed King James and fatally shot him. Even before Strang's murder, moreover, several prominent Strangites who objected to the king's polygamous proclivities broke away to form the Reorganized Church of Jesus Christ of Latter-day Saints. Joseph's widow, Emma Smith, joined these "Reorganites," and her son Joseph III became the group's president and prophet. Today this church—now called the Community of Christ and headquartered in Independence, Missouri, in a striking $60 million temple designed by Gyo Obata—has 250,000 members, making it by far the largest of the Mormon spin-off sects.

sand Saints were plodding westward through the axle-deep spring mud, drawn by the promise of Zion.

The thirteen-hundred-mile emigration from Nauvoo was a grueling trial. On the journey west they were plagued with frostbite, diphtheria, scurvy, starvation, stillborn babies, tick fever, hostile Gentiles, and an epidemic of whooping cough that killed dozens of young children. More than six hundred Saints perished during that first grim winter. But Brigham proved to be a masterful manager of men, and he possessed a formidable will. On July 21, 1847, an advance party crested a ridge and caught the Saints' first glimpse of "the valley where the broad waters of the Great Salt Lake glistened in the sunbeams." The next morning this group, with scout Porter Rockwell leading the way, descended the western slope of the Wasatch down what is now called Emigration Canyon. At its mouth they emerged into the Saints' new Zion, near the southern end of the vast body of water they had spied earlier that day—a lake with no outlet, and saltier than the Pacific Ocean.

Although most of this bottomland was a relentlessly barren desert, along its eastern margin flowed streams of sweet, crystalline snowmelt that rushed down from the Wasatch Range through all seasons. These imposing granite mountains, moreover, served as a natural barrier that would help keep the godless at bay. All things considered, the Great Salt Lake Valley struck the scouting party as a fine site on which to erect a capital city for the Kingdom of God on earth. After conducting a two-hour tour of the immediate environs, they rode back up Emigration Canyon to share the joyous news with Brigham and their brethren.

Brigham, weak and aching from tick fever, arrived in the valley with the main company of Saints on July 24, 1847, the date now venerated throughout Mormondom as Pioneer Day (and the holiday Ron Lafferty would choose, 137 years later, on which to fulfill his removal revelation). Before the sun had set that first evening, they had planted a crop of potatoes and diverted the waters of City Creek to irrigate them. A stone's throw from the creek they began laying the foundation for a temple, at the center of what would become Salt Lake City. The long, seventeen-year journey from Palmyra was over. The Mormons had finally found their home.

Many had died en route. But those who survived the hardships and completed the exodus were more devoted to the church than ever. The wafflers and whiners, the doubters, the malcontents—those of weak faith—had been filtered out by the myriad trials of the preceding years, leaving behind the truest of the true believers. The grueling emigration from Nauvoo, on top of the violence directed at them in Missouri and Illinois, had forged an exceptional bond among the first waves of Saints to arrive in Utah. Adversity had welded them into a close-knit tribe whose loyalty to their leader, Brigham Young, was unconditional. They would do whatever he asked of them.

When the first wagon trains left Nauvoo in the bitter days of February 1846, only a handful of the emigrants knew anything about the doctrine of plural marriage, or that it was already being practiced by their leaders. Nine miles beyond the western banks of the Mississippi, safely beyond the reach of the murderous vigilantes who roamed the Illinois shore, the Saints paused to regroup at Sugar Creek, Iowa, before continuing their trek to the Rocky Mountains. And there, in that snowbound camp, the sacred secret of polygamy was first shared openly with the rank and file.

To the world beyond the confines of their tribe, however, Brigham Young and his counselors vigorously denied that Mormons engaged in polygamy. And they would continue to deny it for years to come, even after the Mormons were established in the Great Salt Lake Valley. Historian D. Michael Quinn refers to the Saints' bald-faced dissembling as "theocratic ethics." The Mormons called it "Lying for the Lord."*

Their decision to keep polygamy in the closet was made necessary by the rapidly expanding boundaries of the American empire. After two decades of the Saints' difficult and often vicious relations with the United States, Brigham had moved his people outside the national borders to escape the strife. But scarcely a year after they landed in Utah, the American republic followed the Saints west and took possession of their new Zion. The Mormon homeland was annexed to the United

---

* Brigham once famously bragged, "We have the greatest and smoothest liars in the world."

States following the conclusion of the war with Mexico, as part of the 1848 Treaty of Guadalupe Hidalgo.

This development greatly complicated Brigham's plan to establish a theocratic kingdom unfettered by Gentile laws. And the Saints' grand dream of dominion over a vast chunk of the Great Basin was further imperiled when gold was discovered in California, prompting swarms of Gentile prospectors to stream through Salt Lake City, which became a crucial way station on the shortest route to the gold fields. The gold rush did have an upside; as the only game in town, Brigham was able to extort exorbitant prices from the Gentiles for provisions they needed to complete the long journey to California, giving the Saints desperately needed capital.

Following the annexation of Utah Territory by the United States, Brigham—ever the pragmatist—proclaimed the Mormons' allegiance to the American republic, then promptly petitioned Washington for statehood, which he considered the best way for the Saints to secure some measure of sovereignty. After all that had happened in Nauvoo, however, officials in Washington were leery of giving Brigham autonomy. So the Mormons were granted territorial status for their homeland instead of statehood, which allowed Washington, in theory, to keep the Latter-day Saints on a much tighter leash. Utah Territory was formally established on September 9, 1850, with Brigham appointed governor.*

On February 4, 1851, the new governor finally felt secure enough about the Saints' prospects to come clean about the number of wives he had. "I have many," he boasted during an address to the territorial leg-

---

* The Saints proposed naming the new territory Deseret, a neologism from *The Book of Mormon* meaning "honeybee," which struck Brigham Young as an apt symbol of the Mormons' industry and their belief that personal freedom should yield to the welfare of the collective whole. But a skeptical Congress nixed this suggestion and named the territory Utah instead, after the Ute Indians who populated the region. Among themselves, nevertheless, the Mormons pointedly continued to call their homeland the Kingdom of Deseret, and it became the name they inscribed on all their maps. Today, the beehive remains prominent on the official state seal of Utah, as well as on road signs designating state highways. Additionally, the second-biggest newspaper in Utah, which is owned by the LDS Church, is called the *Deseret News*.

islature, "and I am not ashamed to have it known."* It was his first public admission that Mormons practiced polygamy. A year later, he decided it was time to announce the "peculiar doctrine" to an even wider audience. On August 29, 1852, at a churchwide assembly in Salt Lake City, he told of Joseph Smith's 1843 revelation concerning "celestial marriage," predicting that one day it would be "fostered and believed in by the more intelligent portions of the world, as one of the best doctrines ever proclaimed to any people."

The cat was out of the bag. To Brigham's dismay, very quickly it proved to be a public-relations disaster for the Mormon Church. In France and England, recently converted Mormons were shocked and appalled by the revelation. The once-robust flow of fresh converts from Europe to Utah slowed to a trickle. A missionary reported that 1,776 British Saints abandoned the church during the six months following the 1852 announcement.

Most of the Utah Mormons, on the other hand, were amenable to the idea of plural marriage once it was made known to them. Although polygamy was never practiced by more than a minority of Saints, it would have been hard to find many inhabitants of Deseret in the mid-1850s who didn't consider plural marriage a lofty ideal to which all righteous men and women should aspire. By 1855, polygamy was not only being practiced openly, it was being urged on the faithful with an unrelentingly hard sell that included dire warnings to the recalcitrant. "If any of you will deny the plurality of wives, and continue to do so," Brigham threatened, "I promise that you will be damned."

This adamant promotion of polygamy grew out of a white-hot burst of religious fanaticism known as the Mormon Reformation, which peaked in the years 1856 and 1857. As Will Bagley observed in his provocative, meticulously researched history *Blood of the Prophets,* "Perhaps the most troubling aspect of the Reformation was the Mormon

---

* Brigham Young took at least twenty women as wives, perhaps as many as fifty-seven. He sired an estimated fifty-seven children, and his direct descendents now number in the thousands. The most famous of them is Steve Young, Brigham's great-great-great-grandson, a star quarterback for both Brigham Young University and the San Francisco 49ers of the National Football League, and the Super Bowl MVP in 1995.

leadership's obsession with blood. . . . Joseph Smith taught that certain grievous sins put sinners 'beyond the reach of the atoning blood of Christ.' Their 'only hope [was] to have their own blood shed to atone.' . . . Of all the beliefs that laid the foundation of Utah's culture of violence, none would have more devastating consequences."

The Reformation was spearheaded by the God-besotted Jedidiah Grant, Brigham's immensely popular second counselor, whom the Saints affectionately called "Jeddy, Brigham's Sledge Hammer." Grant explained to the Lord's chosen that they had the "right to kill a sinner to save him, when he commits those crimes that can only be atoned for by shedding his blood." In September 1856 he sermonized that there were sinners even then in their midst who needed "to have their blood shed, for water will not do, their sins are of too deep a dye."

Grant preached as fervently about the Saints' duty to marry profusely as he did about blood atonement, and his aggressive campaign on behalf of plural marriage achieved the desired effect. Mormon men started taking on wives at a frantic rate. Apostle Wilford Woodruff observed in 1856, "All are trying to get wives, until there is hardly a girl fourteen years old in Utah, but what is married, or is just going to be."

The Saints readily accepted their prophet's avowal that plural marriage was a divinely ordained and crucially important doctrine. But Brigham had badly miscalculated how the rest of the republic would react to the Mormons' embrace of polygamy. After the sacred doctrine became known outside of Utah, a nearly hysterical barrage of condemnation rained down on the Saints from afar—a barrage that would continue unabated for half a century.

Most Americans considered polygamy to be morally repugnant, even as they were secretly fascinated by it. These remarks from Congressman John Alexander McLernand of Illinois, speaking before the U.S. House of Representatives, are a fair characterization of the Gentile reaction to the Mormon doctrine: "As to polygamy, I charge it to be a crying evil; sapping not only the physical constitution of the people practicing it, dwarfing their physical proportions and emasculating their energies, but at the same time perverting the social virtues, and vitiating the morals of its victims. . . . It is a scarlet whore. It is a reproach to the Christian civilization, and deserves to be blotted out."*

Brigham rebutted such criticism, at least on some occasions, with the counterintuitive argument that plural marriage was actually an antidote to immorality, because men with a multitude of wives wouldn't be tempted to engage in adulterous liaisons or visit prostitutes. Other times he maintained that polygamy actually had nothing to do with sexual gratification whatsoever: "God never introduced the Patriarchal order of marriage with a view to please man in his carnal desires," Brigham insisted. "He introduced it for the express purpose of raising up to His name a royal Priesthood, a peculiar people." The Mormon leader insisted, as well, that the marital customs of the Saints were a religious freedom protected by the First Amendment to the U.S. Constitution. The rest of the country, he thundered, had no right to require the residents of Deseret to abandon one of their most sacred religious doctrines: "If we introduce the practice of polygamy it is not their prerogative to meddle with it."

The fact that polygamy was a felony everywhere else in the Union did not impress Brigham. In his view the laws of God took precedence over the laws of men—particularly the laws of Gentile men. To this end, in Deseret the Saints installed a legal system of their own singular design, which very cleverly ensured that whenever the two bodies of law clashed, God's laws would prevail.

Because Utah remained a territory rather than a state, legal power was supposed to reside in the federal courts. The Utah Territorial Legis-

* McLernand's remarks were almost certainly influenced by a pseudoscientific study—patently preposterous yet widely accepted by both the medical profession and the general public—first published by the U.S. Senate and later republished in numerous periodicals and professional journals, in which a surgeon named Roberts Bartholow claimed that the sexual depravities of Mormonism resulted in a whole host of readily visible physical deformities. The Mormon "countenance," according to Dr. Bartholow, was "compounded of sensuality, cunning, suspicion, and a smirking self-conceit. The yellow, sunken, cadaverous visage; the greenish-colored eyes; the thick, protuberant lip; the low forehead; the light, yellowish hair; and the lank, angular person, constitute an appearance so characteristic of the new race, the production of polygamy, as to distinguish them at a glance."

lature, dominated by Mormons, got around this insufferable insult by radically expanding the powers of the local probate courts, which Brigham controlled, thereby usurping the jurisdiction of the federal government. Most probate judges were Mormon bishops, and the juries who assembled in their courtrooms were made up almost entirely of good Mormons who obediently based their verdicts on instructions received from church leaders.

Federal officials dispatched to Utah to ride herd over the Saints were aghast by what they witnessed, and complained to their superiors in Washington that Brigham had transformed the territory into a theocratic dictatorship. But the majority of these Gentile officials (many of whom were corrupt to the core and had come to Utah intending to enrich themselves on graft) faced such unrelenting harassment that all but two of them eventually fled Utah altogether, fearing that if they stayed they would receive an unannounced visit from Porter Rockwell and turn up dead—which, in fact, happened to an undocumented number of federal agents.

A rising chorus of non-Mormon voices declared Brigham to be a dangerous tyrant who wielded absolute power over his followers. One Gentile visitor warned that "on the face of the whole earth there is not another people to be found, so completely under the control of one man."

Brigham was unmoved. As far back as 1851 he had blustered that "any President of the United States who lifts his finger against this people shall die an untimely death and go to hell!" Five years later he was no less ornery, declaring that he intended to make Utah "a sovereign State in the Union, or an independent nation by ourselves, and let them drive us from this place if they can; they cannot do it."

Such rhetoric, on top of ever more numerous reports of Mormon belligerence, alarmed the rest of the nation. The more Washington tried to rein Brigham in, however, the more brazen his insubordination became. In March 1857, shortly after James Buchanan was inaugurated as president, the Utah Territorial Legislature sent a truculent missive to Washington announcing that the Saints would ignore any and all federal statutes they determined to be unjust and would expel from their midst any federal officers who didn't meet the rigorous moral standards of the Mormon Church.

It proved to be bad timing on the part of the Saints. Utah Territory was an annoying problem for the new leader of the nation, but compared to other national problems then looming it was a relatively small one, which President Buchanan thought he could handle quickly and easily. And in the Mormon insurrection he saw a means to distract Americans from much larger, much less tractable issues—the increasingly divisive rancor over slavery, for instance, which was threatening to tear the country to tatters. As a pro-slavery Democrat, Buchanan figured that by coming down hard on pro-slavery Utah,* he could gain favor with abolitionists without having to sacrifice much political capital, because the Mormons were so widely reviled. So he followed the counsel of lawyer Robert Tyler—the son of former president John Tyler and an influential operative within the Democratic Party—who urged him to "supersede the Negro-Mania with the almost universal excitements of an Anti-Mormon Crusade."

Launching a nice little war to divert national attention was a gambit no less appealing to nineteenth-century politicians than it is to their present-day counterparts. As historian Will Bagley noted, "Of all the

---

* Although Joseph Smith had been opposed to slavery on moral grounds (in 1836 he'd even ordained an African-American man, Elijah Abel, as an elder in the Mormon priesthood), Brigham Young was an unapologetic racist (as were a great many other nineteenth-century Americans) whose interpretations of scripture institutionalized racism within the LDS Church. Under his leadership, Utah became a slave territory, and the Mormon Church supported the aims of the Confederacy during the Civil War. Brigham's lasting impact on LDS doctrine made blacks feel exceedingly unwelcome in the church until more than a century after his death. Through most of the twentieth century, African-Americans were strictly banned from the priesthood, and black-white marriages were considered an outrage against God. Then, in 1978, President Spencer W. Kimball had a revelation in which the Lord commanded that the LDS priesthood be open to males of all races, initiating a slow but profound shift in Mormon attitudes about race. In February 2002, the student body of Brigham Young University, though only 0.7 percent African-American, elected a black man, Rob Foster, as their president—the first black student president in the school's history. Given the strongly held views of BYU's namesake, Foster's victory was regarded as an especially potent symbol.

complex difficulties facing the new administration, the Mormon problem offered the most tempting political opportunity and promised the most beguiling of solutions—military action, a course that might unify the nation in a popular crusade against the evils of Mormonism."

Alleging that the Mormons had committed a long list of treasonous acts, in May 1857 Buchanan dispatched a contingent of federal officials to restore the rule of law in Utah, including a new territorial governor to replace Brigham Young. More ominously, the new president ordered twenty-five hundred heavily armed soldiers to escort these officials into Salt Lake City and subdue the Saints if necessary. For all intents and purposes, the United States had declared war on the Mormons.

The Utah War, as it was known, has been compared by more than one historian to a comic opera. As Leonard Arrington and Davis Bitton wrote in *The Mormon Experience: A History of the Latter-day Saints,* "The President of the United States had dispatched the largest peacetime army in the nation's history to oversee the installation of half a dozen officials in a minor territory." It turned out to be a war that generated much more smoke than heat, and a concord was ultimately negotiated before the Saints and American soldiers exchanged a single shot.

The amicable resolution came too late, however, for members of a Gentile wagon train traveling to California through a lovely valley in Utah's remote southwest corner, high on the rim of the Great Basin. This bucolic sanctuary, named the Mountain Meadow, is now synonymous with one of the most chilling episodes in the history of the American West—an episode that exemplified the fanaticism and concomitant brutality of a culture that would be so enthusiastically idealized a century later by Dan Lafferty and his fundamentalist brethren.

EIGHTEEN

FOR WATER WILL NOT DO

*Mormons were different because they said they were different and be-
cause their claims, frequently advanced in the most obnoxious way possible, prompted others to agree and treat them as such. The notion of
Mormon difference, that is, was a deliberate invention elaborated over
time. It was both cause and result of a conflict in which all parties
discovered reasons to stress not what Mormons had in common with
other Americans, which was a great deal, but what they did not have
in common. One result of the conflict was an ideology that sought to
turn the self-advertised differences of the Mormons into a conspiracy
against the American republic.*

R. Laurence Moore,
Religious Outsiders and the Making of Americans

By the time it reached the uplands of southern Utah, 280 miles beyond
Salt Lake City, the wagon train that would be known to history as the
Fancher party included some 130 emigrants, mostly from Arkansas, as
well as a thousand head of cattle and two hundred horses.* Over the pre-

---

* Although the wagon train took its name from forty-five-year-old Alexander Fancher, who
headed one of the company's most prominent families, the "Fancher party" was actually a
loose affiliation of at least four distinct groups, including one led by Captain John T.
Baker—hence the other name by which the wagon train was commonly known: the Baker-
Fancher party.

ceding weeks, a downtrodden assortment of "backouts"—apostate Mormons eager to leave the territory after acrimoniously quitting the church—had joined the Fancher group as well, swelling the company's ranks to approximately 140.

This unusually large train, spread out along miles of the Old Spanish Trail (the southern route to California), rolled into the Mountain Meadow* over several hours on the evening of September 6, 1857, and the travelers stopped for the night beside a clear artesian spring. Their campsite was in the middle of a shallow valley, fifty-eight hundred feet above sea level, carpeted with lush green sedges and bunchgrass gone to seed. Just beyond this high oasis on the edge of the Great Basin, the trail dropped sharply down into the scorching wastes of the Mojave Desert. Given the hundreds of miles of hot, hard country that stretched ahead of them, the emigrants must have been grateful for the opportunity to rest and graze their stock in such a verdant setting.

The temperature dipped into the forties when the sun went down. At daybreak, after rousing themselves from their bedrolls, the group huddled around campfires to warm their hands and to cook. The crisp morning air smelled of sagebrush and juniper smoke. No one suspected they were about to be attacked; the Arkansans hadn't even bothered to circle their wagons the night before, as they customarily did on the trail.

"Our party was just sitting down to a breakfast of quail and cottontail rabbits when a shot rang out from a nearby gully," Sarah Frances Baker Mitchell recalled eighty-two years after the event, "and one of the children toppled over, hit by the bullet." That first gunshot was the beginning of a furious surprise assault that would fatally wound seven Arkansans before the day was out. Although Mitchell was only three years old at the time, the horrors of that morning—and the even greater horrors of the week to come—were seared into her memory.

The emigrants quickly circled their wagons into a defensive corral, dug in as best they could, and returned fire, repelling the first wave of assailants. They assumed they were being ambushed by Indians, a conjec-

---

* Although the valley seems originally to have been named the Mountain Meadow, most maps refer to it as "the Mountain Meadows," in the plural, and the slaughter that took place there is almost universally known as "the Mountain Meadows massacre."

ture that seemed to be confirmed by glimpses of dark-skinned men in war paint shooting at them. As it happened, most of the attackers on that initial morning of what would become a five-day siege were indeed Paiutes, but others were Mormons from nearby settlements who had simply painted their faces to look like Indians. And commanding the assault was a well-known Latter-day Saint: forty-four-year-old John D. Lee, a battle-tested veteran of the troubles in Missouri and Illinois, as devoted to the church and its leaders as any Mormon alive.

Although Lee was a blustery, brown-nosing martinet beloved by few of his peers, Brigham Young felt genuine affection for him and valued his unfaltering obedience. Back in Nauvoo, shortly after assuming leadership of the church, Brigham had adopted him in an esoteric Mormon ritual, making Lee his symbolic son, and in 1856 he'd appointed Lee "Farmer to the Indians," the prophet's personal ambassador to the Southern Paiute tribe.

To comprehend why Lee—an American citizen—would be leading an attack on an American wagon train, one has to look back to the beginning of that summer and consider the shock waves of panic and fury that roiled Deseret when word arrived that a hostile army was amassing to the east.

Porter Rockwell was carrying a load of mail from Utah to Missouri when he learned of the impending American military action against the Saints. Near what is now the eastern border of Wyoming, he encountered the mayor of Great Salt Lake City (as the capital of Utah was then known), his friend Abraham Smoot, who was headed west with a herd of cattle. Smoot told Rockwell that the Mormons' mail contract with the U.S. Postmaster had been abruptly canceled, and that federal troops were mustering at Fort Leavenworth, Kansas, with orders to march on the Kingdom of God.

Rockwell immediately turned around and, accompanied by Smoot and two other companions, headed back to Utah to alert Brigham. Pausing at Fort Laramie, the Destroying Angel hitched a buckboard to the two fastest horses in the Mormon corral, then drove the animals hard all the way to Great Salt Lake, making the 513-mile trip in just over five days. On July 24, Pioneer Day, Rockwell and Smoot told Brigham of the coming invasion just as the Saints were kicking off a huge celebration to mark the tenth anniversary of their arrival in Zion; Brigham announced the electrifying news to the Pioneer Day gathering just after sunset. The crowd reeled, reacting with a mix of confusion, apprehension, and rage.

Standing before twenty-five hundred of his subjects, Brigham assured them that they need not fear the army of the United States, for the Saints were sure to prevail. "We have borne enough of their oppression and hellish abuse," he bellowed, "and we will not bear any more of it. . . . In the name of Israel's God, we ask no odds of them." The commonwealth of the Latter-day Saints, he brashly declared, "henceforth constituted a new and independent state, to be known no longer as Utah, but by their own Mormon name of Deseret."

Brigham had actually been aware for more than a month that federal troops were en route to Utah, but had withheld the news until Pioneer Day for maximum dramatic effect. For the better part of a year, in fact, he'd been stockpiling arms and drilling his crack militia, the Nauvoo Legion. After the Pioneer Day announcement, he simply accelerated preparations for the defense of Deseret. And the cornerstone of this defense, says historian Will Bagley, "was to rally Utah's Indians to the Mormon cause."

The inspiration for Brigham's military strategy came directly from Mormon scripture: according to *The Book of Mormon,* the Indians of North America were descended from the Lamanites, and as such they were remnants of the same ancient tribe of Israel to which Nephi, Mormon, and Moroni had belonged. The Lamanites, of course, had rejected the teachings of Jesus, waged war on the Nephites, and eventually killed every last one of them—crimes that had resulted in God cursing the Lamanites with dark skin. Scripture nevertheless taught that the Lamanites/Indians would once again become "a white and delightsome people" when, during the Last Days before the return of Christ, the Latter-day Saints converted them to Mormonism. *The Book of Mormon* indeed prophesied that the Lamanites, once redeemed, would join forces with the Mormons to vanquish the Gentiles, and thereby usher in the Great and Dreadful Day of the Lord.

This momentous alliance between Mormon and Lamanite, Brigham was certain, was about to become a reality, paving the way for the Second Coming. He had reached this conclusion as soon as the Saints had arrived in the Great Salt Lake Valley, when he'd realized that the Mormons' new homeland was in the midst of the Lamanites. God's plan seemed to be unfolding just as it had been prophesied in *The Book of Mormon*.

It hadn't occurred to Brigham, though, that the Lamanites might balk at playing their divinely ordained role. The Indians were sometimes willing to act as mercenaries and attack "Mericats" on behalf of the "Mormonee"* in return for a share of the plunder, but they never considered the Saints to be their allies. The Indians regarded the Big Captain and the rest of the Mormonee as merely the lesser of two hideous evils—and sometimes not even that.

Despite the Indians' lack of enthusiasm for fulfilling their prophetic calling, Brigham used every means at his disposal to enlist them in his campaign against the Gentiles. And when the spoils were sufficiently enticing, the Indians obliged. Numerous Gentile emigrants passing through Utah reported that their horses and cattle were driven off by Indian raiders, only to show up later in Mormon corrals. If the Indians fell short of the Saints' millennial expectations that they would function as "the battle axe of the Lord," when the Lamanites could be induced to do the Mormons' bidding they were, nevertheless, a potent weapon.

While they awaited the arrival of the federal army, Brigham and other church leaders did their utmost to inflame passions against the Gentiles. The Saints were reminded again and again of the murders of so many of their brethren in Missouri and Illinois, and how their beloved prophet, Joseph Smith, had been shot dead by a godless mob in Hancock County. Rumors were spread that the approaching troops had orders to hang

---

* Indians made a clear distinction between Mormons (whom they called "Mormonee") and other Americans (referred to, in the phonetic rendering of the Paiutes, as "Mericats").

Brigham and exterminate the Mormons altogether. As the sweltering summer of 1857 crept toward fall, observed Juanita Brooks in her courageous, groundbreaking book *The Mountain Meadows Massacre,**

> speeches became more and more inflammatory, such speeches as have been used by patriots and zealots in many causes to stir the heart to anger and strengthen the arm for battle. From one end of the territory to the other, the people of Utah retold and relived their past sufferings, the mobbings and burnings and final expulsion from Nauvoo. They would never be driven again; they would fight first.

By August, hatred for the Gentiles had been raised to a fever pitch. Militias had been organized and drilled in each of the hundred towns and villages across Utah Territory. Men from distant Mormon outposts in Nevada and California had been summoned back to Utah to help defend the commonwealth. Saints were instructed to supply no provisions whatsoever to the Gentile wagon trains that continued to roll through Utah on their way to California; in a letter distributed across the territory, Mormon bishops were admonished not to let so much as a kernel of grain "be sold to our enemies." And if the wicked Gentile army somehow managed to march into Deseret, Brigham demanded to know of his Saints, were they prepared to torch their own towns, burn their own crops, "lay waste to and desolate everything before them?" The answer was a unanimous, unequivocal "Yes!"

This was the explosive atmosphere that greeted the Fancher company when their wagon train crested the Wasatch Range and rolled down Emigration Canyon into the Great Salt Lake Valley on August 3,

---

* *The Mountain Meadows Massacre,* published in 1950, is an extraordinary work of history, the seminal portrait of Mormondom under Brigham Young. Will Bagley's updated treatment of the same subject, *Blood of the Prophets,* published in 2002, must now be considered the definitive work, but as Bagley acknowledges, he owes an immeasurable debt to Juanita Brooks, whom he praises as "one of the West's best and bravest historians." In a very discernible sense, every book about the Mormon experience in nineteenth-century Utah published after 1950 is a response to Brooks's book—just as every post-1946 treatment of the Mormons under Joseph Smith was written in the immense shadow cast by Fawn Brodie's masterpiece, *No Man Knows My History.*

1857. Noting the intensity of the Mormon hostility, the Arkansans rested only two days in the territorial capital before continuing south and west on the Old Spanish Trail to California.

The Arkansas emigrants, it seems, were marked as victims from the moment they entered Utah. One of them later claimed that as soon as they arrived in Great Salt Lake City, it was obvious to him that the Saints were looking for "an excuse to slaughter the entire train." One reason the Fancher party may have been singled out was the Arkansans' conspicuous wealth: it was reputed to be "the richest and best equipped train that ever set out across the continent." Among the group's twelve hundred head of stock were prize Texas longhorns and a strikingly beautiful Thoroughbred racehorse that was alone worth $3,000 in the currency of the day—the equivalent of many hundreds of thousands of twenty-first-century dollars. Additionally, it was rumored that the Fancher party was carrying a strongbox filled with thousands of dollars in gold coins. In Utah, where plagues of crickets and an extended drought had left many Saints contemplating starvation, such riches could not have failed to arouse the interest of people who considered it righteous to steal from the godless.

But the wagon train from Arkansas was probably imperiled less by its affluence than by the Saints' carefully nurtured sense of persecution— a mood that was stoked relentlessly from the pulpit that entire summer. More than ever, the Mormons wanted payback for the assassinations of Joseph and Hyrum Smith. And they had just learned of another, more recent crime to avenge, as well: the slaying of Mormon Apostle Parley Pratt, who had been hunted down like an animal and savagely killed in the same part of Arkansas where the Fancher train originated, just two weeks after the Fanchers embarked for Utah.*

The seeds of Pratt's demise had been planted by an act of charity, when he'd provided succor to a troubled woman from New Orleans named Eleanor McLean. A recent convert to the faith, Eleanor was mar-

---

* Parleys Canyon, the valley Interstate 80 now follows between Salt Lake and Park City (the site of a ski resort and celebrated film festival), was named in honor of the martyred apostle, one of the most popular figures in Mormondom after Joseph Smith, and an estimable man by any measure.

ried to a nasty drunk, a Gentile named Hector McLean, who disapproved of her conversion and regularly beat her. Touched by Pratt's kindness, Eleanor fell in love with him, abandoned her husband, left her three children in the care of her mother, and then found passage to Salt Lake City working as a cook for a party of Mormon emigrants. Although Eleanor remained legally married to Hector McLean, in Deseret Brigham sealed her to Parley Pratt for time and eternity, making her the twelfth of the apostle's plural wives. In 1856, while Pratt was in St. Louis doing missionary work, she returned to New Orleans and absconded with her three children, inducing murderous rage in her first husband, who blamed Pratt for wrecking his marriage.

McLean set out in hot pursuit of Pratt and managed to intercept a letter from Pratt to Eleanor in which the apostle described his plans to meet her on the Arkansas River. Armed with this information, and working in cahoots with a federal marshal who hated Mormons, McLean had Pratt arrested and jailed in Van Buren, Arkansas. The non-Mormon magistrate assigned to hear the case quickly saw that the charges against Pratt were without merit. Concerned that the Mormon apostle would be lynched by vigilantes if he remained locked up, the brave magistrate surreptitiously released Pratt, but McLean was notified immediately by jailhouse spies.

The obsessed McLean and two accomplices tracked Pratt down twelve miles outside of Van Buren, where they stabbed him, shot him for good measure, and then left him by the side of the road to slowly bleed to death. Afterward, McLean boasted that killing Parley Pratt was "the best act of my life," and he was cheered as a hero across western Arkansas for the deed. He was never arrested or charged with any crime.

After her husband's death, Eleanor Pratt gradually made her way back toward Utah, destitute and dispirited. On the trail near Fort Laramie, she crossed paths with Porter Rockwell, who gave her a ride to Great Salt Lake City as he hurried to inform Brigham, on Pioneer Day, of the invading army. About the time the Fancher wagon train was crossing the border into Utah Territory, Eleanor delivered a detailed account of her husband's murder to the leaders of the church. Her report heaped blame on the entire state of Arkansas and implored the Saints to avenge Parley's innocent blood.

On August 3, 1857, the same day the Fancher train arrived in the Great Salt Lake Valley, Apostle George A. Smith (first cousin to Joseph Smith), who held the rank of general in the Nauvoo Legion, rode out of Great Salt Lake City in a carriage bound for southern Utah. Six years earlier, General Smith had led the settlement of this distant corner of the territory.* The Saints who had colonized the region under his direction were known to be the most fanatical in all of Mormondom. The general paused to address the brethren in every town he passed through, inflaming their fanaticism to even greater levels, urging the southern settlements to prepare for holy war.

By late August, Smith was completing the outermost arc of his swing through the south, where he visited Jacob Hamblin, the "Mormon Leatherstocking," a gifted missionary to the Lamanites who had built a summer cabin just a few miles north of the Mountain Meadow. Renowned for his rapport with the Indians, Hamblin was especially respected by the region's Paiutes, who treated him as a father figure. Smith delivered a letter to Hamblin from Brigham Young, dated August 4, in which the missionary was told that the Indians "must learn that they have either got to help us or the United States will kill us both."

Around the same time General Smith met with Hamblin, he also had a long powwow with hundreds of Paiutes on the Santa Clara River, some twenty miles from the Mountain Meadow, employing John D. Lee as his interpreter. According to Lee, Smith told the Indians "that the Americans had a large army just east of the mountains, and intended to kill all of the Mormons and Indians in Utah Territory; that the Indians must get ready and keep ready for war against all of the Americans, and . . . obey what the Mormons told them to do—that this was the will of the Great Spirit."

---

* St. George, the largest city in southern Utah, was named after George A. Smith.

Afterward, as the Mormons were riding away from the powwow, Smith told Lee, "Those are savage looking fellows. I think they would make it lively for an emigrant train if one should come this way." If such a wagon train did arrive in the area, Smith then asked Lee, did he think the Saints of the southern settlements would join the Indians in attacking it? "Would the brethren pitch into them and give them a good drubbing?"

Lee gave the question careful thought, then answered, "I really believe that any train of emigrants that may come though here will be attacked, and probably all be destroyed." This reply, Lee said, "served to cheer up the General very much; he was greatly delighted, and said, 'I am glad to hear so good an account of our people. God will bless them for all that they do to build up His Kingdom in the last days.' "

"I have always believed, since that day," Lee wrote of this conversation twenty years after the event, "that General George A. Smith was then visiting Southern Utah to prepare the people for the work of exterminating Captain Fancher's train of emigrants, and I now believe he was sent for that purpose by the direct command of Brigham Young."

Shortly after this, Smith hurried back to Great Salt Lake City with Hamblin and about a dozen Paiute leaders in order to meet with Brigham. On the night of August 25, as they were on their way north, Smith, Hamblin, and the Indians actually camped within shouting distance of the southbound Fancher wagon train, and three of the Arkansans walked over to visit with the Mormons. In reply to the emigrants' query about where they might rest and graze their massive herd of livestock before striking out across the Mojave Desert, Hamblin recommended a lovely little valley near his cabin called the Mountain Meadow.

The notorious conference between Brigham Young and the Paiute chiefs took place in Great Salt Lake City on the evening of September 1. It lasted for about an hour, with Brigham's son-in-law Dimick B. Huntington acting as interpreter. According to Huntington's notes of the encounter, Brigham explicitly "gave" the Indians all the emigrant cattle on the Old Spanish Trail—that is, the Fancher's prize herd, which the Paiutes had covetously gazed upon when they'd camped next to the emigrants exactly one week earlier. The prophet's message to the Indian leaders was clear enough: he wanted them to attack the Fancher wagon train. The morning after the meeting, the Paiutes left the City of the Saints at first light and started riding hard for southern Utah.

The Arkansans passed through Cedar City, thirty-five miles north of the Mountain Meadow, on September 4, where they asked to buy food from the Saints but were pointedly refused. By this time Cedar City was "a craze of fanaticism," one Mormon resident recalled, where numerous false rumors had been circulating about the Fancher train. It was said, for example, that some of the emigrants had directly participated in the murder of Mormons at Haun's Mill, Missouri, in 1838, and that one of the Arkansans had bragged that he was among the mob that had killed Joseph Smith. As far as the Saints of southern Utah were concerned, the emigrants were the personification of evil.

According to John D. Lee, on or around the day the Arkansans arrived in Cedar City, he received orders to attack the emigrants from Lieutenant Colonel Isaac Haight, the mayor of Cedar City, president of the LDS stake, and commander of the local battalion of the Nauvoo Legion. Lee was told to gather the Indian chiefs who had met with Brigham three days earlier, arm their warriors, and lead them in an ambush on the Fancher train in the mountains south of Cedar City; Lee reported that Haight had emphasized that this directive was "the will of all in authority."

On September 5, Lee headed for the Mountain Meadow with a large contingent of Saints and Paiutes. They arrived in the hills above the meadow on September 6, where they hid among the stunted trees and watched the Arkansans make camp near the spring below, and the Saints painted their faces so they would look like Indians. The next morning before dawn, while the emigrants were sleeping, these painted Mormons and the genuine Paiutes stole toward the Fancher camp and took cover behind rocks and brush. As the sun crept over the serrated, ten-thousand-foot crest of the Pine Valley Mountains, the unsuspecting Arkansans gathered to cook breakfast. Lee's snipers carefully aimed their muskets to inflict maximum casualties, then fired.

· · ·

Lee had assumed the Arkansans would quickly succumb to the surprise assault. The Saints had been so confident of a quick victory, in fact, that they had promised, in Lee's words, that the Paiutes "could kill the emigrants without danger to themselves." But the Fancher party was disciplined, very brave, and well armed, and their ranks included many expert riflemen. After the initial volley of gunfire, the Arkansans quickly circled their wagons, dug into bunkers, and then immediately initiated a counterassault, utterly confounding their attackers.

At least one Paiute brave was killed that morning, two Paiute chiefs were mortally wounded, and the Indian and Mormon forces were decisively repulsed, dealing a completely unanticipated blow to their resolve. As they regrouped at a safe distance, the Indians expressed their displeasure with the bungled operation in no uncertain terms: they threatened angrily to go home and leave the Mormons to their own devices. "Now we knew the Indians could not do the work," Lee was forced to acknowledge after their surprise attack failed, "and we were in a sad fix." After ordering his men to keep the emigrants pinned down, Lee rode off to summon Mormon reinforcements, and to seek the counsel of his superiors.

Down in Cedar City, Isaac Haight had heard by Monday afternoon that things were not going as planned on the Mountain Meadow. Haight was itching to send a deputation of Mormon militiamen up to the high country to finish off the emigrants, but vocal members of the community argued that such a grave action shouldn't be undertaken until they'd received the explicit endorsement of Brigham Young. That evening Haight dispatched a rider on a fast horse to Salt Lake City, bearing a letter to the prophet explaining that Lee had the Fancher party surrounded at the Mountain Meadow and asking what should be done with them.

In the meantime, the Mormons and their Paiute mercenaries kept pressure on the Arkansans by harassing them with sniper fire, preventing them from collecting water from the nearby spring. By now, having glimpsed numerous fair-skinned men among those shooting at them, the emigrants had probably deduced that their attackers included Mormons as well as Paiutes. Hungry and tormented by thirst, the Gentiles knew that their situation was growing increasingly grim. Their ammunition was running out. They could neither bury their dead nor provide much comfort to the many who were seriously wounded. Most of their horses and cattle had been driven off by the attackers, but some sixty animals had been killed in the crossfire; the carcasses of these beasts were now putrefying around the Arkansans in the late-summer sun, creating a sickening stench.

On the night of September 10, two bold emigrants made a desperate attempt to sneak through the siege lines and summon help. One of them, a nineteen-year-old artist from Tennessee named William Aden, who had joined the Fancher train in Provo just a few weeks earlier, somehow made it out of the meadows and had ridden to within several miles of Cedar City when he came upon a group of men camped beside a spring. Believing them to be another party of Gentile emigrants en route to California, Aden rushed into their midst and blurted out a plea for help. The men, however, were Mormons, not emigrants, and upon hearing young Aden's appeal they drew their weapons and shot him dead.

Isaac Haight's messenger had arrived in Salt Lake City early that same morning, and promptly turned around to carry Brigham's reply back to southern Utah. The prophet's instructions were that the Saints "must not meddle" with the Fancher party. "The Indians," Brigham wrote, "we expect will do as they please but you should try and preserve good feelings with them." This letter has been intensely pondered by scholars, yet historians remain sharply divided about what Brigham really intended by it.* Whatever its meaning, the missive didn't arrive in Haight's hands until September 13, two days after the Mountain Meadows massacre had been carried out.

In the absence of word from Brigham Young, Isaac Haight sought guidance from his immediate superior, Colonel William Dame, the thirty-

---

* The actual text of Brigham's letter remains in some doubt, because the original has disappeared (along with almost every other official document pertaining to the Mountain Meadows massacre). The excerpt quoted above is from a purported draft of the letter that didn't surface until 1884, when an LDS functionary came upon it in the pages of a "Church Letter Book."

eight-year-old military commander of all the southern Utah militias. Haight rode twenty miles north to the settlement of Parowan, where he woke Dame in the middle of the night to ask him what to do about the besieged Fancher train. Colonel Dame impatiently insisted that Haight needed no further word from Great Salt Lake to take decisive action. "My orders," Dame declared, "are that the emigrants *must* be done away with." This directive was conveyed to John D. Lee at the Mountain Meadow by Major John Higbee of the Nauvoo Legion, a thirty-year-old zealot who arrived on the scene with more than fifty elite militiamen from Cedar City.

By the night of September 10, most of the Paiutes had ridden away from the Mountain Meadow in disgust, leaving the Saints with perhaps as few as forty Indian mercenaries. Fearing that they no longer had sufficient manpower to overwhelm the emigrants' position by force, the Saints decided to end the standoff by means of subterfuge.

The next morning, September 11, Lee sent an English convert named William Bateman toward the encircled emigrants under a white flag; Bateman was instructed to tell them that the Mormons were there to intercede with the Indians on the Arkansans' behalf, and would escort them to safety past the hostile Paiutes if the emigrants would hand over their weapons. After Bateman indicated that the emigrants were willing to parley, Lee approached the emigrant stronghold to "arrange the terms of the surrender."

"As I entered the fortifications," Lee reported, "men, women, and children gathered around me in wild consternation. Some felt that the time of their happy deliverance had come, while others, though in deep distress, and all in tears, looked upon me with doubt, distrust and terror." It took Lee at least two hours to win the emigrants' confidence, but eventually, seeing no alternative, they agreed to his terms and gave up their weapons.

The youngest children and several of the wounded were placed in a wagon and driven away. They were followed on foot by the emigrant women and the older children. A few hundred yards behind this group, the men of the Fancher party were led away in single file, with each emigrant escorted closely by a Mormon guard. After approximately thirty minutes, Major Higbee, bringing up the rear on horseback, discharged a firearm to get the Saints' attention. "Halt!" he ordered according to a prearranged plan. "Do your duty!"

At this infamous command, each of the Mormons immediately fired a bullet point-blank into the head of the captive under his purview. Most of the emigrant men died instantly, but one of the Saints recalled seeing an apostate Mormon—one of the "backouts" who had joined the Fancher train in Utah and was a close acquaintance of the Mormon executioners—lying wounded on the ground, pleading to Higbee for his life. According to a Mormon witness, Higbee told the apostate, "You would have done the same to me, or just as bad," and then slit the apostate's throat.

Another Saint who participated in the massacre later reported that while the men from the Fancher party were being executed by their Mormon escorts, the women and children were attacked "by the Indians, among whom were Mormons in disguise." Painted Saints and Paiutes rushed upon these victims with guns and knives and began shooting and bludgeoning them to death and slashing their throats. An Arkansan named Nancy Huff, who was four years old at the time, later reported, "I saw my mother shot in the forehead and fall dead. The women and children screamed and clung together. Some of the young women begged the assassins after they had run out on us not to kill them, but they had no mercy on them, clubbing their guns and beating out their brains." According to Nephi Johnson, a Mormon who later confessed his own culpability to historian Juanita Brooks, "White men did most of the killing."

The slaughter was over in a matter of minutes, leaving an estimated 120 emigrants dead. Approximately fifty of the victims were men, twenty were women, and fifty were children or adolescents. Out of the entire Fancher wagon train, only seventeen lives were spared—all of them children no more than five years old, deemed too young to remember enough to bear witness against the Saints.*

---

* Those children not killed were taken to Mormon homes to be raised as Latter-day Saints; some were placed in the households of the very men who had murdered their parents and siblings. In 1859 an agent of the federal government managed to find all seventeen survivors and return them to their Arkansas kin, but before handing the kids over, their Mormon keepers had the audacity to demand thousands of dollars in payment for feeding and schooling the youngsters while they were in the Saints' care.

When quiet settled over the killing field, the Mormons looted the corpses for valuables; after the Saints had gathered what they wanted, they allowed the Indians to take the rest. The dead emigrants were soon stripped of everything, including every shred of clothing they'd been wearing. Very little of the plunder went to the Indians, however. According to historian Will Bagley, "The Paiutes only got about twenty horses and mules while the Mormon officers claimed the best animals for themselves, a measure of contempt for their allies. . . . In the desperately poor country of southern Utah, the spoils of the slaughtered immigrants became a source of envy and conflict. Some of his neighbors felt that Lee had swindled them out of their share."

Colonel William Dame and Lieutenant Colonel Isaac Haight—whose orders had prompted the slaughter—arrived at the Mountain Meadow from Cedar City on the morning after the killing had ended. It was the forty-fifth birthday of John D. Lee, who escorted his commanding officers to the site of the butchery, where they were confronted with the naked, horribly brutalized bodies of men, women, and children scattered across the landscape in twisted poses of rigor mortis. "Colonel Dame was silent for some time," recalled Lee. "He looked all over the field, and was quite pale, and looked uneasy and frightened. I thought then that he was just finding out the difference between giving and executing orders for wholesale killing."

Dame expressed shock at the carnage and tried to absolve himself of any responsibility for it. This infuriated Haight. "You ordered it done," he spat back at his superior officer. "Nothing has been done except by your orders, and it is too late in the day for you to order things done and then go back on it."

Confronted with this irrefutable statement of fact, Dame lost his composure and appeared as though he might burst into tears. According to Lee, Dame vehemently protested, "I did not think there were so many of them, or I would not have had anything to do with it."

Losing his patience with Dame's lack of spine, Haight turned to Lee and said, "Colonel Dame counseled and ordered me to do this thing, and now he wants to back out, and go back on me, and by God he shall not do it. . . . I will blow him to hell before he shall lay it all on me. He has got to stand up to what he did, like a man. He knows he ordered it done, and I dare him to deny it."

Having no adequate answer for this charge, Dame fell silent and turned his attention to supervising the disposal of the corpses. The Mormon militiamen, Lee reported, "piled the dead bodies up in heaps, in little gullies, and threw dirt over them. The bodies were only lightly covered, for the ground was hard, and the brethren did not have sufficient tools to dig with." Within days, wolves and other scavengers had unearthed the dead emigrants from the shallow graves and scattered their remains across the meadow.

Upon completion of this halfhearted, hastily undertaken burial, according to Lee, the Saints gathered in a circle at the site of the mass murder to offer "thanks to God for delivering our enemies into our hands." Then the overseers of the massacre reiterated "the necessity of always saying the Indians did it alone, and that the Mormons had nothing to do with it. . . . It was voted unanimously that any man who should divulge the secret, or tell who was present, or do anything that would lead to a discovery of the truth, should suffer death."

NINETEEN

SCAPEGOATS

Brigham Young saved his Church when Joseph was lynched, brought it to the Missouri, took it to Great Salt Lake, gave it safety, wealth and power. The state of Utah is his monument. . . . He was a great man, great in whatever was needful for Israel. Great in understanding, in will and fortitude and resolution, in finding the means which others could not find. Great in remembering also, in the command and management of men, the opposition and hostility and hate. A great leader, a great diplomat, a great administrator, and at need a great liar and a great scoundrel.

BERNARD DeVOTO,
THE YEAR OF DECISION

"Look! Over here!" shouts six-year-old Randy Bateman. A pint-size tornado with a pertinacious blond cowlick, he kneels in the dirt to prop up a rock with one tiny hand while gesticulating furiously with the other. "Come see!" he yells again, with even greater urgency. "A scorpion hole!" A minute later he's deftly plucked the sinister-looking arachnid from its lair and placed it in an empty Gatorade bottle. Then he scurries up the trail in a burst of dust to show off the prize to his father, DeLoy Bateman, the Colorado City teacher who has apostatized from the Fundamentalist Church of Jesus Christ of Latter Day Saints. As the crow flies, Colorado City is less than fifty miles from the site of the Mountain

Meadows massacre. William Bateman—the Mormon who approached the Fancher party under a white flag at the Mountain Meadow in order to arrange the false truce that persuaded the emigrants to surrender their weapons and walk into John D. Lee's homicidal trap—was DeLoy Bateman's great-great-great-uncle.*

Although DeLoy isn't proud of his ancestor's notorious role in the massacre, he believes it shouldn't be swept under the rug. To the contrary, he'd like to know all there is to know about it. "I've always been a curious person," he says. "Even when I was still in the religion. Uncle Rulon has always restricted what the people in Colorado City can learn, and what books they can read, but that actually kind of runs against the grain of what Joseph Smith originally taught. In *D&C* 90, I think it is, there's a revelation from Joseph which says something like, 'Study and learn, and become acquainted with all good books.' In any case, I've always been interested in learning as much as I can about everything I can, and I've tried to instill that same love of learning in my kids."

The Bateman clan is on a weekend camping trip, planned around a climb of Mount Dellenbaugh, an extinct volcano that stands at the southern edge of the Arizona Strip. The objective of the ascent is to track down a 132-year-old signature said to be etched on the rim of the crater that forms Dellenbaugh's rocky crest—a signature that may help explain a puzzling series of events that happened in the aftermath of the Mountain Meadows massacre, and might conceivably have involved some of DeLoy's ancestors or their cohorts. In addition to DeLoy and Randy Bateman, the team presently en route to the summit includes one of DeLoy's two wives and nine more of his seventeen children; four other kids, a grandchild, and a son-in-law have stayed behind at base camp in support.

---

* Several Saints who took an active part in the 1857 slaughter were the forebears of modern Americans of some renown. Current Utah governor Mike Leavitt, for example, is a direct descendent of massacre participant Dudley Leavitt, as was Juanita Leavitt Brooks, the author of *The Mountain Meadows Massacre*. And among the descendants of John D. Lee are members of the Udall political dynasty: Stewart Udall was a three-term congressman from Arizona and served as U.S. secretary of the interior under President Kennedy; his younger brother, the late Morris Udall, succeeded Stewart to serve fifteen terms in the U.S. House of Representatives; and Morris's son Mark Udall currently represents Colorado's Second District in the U.S. House.

Because today's expedition includes DeLoy's two six-year-old boys, Randy and Kevin, and his two eight-year-old daughters, Maria and Sarah, the pace up the mountain is less than brisk. The kids are strong hikers and completely at home in this unforgiving environment, but they stop constantly to peer under rocks in search of snakes and other interesting creatures or to marvel at desert plants and identify geologic specimens. "I encourage it," DeLoy says with an unapologetic shrug. "The idea is to turn every trip outdoors into a biology lesson." The only problem is, by the time the party finally arrives on the summit, the sun is within minutes of disappearing behind the majestic curve of the western horizon, leaving precious little daylight for locating the signature DeLoy hopes to find.

The top of Dellenbaugh is a spiky crown of basalt swept by a hot, dry wind. Hundreds of giant megaliths bristle from the summit crater, and any of them might conceivably be imprinted with the relevant graffito. Finding the right rock before the mountain is swallowed in darkness seems like a long shot, but should the expedition fall short of its goal, the view from the top is a fine consolation. To the south, the earth is covered in a rolling sea of piñon and scraggly juniper that washes right up to the very lip of the Grand Canyon, which appears as a huge, shadowy gash rimmed with cliffs of pale Kaibab limestone.

Just before daylight vanishes altogether, somebody yells, "Here it is!" And lo, scratched onto a brownish, flat-faced chunk of basalt the size of a washing machine is the name DeLoy has been looking for, faintly but unmistakably printed in crude, inch-and-a-half-high letters: "W Dunn." Immediately below is the date 1869 and an arrow pointing north toward the Utah line. "I'll be darned," DeLoy exclaims. He brushes his fingertips across the inscription, then looks up to consider what the man who carved his name into this rock would have seen more than a century earlier from this mountaintop.

The inscription was made by one William Dunn, a shaggy-haired mountain man, not yet thirty years old, whose buckskin clothing was distinguished by its "dark oleaginous luster." This latter description comes to us from Mr. Dunn's employer at the time, Major John Wesley Powell, the eminent explorer of the American West celebrated for making the first descent of the Grand Canyon. Dunn, a member of that astounding expedition, vanished with two companions, the brothers Oramel Gass Howland and Seneca Howland, near the conclusion of the journey. Dunn's signature atop Mount Dellenbaugh is the last trace of the missing explorers known to exist.

After taking a few photos of Dunn's etching, DeLoy and his family admire the view from the summit for as long as the twilight lingers, then descend to their camp beneath a sky smeared with stars. The next morning on their way back to Colorado City, the Bateman caravan unexpectedly rolls past a memorial to the lost men from Powell's expedition, and DeLoy pulls off the road to examine it. The handsome wooden sign declares:

> WILLIAM DUNN, O. G. HOWLAND AND SENECA
> HOWLAND, AFTER LEAVING MAJOR POWELL'S PARTY
> CAME UP SEPARATION CANYON AND CROSSED OVER MT.
> DELLENBAUGH. THEY WERE KILLED BY INDIANS EAST
> OF THIS MARKER THE LAST OF AUGUST, 1869.

The memorial reflects the prevailing view of what happened to Dunn and the Howland brothers. DeLoy has recently arrived at a different opinion, however. He's decided that the three explorers were murdered not by Native Americans but by the Mormons of southern Utah. And the bloodshed, he believes, stemmed from an unfortunate misunderstanding that grew out of the Mountain Meadows massacre.

In 1858, a year after the massacre, Brigham Young reluctantly agreed to admit federal troops into Utah and to step down as territorial governor, bringing an end to the threat of all-out war between the Saints and the United States. But persistent rumors that Mormons had committed unspeakable atrocities against the Fancher wagon train kept drifting up from the southern settlements, threatening the fragile peace.

President Buchanan's secretary of war ordered army brevet major James H. Carleton to investigate the matter. Arriving at the Mountain Meadows in the spring of 1859, Carleton was sickened to discover that, nearly two years after the event, the valley was littered with skulls, bones, clumps of women's hair, and scraps of children's clothing bleaching in the sun. An army surgeon reported that many of the skulls "bore marks of violence, being pierced with bullet holes, or shattered with heavy blows, or cleft with some sharp-edged instrument." The nature of the bullet wounds, he concluded, "showed that fire-arms had been discharged close to the head."

"There has been a great and fearful crime perpetrated," Carleton declared. His soldiers gathered up whatever bones they could find, interred them in a common grave, and then laboriously hauled stones from the surrounding hillsides to build a massive, if crude, monument above it. At the apex of this rock pile, which was twelve feet high and fifty feet in circumference, they placed a wooden cross inscribed with the epigraph "Vengeance is mine: I will repay, saith the Lord."

In May 1861, Brigham Young happened upon this memorial as he was passing through the meadow during a tour of his southern settlements. According to Apostle Wilford Woodruff, who was accompanying the prophet, when Brigham read the inscription on the cross he pondered it for a short while and then proposed an emendation: "Vengeance is *mine,*" the prophet smugly asserted, "and I have taken a little." A moment later one of the Saints in his entourage threw a rope over the cross and pulled it down, while others began dismantling the stones and scattering them. By the time Brigham's party departed the Mountain Meadows, the monument to the slaughtered emigrants had been obliterated.

Things had lately been looking up for the Kingdom of God, leaving the prophet in a cheerful frame of mind. The territorial governor installed by President Buchanan as Brigham's replacement, a bureaucrat from Atlanta named Alfred Cummings, had turned out to be a patsy who was easily manipulated to do the Saints' bidding. The despised Buchanan, moreover, had himself been replaced in the White House by Abraham Lincoln; after taking office, Honest Abe told a Mormon emissary, "You go back and tell Brigham Young that if he will let me alone, I will let him alone." Brigham thus had good reason to be in an expansive mood.

The Saints' capital city had even become a popular travel destination for intrepid luminaries from afar, including the French botanist Jules Remy, the famous newspaperman Horace Greeley, and the English ex-

plorer Sir Richard Francis Burton. Greeley—the most influential journalist of the era—had interviewed Brigham in 1859 and then published
a largely favorable piece in the *New York Tribune,* noting that the prophet
spoke "with no apparent desire to conceal anything" and had "no air of
sanctimony or fanaticism." After Sir Richard Burton rubbed shoulders
with Brigham, Porter Rockwell, and other Mormon eminences in 1860,
the celebrated English adventurer had written,

> The Prophet is no common man, and . . . he has none of the weakness
> and vanity which characterize the common uncommon man. . . .
> There is a total absence of pretension in his manner, and he has been
> so long used to power that he cares nothing for its display. The arts by
> which he rules the heterogeneous mass of conflicting elements are in-
> domitable will, profound secrecy, and uncommon astuteness.

Such flattery from prominent Gentiles no doubt buoyed Brigham's dis-
position, but most of his ebullience was attributable to the advent of the
Civil War. The momentous conflict erupted at Fort Sumter, South Car-
olina, just a month before his 1861 tour of the southern Utah, inspiring
in the prophet an attitude of renewed insolence toward the United
States. When federal troops were yanked out of Utah to buttress the
Union forces fighting the Confederacy, he couldn't have been happier.

All the news from the East, moreover, seemed to confirm that
the Gentile nation was teetering precariously on the brink of self-
destruction, exactly as Joseph Smith had prophesied back in 1832.*

---

* On December 25, 1832, Joseph received a revelation, later canonized in *The Doctrine and
Covenants* as Section 87, in which God explained that civil war

> *will shortly come to pass, beginning at the rebellion of South Carolina, which will eventu-
> ally terminate in the death of many souls. . . . For behold, the Southern States shall be di-
> vided against the Northern States. . . . And it shall come to pass, after many days, slaves
> shall rise up against their masters, who shall be marshaled and disciplined for war. . . .
> And thus, with the sword and by bloodshed the inhabitants of the earth shall mourn; and
> with famine, and plague, and earthquake, and the thunder of heaven, and the fierce and
> vivid lightning also, shall the inhabitants of the earth be made to feel the wrath, and in-
> dignation, and chastening hand of an Almighty God, until the consumption decreed hath
> made a full end of all nations.*

Although their bitterness toward the government in Washington, D.C., moved the Mormons to cheer each Confederate victory on the battlefield, Brigham was certain that Union and Confederate forces would eventually annihilate each other, leaving the Latter-day Saints triumphant and unmolested when the Civil War came to an end, eagerly awaiting the Great and Dreadful Day of the Lord.

Seeing no reason to doubt this outcome, Brigham felt assured that the United States would no longer be meddling in the affairs of Deseret. His confidence, however, proved to be distressingly short lived. Just sixteen months after Union forces pulled out to fight the Confederacy, President Abraham Lincoln replaced them with a regiment of California infantry to ensure federal control of Utah. For the remainder of the war, according to historian D. Michael Quinn, some of these troops "literally had their guns trained on Brigham Young's home, so that if there was going to be a civil uprising, his home would be the first to receive cannon shots."

Compounding the prophet's woes, in 1862 Lincoln signed into law the Morrill Anti-Bigamy Act, which had been drafted specifically to "punish and prevent the practice of polygamy in the Territories of the United States and to disapprove and annul certain acts of the territorial legislature of Utah." Just months after taking office, Lincoln demonstrated that he intended to be at least as tough on the Mormons as Presidents Fillmore, Pierce, and Buchanan had been before him, prompting Brigham to lash out against "such cursed scoundrels as Abe Lincoln and his Minions." (Which is ironic, because the second Mormon prophet shared many of the attributes that distinguished the sixteenth American president; had Brigham's life been diverted onto a different track—had his ambitions been less millennial and more secular—it is easy to imagine him in the White House. He certainly had what it takes to become president, and he would have made a memorable one, a national leader in the mold of Lyndon Johnson, say, or Franklin Roosevelt, or even Lincoln himself.)

In April 1865 Brigham's comforting pipe dream of the North and South's mutual destruction came to an end with the surrender of General Robert E. Lee at Appomattox. The Civil War concluded with the Union not only intact but in important ways stronger than ever. Brigham was forced to acknowledge that the United States would thereafter be increasingly involved in the business and governance of Deseret.

This eventuality was underscored in 1869 with the ceremonial driving of the golden spike at Promontory Summit, near the north end of the Great Salt Lake, marking completion of the transcontinental railroad. Now all that separated Utah from the ungodly reach of the whole Gentile nation was a relatively short, comfortable train ride. And 1869 also saw another major event that signified the end of Utah's isolation: the first descent of the Green and Colorado Rivers by Major John Wesley Powell, a Civil War hero who had lost his right arm at the battle of Shiloh.

Powell's expedition cast off in puny wooden boats from Green River Station, Wyoming, on May 24, 1869, planning to float the Green River to its confluence with the Colorado River,* then continue downstream through the treacherous, completely uncharted chasms of the Grand Canyon, thereby traversing the last vast expanse of unexplored wilderness in the contiguous United States—the final blank spot on the map. It was a trying voyage, marked by danger, hardship, and acrimony between Powell and some of his men.

On August 27, near the lower end of the Grand Canyon, the boatmen beached their vessels on the riverbank immediately above what would turn out to be the last set of dangerous rapids on the entire journey. Seneca Howland, his brother Oramel Howland, and William Dunn announced that they were leaving the expedition. Ignoring Powell's pleas that they remain with the main group, the three disgruntled adventurers told him they intended to climb four thousand vertical feet from the river to the canyon's north rim, then walk across more then a hundred miles of barren desert to the Mormon settlements of southern Utah.

By this point the expedition had traveled nearly a thousand perilous river miles. All nine men were battered and hungry, and they had only five days of provisions left, mostly consisting of dried apples and coffee.

---

* In those years it was called the Grand River, rather than the Colorado.

The party's greatest problem, however, was the rift that had developed between Major Powell and his mentally unstable brother, Captain Walter Powell, on the one hand, and five free-spirited trappers on the other: Dunn, the Howland brothers, Jack Sumner, and Billie Hawkins.* As Wallace Stegner noted in his classic biography of Powell, *Beyond the Hundredth Meridian,* the major and his brother "represented military discipline and the officer class," while the five trappers "represented frontier independence and a violent distaste for discipline of any kind."

On August 28, after Dunn and the Howland brothers watched their companions crash through Separation Rapids and then disappear around a bend in the river, the three deserters began the arduous climb out of the Grand Canyon, carrying two rifles and a shotgun, a duplicate set of expedition papers, and a silver watch Jack Sumner had asked them to deliver to his sister in case he drowned. Dunn and the Howlands ascended a steep gulch (later named Separation Canyon) to reach the north rim, then set out across the Shivwits Plateau. Thirty arduous miles from the river's edge, they climbed the gentle slopes of an extinct volcano, now called Mount Dellenbaugh, in order to get their bearings and plot a course across the harsh country that stretched ahead of them. On Dellenbaugh's 6,990-foot summit, Dunn scratched his name on the face of a boulder, and then the trio presumably headed north for the Mormon settlements. Nobody knows for sure, though, because Dunn and the Howlands never reappeared.†

---

* The nine-man expedition also included a melancholic Civil War veteran named George Bradley and twenty-year-old Andy Hall; both these men maintained good relations with the two disputatious factions. The expedition had embarked from Green River with a tenth member, as well, Englishman Frank Goodman, but after Goodman's boat capsized and he nearly drowned in Disaster Falls, he told Powell on July 5 that he "had seen danger enough" and left the expedition—well before the group entered the Grand Canyon.

† Evidence corroborating the authenticity of Dunn's inscription atop Mount Dellenbaugh was discovered in 1995: a young man from Cedar City named Wynn Isom was looking for arrowheads on the eastern slope of Mount Dellenbaugh, well off the trail, when he caught sight of "a little glint" on the ground, perhaps thirty feet away. It turned out to be a thin piece of badly tarnished brass, two inches long and just over an inch wide, with the name William Dunn engraved on its face in cursive script. From indentations at the plate's corners, it appears to have been riveted to a gun stock, perhaps, or some leather article that belonged to Dunn.

. . .

After Powell and the rest of his team had made it through Separation Rapids without flipping their boats, they pulled ashore, "waited about two hours, fired guns, and motioned for . . . the Howlands and Dunn to come on," Jack Sumner recalled, "as they could have done by climbing along the cliffs. The last thing we saw of them they were standing on the reef, motioning us to go on, which we finally did."

Two days after floating away from the three deserters, Powell's group arrived safely at the confluence of the Virgin River, where they encountered a group of Mormons netting fish. The Saints generously fed the emaciated explorers, then escorted Powell over the Beaver Dam Mountains to St. George, the principal city of southern Utah. On September 8, as Powell was traveling via carriage from St. George to Great Salt Lake City, a story appeared in the *Deseret News,* the Mormon newspaper, under the headline "Three of the Powell Expedition Killed by Indians":

> We have received a dispatch through the Deseret Telegraph Line from St. George of the murder of three of the men belonging to the Powell Exploration Expedition. It appears according to the report of a friendly Indian that about five days ago the men were found by peaceable Indians of the Shebett [Shivwit] tribe very hungry. The Shebetts fed them, and put them on the trail leading to Washington in Southern Utah. On their journey they saw a squaw gathering seed, and shot her; whereupon they were followed by three Shebetts and killed. A friendly Indian has been sent out to secure their papers. The telegraph does not give us the names of the men.

When Powell heard the news, he refused to believe that Dunn and the Howlands had been killed by the Shivwits—a retiring, relatively small band of Indians belonging to the Southern Paiute nation. His skepticism was based largely on reports that the woman, who had allegedly been raped before she was murdered, was alone and unarmed. "I have known O. G. Howland personally for many years," Powell explained, "and I have no hesitation in pronouncing this part of the story as a libel. It was not in the man's faithful, genial nature to do such a thing."

The first report of any kind that Dunn and the Howland brothers had been killed by Indians was the mysterious telegram alluded to in the *Deseret News* story. The telegram had been sent anonymously to Mormon Apostle Erastus Snow in St. George on the evening of September 7, 1869, shortly after Powell had passed through town and asked the local Saints to keep a sharp eye out for the missing members of his team. The telegram read:

> Powell's three men killed by three She-bits, five days ago, one Indian's day journey from Washington. Indians report that they were found in an exhausted state, fed by the She-bits, and put on the trail leading to Washington; after which they saw a squaw gathering seed and shot her, whereupon, the She-bits followed up and killed all three. Two of the She-bits who killed the men are in the Washington Indian camp with two of the guns. Indian George has gone to secure what papers and property there is left.

Jack Sumner—one of the expedition members who'd emerged safely from the Grand Canyon with Major Powell, and a close pal of William Dunn and the Howland brothers—didn't see eye to eye with Powell on most matters, but he shared the major's skepticism that Indians had killed their companions. The night after separating, the men who had stayed on the river with Powell had speculated around their campfire about "the fate of the three men left above." According to Sumner, everyone else in Powell's group "seemed to think the red bellies would surely get them. But I could not believe that the reds would get them, as I had trained Dunn for two years in how to avoid a surprise, and I did not think the red devils would make open attack on three armed men. But I did have some misgiving that they would not escape the double-dyed white devils that infested that part of the country. Grapevine reports convinced me later that that was their fate."

Sumner was of course talking about the Mormons of southern Utah. He knew all about the Mountain Meadows massacre and the Mormons' continuing insistence that Indians alone had been responsible for the murder of the Arkansans, despite ample evidence to the contrary. When Sumner heard the Mormons claiming that Indians had killed his friends, he was skeptical. Later he reported, "I saw some years afterwards the silver watch I had given Howland" during a drunken brawl with some white men, one of whom "had a watch and boasted how he came by it. . . . Such evidence is not conclusive, but all of it was enough to convince me that the Indians were not at the head of the murder, if they had anything to do with it."

A year after emerging from the Grand Canyon and departing Utah for his home in Chicago, Major Powell—now an international celebrity— returned to the region to conduct further explorations of the Colorado River and its tributaries. In the interim, he had been contacted by the Howland brothers' family, who implored him to find out what had really happened to Oramel and Seneca. Toward these ends Powell sought the assistance of Brigham Young, who volunteered his main man in southern Utah, Jacob Hamblin, Indian missionary extraordinaire, to serve as Powell's guide.

On September 5, Powell rendezvoused in Parowan with Brigham, Hamblin, and approximately forty local Saints—including two of the leading perpetrators of the slaughter at Mountain Meadows: William Dame and John D. Lee. The entire group accompanied Powell as far as the Mormon outpost of Pipe Spring, where Powell and Hamblin bid farewell to Brigham and the other Saints and headed south across the Arizona Strip with an escort of Kaibab Indians. On the evening of September 19, just northeast of Mount Dellenbaugh, Hamblin arranged a parley between Powell and members of the Shivwit tribe who had supposedly killed his men.

According to Powell's account of the meeting, the Shivwit chief— relying on Hamblin to translate for him—freely confessed that "we killed three white men." Another member of the tribe then explained (outside of Powell's hearing) that Dunn and the Howland brothers had stumbled into the Shivwits' village

almost starved and exhausted with fatigue. They were supplied with
food and put on their way to the settlements. Shortly after they had
left, an Indian from the east side of the Colorado arrived at their village and told them about a number of miners having killed a squaw in
a drunken brawl, and no doubt these were the men. . . . In this way he
worked them into a great rage. They followed, surrounded the men in
ambush, and filled them full of arrows.

The murders had resulted from a terrible misapprehension, in other
words. Powell forgave the Shivwits and made no effort to punish them
or take revenge.

Over the years, a handful of voices persisted in challenging this version
of the tragedy, most prominently those of Dunn's friend Jack Sumner
and a grizzled Colorado River guide named Otis "Dock" Marston, who
claimed he had heard from a Mormon privy to confidential information
that "it was the Mormons that shot these men." But Sumner, Marston,
and the other skeptics were roundly dismissed by the majority of historians and scholars, Mormon and Gentile alike, including such eminences
as Wallace Stegner. Then, in 1980, a former dean of the college of science at Southern Utah University, a Latter-day Saint named Wesley P.
Larsen, came across a letter that had been squirreled away for ninety-
seven years in an old trunk in the hamlet of Toquerville. Dated February
17, 1883, the letter suggested that Dunn and the Howlands had been
killed in Toquerville—inside the LDS ward house, no less—by one of
the local Saints.

The letter was written to John Steele—a highly respected judge and
ecclesiastical leader, as well as Toquerville's preeminent doctor and boot-
maker—by William Leany, Steele's friend of thirty-seven years. Leany
had been a faultless Saint (he had once even been a trusted bodyguard to
Brigham Young) until the volatile, hate-soaked summer of 1857, immediately prior to the Mountain Meadows massacre, when he'd committed the unforgivable sin of providing food to a Gentile member of

the Fancher wagon train as it passed through Parowan. The Gentile in question was William Aden, the nineteen-year-old artist from Tennessee who would be shot a week later trying to summon help for the besieged Arkansans.

Aden was the son of a doctor who years earlier had saved Leany from the clutches of an anti-Mormon mob that threatened to do him mortal harm in the town of Paris, Tennessee, where Leany was serving as a missionary. Following his rescue, Leany was taken to the Aden residence, where he met young William. Recognizing the Aden boy when the Fancher party stopped for the night in Parowan, Leany invited him into his home, gave him dinner, and then sent Aden away with some onions from his garden. Upon learning of this treasonous act, William Dame dispatched a thug to Leany's house, who pried a post from Leany's fence and clubbed him in the side of the head with it, fracturing his skull and nearly killing him.

In 1883, when he wrote the long, rambling letter discovered by Professor Larsen, Leany was sixty-eight years old. The correspondence to Judge Steele was apparently prompted by a suggestion from the judge that before he passed into the hereafter, Leany might want to repent for certain sins some of the Toquerville brethren had accused him of committing. Leany replied angrily that "God shall bear me witness that I am clean of all of which they accuse me & they guilty of all that I accuse them & much more."

What Leany accused his fellow Saints of, the letter revealed, was "thieving whoredom murder and Suicide & like abominations." He reminded Steele, moreover, that "you are far from ignorant of these deeds of blood from the day the picket fence was broke on my head to the day those three were murdered in our ward & the murderer killed to stop the shedding of more blood." Five paragraphs later, Leany made another allusion to "the killing the three in one room of our own ward."

Baffled and intrigued by these provocative references to murder, Wesley Larsen deduced from historical records that the killings alluded to by Leany had occurred in 1869. Then he determined that only three men had been murdered that year in southern Utah: William Dunn and the Howland brothers. But why would the good Saints of Toquerville want to take the lives of three wayward explorers?

Toquerville was founded in 1858, a year after the Mountain Meadows massacre, and most of the first families to settle there were headed by men who had participated in the slaughter. Many of these same men were living in Toquerville in 1869 when Powell floated down the Grand Canyon. The year prior to Powell's expedition, Ulysses S. Grant had been elected president, and his administration had made it a priority to capture the perpetrators of the massacre and bring them to justice. Even before this new dragnet, moreover, a $5,000 bounty had been placed on the heads of Isaac Haight, John Higbee, and John D. Lee. By the time Dunn and the Howlands decided to abandon Powell's expedition and walk to the Mormon settlements, many of Toquerville's leading citizens were living in constant fear of arrest.

The climate of paranoia that pervaded the region was at a particularly high pitch in the summer of 1869 thanks to Brigham Young, who had made a trip through southern Utah that season stoking hatred for the Gentiles. Cautioning that federal troops were about to launch a new invasion of Deseret, Brigham ordered sentries to stand watch at strategic points along the territory's southern border. This was the volatile atmosphere that awaited Dunn and the Howlands as they walked north from Mount Dellenbaugh toward the Mormon settlements.

Larsen speculates that somewhere on the Shivwits Plateau they encountered one or more Mountain Meadows fugitives, who assumed that Powell's men must be federal agents or bounty hunters; their preposterous claim to be harmless explorers who had just completed the first descent of the Grand Canyon—which was known by everyone in Utah to be completely impassable—would only have confirmed their treacherous intentions in the eyes of the Saints. So (according to this scenario) the Mormons hauled Dunn and the Howlands into Toquerville, where they were tried by a kangaroo court and summarily executed.

Within a few days of this presumed lynching, Major Powell happened to turn up in St. George, asking the good people of the southern settlements to keep an eye out for his missing men, and the Saints of Toquerville realized they'd committed a serious mistake. Magnifying their blunder, Powell was a friend and vocal admirer of the Mormons, in sharp contrast to almost all other agents of the Gentile government in Washington. In a rising panic over what they'd done, the Toquerville residents sent a bogus telegram to Apostle Erastus Snow, blaming the murders on their usual whipping boys, the Indians. Five months later, these same Saints killed the unfortunate fellow who had volunteered to carry out the executions, electing to sacrifice the executioner in order "to stop the shedding of more blood," as Leany's letter described it. Then, just as they had done in the wake of Mountain Meadows, the conspirators swore an oath to say nothing about the abominable deed to anyone.

Larsen theorizes that this last victim, the presumed executioner, may have been a Mormon named Eli N. Pace. "I understand that Pace had three wives," says Dr. Larsen, "one of whom was the daughter of John D. Lee. It seems possible that Pace killed Powell's men because he thought they were bounty hunters closing in on his father-in-law, who had a $5,000 reward on his head at the time." Adding weight to Larsen's conjecture is the fact that Eli Pace died on January 29, 1870, "under very mysterious circumstances": an inquest conducted by local Mormons determined that Pace had committed suicide, but his family took strenuous issue with this finding and demanded another, more rigorous investigation. The second inquest, presided over by Erastus Snow himself and weighed by a three-man jury that included Isaac Haight, corroborated the initial finding—to the surprise of absolutely nobody beyond Pace's immediate family. The matter was pronounced closed by the LDS Church and the local judiciary, which were one and the same.

Larsen's hypothesis that Dunn and the Howland brothers were killed by Mormons, rather than Shivwits, has been disparaged by most historians, as have all previous suggestions that the Indians weren't responsible. The majority view is based almost entirely on accounts by both Jacob Hamblin and Major John Wesley Powell that describe, with convincing detail, how the Shivwits freely confessed to murdering

Powell's men. But such accounts, it turns out, should be taken with a large grain of salt.

Hamblin enjoyed a reputation of unimpeachable integrity among the Saints of southern Utah, who called him "Honest Jake." The historical record plainly shows, however, that Hamblin had no compunction about "lying for the Lord" when he thought it would advance the goals of the Kingdom of God. Indeed, the record also shows that Hamblin was quite willing to lie through his teeth simply to enrich himself. It's worth noting that John D. Lee had his own nicknames for Hamblin: "Dirty Fingered Jake" and "the fiend of Hell."

In September 1857, immediately following the Mountain Meadows massacre, Hamblin orchestrated the shakedown and robbery of the William Dukes wagon train, among the first parties of emigrants to travel through southern Utah after the slaughter. Despite paying Mormon guides $1,815 to be escorted safely through the region, the Dukes party was attacked by a band of Paiutes, who let the emigrants escape to California but stole everything they had of any value, including more than three hundred head of cattle. The emigrants noticed, moreover, that many of the marauding "Indians" had blue eyes, curly hair, and splotches of white skin at the corners of their eyes and behind their ears. In actuality, the thieves had been led by Mormons who had painted their faces to resemble Paiutes, according to the instructions of Jacob Hamblin (which was, of course, the same ruse employed by the Saints during the Mountain Meadows massacre, and on numerous other occasions).

The Paiutes were given a few of the stolen cattle as payment for their supporting role in the shakedown, but Hamblin kept the bulk of the plunder for himself, professing to be safeguarding the large and very valuable herd of livestock for the Dukes party until the emigrants were able to return to Utah and take possession of them. But when William Dukes called Hamblin's bluff and recruited a brave soul to reclaim the rustled cattle, Hamblin hid most of the animals in the mountains for three weeks, until the representative for the emigrants finally gave up in frustration and departed, nearly empty-handed.

Although Hamblin was absent from the Mountain Meadow when the Fancher train was attacked, and thus did not directly participate in the massacre, after the fact he brazenly lied about what he knew about it in order to protect the LDS Church. Thus, when Hamblin reported that the Shivwits admitted to killing Major Powell's men in 1869, there is little reason to trust his word. John Wesley Powell, however, was also present when the Indians made their confession, and he corroborated Hamblin's version of the event. But did Powell understand what the Shivwits were saying? Or was he simply parroting Hamblin's translation?

In *A River Running West,* his excellent biography of Powell, Donald Worster—a distinguished professor at the University of Kansas—speculates that Powell was sufficiently fluent in the Numic dialects spoken by the Southern Paiute tribes to have known whether Hamblin was translating accurately. If Hamblin fabricated the confession, Worster argues, he had to have done it "without Powell suspecting, and that fabrication had to have been part of a well-orchestrated conspiracy directed from above. None of these hypotheses seem plausible."

Wesley Larsen, not surprisingly, begs to differ with Worster and the majority who share his view. A devout Mormon, Larsen has no trouble believing that a fabrication could have been part of "a well-orchestrated conspiracy directed from above"; the Saints' tenure in Utah is rife with such conspiracies. Moreover, Larsen points out that "Powell certainly wasn't fluent in the Paiute language. The Shivwit dialect was sufficiently different that they had trouble making themselves understood even to other tribes in the area. . . . Powell would only have understood what Hamblin translated for him, which is of course why Hamblin was translating in the first place."

And Powell's colorful retelling of his momentous parley with the Shivwits must itself be regarded with a healthy dose of skepticism. The best-selling book by Powell from which the account is drawn, *The Exploration of the Colorado River and Its Canyons,* is universally acknowledged to include numerous embellishments, as well as the omission of many pertinent events. In his book, Powell even conflates anecdotes drawn from three different visits to Utah Territory—the original 1869 expedition, the 1870 excursion in which he met with the Shivwits, and an extended exploration of the Colorado Plateau conducted from 1871 through 1873; striving for a more dramatic narrative, he shamelessly presents events from 1872 as having occurred in 1870.*

Perhaps the greatest reason to doubt the accepted version of what happened to Powell's men is that it simply doesn't stand the test of common sense. Both Mormonee and Mericats were typically quick to avenge Indian depredations, yet nobody ever attempted to punish the Shivwits who'd allegedly killed Dunn and the Howlands—no real effort was even made to recover their valuable guns, scientific instruments, or papers from the Indians. This despite the fact that the telegram sent by an anonymous Saint on September 7, 1869, which first reported the murders, also stated that "two of the She-bits who killed the men are in the Washington Indian camp with two of the guns." The Washington Indian Camp was less than ten miles from St. George, but no Saints ever made the short trip up the hill to arrest the alleged perpetrators, or even to ask them where they had left the bodies of Powell's men.

Curiously, the telegram included no mention of who had composed it or from where it was sent; Larsen points out that it very well could have originated in Toquerville, where a telegraph office was situated in the same ward house in which the murders were alleged to have occurred. "It seems strange," he adds, "that after Apostle Snow received the telegram, none of the locals tried to bring the Indians to justice. I've

---

* In his fascinating book *Colorado River Controversies,* the surveyor, engineer, and amateur historian Robert Brewster Stanton (1844–1922) wrote,

> When I first became acquainted with Major Powell's Report giving his account of that first exploration, it was to me the most fascinating story I had ever read. Even after completing the railway survey and finding many of his descriptions of the conditions of the canyon and the river, to say the least, misleading, I found the narrative of the adventures of the party as beautiful and as fascinating as ever. . . . With all this in mind, however, I nevertheless experienced one of the greatest regrets of my life when I learned in later years . . . that a large part of the story credited to the exploration party of 1869 was taken from the experiences and notes of the expedition of 1871 and 1872.

When, in 1889, Stanton interviewed Jack Sumner, Sumner told Stanton "with a trace of bitterness in his voice . . . , 'There's lots in that book besides the truth,' and turned away."

never heard of Indians being left alone after committing a deed like that during this period of Utah's history."*

It also strains belief that three Shivwits would have been able to surprise and kill three seasoned, well-armed mountain men. The Shivwit tribe had no firearms of any kind; they were known to be a docile, dirt-poor band of "seed gatherers and bug eaters." Dunn and the Howland brothers, on the other hand, had two rifles and a shotgun and were ever alert to the possibility of an ambush after years of tangling with Indians. Before joining Powell's expedition, William Dunn had been wounded four times by Comanches, and as a consequence was especially wary of further attacks.

While the evidence may not be conclusive that the three men who disappeared from Powell's expedition were murdered by the inhabitants of Toquerville, credible evidence that Powell's men were shot full of arrows by Shivwits, as Hamblin reported, is in even shorter supply. It is thus hard to countenance scholars (and their numbers are legion) who blithely assert that Indians killed William Dunn, Oramel Howland, and Seneca Howland—especially given the Mormons' unfortunate (and thoroughly documented) history of framing Indians for crimes that were actually committed by Latter-day Saints.

As for the Shivwits, two decades after their parley with Powell and Hamblin, the Saints forced the Indians to leave their vast ancestral homeland on the Arizona Strip because the range was wanted for grazing Mormon cattle. The Mormons relocated the Shivwits onto a minuscule reservation on the outskirts of St. George, barely six miles across by six miles long.

In the years following the Mountain Meadows massacre, most of the culpable Saints fled to remote desert settlements in order to elude their Gentile pursuers—but not John D. Lee, who had become the wealthiest

---

* Three years earlier, for example, two settlers were killed by Paiutes near Pipe Spring; just eight days after this attack, a group of Mormons rode from St. George onto the Arizona Strip and executed seven Paiutes in retaliation—even though it turned out that none of the seven had been party to the murder of the settlers.

man in southern Utah during this period and was loath to abandon the comforts of his several homes and eighteen wives. In 1869, though, after President Ulysses S. Grant ramped up federal efforts to catch the guilty parties, Brigham Young grew quite concerned that Lee would be arrested, so he advised his adopted son to sell off his property and make himself scarce.

Lee, however, brushed the proposal aside and remained on his old stamping ground, preferring simply to hightail it into the local hills whenever federal agents or bounty hunters approached. During their little jaunt with John Wesley Powell in September 1870, Brigham finally ordered Lee to move far from Washington and Iron Counties and establish residency deep in the wilderness; Brigham feared that if Lee were caught, he might spill secrets that could bring down the entire church. According to Juanita Brooks's biography of Lee, during their 1870 excursion onto the Arizona Strip, the prophet told him, "Gather your wives and children around you, select some fertile valley, and settle out here."

Conveying a distinct lack of enthusiasm for this suggestion, Lee halfheartedly replied, "Well if it is your wish and counsel . . ."

"It *is* my wish and counsel," Brigham impatiently commanded. A month later, for good measure, he excommunicated Lee from the church, eventually exiling him to the upper end of the Grand Canyon to run a shuttle service across the Colorado River. Lee called this forlorn settlement Lonely Dell; today it's known as Lee's Ferry. In the wake of this turn of fortune, eleven of Lee's wives divorced him, and only two of his remaining spouses ever joined him at the desolate outpost that now bears his name.*

The fact that Lee and the massacre's other prime suspects had gone deep into hiding didn't deter authorities in Washington from their pursuit of justice; to the contrary, the feds only turned up the pressure, making it clear that they would not let the matter rest until the guilty were punished.

---

* These days, Lee's Ferry serves as the starting point for most float trips down the Grand Canyon. As a consequence, thousands of boaters now pass through John D. Lee's Lonely Dell each year, few of whom ever learn much about the man whose name is attached to the historic settlement.

In November 1874, a U.S. marshal named William Stokes cornered Lee in the settlement of Panguitch, where he was visiting one of his remaining wives. Stokes discovered the fugitive hiding in a chicken coop under a pile of straw, and arrested him. Lee was put on trial in Beaver, Utah, eight months later, but the jury deadlocked and failed to convict. To the American populace, this outcome was the nineteenth-century equivalent of the 1995 O. J. Simpson verdict. Newspapers from coast to coast expressed rabid outrage, generating a hurricane of anti-Mormon sentiment that did not escape the notice of Brigham and his counselors in Great Salt Lake City.

Conceding the inevitable, Brigham adopted a pragmatic new strategy that was as brilliant as it was callous. He stopped claiming that the Indians were responsible for the massacre and decided to blame the whole thing on Lee, offering up his adopted son as a scapegoat.

Lee was put on trial a second time in 1876. On this occasion the LDS First Presidency carefully screened the jurors, all Mormons, to ensure that Lee, and Lee alone, would be convicted. Jacob Hamblin, who had been far from the Mountain Meadow when the killing took place, proved to be the star witness for the prosecution; his convincing, if perjured, testimony of Lee's savagery sealed the latter's fate. "So carefully had the questions been placed," wrote Juanita Brooks, "so patient and delicate had the lawyers been with the witnesses, that the combined sins of all the fifty men who were present were laid on the shoulders of John D. Lee." On September 20, after considering the witnesses and evidence that Brigham had very selectively provided to the prosecution, Brigham's jury found Lee guilty of first-degree murder.

The court sentenced Lee to die, thereby satisfying Gentile America's demand for justice, or at least the appearance thereof. "Someone had to be sacrificed," one of the jurors admitted afterward, alluding to the passage from *The Book of Mormon* in which Nephi slays Laban (the same passage that had inspired Dan Lafferty to kill): "Better for one man to die than for a whole nation to dwindle in unbelief."

In prison, awaiting execution, Lee used the time remaining to him to pen his life story, which was published posthumously under the title *Mormonism Unveiled,* and became a national best-seller. At the conclusion of his book Lee wrote,

I was guided in all that I did which is called criminal, by the orders of the leaders in the Church of Jesus Christ of Latter-day Saints. I have never knowingly disobeyed the orders of the Church since I joined it at Far West, Missouri, until I was deserted by Brigham Young and his slaves.

On the morning of March 23, 1877, under the watchful eye of his guards, Lee stepped out of a carriage onto the sandy loam of the Mountain Meadow, the first time he had returned to the site of the massacre in twenty years. The condemned man completed his will, sat down on the coffin that would shortly hold his corpse, and listened to a marshal make a formal recitation of his death warrant. Then he stood and calmly addressed the crowd of some eighty people who had traveled to the meadow to watch him die. "A victim must be had, and I am the victim," Lee declared with a mix of resignation and accusation. "I have been sacrificed in a cowardly, dastardly manner."

After Lee finished speaking, the marshal tied a blindfold across his eyes, and Lee sat down again on the edge of the open coffin, imploring of the firing squad, "Let them shoot the balls through my heart! Don't let them mangle my body." A moment later, a deafening blast shattered the peace of the morning and four bullets tore into his chest. John D. Lee tipped back from the waist into the wooden box, his feet still planted on the meadow, as the rifles' report echoed from the surrounding hills.

TWENTY

UNDER THE BANNER OF HEAVEN

*Civil libertarians have consistently insisted on America's sacred duty
to make the country a place of unprecedented religious tolerance. Faced
however, with the realities of religious pluralism—multiplying sects
and excessive fervor for seemingly bizarre religious tenets—they have
reacted with something short of enthusiasm.*

R. LAURENCE MOORE,
RELIGIOUS OUTSIDERS AND THE MAKING OF AMERICANS

In his day, John D. Lee was renowned not only for his role in the Mountain Meadows massacre but also as a gifted healer and oracle. He cured many an ailing Mormon by the laying on of hands. Numerous Saints were awed by the accuracy of his prophecies—and never more so than on the occasion of his final prediction. According to a family memoir, shortly before Lee was executed he prophesied, "If I am guilty of the crime for which I am convicted, I will go down and out and never be heard of again. If I am not guilty, Brigham Young will die within one year! Yes, within six months."

On August 23, 1877, exactly five months after Lee's death, Brigham was overcome with fever, gastrointestinal cramps, diarrhea, and vomiting. Six days later "The Old Boss," as Lee called him, was dead, most likely from a ruptured appendix.

Brigham had hoped that offering up Lee for sacrifice would appease the Gentile powers in Washington and win the Saints at least a modicum of relief from the hounding of federal minions. He was sorely mistaken. From the time Rutherford B. Hayes moved into the Oval Office in 1877 through the end of Grover Cleveland's term in 1897, each successive American president increased pressure on the Mormon Church to forsake polygamy and submit to the laws of the land.

John Taylor, who replaced Brigham as the Saints' president, prophet, seer, and revelator, refused to cede an inch to the government in Washington; if anything, he was even less acquiescent than the Old Boss had been. Taylor had believed passionately in Joseph Smith and his doctrines ever since their first encounter, when Joseph had grasped Taylor's hand and caused "an electric current" to race up his arm. On that bleak afternoon when Joseph was shot dead in the Carthage jail, Taylor had been within arm's reach of the prophet, and had been gravely wounded himself. The truest of true believers, Taylor was not about to compromise the most sacred principles of the Kingdom of God to appease the church's Gentile oppressors.

"God will lay his hand upon this nation," Taylor proclaimed in 1879. "There will be more bloodshed, more ruin, more devastation than ever they have seen before. . . . We do not want them to force upon us that institution of monogamy called the social evil."

A year later Taylor's recalcitrance and rage had only intensified. "W[hen] they enact tyrannical laws, forbidding us the free exercise of our religion, we cannot submit," he pronounced, on January 4, 1880, during a Sunday assembly in Great Salt Lake City.

> God is greater than the United States, and when the Government conflicts with heaven we will be ranged under the banner of heaven and against the Government. The United States says we cannot marry more than one wife. God says different. . . . Polygamy is a divine institution. It has been handed down direct from God. The United States cannot abolish it. No nation on earth can prevent it, nor all the nations of the earth combined; these are my sentiments and all of you who sympathize with me in this position will raise your right hands. I defy the United States; I will obey God.

Every right hand in the vast Assembly Hall instantly shot heavenward. Taylor was a man of the highest integrity who had devoted his life completely to the church. Among the Saints, his words held enormous sway.

Back in Washington President Hayes thought little of Taylor's rhetoric. After paying a personal visit to Great Salt Lake City in 1880, Hayes urged Congress to enact laws ensuring that the "right to vote, hold office and sit on juries in the Territory of Utah be confined to those who neither practice nor uphold polygamy." Over the next fifteen years Congress obliged him by passing legislation that did exactly that, and more. After the Edmunds Act was passed in 1882, Mormons could be prosecuted not only for engaging in polygamy, which was difficult to prove, but also for "unlawful cohabitation," which wasn't.

Thereafter, Utah's polygamists were derogatorily referred to as "cohabs," and swarms of federal agents descended on Utah to carry out "cohab hunts" in virtually every town in the territory. By the late 1880s, some one thousand Saints had been thrown in jail, but still the Mormons remained defiant. Going to prison on a polygamy conviction became something to brag about.

Although they didn't reveal their concern to the brethren, Mormon leaders were nevertheless feeling the heat. John Taylor dispatched increasing numbers of Saints not only to far-flung desert settlements around the American West (such as Lee's Ferry) but also to Mexico and Canada in order to establish safe havens where a man could have a plurality of wives without fear of harassment or arrest. Thriving colonies of cohabs sprung up in such places as Cardston, Canada (in the province of Alberta, just north of the Montana border), and at the foot of the Sierra Madre Occidental in Mexico. Then, in 1885, a warrant went out for Taylor's arrest, forcing the prophet himself to go into hiding. One year after that, he thumbed his nose at the feds by marrying twenty-six-year-old Josephine Roueche, his sixteenth wife. The groom was seventy-eight years old at the time.

The harder the Saints resisted federal control, however, the more Washington resolved to bring them to heel. In March 1887, Congress passed the harshest legislation yet directed at the Mormons, the Edmunds-Tucker Bill. Four months later John Taylor died, still in hiding, and a day after he was laid to rest, federal lawyers initiated a series of legal actions intended to bankrupt the Mormon Church. On May 19, 1890, they achieved their desired end when the U.S. Supreme Court ruled on these actions against the Saints, allowing church holdings to be seized by the government.

The whole of Mormondom was wobbling on the brink. With the death of Taylor in 1887, an eighty-two-year-old apostle named Wilford Woodruff had been installed as the fourth Mormon prophet. And he recognized, with great pain, that the Kingdom of God had no choice but to surrender to Washington's demands. After taking to his bed on the evening of September 23, 1890, Woodruff reported, he "struggled all night with the Lord about what should be done with the existing circumstances of the church."

In the morning he called together five trusted Mormon leaders and, "with broken spirit," informed them that God had revealed to him the necessity of relinquishing "the practice of that principle for which the brethren had been willing to lay down their lives." To the shock and utter horror of the other men in the room, President Woodruff explained that "it was the will of the Lord" that the church stop sanctioning the doctrine of plural marriage.

On October 6, 1890, Woodruff's momentous revelation was formalized in a brief document that became known as "the Woodruff Manifesto," or simply "the Manifesto." It read, in part,

> Inasmuch as laws have been enacted by Congress forbidding plural marriages, which laws have been pronounced constitutional by the court of last resort, I hereby declare my intention to submit to those laws, and to use my influence with the members of the Church over which I preside to have them do likewise. . . .
>
> And I now publicly declare that my advice to the Latter-day Saints is to refrain from contracting any marriage forbidden by the law of the land.

WILFORD WOODRUFF
President of the Church of Jesus Christ of Latter-day Saints.

. . .

The impact of the Manifesto shook Mormondom to its roots, but it did not end polygamy—it merely drove it underground. For the next two decades members of the Mormon First Presidency privately advised Saints that polygamy should be continued, albeit discreetly, and top leaders of the church secretly performed numerous plural marriages. When this casuistry came to light, it unleashed a nationwide howl of indignation. In October 1910, the *Salt Lake Tribune*—which had been established as a rabidly anti-Mormon alternative to the church-owned *Deseret News*—published the names of some two hundred Saints who had taken plural wives after the Manifesto, including six members of the Quorum of the Twelve Apostles.

When the church leadership's deceit about polygamy was made public, it wasn't just Gentiles who were outraged—a number of prominent Mormons were upset as well, sparking a groundswell within the church to enforce the Manifesto and eradicate polygamy altogether. By the 1920s most Saints, including their leaders, had turned against polygamy and were encouraging the prosecution of cohabs.

A significant number of dedicated Saints, however, were convinced that Wilford Woodruff had been grievously mistaken when he'd issued the Manifesto, and that heeding it ran counter to the religion's most sacred principles. These hard-core polygamists argued that the Manifesto had not revoked Section 132 of *The Doctrine and Covenants,* Joseph Smith's 1843 revelation about plural marriage—that it merely suspended the practice under extenuating (and presumably temporary) circumstances. They pointed out that *D&C* 132 was still an accepted part of Mormon scripture (as, indeed, it remains today).

These Mormon Fundamentalists, as they would proudly call themselves, took special inspiration from a revelation dispensed by the Lord to their departed hero John Taylor on September 26, 1886, while he was hiding out from federal cohab hunters.* Perhaps the most contentious

---

* Dan Lafferty is among the modern fundamentalists who still draw inspiration from the third Mormon prophet. "I was favorably impressed with the integrity of John Taylor," Dan says, "and probably at times strengthened in my challenging moments by thinking about him."

revelation in the history of the Mormon Church, it had come in response to a question President Taylor had posed to God, inquiring if His earlier revelation to Joseph concerning the sacred doctrine of plural marriage should be abandoned. God's reply was clear and unambiguous:

> Thus saith the Lord All commandments that I give must be obeyed by those calling themselves by my name unless they are revoked by me or by my authority. . . . I have not revoked this law nor will I for it is everlasting and those who will enter into my glory must obey the conditions thereof, even so Amen.

At the time he received this revelation, Taylor had been hiding out in the home of a Saint named John W. Woolley. During the night, Woolley's son Lorin had noticed an eerie light "appearing under the door leading to President Taylor's room, and was at once startled to hear voices of men talking there. There were three distinct voices." At eight o'clock the next morning, when Taylor emerged from his room, Lorin recalled, "we could scarcely look at him on account of the brightness of his personage."

Young Woolley asked Taylor whom he had been talking to in the middle of the night. "I have had a very pleasant conversation all night with Brother Joseph," the prophet replied cheerfully, adding that the third voice Lorin had heard was that of Jesus Christ himself.

Taylor immediately called a meeting of trusted brethren to discuss his revelation. In addition to Taylor, John W. Woolley, and Lorin C. Woolley, ten others were in attendance, including Samuel Bateman and his son Daniel R. Bateman.* After sharing what God had revealed to him, Taylor placed all present "under convenant that he or she would defend the principle of Celestial or Plural Marriage, and that they would consecrate their lives, liberty, and property to this end, and that they personally would sustain and uphold the principle."

The Mormon prophet warned the twelve wide-eyed Saints who sat before him, "Some of you will be handled and ostracized and cast out

---

* Samuel and Daniel Bateman were DeLoy Bateman's great-great-grandfather and great-grandfather, respectively.

from the Church by your brethren because of your faithfulness and integrity to this principle, and some of you may have to surrender your lives because the same, but woe, woe, unto those who shall bring these troubles upon you." Then Taylor called together five of the assembled Saints, including Samuel Bateman, John W. Woolley, and Lorin C. Woolley, and granted them authority not only to perform celestial marriages but to ordain others to do the same, thereby seeing to it "that no year passed by without children being born in the principle of Plural Marriage."

This historic meeting (the authenticity of which has been angrily disputed by LDS General Authorities ever since) lasted eight hours. As it was winding down, Taylor prophesied that "in the time of the seventh president of this Church, the Church would go into bondage both temporally and spiritually, and in that day the One Mighty and Strong spoken of in the 85th Section of *The Doctrine and Covenants* would come."

And thus were the seeds of Mormon Fundamentalism sown. Four years later, when the LDS Church voted to sustain the Manifesto and end polygamy, Mormon society began to take its first tentative steps toward joining the American mainstream—slowly and ambivalently at first, and then with stunning determination. But the fundamentalists refused to have any part of it. They remained dedicated to the doctrines of Joseph Smith—to his doctrine of plural marriage, in particular. They vowed to uphold John Taylor's covenant with ferocious resolve, regardless of the course taken by the rest of Mormondom or the rest of the world. Today, that same vow has been taken up by the fundamentalists' twenty-first-century brethren, and their fervor is no less resolute.

To Mormon Fundamentalists—to the likes of Dan Lafferty, and the inhabitants of Colorado City, and Brian David Mitchell (the abductor of Elizabeth Smart)—September 27, 1886, is a sacred date. From that moment forward, faithful polygamists have been eagerly anticipating the arrival of the "one mighty and strong," who will, as Joseph prophesied, "set in order the house of God."

PART IV

Both revelation and delusion are attempts at the solution of problems. Artists and scientists realize that no solution is ever final, but that each new creative step points the way to the next artistic or scientific problem. In contrast, those who embrace religious revelations and delusional systems tend to see them as unshakeable and permanent. . . .

Religious faith is an answer to the problem of life. . . . The majority of mankind want or need some all-embracing belief system which purports to provide an answer to life's mysteries, and are not necessarily dismayed by the discovery that their belief system, which they proclaim as "the truth," is incompatible with the beliefs of other people. One man's faith is another man's delusion. . . .

Whether a belief is considered to be a delusion or not depends partly upon the intensity with which it is defended, and partly upon the numbers of people subscribing to it.*

ANTHONY STORR,
FEET OF CLAY

* Reprinted with the permission of The Free Press, a division of Simon & Schuster Adult Publishing Group, from *Feet of Clay: Saints, Sinners, and Madmen: A Study of Gurus* by Anthony Storr. Copyright © 1996 by Anthony Storr.

TWENTY-ONE

EVANGELINE

My mother was born into a world of early twentieth-century Mormon Utah—a place that, in many respects, was dramatically different from the America that surrounded it. The Mormons had long possessed a strong and spectacular sense of otherness and unity: They saw themselves not only as God's modern chosen people, but also as a people whose faith and identity had been forged by a long and bloody history, and by outright banishment. They were a people apart—a people with its own myths and purposes, and with a history of astonishing violence.

MIKAL GILMORE,
SHOT IN THE HEART

For more than fifteen years—ever since Rulon Jeffs became leader of the Fundamentalist Church of Jesus Christ of Latter Day Saints—the inhabitants of Colorado City were sustained by their conviction that he was the "one mighty and strong," the Lord's anointed emissary on earth, a prophet whom God had granted eternal life. But Uncle Rulon had been gravely ill for a long time, and on September 8, 2002, his heart stopped beating and a physician pronounced him dead. That was four days ago; now, as the reality of their leader's death has begun to sink in, the town's residents are desperately trying to reconcile their faith in his immortality with the inescapable fact that he is deceased. Today, on a warm and cloudless Thursday afternoon, more than five thousand people—mostly devout fundamentalists, but a few Gentiles and mainline Mormons as well—have assembled in Colorado City from as far away as Canada and Mexico to pay their respects and bury Uncle Rulon.

The men and boys somberly filing out of the funeral service that has just concluded in the LeRoy Johnson Meeting House are dressed in their Sunday best. The women and girls wear ankle-length dresses in pastel shades of pink, lavender, and blue that could be straight out of the nineteenth century; their hair, pulled back into long, chaste braids, first rises from their foreheads in fabulous crests, painstakingly arranged, that bring to mind breaking surf. Above the grieving throngs, the cliffs of Canaan Mountain glow in the angled sunlight, profiled against a blue autumn sky.

Uncle Rulon, who was three months shy of his ninety-third birthday when he passed on, left behind an estimated seventy-five bereft wives and at least sixty-five children. There is much uncertainty about how the next of kin and the rest of his followers will cope in his absence. An air of vague anxiety hangs over the community.

The same kind of apprehension gripped Colorado City in 1986, when the prophet who preceded Uncle Rulon—LeRoy Johnson, the much adored Uncle Roy—perished at the age of ninety-eight. Uncle Roy was also supposed to live forever. After his death, Uncle Rulon assumed leadership of the sect, but his right to claim Uncle Roy's mantle was furiously contested by those loyal to a prominent bishop named Marion Hammon. Hammon's followers, amounting to nearly a third of the community, left the fold en masse, moved onto a swath of desert just across the highway, and founded their own fundamentalist church—which became known as the Second Ward (the original church was called the First Ward). Each congregation accused the other of being godless apostates and issued impassioned warnings about the eternal damnation that would surely be the other's fate. Which is pretty much how things still stand today.

Now, following Uncle Rulon's demise, the First Ward is threatened by further rifts, even though forty-six-year-old Warren Jeffs—the second son of Rulon's fourth wife—moved swiftly to take the reins of the church. Because his father had been seriously ailing for several years, Warren had already been running things, and had long functioned as prophet in everything but name. But Warren—a tall, bony man with a bulging Adam's apple, a high-pitched voice, and a frightening sense of his own perfection in the eyes of God—has never received anything remotely close to the kind of affection lavished on Uncle Rulon or Uncle Roy by the people of Colorado City and Bountiful, British Columbia. Almost nobody in either town refers to Warren Jeffs as "Uncle Warren."

"My father, and especially Uncle Roy, were warm, loving prophets who taught polygamy for the right reasons," says one of the new prophet's older siblings. "Warren has no love for the people. His method for controlling them is to inspire fear and dread. My brother preaches that you must be perfect in your obedience. You must have the spirit twenty-four hours a day, seven days a week, or you'll be cut off and go to hell. Warren's a fanatic. Everything is black and white to him."

A great many First Warders had hoped that an admired, ninety-five-year-old patriarch named Fred Jessop—known as Uncle Fred—would succeed Uncle Rulon. When Warren was ordained as prophet instead, there was considerable speculation that Uncle Fred's followers would be sufficiently disenchanted to secede from the First Ward and form yet another sect of their own. But the brother of Warren quoted above speculates that this faction may bide their time for a while before deciding to make the break, because they don't think Warren is going to be sitting in the prophet's chair for long: "They're holding on. They believe that it's just a matter of time before God takes this evil man from their midst, leaving the First Ward intact, with one of their own in power. And I agree with them. I think Warren's going to get his comeuppance. I don't know how it's going to happen, or when, but I think he's going to suffer an untimely death. I feel this in my bones."

In the meantime, Warren is still very much in the company of the living, and he has been taking steps to consolidate his power. Up in Bountiful, British Columbia, he has stripped Winston Blackmore (whom he has long resented and distrusted) of his leadership position and has threatened to banish him from the religion altogether. Warren installed a compliant man named Jimmy Oler (the half brother of

Debbie Palmer, the woman who burned her house down to escape Bountiful) as the new bishop of the Canadian branch of the church, but at least half of the Bountiful community has remained loyal to Blackmore. Should he decide to establish an independent sect of his own, many Canadian fundamentalists would probably sever their ties with Warren's church in Colorado City to follow Blackmore.

But schisms of this sort are hardly a new phenomenon. A look backward at the history of Mormon Fundamentalism shows that its adherents have been splintering into rival sects ever since the first group of die-hard polygamists themselves broke away from the main Mormon Church a century ago.

The polygamous roots of Colorado City, née Short Creek, lead back to John D. Lee and the forlorn outpost where he was exiled by Brigham Young after the Mountain Meadows massacre. Lee's Ferry is situated at a sweeping bend in the Colorado River, immediately below the lowermost rapids of Glen Canyon, and just upstream from where the turbulent river surges into the depths of the Grand Canyon. In the nineteenth century, because it was the only place for many miles where the torrent could be crossed, this bit of desert was of great strategic importance to the Kingdom of Deseret. Saints traveling between Utah and Mormon colonies in Arizona and Mexico—as well as the occasional Gentile prospector—relied on Lee to shuttle them across the river in his small wooden scow. Prior to his arrest and subsequent execution, operating this ferry service provided Lee with a meager living.

When Lee was captured and jailed in 1874, the LDS Church recruited a Saint named Warren M. Johnson to resettle with his two wives and children on the north bank of the Colorado River in order to help Lee's wife, Emma, maintain the crucial crossing. On June 12, 1888, one of Johnson's wives gave birth to a boy at Lee's Ferry. The baby was christened LeRoy Sunderland Johnson, but in later years, after he had risen to become prophet of the fundamentalist church, everyone would call him Uncle Roy.

After the Manifesto, the remoteness of Lee's Ferry was considered especially attractive to polygamists, and it became a haven for cohabs, as did another isolated settlement on the Arizona Strip, Short Creek, founded in 1911. By the early decades of the twentieth century, tight bonds had been established between the polygamous inhabitants of Short Creek and Lee's Ferry, a group that included Warren Johnson and his descendents. In 1928, when improved access brought swelling ranks of outsiders through Lee's Ferry, some of the Johnson clan, including LeRoy, pulled up stakes and moved to Short Creek, which remained farther off the beaten track and was thus less likely to draw the attention of cohab hunters.

By the mid-1930s, the fundamentalist movement was being led by a staunch polygamist named John Y. Barlow. Although he lived in northern Utah, when Barlow heard that Short Creek had become a magnet for families devoted to the Work, he cultivated a close relationship with the community as a whole, and LeRoy Johnson in particular. In 1940 Barlow transplanted some of his own families to Short Creek, and later one of his daughters was married to Johnson. DeLoy Bateman happens to be John Y. Barlow's grandson. Another of Barlow's descendents, Dan Barlow, is today the mayor of Colorado City.

In the homes of the present-day residents of Colorado City and Bountiful, it is common to see the portraits of eight ecclesiastical leaders hanging on the walls. Usually arranged in a large, handsomely framed montage, the portraits depict the preeminent stars in the constellation of Mormon Fundamentalism: Joseph Smith, Brigham Young, John Taylor, John W. Woolley, Lorin C. Woolley, John Y. Barlow, LeRoy Johnson, and Rulon Jeffs. Fundamentalists believe the so-called keys to priesthood authority—the divinely ordained power to lead the righteous—have been given to each of these prophets in turn, starting with Joseph and proceeding through Uncle Rulon (and now, with Rulon's death, to Warren Jeffs). This, at any rate, is how the folks in Colorado City and Bountiful view things. Other fundamentalist communities, however, glorify a slightly different pantheon of prophets.

After John Y. Barlow died, in 1949, the fundamentalist leadership was transferred to a respected acolyte named Joseph Musser, who was immediately stricken by a series of crippling strokes, creating the first major schism in the movement. When he became debilitated, Musser was treated by a folksy, gregarious naturopath and fellow polygamist named Rulon Allred, on whom he became utterly dependent. In 1951 Musser, now gravely ill, appointed Allred his "second elder"—his heir apparent—over the strenuous objections of those who believed LeRoy Johnson should succeed Musser as prophet, as John Y. Barlow had specified before his death.

The hatred between Uncle Roy's supporters and the Allred camp was so strong that the fundamentalist movement split into two rival sects. Following Musser's death in 1954, Uncle Roy assumed leadership of the larger splinter group, which remained in Short Creek and called itself the Fundamentalist Church of Jesus Christ of Latter Day Saints, or simply the United Effort Plan (UEP). Allred became prophet of the other splinter, called the Apostolic United Brethren, which was based 280 miles to the north in the Salt Lake Valley.*

After the split, the Short Creekers had little further involvement with their counterparts in the Allred group. Taking care to fly below the radar of the Gentile culture, Uncle Roy and his followers were seldom noticed by the world beyond Short Creek. The Apostolic United Brethren wasn't so fortunate. On the afternoon of May 10, 1977, Rulon Allred was treating patients in his office in Murray, a suburb of Salt Lake City, when two young women walked in, shot him dead, and calmly walked out.

Allred's killers turned out to be members of another breakaway fundamentalist sect known as the LeBaron clan. Founded by a man named Dayer LeBaron, who hailed from one of the Mormon colonies in Mexico, the sect had once maintained a loose association with Allred's group. After Rulon Allred was convicted of polygamy in Utah in 1947 and jumped parole, the LeBarons even gave him refuge in Mexico for a period.

---

* Rulon Allred's polygamist father, Byron C. Allred, was an eminent Mormon who had been Speaker of the Idaho House of Representatives before, in flight from the cohab hunters, relocating to Mexico, where Rulon was born in 1906. Alex Joseph and John Bryant—leaders of independent polygamist communities whom Dan and Ron Lafferty visited in the summer of 1984, shortly before they murdered Brenda and Erica Lafferty—were introduced to Mormon Fundamentalism by Rulon Allred. Both Joseph and Bryant, in fact, were devoted followers of Allred before breaking with him and going out on their own.

Dayer LeBaron had seven sons. Three of the seven LeBaron brothers would eventually claim, at one time or another, to be the "one mighty and strong"; each regarded himself as a divinely ordained prophet comparable to Moses who would return the Mormon Church to the righteous path it had abandoned after the 1890 Manifesto.

The oldest of the brothers, Benjamin, was fond of roaring at the top of his lungs in public to prove that he was "the Lion of Israel." In one legendary incident that occurred in the early 1950s, he lay facedown in the middle of a busy Salt Lake City intersection, bringing traffic to a halt, and did two hundred push-ups. When the police finally persuaded him to get up off the pavement he proudly insisted, "Nobody else can do that many. That proves I'm the One Mighty and Strong." Not long thereafter, Ben was committed to the Utah State Mental Hospital.

In the 1960s, with Ben locked up in a psychiatric institution, two of the other LeBaron brothers emerged as the group's guiding lights: soft-spoken, amiable Joel and tightly wound Ervil, who weighed 240 pounds, stood six feet four inches tall, and knew how to nurse a grudge. A dashing figure, he was found irresistibly attractive by many otherwise sensible women. Another LeBaron sibling, Alma, reported that Ervil "used to dream about having twenty-five or thirty wives so he could multiply and replenish the earth. . . . He wanted to be like Brigham Young, a great man."

Ervil also fancied himself a brilliant writer and scriptorian. According to Rena Chynoweth—who would become his thirteenth wife in 1975 and, two years later, pull the trigger of the gun that killed Rulon Allred*—Ervil would write scripture obsessively, in marathon sessions that might last for a week or more. "He would go for days without shaving or bathing, putting in twenty hours a day," she recalled, sustaining himself "on continuous cups of coffee. When he sweated, that was all you could smell coming out of his pores—coffee."

---

* Chynoweth went to great lengths to conceal her involvement in Allred's murder. Although she was charged with the crime in 1978, she lied under oath at trial and thereby beat the rap. Twelve years later she wrote a breezy, tell-all memoir about the LeBarons titled *The Blood Covenant* (the source of these quotes), in which she revealed her culpability. When the book was published in 1990, Allred's survivors filed a civil action against Chynoweth and won a $52 million wrongful-death judgment against her.

Both Ervil and Joel were imbued with exceptional charisma—and both claimed to be the "one mighty and strong." It was therefore inevitable, perhaps, that the LeBaron brothers would eventually clash.

The terminal rupture began in November 1969, when Joel, the elder brother and nominal presiding prophet, booted Ervil out of the sect for insubordination. Soon thereafter Ervil had a revelation in which God explained that Joel—by all accounts an uncommonly benevolent man, routinely described by his followers as "saintlike"—had become an obstacle to His work and needed to be removed. On August 20, 1972, in the polygamist settlement of Los Molinos, which Joel had established eight years earlier on the Baja Peninsula, he was shot in the throat and head, fatally, by a member of the group loyal to Ervil.*

After he ordered the death of Joel, Ervil initiated a divinely inspired series of murders, resulting in the killing of at least five additional people through 1975 and the wounding of more than fifteen others. In March 1976 he was arrested for these crimes and held in a Mexican jail, but Ervil's followers on the outside continued to do his bidding. Operating out of a post office box in southern California, they distributed pamphlets denouncing taxes, welfare, gun control, and rival polygamists. When Jimmy Carter ran for president in 1976, Ervil's subordinates even issued a decree threatening the candidate with death for his liberal views.

Less than a year after he was incarcerated, Ervil was let out of jail. The official explanation was a "lack of evidence," although everyone assumed that well-placed bribes had more to do with it. Within a few months of his release, he had a disobedient daughter killed, and shortly after that arranged the murder of Rulon Allred, whose followers Ervil coveted and hoped to convert to his own group, the Church of the Lamb of God.

Ervil managed to remain a free man until 1979, when he was finally arrested in Mexico. He was extradited to the United States, convicted, and sentenced to life behind bars in the Utah State Prison at Point of the

---

* Los Molinos was also where, in 1986, thirteen-year-old Linda Kunz married thirty-seven-year-old Tom Green, the Utah polygamist convicted in 2001 after boasting of his polygamous lifestyle on *Dateline NBC*.

Mountain, in the same maximum-security facility where Dan Lafferty now resides. By 1981, as he began to understand that his prospects for ever getting out of the penitentiary were nil, Ervil became increasingly frantic and irrational. According to Rena Chynoweth, he "began having revelations of a miracle that would free him. He envisioned God's wrath striking down the prison walls like the walls of ancient Jericho, because the pagan temporal authorities dared to incarcerate God's Chosen Prophet and Revelator."

In August 1981, Ervil LeBaron was discovered dead in his cell at the age of fifty-six, felled by an apparent heart attack. Before succumbing, however, he had written a rambling four-hundred-page screed, oozing venom from every line, titled *The Book of the New Covenants.* The text was primarily a list of all those individuals who, in Ervil's view, had ever been disloyal to him and thus deserved to die. This catalog of hatred was accompanied by scathing, semicoherent descriptions of the precise nature of each betrayal. Essentially, the book was an overwrought hit list. Some twenty copies were published, most of which wound up in the possession of Ervil's most devoted followers.

These fervent Lambs of God, as they called themselves, were largely drawn from among Ervil's fifty-four children—progeny who remained fanatically devoted to their father long after his death. Led by a son named Aaron LeBaron who was just thirteen when Ervil died, this gang of boys, girls, and young adults—most of whom had been physically and/or sexually abused by older members of the sect and then abandoned—resolved to avenge Ervil's death by systematically spilling the blood of the persons listed in *The Book of the New Covenants.* A prosecutor assigned to the case referred to this pack of parentless kids as the LeBaron clan's "Lord of the Flies generation."

Two men on the hit list were assassinated in 1987. Then, on June 27, 1988—the 144th anniversary of Joseph Smith's martyrdom—three more people on the list, along with the eight-year-old daughter of one of them, were ambushed and gunned down. These latter four murders, which occurred within five minutes of one another at different sites in Texas three hundred miles apart, were carefully planned to occur at almost the exact hour that Joseph was fatally shot in the Carthage jail.

Afterward, the Lambs of God bragged that they were responsible for the deaths of seventeen people all told. Because each of their victims had been killed as an act of blood atonement, the Lambs explained, the exterminations were justified in the eyes of the Lord.

In 1993, two of Ervil's sons and one of his daughters were sentenced to life in prison for their involvement in some of these crimes. Two years after that, Aaron LeBaron, the mastermind of the gang, was captured in Mexico, extradited to Utah, and in 1997 sentenced to forty-five years in prison. The whereabouts of several other LeBaron offspring, who played lesser roles in the murders, remain unknown.

The Mormon presence in Mexico, which remains strong even today, goes back to 1886, when a group of polygamous Saints purchased fifty thousand acres along the Rio Piedras Verdes, about 150 miles southwest of El Paso, Texas, to escape the cohab hunts then sweeping Utah. By the time the first of the LeBarons moved south of the border in 1902, thirty-five hundred Mormons were already residing in the vicinity of this settlement at the foot of the Sierra Madre Occidental, which was called Colonia Juárez.

In 1944, Dayer LeBaron—father to Joel and Ervil—received a revelation in which God commanded him to buy a piece of mesquite-covered desert about thirty-five miles outside of Colonia Juárez. He cleared the land, planted a crop of beans, and christened the place Colonia LeBaron. It was soon the base of operations for Dayer's expanding fundamentalist sect.

A cute teenager named Lavina Stubbs moved to Colonia LeBaron in 1958 after spending the first fifteen years of her life in Short Creek. The Stubbs family name was (and still is) one of the most prestigious pedigrees in Short Creek/Colorado City, but Lavina's father had a falling out with Uncle Roy, converted to the LeBaron group, and moved his brood to Mexico. A year later, at the tender age of sixteen, having caught the eye of Prophet Joel LeBaron, Lavina became one of his plural wives.

"I was married to Joel for fourteen joyful years," Lavina says. "He was an absolutely righteous man, one of the greatest men that ever lived." Before moving away from Short Creek, Lavina's mother had wanted her to marry DeLoy Bateman's father, but the prophet commanded her to become the plural wife of someone else, whom she despised. "I was almost forced to marry a man there who I couldn't stand," she recalls. "I got out by the skin of my teeth. It was a miracle that my father took us away when he did, and God allowed me to marry Joel instead."

In 1972, however, Joel was shot dead on Ervil's orders, and Lavina's life entered an extended rough stretch, from which it has yet to emerge. The worst of her heartache she attributes to Kenyon Blackmore—first cousin of Winston Blackmore, the erstwhile leader of the polygamist community in Bountiful, British Columbia. In 1983, Kenyon Blackmore married Joel and Lavina LeBaron's twenty-two-year-old daughter, Gwendolyn. The marriage not only brought out the worst in both partners, but it has injected misery into the life of almost every person it has touched.

Among these unlucky souls is a Canadian woman named Annie Vandeveer Blackmore. When Kenyon Blackmore wed young Gwendolyn LeBaron, he was already married to Annie. At that point, in fact, Annie had been married to Kenyon for twenty-four years—yet he neglected to tell her that he had taken a second wife.

"See that picture on the wall?" Annie asks with a sour smile, pointing to a framed cover of the September 29, 1956, issue of Canada's *Weekend Magazine* depicting a pair of beautiful seventeen-year-old cowgirls astride equally magnificent horses. "That was how I met Ken." The two cowgirls are Annie and her twin sister, photographed on their family's ranch outside Winnipeg, Manitoba. Upon seeing this magazine cover, twenty-year-old Kenyon Blackmore—an avid horseman from a family of renowned polygamists in western Canada—resolved on the spot to marry at least one of the lovely twins.

"When he come across this article," Annie says, "he started to write us letters and became my pen pal. He was about to go on a mission to South Africa, but he wrote to me the whole time he was gone, and when he got home two years later he took a trip out to Winnipeg to see us. Six months later, in December 1959, Ken and me were married." Exactly nine months after that, Annie gave birth to a baby girl, Lena, the first of seven children she would have with Kenyon, and they moved to Provo so he could attend Brigham Young University.

In 1966, Kenyon took a teaching job in Bountiful. And there, as Annie phrases it, "he started pushing for marrying plural wives. Before we'd gotten married he'd told me about his polygamist relatives, but it didn't mean anything to me at the time. I'd only converted to Mormonism after meeting Ken. I didn't know much about polygamy or anything. I was just a farmer's daughter, a country girl from Manitoba."

Annie tried to approach the idea with an open mind. "I was raised to be a peacemaker," she says. "My whole life I tried to please him, to do whatever he wanted. But I just couldn't accept plural marriage." Annie's refusal to consent to polygamy didn't deter Kenyon, however. Openly and aggressively, he began to pursue a particularly alluring girl coveted by many men in Bountiful: Alaire, the adopted daughter of Kenyon's uncle Ray Blackmore, who was the community's presiding bishop. Kenyon's amorous advances, which had not been sanctioned by either the bishop in Bountiful or the prophet in Colorado City, enraged Ray, who ordered his sons to chase Kenyon out of town—after which Alaire was married to Ray, her own father.*

For the next decade and a half Kenyon shuffled his growing family around western North America, scraping by as a ranch hand, a leather worker, and a carpenter, never settling in any one place for more than a year or two. Annie gradually began to understand, she says, that "the kids and I didn't mean that much to him. Ken did whatever he wanted, with whoever he wanted, whenever he wanted. He'd go away for weeks at a time, wouldn't ever call, wouldn't tell me where he was."

Annie and Kenyon's oldest child, Lena, who is now forty-two, confirms that he was a bad father. "Dad is a mean son of a bitch," she says bluntly, "although it took me until I was in my thirties to really see who he was. He's a mean, mean man who doesn't care about anybody but himself." Kenyon was physically abusive to all his children, but he was

---

* Four years after Ray Blackmore married his adopted daughter Alaire, he took Debbie Palmer (the woman who burned down her own house in Bountiful) as yet another plural wife.

especially vicious to Lena. When she was eleven, he grabbed a heavy tractor fan belt and gave her a particularly brutal whipping, "for no reason at all that I could tell," Lena remembers. "We were living in Las Cruces [New Mexico]. I still have the scars on the backs of my legs."

In the early 1980s, Kenyon's fortunes seemed to take an upward turn. He moved his family to the pious community of Salem, in Utah County, where he entered into a business partnership with an affable Mormon named Bernard Brady. Kenyon converted Brady to fundamentalism, the two men began selling shares in tax-sheltered financial trusts, and as a side venture they invested in the legendary Dream Mine, which dominated the mountainside above Salem. Soon millions of dollars were flowing into the Blackmore-Brady business account. Each man bought a lavish home below the Dream Mine. Life was good.

During this period, Kenyon would make frequent sales trips, roaming across western North America in search of investors. In 1983, during one of these trips, he went to Mexico and secretly married Gwendolyn Stubbs LeBaron, the winsome daughter of Lavina Stubbs and the late Joel LeBaron.

Around this time, as well, Kenyon introduced Bernard Brady to a longtime friend of his from Canada, the Prophet Onias, whom Kenyon had first met when he was working as a schoolteacher in Bountiful seventeen years earlier. Onias, who had just moved to Utah County in order to build his City of Refuge below the Dream Mine, was in the process of launching his School of the Prophets, and he invited Brady to join. Flattered and grateful, Brady returned the favor by recruiting into the school five brothers from an "outstanding" Utah County family: Tim, Watson, Mark, Dan, and Ron Lafferty. Not long thereafter, Kenyon's brief fling with good fortune came to a screeching halt.

Brenda and Erica Lafferty were murdered in American Fork on July 24, 1984, and right away the police considered Kenyon Blackmore and Bernard Brady to be prime suspects, along with everyone else even remotely associated with the School of the Prophets. But law enforcement officers had actually become well acquainted with Brady and Blackmore long before the Lafferty murders: in 1983, a federal grand jury had in-dicted Blackmore, Brady, and nineteen other partners on multiple counts of fraud, charging them with bilking more than $32 million from thirty-eight hundred investors—a swindle described as a "classic Ponzi scheme" by the United States Attorney who prosecuted the case.*

Among those who got burned in the scam was Blackmore's new mother-in-law, Lavina Stubbs LeBaron—Gwendolyn's mom. "Heaven sakes alive," Lavina recalls, "I lost a lot of money in Kenyon's stupid money program. I sold my house and everything else, and gave all the money to him. Every cent of it disappeared." Astonishingly, she doesn't blame Kenyon Blackmore for leaving her penniless. According to Lavina, he "meant well. He was trying to benefit all of us, but then the investments just turned bad or something. I wasn't mad at Ken, not for that. Not until he took my daughter and all my grandkids to Central America and did all those horrible things to them."

Kenyon's partner in crime, Bernard Brady, was arrested, tried, and eventually sent to federal prison for six years. But when Blackmore learned of the indictments, he opted to go into hiding instead of surren-dering to the police. He ran straight to Mexico, where Gwendolyn and Lavina were waiting to shelter him in Colonia LeBaron.

At this point Annie Blackmore, Kenyon's first wife, still knew noth-ing of Gwendolyn, the second wife. "God had commanded Ken not to tell me about her," Annie says bitterly. "The only reason I found out he had married her is because I went down to Mexico to try and talk him into coming back to Utah." It proved to be an exceedingly humiliating

---

* Utah has been called the "fraud capital of the world" by the *Wall Street Journal,* and within the state, no place has more white-collar crime than Utah County. According to FBI agent Jim Malpede, at any given moment the FBI is investigating scams totaling $50 million to $100 million perpetrated by con artists, like Kenyon Blackmore, based in the county. The uncommonly high incidence of fraud is a direct consequence of the uncommonly high per-centage of Utah County residents who are Mormons. When Saints are invited to invest in dubious schemes by other Saints, they tend to be overly trusting. Michael Hines, director of enforcement for the Utah Securities Division, told the *Deseret News* that in Utah County it is common for scammers to ensnare their victims by asking them to evaluate the proposed in-vestment through prayer. "People need to realize," Hines warned, "that God is not a good investment adviser."

experience for Annie. Not only did she discover that Kenyon had a new wife who was the same age as their oldest daughter, but this young woman had just given birth to a baby daughter of her own with Kenyon. Delivered in Colonia LeBaron exactly three days before Dan Lafferty cut the throats of Brenda and Erica Lafferty, the little girl had been named Evangeline.

After failing to persuade Kenyon to return to Utah with her, Annie went home alone, in utter shock. But she couldn't let herself give up on him. "I was committed to the marriage," she says. "I didn't want to be a quitter." So in January 1985 she went back to Mexico and again asked Kenyon to come home. And this time he agreed.

As soon as he crossed the border into El Paso, Texas, however, Kenyon was surrounded by FBI agents and placed in handcuffs. A brother-in-law—one of the investors who had been swindled by Kenyon—had tipped them off. Seeing no alternative, following his arrest Kenyon entered into a plea bargain with the government and was incarcerated in a federal lockup in Tallahassee, Florida.

After his release from prison in late 1991, Kenyon Blackmore returned to the town where he was born—Cardston, Alberta. Annie had given up on him by this point and filed for divorce, but Kenyon made an effort to reunite with their oldest daughter, Lena, in Cardston, the hub of Canadian Mormondom. Although Lena tried to give her father the benefit of the doubt, she wasn't comfortable around Gwendolyn, the wife who had supplanted her mother, or the two children Gwendolyn had had with Kenyon by this point. "It was disturbing to see how my dad and her were raising those kids," Lena says. "They had them on some extremely weird natural diet. And Ken wouldn't let them use soap, or brush their teeth. The kids looked malnourished and smelled bad. My dad and his wife did too. They just stunk. It was disgusting."

Lena might have been able to put up with all that, but then her father stole her vehicle. "I had this nice new truck," she says, "and I was having some financial difficulties. So Dad said he'd make the payments for me and pay the insurance if he could use it for a little while." After driving off in Lena's truck, however, Kenyon didn't bother to make any of the promised payments, which she discovered only when the bank threatened to repossess it. Furious, she called the Royal Canadian Mounted Police, who in turn alerted Kenyon's probation officer, and a warrant was issued for his arrest. "Ken discovered he'd bit into the wrong bone this time," Lena says. Upon learning he was wanted by the law again, Kenyon fled south with Gwendolyn and their kids to his old hideaway, Colonia LeBaron.

Back in Mexico, Kenyon married a third wife, who happened to be Gwendolyn's half sister. He departed Colonia LeBaron soon thereafter with both wives and all their children, and lit out across Central America. Over the years that followed he had four more children with each wife. He supported all these dependents, after a fashion, by doing odd jobs, selling natural foods, working as a massage therapist, and running petty scams. "He got money lots of different ways," says Evangeline Blackmore, the oldest of the kids Ken had with Gwendolyn. Now a tall, blond, exotic-looking eighteen-year-old who speaks English with a trace of a Mexican accent, Evangeline explains that Kenyon "would buy and sell gold once in a while. When we were in Mexico he made saddles and other leather goods for Mexican cowboys. But mostly he would con people. My dad is a very good con artist."

Kenyon Blackmore had always subscribed to weird religious views, but they became notably more extreme after his release from prison, when he disappeared into the shadows of Central America with his two LeBaron wives. "The LeBarons seemed to encourage Dad's strange beliefs," says Lena. "They were convinced he possessed God-like qualities. They would feed his fantasy, and he would feed theirs."

As he dragged his young wives and their pack of semiferal children back and forth across Central America, Kenyon received a series of revelations in which God told him that he was "the last prophet before the return of Jesus Christ." God told him, in fact, that Jesus would come back to earth in the form of a child born of Kenyon's pure seed and his daughter's virgin womb. Heeding the Lord's commandment, in June 1996, on Evangeline's twelfth birthday, he took her as his wife—that is to say, he began raping her on a regular basis. According to Evangeline, her father believed that he should start having sexual intercourse with her when she turned twelve "because this is when Mary, the first mother of Jesus, was impregnated." Kenyon was convinced, she says, that "nobody else's blood was good enough" to sire the Son of Man.

When Kenyon forced himself on Evangeline, she remembers him telling her that "I was going to hell because I wasn't being submissive." As she continued to resist, "he would throw me on the ground, punch me, and cover my mouth when I would try and scream." Eventually, to keep from being beaten, she started yielding passively to her sixty-year-old father's incestuous assaults.

"I was barely twelve years old," Evangeline states with astounding composure. "I didn't know what was happening to me, but I knew I didn't like it. I felt gross. My father wouldn't allow me to have friends, or even talk to anybody."

During Evangeline's ordeal at her father's hands, Blackmore often fasted, and would force his family to fast along with him. "He was always going on liquid diets of pure orange juice, or lemon water," says Evangeline. He came to believe that "if he makes his body pure enough, that he can move mountains, and walk through walls." He also believed that almost everyone in the world except himself had been corrupted and was evil. Evangeline recalls Blackmore talking "about finding some innocent naive Indian tribe and converting them to his beliefs," then systematically improving their blood by impregnating their women "with his own pure seed."

After being raped by her father for the better part of a year, Evangeline became pregnant, but she miscarried the baby two months later. In April 1997, when she failed to conceive again, Kenyon cast Evangeline out and abandoned her in Guatemala; she was two months shy of her thirteenth birthday. "I lived by myself for about four months," she recalls. "When I ran out of food I went to stay with some friends in Guatemala City." After about six months, these Guatemalan acquaintances managed to contact her grandmother, Lavina, in Colonia LeBaron, and Lavina drove down to Guatemala and rescued her.

Evangeline currently lives in the American Midwest; she is married and has a baby son. She's doing well, all things considered, but she's extremely worried about her younger siblings, six of whom are girls, all of them still traveling with Kenyon Blackmore, presumably, somewhere in

Central or South America. Her father, she reports, intends to "marry" each of his daughters when they turn twelve years old. "I'm concerned about my sisters," Evangeline says. "I don't want them getting raped. I'm still not over it. It's something that . . . haunts you, something that's always there."

The oldest of Evangeline's sisters had her twelfth birthday in May 2001, the next in February 2003; another will turn twelve in July 2004.

TWENTY-TWO

RENO

Joseph Smith bequeathed his followers a troublesome legacy, the conviction that it was "the Kingdom or nothing" and the belief that any act that promoted or protected God's work was justified. Some have tried to dismiss Mountain Meadows as an isolated event, an aberration in the otherwise inspiring history of Utah and Mormonism, but it was much more a fulfillment of Smith's radical doctrines. Brigham Young's relentless commitment to the Kingdom of God forged a culture of violence from Joseph Smith's theology that bequeathed a vexatious heritage to his successors. Early Mormonism's peculiar obsession with blood and vengeance created the society that made the massacre possible if not inevitable. These obsessions had devastating consequences for Young's own family. In New York in 1902, William Hooper Young, the prophet's grandson, slit the abdomen of an alleged prostitute and wrote the words "Blood Atonement" in his father's apartment.

WILL BAGLEY,
BLOOD OF THE PROPHETS

It was around two o'clock on the afternoon of July 24, 1984, when Dan Lafferty cut Brenda Lafferty's throat and let her life drain across the floor of her kitchen in a viscous crimson flood. Since he'd already killed Brenda's baby, the first half of the removal revelation had been completed. Ron Lafferty then drove Dan, Chip Carnes, and Ricky Knapp to the home of Chloe Low, which was located on an unpaved, out-of-the-way street in Highland, Utah. Their immediate plan was to "remove" Low, as God had commanded in the second part of Ron's revelation, then go to the nearby residence of Richard Stowe—president of the Highland LDS Stake—and slash his throat as well. Once they'd thus fulfilled the entire commandment, the path would be clear for work to commence on the City of Refuge, which was to be built next to the Dream Mine in preparation for the Last Days.

When they arrived at the Low home, Ron parked his Impala station wagon out of sight on a side street and he and Dan crept up to the house to determine who might be inside. As it happened, nobody was there: the Lows had gone to their summer home on Bear Lake, up near the Utah-Idaho border, for the Pioneer Day holiday. Ron returned to the car and told Carnes and Knapp, "Well, there ain't nobody here, so we're just going to rip it off and see if we can find any guns and some money or whatever we can get." After backing the car into the Lows' carport, Ron grabbed his 20-gauge shotgun and told Carnes to act as a lookout while he and Knapp returned to the house, where Dan was waiting for them.

Ron, having been a guest in the Low home many, many times over the previous dozen years, knew it well. After removing a window, he, Dan, and Knapp disabled the burglar alarm, entered the house, and ransacked it. While they were inside, two boys from the neighborhood drove up on a noisy all-terrain vehicle. Carnes, who was conspicuously holding a .30–30 Winchester rifle and wearing a ski mask in the suffocating July heat, dove out of the station wagon and hid in some nearby brush as the neighborhood kids approached the front door and then knocked for a long time, over and over. Inside the house, Dan and Ron heard the boys knocking but simply ignored it, calmly continuing their search for valuables. After a few minutes the boys quit pounding on the door and roared away in a cloud of blue smoke.

Dan, Ron, and Knapp stole a hundred-dollar bill, a watch, car keys, and some jewelry, and then, in an act of spite, Ron destroyed Chloe Low's collection of porcelain figurines from Dresden, Germany, which he knew she treasured for sentimental reasons. The burglars exited the home via a back window, picked up Carnes, who was still hiding in the scrub, and drove off.

The next item of business on their agenda was the murder of Richard Stowe. Knapp was driving. Ron gave him directions to Stowe's home, but the route was complicated and Knapp missed one of the turns. According to Dan, "Ron yelled something to Ricky like, 'Hey, that's where we were supposed to turn!' But by that point there wasn't much enthusiasm for continuing to fulfill the revelation right then."

The four men briefly discussed whether to turn around and go back to the Stowe home. Carnes, who was growing increasingly anxious, begged Ron to forget about the remainder of the revelation. "If the Lord wanted you to kill someone else today," Carnes pleaded, "you'd already be there." To his surprise and immense relief, Ron concurred without argument and told Knapp to continue in the direction he was heading, which would take them to Interstate 15.

Had they turned around and driven to President Stowe's residence that afternoon, they would have found him, unlike Chloe Low, at home. He was taking advantage of the holiday to do some work on his house with his son, using a tractor to remove a set of concrete steps. It's impossible to know what would have occurred had the Lafferty brothers gone on to Stowe's property, but considering the number of guns in their possession, it's not difficult to imagine the bloodshed that might have ensued if Ricky Knapp hadn't missed the turn.

But he did miss the turn, so instead of going back to kill Stowe, the four men drove on to Salt Lake City, where Knapp exited Interstate 15 and steered the car west onto Interstate 80. As they drove, Dan held the sawed-off 12-gauge shotgun in his lap so it would be ready in case they were pulled over by the police. Their destination was Reno, Nevada.

As the Impala sailed down the freeway, Knapp finally mustered the courage to ask Ron and Dan what, exactly, had happened inside the apartment of Allen and Brenda Lafferty, back in American Fork. According to Dan, he described to Knapp in considerable detail how he had killed Brenda and her baby, recounting the murders exactly as he would later recount them in chapter 16 of this book—which also matches his sworn testimony during a 1996 trial in every important detail. Dan says he made it very clear to Knapp and Carnes that he, not Ron, actually wielded the knife that ended the lives of both Brenda and Erica.

But Chip Carnes remembers this episode differently. In his own sworn testimony during the same 1996 trial, Carnes insisted in an entirely believable manner that it was Ron, not Dan, who told Knapp and him about the murders during the long, sweltering drive from Salt Lake to Nevada. And Ron's story differed from Dan's in one crucial regard. According to Carnes, Ron said that

> as soon as he went in the house, he punched [Brenda] as hard as he could, and she fell down again on the floor. And he said that he was calling her a bitch, and, you know, telling her what he thought about her.
>
> And he said that she was begging him and pleading with him, you know, to stop. And he said he just kept beating her and beating her; said she wouldn't go down and stay down.
>
> So while he got Dan to hold her on the floor, he said that he got up and cut a vacuum-cleaner cord off and proceeded to tie it around her neck, kept it there until Dan told him—to let him know that she had went limp.
>
> And he said at that time he removed the cord, and him and Dan picked her up, took her into the kitchen, laid her on the floor, and cut her throat. He said he cut her from ear to ear, and he demonstrated how. . . .
>
> A little bit later on after that, Ron had pulled a knife out of his— removed the knife from his boot. And he started banging it on his knee, and said, "I killed her. I killed her. I killed the bitch. I can't believe I killed her." He went on to brag about his knuckle being swelled up, you know, maybe broke, you know, from hitting her.

Carnes testified that when Ron boasted of cutting Brenda from ear to ear, he had also described, in repugnant detail, how after he drew the knife across her throat, he yanked her head back and

opened her neck so the blood would flow freely and everything. And
he then said he handed the knife to Dan. He turned and he kind of
glanced at me, and then he looked back at Dan and said, "Thank you,
brother, for doing the baby, because I don't think I had it in me." And
Dan replied and said, "It was no problem."

Dan doesn't dispute the essential facts in the last two sentences of
Carnes's testimony, but he says the rest of it is fiction. Dan is adamant
that he, not Ron, killed Brenda, pointing out that he has no reason to lie
about this—unlike Carnes. After the police arrested Carnes, the state
told him they would charge him with capital homicide and seek a death
sentence unless he provided them with evidence that led to the conviction of both Ron and Dan on first-degree murder charges. If Carnes's testimony turned out to be sufficiently helpful to the prosecution, the state
assured him, "we will make you one heck of a deal."

Dan Lafferty says he was "a little surprised" that Chip Carnes misunderstood Ron's involvement in the murders, "unless he was encouraged in some way by the prosecution. Or maybe he was just confused. I
don't blame Chip, either way. It was a pretty intense scenario, and when
I explained it in the car to him and Ricky, probably a lot of it didn't
make a lot of sense."

Perhaps the question of who actually used the knife is a relatively
unimportant distinction; when they forced their way into Brenda's
apartment in American Fork, the hands of both brothers got bloody, literally and metaphorically. The murders were a team effort. Ron and Dan
were equally culpable. A big-hearted young woman and her baby girl
were dead, and nothing was going to change that fact as Ron, Dan,
Carnes, and Knapp drove west into the blinding white glare of the Bon-
neville Salt Flats.

The fugitives reached the Nevada state line around six in the
evening. As soon as they were out of Utah they pulled off the interstate
and rented a bungalow at a cut-rate motel in the border town of
Wendover. It had been a long day. Everybody was tired and frazzled.
Dan rinsed out their bloody clothes in the bathtub, and then all four
men walked to a cheesy little gambling parlor–cum–convenience store,

where they bought beer and hot dogs to take back to the motel for dinner.

Around 11:00 they were sitting around the motel room drinking beer when "all of a sudden Ron decided it was time to go," Carnes said. They hastily repacked everything into the Impala and took off, with Knapp at the wheel. Immediately he saw flashing lights in the rearview mirror. It was the Nevada Highway Patrol.

Knapp pulled over and got out of the car to talk to the officer while the others sat with their guns at the ready, prepared to open fire if it looked like the cop had figured out who they were and why they were wanted by the law. But the officer never realized they were fugitives. Instead of attempting to arrest the men, he simply told Knapp that the Impala's taillights were out and that the car was leaking gas. Knapp, betraying nothing, politely assured the officer that they'd get everything fixed right away. The cop told him just to drive the car back across the Utah line and out of his jurisdiction because he didn't want it blowing up in Nevada, and then drove off into the night.

The four fugitives let out a collective sigh of relief, then replaced the fuse for the taillights. The fuse blew again as soon as they switched the lights back on, however, so they returned to the motel to wait for daylight. Leaving all their belongings in the car, Ron and Dan lay down to get some rest. But Knapp and Carnes were still way too freaked by their encounter with the policeman to even think about sleeping, so they left the room to buy cigarettes.

"We went out walking around," said Carnes. The twenty-three-year-old had a really bad feeling about what was going down. "I told Ricky how I felt about what, you know, I thought was happening. And he told me that he was pretty much feeling the same way." Carnes then confessed to Knapp that he was about to make a run for it: "I'm out of here. As soon as they go to sleep, I'm gone."

Carnes and Knapp went back inside the motel room, playing it cool, so that Ron and Dan wouldn't suspect that something was up. "As soon as I was sure they were asleep," said Carnes, "I took the keys and told Ricky, 'I'll see you later.' Ricky said, 'Wait a minute. I'm coming with you.' "

Carnes and Knapp pushed the Impala far enough down the road so that the brothers wouldn't hear them turning the engine over, then started it up and got the hell out of there. Knapp drove, keeping his foot lightly on the brake pedal so that the brake lights would stay on, thereby preventing them from being pulled over again.

They went west on Interstate 80, then turned north on U.S. 93 toward Twin Falls, Idaho, eventually deciding to take a roundabout route, mostly on back roads, to Cheyenne, Wyoming, where Carnes's brother Gary lived. As they drove, they kept finding evidence of the crime in the station wagon—the boning knife used to kill Brenda and Erica; a garbage bag holding the bloody clothes Dan had rinsed out in the motel bathtub; a green suitcase with two straight razors in it—and whenever they came across this stuff, they chucked it out the window.

Carnes and Knapp arrived at Gary Carnes's home in Cheyenne on Thursday morning. Four days later police spotted the Impala parked out front, raided the house, and arrested them. Because they had been drawn into the Laffertys' orbit and become entangled in the brothers' murderous crusade, the odds were good that both Carnes and Knapp would be convicted and sentenced to death. When the cops explained this to them, they quickly agreed to reveal everything they knew in return for a promise of leniency. Police officers were thereby able to recover the murder weapon, as well as most of the other evidence that had been dumped during the fugitives' panicked drive across Nevada, Idaho, and Wyoming. Knapp and Carnes also provided detectives with an important lead about the whereabouts of the Lafferty brothers, revealing that they had talked about going to Reno.

Bernard Brady, the Dream Mine investor and business partner of Kenyon Blackmore who had introduced the Lafferty boys to the Prophet Onias, arrived home from work on Wednesday afternoon, July 25, he remembers, to find "all these cop cars in front of my house. Just up and down the street—cop cars everywhere. So I went inside to see what was going on, and my house was filled with cops. My family was seated on the couch, having been told if they moved they would be shot. They were terrorized."

The horde of police officers was literally ripping apart the house, looking for evidence. As soon as Brady walked in the door, a grim-faced detective told him to "sit down and shut up."

Annoyed at being treated as a suspect, Brady asked to see their search warrant. "When they showed it to me," he says, "I noticed they had the address wrong. The warrant authorized them to search an address across the street and a couple of houses down, not my house. So I went over to one of the cops and pointed out that they were conducting an illegal search. He showed it to the sheriff, who came back and insisted it was a valid warrant anyway, and they kept on tearing the house apart."

It proved to be a fruitful search. In a drawer the officers found the affidavit Brady had notarized back on April 9, stating that he had been shown the removal revelation but wanted to have nothing more to do with it. They also took into evidence some files about the School of the Prophets, as well as the computer on which Ron had typed out most of the revelations he had received—although it did not contain the removal revelation. Soon thereafter, however, the police obtained another search warrant, for an unoccupied house where Ron had been squatting before he and Dan embarked on their road trip. One of the closets inside this home yielded a flannel shirt, and in the breast pocket of the shirt was a note written on a sheet of yellow legal paper, in Ron's tidy hand. It turned out to be the original copy of the removal revelation.

When the Lafferty brothers went to bed in their Wendover motel room late on the night of July 24, they both fell into a deep sleep. They awoke the following morning to discover that Knapp and Carnes had vanished with the Impala and everything inside it, leaving them flat broke, with little more than the clothes they were wearing. Instead of being angry, Dan says, "I thought that maybe it was a good thing in some ways. I certainly didn't blame them, all considered, and I was inclined to think it was meant to be because Ron and I had slept so soundly." After pondering their options, Ron suggested they split up, hitchhike across Nevada, and rendezvous in the Reno area at John Ascuaga's Nugget, a casino in Sparks they'd visited during their road trip earlier that summer.

Dan stuck out his thumb beside the westbound on-ramp to Interstate

80 and was immediately picked up by a trucker in an eighteen-wheeler, who gave him a ride all the way to Reno. He spent that night huddled in a historic steam locomotive on display in a city park, then passed the following day skulking around the Nugget until Ron showed up.

After they found each other, Ron and Dan were standing outside the entrance to the casino, Dan says, "when this big guy named Bud staggered out and kind of puked a little by the curb, and when he did his wallet fell to the ground. . . . It was about the fattest wallet I've ever seen." Instead of keeping it, Dan handed the wallet back to Bud, who in gratitude let the brothers sleep on his floor that night, then invited them to go water-skiing with him the next morning. They spent the day relaxing above the crystalline depths of Lake Tahoe, drinking beer and eating Bud's sandwiches. He bought them a big dinner in Truckee that evening, then drove them back to downtown Reno.

For the next two weeks Ron and Dan hung around Sparks and Reno, riding back and forth on the free double-decker shuttle bus, subsisting on the promotional largesse of the gambling industry. They became acquainted with the driver of the shuttle, and he allowed the brothers to sleep in his bus each night, "which was a real blessing," Dan says. After his final run in the evening, the driver would have Dan and Ron hide under the seats while he drove into a secure, fenced-in lot in downtown Reno, where he parked the bus overnight. According to Dan, "The long padded seats in the back of the bus were real nice for sleeping, considering the alternative."

Most days, Dan and Ron bided their time in the cavernous, air-conditioned chambers of the Peppermill Casino. Dan recalls that "the Peppermill had a big screen on which they showed the [Los Angeles] Olympics while we were there, and they also had coupons you could get each day if you had an I.D., which gave you a few chips to gamble with and a coupon for a plate of free nachos. I didn't have an I.D., but Ron did, and it was our plan to gamble with the free chips to make enough to buy food, which sometimes happened but usually didn't."

After they'd been in Reno a couple of days, the Laffertys were approached by "a strange man," according to Dan, who "had a beard and rose-colored glasses so you couldn't see his eyes." The fellow gave the brothers a reefer rolled from "some excellent weed," asked them "a few strange questions," then loaned Dan his I.D. card, enabling Dan to obtain free gambling chips and nachos. From that point on, Dan says, "we had at least two plates of nacho chips each day," although that was often all they ate.

"We were pretty hungry most of the time," Dan concedes, "but just when we needed food, someone would offer us something to eat. One couple invited us to their place for a Saturday barbecue, and this kid who was fishing in the little creek that ran through Reno took us for soup and salad at one of the casino specials when we really needed it." And every few days, the strange man in the psychedelic glasses "came by to see us and get us high and ask how we were doing." Dan believes, even now, that this person was an angel sent by God to look after them.

During their visit to Reno earlier that summer, Ron and Dan had made the acquaintance of a woman named Debbie who worked as a blackjack dealer at Circus Circus. She had befriended the brothers and let them crash on her floor; they'd returned the favor by baby-sitting her young child when she went to work. According to Dan, the brothers "had a rather curious miraculous experience while we were visiting with her": Debbie had bought a puppy for her little boy, and the dog was quite sick with canine parvovirus—a disease much like distemper in cats, usually fatal. Dan placed his hands on the dog's head and gave it a blessing, he says, "and it appeared to be instantly healed. I remember how impressed Debbie was—I was, too, but tried to act like it was no big deal."*

* Although it might sound like yet another manifestation of Dan's extreme fundamentalist beliefs, performing blessings is an entirely ordinary ritual among mainstream Latter-day Saints. Mormon men will commonly lay hands on the head of a family member or fellow Saint and pronounce a blessing in order to heal or to provide comfort in times of stress. Countless Mormons have testified that they were cured of serious illnesses through the laying on of hands. As Kenneth Anderson wrote in a 1999 *Los Angeles Times* article,

> This peculiar commingling of mystical (as well as historically unsupported) doctrines on the one hand and pragmatic rationality on the other is a strong feature of contemporary Mormons as individuals. Educated Mormon culture has long been characterized, for example, by outstanding physical scientists and engineers, as strictly rational as possible in their worldly work yet devout in their adherence to many historical beliefs that would not pass the test of rational science, and believers, moreover, in deeply mystical ideas, even if they would not rep-

When they returned to Reno after the murders, on the run, Ron suggested they stop by Circus Circus and look up Debbie again. Dan warned that he had written about Debbie in his journal—a journal he surmised was by then almost certainly in the possession of the police—so she was probably under surveillance. "If we go," he assured Ron, "you know we will be arrested."

"As best I can recall," Dan says, "Ron didn't really answer me, but just kept walking" toward the casino, where they assumed Debbie would be working her shift—and Dan figured the police would be waiting for them. "So," Dan recalls, "I said, 'If it's that time, that's cool.' "

The Lafferty brothers visited Circus Circus early on the afternoon of August 7, but they didn't see Debbie dealing cards at any of the black-jack tables. According to Dan, he inquired of Ron, " 'Should I go and ask for her?' which I knew would spring the trap." Ron told him to go ahead and do it. When Dan approached a pit boss and asked to speak with Debbie, Dan says, "his eyes got big and he quickly disappeared."

At that point Ron and Dan strolled over to one of the casino's eateries and got in line for the lunch buffet. As they stood in the queue, Dan says, he could see men who appeared to be FBI agents "peeking around corners and stuff." A moment later a swarm of police officers "rushed up from behind and put guns to our heads and said, 'Don't move or we'll blow your brains out.' I just smiled. It was kind of fun." Both Lafferty brothers surrendered without a fight and were placed in the Reno jail under extraordinary security.

_____

resent them as such. My own father spent his career as a chemistry professor and university dean, a dedicated and rational teacher of science. Yet in the Mormon Church his function . . . for many years has been to deliver blessings, to put his hands on the heads of church members and tell them things as moved by God, which are recorded, transcribed and kept by the church member as a meditative guide to God's intentions for him or her in life. Surely, to an outsider, this is very close to wild mysticism, yet my father is far indeed from being a wild mystic. Nor is it that he bifurcates his rational life from this mystical experience and has some sort of existential disconnect between them. On the contrary, his experience of giving these Mormon blessings is that the process of "following the spirit" is itself "reasonable," in a way that is highly characteristic of the Mormon trait of perceiving mysticism as a rational practice.

TWENTY-THREE

JUDGMENT IN PROVO

Critical examination of the lives and beliefs of gurus demonstrates that our psychiatric labels and our conceptions of what is or is not mental illness are woefully inadequate. How, for example, does one distinguish an unorthodox or bizarre faith from delusion? . . .

Gurus are isolated people, dependent upon their disciples, with no possibility of being disciplined by a Church or criticized by contemporaries. They are above the law. The guru usurps the place of God. Whether gurus have suffered from manic-depressive illness, schizophrenia, or any other form of recognized, diagnosable mental illness is interesting but ultimately unimportant. What distinguishes gurus from more orthodox teachers is not their manic-depressive mood swings, not their thought disorders, not their delusional beliefs, not their hallucinatory visions, not their mystical states of ecstasy: it is their narcissism. *

ANTHONY STORR,
FEET OF CLAY

It's August 5, 2002, a Monday morning, and outside Utah's Fourth Judicial District Courthouse merchants and businessmen are striding

---

* Reprinted with the permission of The Free Press, a division of Simon & Schuster Adult Publishing Group, from *Feet of Clay: Saints, Sinners, and Madmen—A Study of Gurus* by Anthony Storr. Copyright 1996 by Anthony Storr.

purposefully to work in downtown Provo. Although it's still early in the day, the heat is already rising from the pavement in visible waves. Inside the courthouse, the clock on the wall shows 9:21 when the bailiff abruptly shouts, "All rise! The Honorable Steven Hansen presiding!" The murmur from the gallery subsides, and a moment later a side door swings open, through which sixty-one-year-old Ron Lafferty, attired in orange coveralls with UDC INMATE stenciled across the back, is hustled into the courtroom by four armed sheriff's deputies.

Ron's reddish-brown hair, now streaked with gray and thinning across the crown, is neatly trimmed. Except for a bushy, Yosemite Sam mustache, he is clean-shaven. For the past few months, according to the prison grapevine, he has been obsessively lifting weights and working out; his bulging forearms and thick shoulders appear to confirm the rumor. Ron sits at the defense attorneys' table with his hands manacled awkwardly behind his back, staring defiantly at the judge.

Looking edgy and hyperalert, the deputies guarding Ron are taking their responsibilities very seriously. The inmate in their custody has been sentenced to die for viciously murdering a young woman and her baby. They know that, at this point, he doesn't have a whole lot left to lose.

"Good morning, Mr. Lafferty," Judge Hansen says in a formal but amiable voice.

"What's up, Stupid Stevie?" Ron fires back with an insolent sneer. The judge has started explaining to the inmate why he was summoned from death row to appear before the court this morning when Ron cuts him off: "I know what it's about, you fucking retard!"

Unruffled, the judge informs Ron that a warrant for his imminent execution has been filed by the state and that he has thirty days to tell the court whether or not he intends to make a last-ditch challenge to his conviction and sentence; if not, an execution date will be set. Judge Hansen also tells Ron that the state will appoint new counsel to shepherd him through the remainder of the appeals process. Ron indicates that his first choice for a new attorney would be Ron Yengich, the lawyer who engineered the controversial plea bargain that spared the life of forger and murderer Mark Hofmann, Dan Lafferty's good friend and cell mate. Ron Lafferty then emphatically declares that he intends "to pursue any appeals that are available to me." He makes it clear that he is going to fight the state's efforts to kill him all the way to the bitter end.

More than seventeen years have passed since Ron was first sentenced in this same courthouse to be shot to death for murdering Brenda and Erica Lafferty, yet here he is, still belligerently among the living. His ongoing legal maneuvers ensure that the agony of Brenda's family is refreshed on a regular basis. "The trials dragging on and on have been hard," admits LaRae Wright, Brenda's mother. "Some of our children have had quite a struggle. And my husband, especially. But that's just the way it goes. We're doing okay now. And we're glad that Brenda's in a better place, out of this cruel world."

"Brenda would be forty-two now," says Betty Wright McEntire, Brenda's older sister. "We all still miss her a lot. When they had that first trial, the prosecutors asked us not to attend. They were worried about my dad. They didn't think he could handle it."

Immediately following the murders, detectives removed most of Brenda's possessions from the apartment she'd shared with Allen Lafferty, as evidence. "After the police had gone through it all, they put the things they didn't need for the investigation into a storage unit," Betty says. "But Allen never paid the rental fee, so the storage company called, and my mother and I drove down to American Fork to take possession of Brenda's stuff. Eventually my dad started looking through it—her journals and scrapbooks and personal items. And that's when he fell apart. He just cried and cried.

"Reading what she wrote in her journals, my dad started thinking, 'Why didn't I do something to save her? Why didn't I get her out of there?' As her father, he thought he should have been able to protect her somehow, but he couldn't. And now his little girl was gone, and his first grandchild, too. I think he struggled with that for a long time." Capital murder cases must inevitably proceed carefully and deliberately to avoid any chance of a wrongful execution. But the long, slow machinations of

American jurisprudence have done little to ease the ongoing suffering of Brenda's father, mother, or siblings.

During the original trial back in 1985, Ron's court-appointed attorney had attempted to mount an insanity defense, hoping for a manslaughter conviction rather than first-degree murder, but Ron had objected to such a stratagem, even though it stood a reasonable chance of saving him from the firing squad. He'd refused to allow any psychiatric testimony to be presented on his behalf. The judge on that occasion, J. Robert Bullock, was concerned that Ron might not fully comprehend the probable outcome of his refusal to consider an insanity defense, so he demanded, "You do understand, Mr. Lafferty, that you are probably leaving the jury with only two choices: to find you guilty of first-degree murder or not guilty?"

"I do, your honor," Ron answered.

"And you understand that if there is a guilty verdict there will be a penalty hearing," Judge Bullock asked further, "and at that hearing the jury could impose the death sentence?"

"I understand that," Ron replied, "but I can't in good conscience, Your Honor, plea-bargain. It seems to me that is an admission of guilty." Ron remained resolute in insisting that he wasn't crazy, and he wasn't going to let his lawyer claim otherwise in order to negotiate the murder-one charges down to manslaughter.

Hamstrung by Ron's obstinacy, his lawyer had to cancel plans to present several witnesses whose testimony would have made a strong case that the defendant was a religious kook. The only witness left for the defense to call was Ron's mother, Claudine Lafferty, who broke down and cried on the stand, then blatantly perjured herself by professing to be unaware that Ron and Dan had talked openly in her presence of killing her daughter-in-law and grandchild. It probably surprised nobody but Ron when the jury returned after deliberating for just two hours and forty-five minutes and announced that they had found him guilty of all charges, including two counts of first-degree murder.

Following his conviction, Ron was given a new team of attorneys, who appealed to both the U.S. District Court and the Utah Supreme

Court. Ron was rebuffed on each occasion, but his lawyers persisted. By 1991 his case had landed in the Tenth U.S. Circuit Court of Appeals in Denver, Colorado. And this court, in a ruling that shocked most of Utah, tossed out Ron's 1985 convictions. In vacating the findings of the state trial court, the Tenth Circuit declared that the lower court had bungled things right out of the gate by applying a faulty legal standard when it determined that Ron had been mentally competent to stand trial.

Although the judges of the Tenth Circuit agreed that Ron understood the charges against him and their possible consequences, they concluded that "he was unable as a result of his paranoid delusional system to interpret them in a realistic way." The bench was troubled by Ron's belief that because he answered to the laws of God, he need not answer to the laws of man. They thought this was a pretty clear indication that the guy was not in his right mind. If the state of Utah wanted to keep him locked up, the judges announced, it was going to have to try him again, from scratch, after first redetermining whether he was crazy or sane according to accepted legal criteria.

The Tenth Circuit's ruling had a profound effect on Ron Lafferty and the families of his victims, obviously, but it potentially had even greater ramifications for the manner in which American courts would deal thereafter with violent crimes inspired by religious belief. As Utah Solicitor General Jan Graham explained, "We are concerned about what this decision means not only for the Lafferty case but for other cases." She warned that it might set a precedent that would "immunize" religious fanatics from criminal prosecution.

Theologians mulled other potential consequences of the Tenth Circuit's ruling, as well. As Peggy Fletcher Stack, a highly regarded religion writer for the *Salt Lake Tribune,* pointed out, "Saying that anyone who talks to God is crazy has enormous implications for the whole world of religion. It imposes a secular view of sanity and means that all religions are insane." This issue was especially germane for Latter-day Saints, given the unusual importance Mormons have always placed on communicating directly with the Almighty. Their entire faith is based on talking to God.

· · ·

The state of Utah was not happy about having to toss out Ron Lafferty's conviction and give him a new trial, but it complied with the Tenth Circuit Court's edict—the first phase of which entailed rigorously reassessing Ron's mental competency. The upshot was a hearing in late 1992 wherein a trio of doctors, after examining Ron, convinced the Fourth District Court in Provo that he was not fit to stand trial.

Having been found incompetent, Ron was transferred from death row at Point of the Mountain to the Utah State Hospital, but the state had no intention of abandoning its efforts to convict and execute him for murder. Following sixteen months of psychotherapy, which included putting Ron on a course of antidepressant and antipsychotic medications, another competency hearing was held in February 1994. This time around, the team of shrinks assembled by the prosecution proved more persuasive than the shrinks marshaled by the defense, and Judge Steven Hansen ruled that Ron was now sufficiently competent to be tried all over again for slaying Brenda and Erica Lafferty.

After Ron and Dan had initially been arrested, each of them had made a point of being exceedingly uncooperative with the prosecution. When questioned about the murders, the brothers never failed to be coy and evasive. From the time of their arrest through their 1985 convictions, neither man would confess to anything. By the mid-1990s, however, Dan's attitude and outlook had changed. He accepted that he was going to spend the rest of his life behind bars—indeed, he believed that his conviction and imprisonment were crucial components of God's plan for mankind. As a consequence, Dan became quite willing—eager, even—to talk honestly and openly about exactly what had happened on July 24, 1984.

According to Dan's version of events—a narrative considered quite credible, for the most part, by almost everyone who has heard it—he was the one who cut not only Erica Lafferty's throat but Brenda's throat as well. Dan insists that Ron didn't actually kill anybody. But even if Ron hadn't wielded the murder weapon, Dan's account clearly placed Ron inside the apartment when the killings happened. Furthermore, Dan now told—in sickening detail—how Ron had savagely beaten Brenda, ignoring her pleas for mercy, until her face had been transformed into a pulp of bloody, disfigured flesh. Dan's vivid testimony left no doubt that both brothers were equally culpable for the American Fork murders. Once the jury had an opportunity to hear Dan's testimony during the re-trial, Ron would no longer be able to claim—as he had during his 1985 trial—that he'd known nothing about the murders.

The retrial was scheduled to commence in March 1996. Ron's attor-neys were left with just a single legal option in their attempt to save him from the firing squad: an insanity defense—the same defense they had wanted to use during the 1985 trial but Ron had forbidden them to em-ploy. As the trial date approached, Ron continued to tell anyone who would listen that he wasn't the least bit crazy, but this time he stopped short of actively preventing his lawyers from arguing to the court that he was insane.

Whether Ron lived or died would hinge entirely on whether a jury could be convinced that his religious beliefs—including his certainty that God had commanded the removal of Brenda and Erica Lafferty—were not only sincerely held but also so extreme as to be a delusional artifact of a diseased mind.

Such a defense would unavoidably raise the same difficult epistemo-logical questions that had come to the fore after the Tenth Circuit Court's ruling in 1991: if Ron Lafferty were deemed mentally ill because he obeyed the voice of his God, isn't everyone who believes in God and seeks guidance through prayer mentally ill as well? In a democratic re-public that aspires to protect religious freedom, who should have the right to declare that one person's irrational beliefs are legitimate and commendable, while another person's are crazy? How can a society ac-tively promote religious faith on one hand and condemn a man for zeal-ously adhering to his faith on the other?

This, after all, is a country led by a born-again Christian, President George W. Bush, who believes he is an instrument of God and charac-terizes international relations as a biblical clash between forces of good and evil. The highest law officer in the land, Attorney General John Ashcroft, is a dyed-in-the-wool follower of a fundamentalist Christian sect—the Pentecostal Assemblies of God—who begins each day at the Justice Department with a devotional prayer meeting for his staff, periodically has himself anointed with sacred oil, and subscribes to a vividly apocalyptic worldview that has much in common with key millenarian beliefs held by the Lafferty brothers and the residents of Colorado City. The president, the attorney general, and other national leaders frequently implore the American people to have faith in the power of prayer, and to trust in God's will. Which is precisely what they were doing, say both Dan and Ron Lafferty, when so much blood was spilled in American Fork on July 24, 1984.

During pretrial hearings, Ron's behavior in the courtroom served to underscore his lawyers' contention that he was mentally incompetent. He appeared with a cloth sign attached to the seat of his prison jumpsuit that read, EXIT ONLY; his attorneys explained that he wore the sign to ward off the angel Moroni, who Ron believed was an evil homosexual spirit trying to invade his body through his anus. He believed that this same sodomizing spirit had already taken possession of Judge Hansen's body, which is why Ron made a point of shouting profanities at the judge and addressing him with such epithets as "Punky Brewster" and "fucking punk."

The defense team would try to spare Ron's life by calling as expert witnesses three psychiatrists and one psychologist who would testify that, after examining the defendant, they were utterly convinced that he was deranged. The prosecution, on the other hand, would attempt to have Ron executed by presenting one psychiatrist and three psychologists who would argue with no less conviction that Ron was quite sane and had known exactly what he was doing when he'd participated in the murders of Brenda and Erica Lafferty.

The first witness to appear was C. Jess Groesbeck, M.D., a psychiatrist who testified for the defense that Ron had slipped over the edge of sanity when his wife, Dianna, took their children and left him. "It's clear," said Dr. Groesbeck, "that he could not tolerate her loss," triggering the onset of what Groesbeck alternately termed a "schizo-affective disorder" and a "delusional disorder."

He based this diagnosis on the fact that Ron's bizarre beliefs could not be "changed with reason" and "are so fantastic and so beyond any kind of rational acceptance by anyone in the culture, that they would be categorized as delusional." When Dianna Lafferty left him, Dr. Groesbeck speculated, Ron suffered "a total loss of self-esteem or self-image," which prompted him to compensate "by creating a new but unreal view of himself and the world."

Mike Esplin, Ron's lead attorney, asked Groesbeck, "Do you feel that based on your evaluations that these mental disorders affect his ability, his capacity to comprehend and appreciate the charges or allegations against him?"

"I do," Groesbeck answered. "He can't, number one, even evaluate the reality of, for example, the case the State has against him. And, number two, I think that even when he can hear a few of those facts, his delusional system is so strong . . . for example, he absolutely believes that every piece of evidence that has been brought up against him had been planted. And I think that's a product of his delusional thinking. And because of that . . . in my opinion he does not meet the criteria of being able to appreciate the charges."

The next defense witness, a clinical and forensic psychologist named Robert Howell, seconded Dr. Groesbeck's opinion that Ron suffered from a delusional disorder, "a schizophrenic illness" that rendered him mentally incompetent to stand trial.

Esplin asked Dr. Howell if he had "seen evidence of delusion in Mr. Lafferty?"

Howell replied, "Oh, yes, clear back in 1985 and continuing on until now." He pointed out that many of Ron's delusions concerned "the State and the family": Ron didn't understand why he was being tried by the State instead of his own family. According to Dr. Howell, Ron considered the issue of his guilt or innocence to be "a family matter" that could best be resolved by having him "duke it out with Allen, the husband of the deceased woman."

Dr. Howell went on to describe other delusional behaviors on Ron's part: that he believed Moroni was trying to invade his body through his rectum; that he sometimes heard Christ speaking to him; that he heard

a buzzing sound when spirits were present; and that he saw sparks shooting from his fingertips.

When it was the prosecution's turn to make its case, however, the
battery of expert witnesses the state put on the stand moved quickly to
throw cold water on the notion that such behavior demonstrated that
Ron was crazy or in any way unfit to stand trial.

The first of these experts was Noel Gardner, M.D., a psychiatrist affiliated with the University of Utah Medical School. Dr. Gardner admitted that Ron's belief in "travelers," evil spirits, reflector shields, and the
like was due to "very odd, very strange ideas. The first time I read the defense memorandum describing them, . . . I thought this man may have
become psychotic in some way, because they sounded so strange. What
is interesting, though, is in an in-depth exploration of where those ideas
came from, and how he uses those ideas and thinks about them, it is very
clear to me they are not psychotic ideas. . . . [They are] very consistent
with things he's learned as a child."

Gardner explained that Ron described "travelers" as being spiritual
entities with the ability to "inhabit different bodies at different times."
Gardner pointed out that this belief wasn't really very different from the
notion of reincarnation, and that Ron simply "used some very unusual
labels" for a "rather conventional set of ideas. There are millions, literally, probably billions of people who believe in a spirit world."

Ron "talks about what he calls reflector shields," Dr. Gardner testified, "warding off or defending against evil forces. And in talking about
that, it has the quality that might suggest a psychotic, paranoid set of
ideas." But, Gardner continued, Ron actually "describes these forces in
very much the same kind of language that ordinary religious people
would. For example, I asked him how these spirits were alike or different than the idea of guardian angels, and I said I grew up in a family
where we believe in guardian angels."

Ron responded that his "reflector shields" were very much like
guardian angels, which struck Dr. Gardner as "very non-psychotic." It
seemed to him to be nearly identical to the ordinary Christian concept of
erecting defenses "against the temptations or influences of Satan. It's not

all that different in many ways than a common New Testament text. . . .
And it's real clear that many of his ideas have come from his early Mormon religious teachings."

Prodding Dr. Gardner to continue in this vein, Utah Assistant Attorney General Creighton Horton asked him, "Are people who believe
in divine guidance, or believe God sends guardian angels to protect us,
mentally ill?"

"I would hope not," Gardner replied. "Certainly, the majority of
people in our country believe in God. Most people in our country say
they pray to God. It's a common experience. And while the labels that
Mr. Lafferty uses are certainly unusual, the thought forms themselves are
really very common . . . to all of us."

Horton: "From what the defendant told you, does the defendant say
that he thinks travelers can enter humans?"

Gardner: "Yes, he does believe that travelers can enter humans."

Horton: "Is there a Judeo-Christian parallel to that?"

Gardner: "The idea that Christians should pray to have the Holy
Spirit fill their lives, to come in and control their lives, possess them, . . .
is a very common notion. . . . The idea that people can be influenced by
evil, and that Satan is a personal being who can influence us, and that Satan can take control of our minds and influence our behavior, is a very
common notion to Christians and non-Christian religious people."
Gardner reminded the court that a number of religions still engage in
exorcisms, to remove evil spirits that have taken possession of individuals.

"Are people who practice exorcisms," Horton asked, "are they mentally ill, necessarily, because they believe in evil spirits?"

"Certainly not," Gardner answered.

Later, Gardner expounded further on the distinction between believing in preposterous religious tenets and clinical delusion. "A false
belief," he reiterated, "isn't necessarily a basis of a mental illness." He
emphasized that most of mankind subscribes to "ideas that are not particularly rational. . . . For example, many of us believe in something referred to as trans-substantiation. That is when the priest performs the
Mass, that the bread and wine become the actual blood and body of

Christ. From a scientific standpoint, that is a very strange, irrational, absurd idea. But we accept that on the basis of faith, those of us who believe that. And because it has become so familiar and common to us, that we don't even notice, in a sense, it has an irrational quality to it. Or the idea of the virgin birth, which from a medical standpoint is highly irrational, but it is an article of faith from a religious standpoint."

Gardner explained that what makes Ron Lafferty's religious beliefs "so striking is not that they are somewhat strange or even irrational, because all religious people have . . . irrational ideas; what makes them different is that they are so uniquely his own." And although Ron had constructed his own idiosyncratic theology, Gardner insisted that he did so "in a very non-psychotic way. . . . He created it by whatever feels good to him. He says, 'It just gives me a sense of peace, and I know it's true,' and it becomes a part of his own unique article of faith. That is not a product of a schizophrenic, broken brain."

When defense attorney Mike Esplin was given an opportunity to cross-examine Dr. Gardner, he attempted to make Gardner concede that because Ron's theology was so outlandish, and "non–reality based," it must be psychotic. But the psychiatrist stood his ground.

"There are many irrational ideas that are shared in the community that are non-psychotic," Gardner replied. "We all hold to non–reality based ideas." Then, in a fascinating digression, he used as an example his own upbringing in a conservative Protestant family that adhered to the teachings of Archbishop James Usher, the Irish theologian who came to prominence in the seventeenth century. His family's beliefs, Gardner explained to the court, were "somewhat fundamentalist, not Mormon." Although his father was an intelligent and very well-read physician, "a highly respected person and scientist in the community," he raised his children to believe "the world was created in six literal days, 6,000 years ago." Gardner recalled being taken, as a small child, to the American Museum of Natural History in New York, where his father scoffed at the exhibits, insisting that the world wasn't nearly as old as the museum placards claimed—that the archaeological and geological evidence indicating the earth was many millions of years old was simply "a deception of Satan," intended to fool the gullible.

His father's stubborn belief that the world was created six thousand years ago, in just six days, was "a pretty irrational idea," Gardner testified, "but he learned the idea just the way we do all other ideas": from his family, and from the culture in which he was raised. And by these very means, Gardner said, his dad instilled that same irrational idea in him when he was a boy: "I learned the earth was 6,000 years old, just like two plus two is four."

Ron Lafferty's theology, Gardner argued, is definitely strange, but it is not an outgrowth of schizophrenia, or some other sickness of the brain. Ron's beliefs are rooted in things he was taught at an early age from his family and his community, just as Gardner's own beliefs are. And although Ron's theology amounts to "an odd set of ideas," as Gardner phrased it, those ideas nevertheless have "a kind of cohesive coherence that is not unlike the coherence of other non-verifiable belief systems, other sorts of religions."

The next expert to testify for the prosecution was a psychologist from Utah County named Richard Wootton, a practicing Mormon who was educated at Brigham Young University. Hoping to persuade the jury that Ron's beliefs were so kooky as to be certifiably mad, defense attorney Mike Esplin asked Wootton what he thought of Ron's assertion that not only was the angel Moroni a homosexual "traveler" who invaded people through the anus but the reason a statue of Moroni adorns most modern LDS temples is that the angel made a deal with Brigham Young back in 1844, after the death of Joseph Smith. According to Ron, Moroni agreed to make Brigham the next leader of the LDS Church if Brigham would promise to render the angel's likeness in gold atop the highest spire of the Mormon temple.

Dr. Wootton agreed that this was a bizarre belief on Ron's part, but he insisted that it was no more bizarre than many notions held to be true by religious folk, including members of his own faith, Mormonism. All kinds of things are accepted by one culture or another that would appear crazy or extreme to those outside the culture, Wootton argued. Asked for an example, he mentioned the multitude of visions and other supernatural experiences Joseph Smith had had throughout his lifetime. "Some outsiders," Wootton observed, "might see that as being delusional."

If one were to compare Ron's revelations and belief in spirits to "material from LDS doctrine," Dr. Wootton continued, "you'd find that his statements were not as extreme as some people might think." Wootton explained to the court that spirits were a frequent topic of conversation among ordinary Mormons: "We talk about spirits being on 'the other side.' It's not unusual to talk about what is 'beyond the veil' and what is on 'the other side' in the spirit world."

Wootton acknowledged that Ron "has a tendency to take things of a religious nature and carry them to a real extreme. However, I would add that I know dozens and dozens of people who do the same thing and never commit any crime. So it's not unusual to find people who take some religious ideas or other ideas to an extreme."

The final expert to testify for the prosecution was Stephen Golding, a forensic psychologist who in 1980 coauthored a much-praised book about the legal parameters of mental competency and helped develop the leading methodology for determining fitness to stand trial. Challenging Dr. Golding during his cross-examination, Mike Esplin pointed out that the *Diagnostic and Statistical Manual of Mental Disorders*, fourth edition (commonly referred to as *DSM-IV*)* stated that "false beliefs," by definition, are delusions. Because everyone seemed to agree that Ron Lafferty's beliefs were not based on fact, and were therefore false, Esplin demanded to know why Golding refused to characterize Ron Lafferty as delusional.

"You can't take a word in a diagnostic manual and lift it out of context," Golding answered. "Almost every religious belief system that I know of is made up ninety percent of things that are articles of faith and cannot be reduced to fact. So by using your definition they would all be false—they would all be delusional." Whether Ron's beliefs were true or false, he explained, was irrelevant in determining whether he was mentally competent. One had to consider other criteria.

---

* Published by the American Psychiatric Association, *DSM-IV* functions as the bible of the mental-health professions.

"Mr. Lafferty's approach to the world," said Dr. Golding, "is no different than other kinds of political or religious zealots in this country, in Iran, in Montana, in a variety of places."

When Esplin continued to press Golding, arguing that Ron's brand of religious zealotry was so excessive that it must be considered a symptom of psychological instability, Golding stated, "I do not believe that zealots are mentally ill, per se." He explained that there were "zealots of all stripes and colors" in the world—political, religious, and otherwise: "A zealot is simply someone who has an extreme, fervently held belief" and is willing to go "to great lengths to impose those beliefs, act on those beliefs. . . . For example, the Palestinian terrorist organization, Hamas. Hamas means 'zeal.' " Golding reiterated, "I guess my actual point, to try and say it again, is the existence of an extreme religious, personal, or political belief system is not, per se, an indication of mental illness."

As part of the prosecution's efforts to portray Ron as fanatical but utterly sane, at one point Assistant Attorney General Michael Wims asked Dr. Noel Gardner to compare Ron to schizophrenics he had examined. Gardner was adamant that Ron bore little resemblance to such seriously ill individuals. "You can't interview Mr. Lafferty without sensing the vibrancy and intensity of his affect," he testified. "This is a man who enjoys a good joke." Gardner recalled that Ron laughed a lot, and "laughter is always something that is a shared experience. . . . One thing I can tell you in working with hundreds of schizophrenics over my lifetime, is schizophrenics don't have shared humor with people around them. Most of the time they are quite humorless. Once in a while, they'll have their own idiosyncratic humor, laughing with themselves at things that have nothing to do with their environment. But a rather sensitive marker of psychosis is whether people have enough of the same shared reality to not only understand the facts of one's reality, but the subtle and social meaning and significance that is irony."

Dr. Gardner made it very clear that Ron Lafferty "is a man who enjoys and seeks out engagement with other people. Schizophrenics by nature do not seek out relationships; they're isolated, lonely, very self-contained."

Gardner pointed out, "Mr. Lafferty had stacks of books in his cell.

Show me a schizophrenic at the State Hospital who actually has the books and actually reads them. You know why? They can't stay focused. Their thoughts keep getting distracted. You don't find schizophrenics that can read the books, and then discuss the details about the content of the book. Mr. Lafferty can do that wonderfully. He can show you where he accepted this idea, rejected that idea, . . . the way all of us do."

"Now, when you read in the newspaper Mr. Lafferty had revelations from God to do something, it sounds like he's crazy," Dr. Gardner admitted. But Ron didn't strike him as the least bit crazy, Gardner quickly added, when one considered that Ron's revelations occurred within the context of the School of the Prophets: a group of devout, like-minded individuals who regularly met to evaluate those revelations. "That is a very different thing," Gardner said, "than the psychosis of somebody who believes that God is talking to them when they're schizophrenic. And the difference is this: These are six people who shared the same reality, doing the same thing; praying together, reading together, talking together, weighing whether these really came from God or not, whether they were genuine.

"That's exactly the tradition of the Christian church," Gardner asserted, in which people tried to determine whether spirits they encountered "were from God or not. It's a communal experience, the real world of six or seven people getting together, sharing the same ideas, talking about them in the real world. You do not find schizophrenics sitting in a group together talking about shared experiences."

If Ron wasn't insane—or at least no more insane than anyone else who believes in God—what was he? Why had the Lafferty brothers' religious beliefs turned them into ruthless killers? Dr. Gardner told the court that although Ron was not psychotic, he did exhibit the symptoms of a psychological affliction called narcissistic personality disorder, or NPD. According to *DSM-IV,* NPD is distinguished by

a pervasive pattern of grandiosity (in fantasy or behavior), need for admiration, and lack of empathy . . . , indicated by five (or more) of the following:

1. An exaggerated sense of self-importance . . .
2. Preoccupation with fantasies of unlimited success, power, brilliance, beauty, or ideal love
3. Believes that he or she is "special" and can only be understood by, or should associate with, other special or high-status people . . .
4. Requires excessive admiration
5. Has a sense of entitlement . . .
6. Selfishly takes advantage of others to achieve his or her own ends
7. Lacks empathy
8. Is often envious of others or believes that others are envious of him or her
9. Shows arrogant, haughty, patronizing, or contemptuous behaviors or attitudes

Although narcissistic personality disorder was not even listed as a formal diagnosis in the *Diagnostic and Statistical Manual of Mental Disorders* before 1980, it has been estimated that 1 percent of the American population is afflicted with it; NPD is a disconcertingly common ailment. Indeed, to a noteworthy degree, narcissists fuel the cultural, spiritual, and economic engines of Western society, as Dr. Gardner readily acknowledged from the witness stand. "Many successful people are narcissistic," he said, stressing that narcissism is especially prevalent among accomplished businessmen, attorneys, physicians, and academics. Such people have a sense of vast self-importance, Gardner explained, and believe "they're smarter and better than anybody else. They're willing to work incredible hours to provide confirmation to support their grandiose ideas."

As examples, Gardner cited some of his own colleagues at the University of Utah Medical School: "I can go through the school of medicine and just pick them out at the tops of many of the departments . . . they'll work three or four times as hard as anybody else. . . . So it can be adaptive in the sense of making them high performers. On the other hand, it really impairs their ability for intimacy and closeness, because they lack empathy, and can't understand the importance of other people's life experiences, so they'll work and ignore their wives and children because they're pursuing this grandiose vision of themselves, which may make them successful . . . but really impair their social and interpersonal interactions."

Grandiosity and lack of empathy, Dr. Gardner emphasized, were the hallmarks of NPD, and Ron Lafferty was nothing if not grandiose and emotionally cold. Ron had readily volunteered that Brenda's death had aroused in him no feelings whatsoever. And he'd insisted to one and all that he was an especially important person in the eyes of God—that God had anointed him, Ron Lafferty, the "one mighty and strong."

Although an exaggerated desire to mete out justice is not listed among the defining characteristics of narcissistic personality disorder in *DSM-IV,* it probably should be. Narcissists erupt with self-righteous indignation whenever they believe others are breaking rules, acting unfairly, or getting more than their fair share of the pie. They have no compunction about breaking the rules themselves, however, because they know they're special and the rules don't apply to them. In Ron's case, he was quick to castigate anyone he thought was behaving selfishly or unrighteously—indeed, in the case of Brenda and Erica Lafferty, he didn't hesitate to assume the role of judge, jury, and executioner. Yet nobody howled louder about unfair persecution when he was accused of moral, ethical, or legal lapses by others.

When narcissists are confronted by people who disparage the legitimacy of their extravagant claims, they tend to react badly. They may plunge into depression—or become infuriated. As Gardner explained to the court, when narcissists are belittled or denigrated "they feel horrible. . . . They have this sense they're either grandiose, perfect, and beautiful people, or absolutely worthless. So if you challenge their grandiosity—these are the words in the diagnostic manual—'They respond with humiliation or rage.' Their reaction to criticism is intense. And I think that is a characteristic that's very clearly demonstrated by Mr. Lafferty."

Gardner described Ron as "a man whose grandiose self had been severely challenged by divorce and by rejection by his community. He was excommunicated. And in those moments of sitting quietly and think-ing, he came up with a set of ideas that gave him a sense of release and relief. They're logical. They may not be based in fact, but it has a logical quality, because it serves his purposes in a very logical way."

A skeptical Mike Esplin demanded, "It's logical for him?"

"For him," Dr. Gardner asserted. "Any psychiatrist looking at that would say this is a set of defenses he's using so he doesn't feel the pain of his loss so much. So he's created some ideas that are soothing to him. Many people looking at religion would say religion is a set of ideas cre-ated by people as a way to soothe them, because we live in a very uncer-tain and oftentimes tragic world."

Many people would also argue that virtually everyone who has in-troduced a new framework of religious beliefs to the world—from Jesus to Muhammad to Joseph Smith to Ron Lafferty—fits the diagnosis for narcissistic personality disorder. In the view of psychiatrists and psy-chologists, any individual who proclaims to be a prophet or guru—who claims to communicate with God—is, almost by default, mentally or emotionally unbalanced to some degree.* As William James wrote in *The Varieties of Religious Experience,*

> There can be no doubt that as a matter of fact a religious life, exclu-
> sively pursued, does tend to make the person exceptional and eccen-
> tric. I speak not now of your ordinary religious believer, who follows
> the conventional observances of his country, whether it be Buddhist,
> Christian, or Mohammedan. His religion had been made for him by
> others, communicated to him by tradition, determined to fixed forms
> by imitation, and retained by habit. It would profit us little to study
> this second-hand religious life. We must make search rather for the
> original experiences which were the pattern-setters to all this mass of
> suggested feeling and imitated conduct. These experiences we can
> only find in individuals for whom religion exists not as a dull habit,
> but as an acute fever rather. But such individuals are "geniuses" in the
> religious line; and like many other geniuses who have brought forth

---

* Of course, many have argued that psychiatry is itself simply a variety of secular faith—religion for the nonreligious.

fruits effective enough for commemoration in the pages of biography, such religious geniuses have often shown symptoms of nervous instability. Even more perhaps than other kinds of genius, religious leaders have been subject to abnormal psychical visitations. Invariably they have been creatures of exalted emotional sensibility. Often they have led a discordant inner life, and had melancholy during part of their career. They have known no measure, been liable to obsessions and fixed ideas; and frequently they have fallen into trances, heard voices, seen visions, and presented all sorts of peculiarities which are ordinarily classed as pathological. Often, moreover, these pathological features in their career have helped to give them their religious authority and influence.

But if all self-proclaimed prophets are narcissists, few narcissists believe they are prophets of God. And fewer still are murderers. These were among the nuances the state asked the jurors to ponder as it tried to persuade them that Ron Lafferty was merely narcissistic and devoutly religious, not crazy, and should therefore be put to death for his role in the killing of Brenda and Erica Lafferty.

On April 10, 1996, after hearing four weeks of testimony and then deliberating for five hours, the jury agreed with the state. Ron was convicted of first-degree murder and related charges—reprising the outcome of his first trial, eleven years earlier, exactly.

Judge Steven Hansen called the court to order on May 31 to impose a sentence. Before doing so, he asked Ron if there was anything he wanted to say. Ron replied to the judge, "Go ahead and do what you gotta do, you little political punk, because that's all you are is a fucking punk, Stevie Wonder." Ron continued in this vein for several minutes, calling the judge, among other things, a "fucking idiot" who "comes to work in a dress."

When Judge Hansen calmly inquired if Ron had made his final statement, Ron said, "Well, my final statement is you can kiss my butt, pal. . . . That will pretty well cover it. Wouldn't do any good to go any further. Hell, I'm talking to myself right now, probably."

After confirming that Ron had finished addressing the court, the judge declared, "It is hereby adjudged and ordered that the defendant be sentenced to death." He then asked Ron whether he preferred to be executed "by firing squad or by a lethal intravenous injection."

"I don't prefer either one," Ron answered. "I prefer to live. That's what I prefer."

"If you don't indicate to me what you prefer," Judge Hansen explained, "I'm going to impose lethal injection as the method of execution."

"I've already had the lethal injection of Mormonism," Ron barked back. "And I kind of wanted to try something different this time. . . . I'll take the firing squad. How's that? Is that pretty clear?"

"That's clear," said the judge, and then sentenced Ron to be shot to death for his crimes—underscoring the fact that Mormon Fundamentalists are by no means the only modern Americans who believe in blood atonement.

Attorney Mike Esplin filed a series of appeals on Ron's behalf, eventually taking the case all the way to the U.S. Supreme Court. In November 2001, the justices of the nation's highest judicial body declined to hear Ron's appeal, virtually assuring that he will be killed by the state of Utah. Ron Yengich, a shrewd and aggressive attorney, replaced Esplin as defense counsel in September 2002. The execution will wait until Yengich exhausts every possibility for reversal, but the sentence is expected to be carried out as early as 2004. Almost nobody, including Dan Lafferty, believes that Ron has any chance of escaping death at the hands of a firing squad.

"I don't think there is any realistic possibility that my brother will ever beat the death penalty," Dan confirmed in November 2002. He considers Ron's execution to be a key piece in God's blueprint for humankind. In fact, Dan thinks it may well be an indicator that Armageddon is right around the corner—or, as he puts it, "a sign that the Big Party is getting close."

TWENTY-FOUR

THE GREAT AND DREADFUL DAY

CREIGHTON HORTON, UTAH ASSISTANT ATTORNEY GENERAL:

And, essentially, you say that Ron got a revelation indicating that there were people that the Lord wanted to be killed, and you helped him kill those people?

DAN LAFFERTY:

I don't think there's anything wrong with that statement, saying yes.

CREIGHTON HORTON:

You also indicated to our investigators that you weren't ashamed to be characterized as a religious fanatic?

DAN LAFFERTY:

No, I have no problem with that. *

In August 1995, during the endless rounds of motions and hearings that preceded Ron Lafferty's retrial, there happened to be an occasion when both Dan and Ron were hauled into Judge Steven Hansen's Provo court-

---

* This exchange took place in the Provo Courthouse on April 2, 1996, with Dan Lafferty on the witness stand, during the retrial of Ron Lafferty.

room at the same time. Their eyes met, and Ron offered a friendly greeting: "Hey, Bro, what's happening?"

"Good to see you," Dan replied with a smile. It was the first time the brothers had spoken to each other in eleven years, since they were confined together in the Utah County Jail. Despite the cordial exchange in Judge Hansen's court, by 1995 Dan had come to believe that Ron was a "child of the devil"—an agent of Satan who was bound and determined to kill Dan in order to prevent him from fulfilling the rest of the vital mission God has given Dan to carry out.

Dan actually had good reason to believe that Ron wanted to end his life, because the last time they were together he had tried to do just that, and very nearly succeeded. It had happened in December 1984, five months after the murders, while they were sharing a cell in the Utah County Jail as they awaited trial. Dan was lying in his bunk trying to sleep, he remembers, when "I had a funny feeling and opened my eyes to catch Ron creeping up on me." Discovered in the act, Ron stopped and went back to his own bunk. "But then," Dan says, "curiously, he asked me if I thought he would be able to kill someone as big as me, and I answered, 'Yes, I suppose so.' " From that moment, Dan resolved to watch his back.

The rest of that night passed without incident. The next day, however, while Dan was standing in their cell, he says, Ron "blindsided me in the left temple with a roundhouse haymaker that stunned me but didn't knock me out." As Dan turned to face his attacker, Ron unleashed a flurry of blows, smashing Dan's nose, loosening several of his teeth, and breaking a rib. Dan, who kept his hands by his sides and offered no resistance, says Ron didn't stop beating him "until his hands hurt too bad to hit me anymore. There was blood all over the floor and walls." At the time, Dan attributed the assault to problems Ron was having with "bad spirits."

After the beating, their jailers separated the brothers, placing them in adjoining cells. Not long thereafter, Ron handed Dan a piece of paper through the bars. Written on it was a revelation Ron said he'd just received, in which God commanded Dan to let Ron kill him. After praying for guidance, Dan says, "I felt that I should submit to what it said, and we discussed how it might be done. We thought the best way might be for me to back up to the bars and let him put a towel around my neck and choke me out."

As soon as Dan agreed to let Ron kill him, he remembers, "I felt the urge to vacate my bowels," which he interpreted as a further sign that the revelation was valid and should be followed. He understood that going to the commode was part of God's meticulous plan, Dan says, so that "I wouldn't make a mess when I died and my muscles relaxed—actually the bowel goes into spasm but the bladder muscles relax when you are throttled." After finishing up his business on the toilet, Dan "said good-bye to Ron and anticipated seeing God as I backed up to the bars and Ron put a towel around my neck."

Over on his side of the partition, Ron stood on one foot, braced the other foot against the bars, and then yanked the towel against Dan's throat as hard as he could and held it there, cutting off the oxygen to Dan's brain and bursting thousands of tiny blood vessels in his eyes. Just before Dan lost consciousness, he recalls, he experienced "a moment of desperation that was extremely intense. . . . The next thing I remember was coming to on the floor of the cell and slowly recognizing my surroundings" as Ron tried "to explain why he hadn't carried out the deed."

It turns out that after Dan blacked out and went limp against the bars, Ron felt God telling him that if Dan took another breath it was a sign that he was supposed to live. When Ron saw Dan's chest rise and his lungs fill a moment later, he let Dan drop to the floor. Dan's eyes had turned bright red from all the ruptured blood vessels, and the skin had been scraped off the back of his neck by a horizontal bar, but he kept breathing and regained consciousness.

The next day, Dan says, "Ron started showing signs of torment even worse than he had before. He was pacing back and forth in his end of the cell, mumbling to himself that he would get one more chance and he would have to do it right this time. A couple of days later or so, he handed me another revelation that said I was supposed to let him kill me again, but when I prayed about it I didn't feel like I was supposed to submit myself to let him do it again." When Dan indicated that he wasn't going to comply with the revelation this time, he says, Ron "seemed to get increasingly worse with his personal demons and his torment."

Immediately thereafter, on December 29, Ron hung himself from a towel rack when Dan was taken away from his cell for questioning; Ron would certainly have died if Dan had returned to find him even a few minutes later. By the time paramedics got to Ron he wasn't breathing and had no pulse. "His recovery in the hospital was rather miraculous, apparently, which caused a lot of talk," Dan says. "I also wondered about it. . . . Now, these many years later, I believe I understand at least part of why things have happened the way they have."

During Ron's 1996 retrial, the state convinced a twelve-person jury that Ron wasn't psychotic—that he was fully aware of what he was doing when he participated in the murders of Brenda and Erica Lafferty and was thus mentally competent to stand trial. "Is Ron crazy?" asks Utah Assistant Attorney General Michael Wims, six years after that conviction. "Yeah, sure, he's crazy. Crazy like a fox."

Many Utahans share Wims's view that Ron's outbursts in court and his weird religious pronouncements were less than sincere. People think he was merely acting crazy to avoid a death sentence. And they likewise speculate that Ron's claims to have received revelations from God were a cynical attempt to manipulate and deceive. But almost nobody doubts the sincerity of his brother's religious faith. Most folks in Utah regard Dan Lafferty's theology as both preposterous and horrifying, but they concede that he seems to be a true believer.

As it happens, what Dan believes today is not exactly what he believed when he killed Brenda and Erica. "After I arrived in the monastery—after I arrived here in prison—my beliefs went through this major evolution," he says. No longer does he subscribe to the tenets of Mormon Fundamentalism. "I changed Gods," he says. "I'd forsaken the LDS Church to go into fundamentalism, and now I've forsaken fundamentalism." These days his theology is a disturbing potpourri assembled from the Old Testament, the New Testament, *The Book of Mormon,* fundamentalist scripture, and the hyperkinetic machinations of Dan's own mind.

"When you put your whole heart into a search for the truth," Dan says, "in due course you start to see the contradictions in what you've been taught. You start to realize that something doesn't feel right and doesn't look right. Something starts to stink. . . . I used to refer to myself as a religious fanatic, but I realize I was kicked out of the LDS Church because I was really a truth fanatic. I have the need to resolve contradictions, which is what got me excommunicated."

All modern religions are fraudulent, Dan contends, not just the LDS Church. "Organized religion is hate masquerading as love. Which inevitably leads you back to the religion as it originally existed, before it was corrupted. It leads you to become a fundamentalist. You can see where the Church lost the answers by giving up its fundamental principles. So you find your beliefs evolving toward fundamentalism.

"But then I found out that there weren't answers in fundamentalism, either. You see some of the same contradictions. Fortunately for me, I saw this about the time I came here to the monastery. That's when everything started to slowly distill and come together."

At the core of Dan's transmogrified faith is his newfound conviction that he is Elijah, the biblical prophet known for his solitary ways and unyielding devotion to God. And as Elijah, Dan is certain, it will be his job to announce the Second Coming of Christ in the Final Days. According to Dan, "In my role as Elijah, I'm like John the Baptist. Elijah means 'forerunner,' the one who prepares the way. John the Baptist prepared the way for the First Advent of Christ. I'm here to prepare the way for the return of the Son of Man."

Dan believes, as he did when he was a fundamentalist Mormon, that the most salient fact of existence is the immutable division of humankind into those who are inherently righteous and those who are inherently evil. "Some people were chosen to be children of God," Dan explains, "and others became children of the devil. Either you're a brother—a child of God—or an asshole—a child of the devil. And you can't do anything to change it.

"'There are two fathers, God and the devil. And all the children of God possess something none of the children of the devil possess, which is the gift of love. The devil could not program love into his children because love is something he doesn't possess or understand. It's beyond his knowledge. All the children of the devil possess is greed, hatred, envy, and jealousy."

According to Dan, at a certain point Christ gathered all His children around Him and announced, " 'I want to have a party that's gonna last for a thousand years. You interested? You want to party with Me on this earth for a thousand years?' And we said, 'Hell, yeah!' So He said, 'Okay, that's the good part. Here's the bad part: you can't have something for nothing. . . . For six thousand years I'm gonna let the earth become hell before I turn it into heaven. And hell, by definition, is where the devil and his children are running shit. So what I'm gonna do is, I'm gonna let the devil populate the earth with all of his assholes, and then I'm gonna sprinkle you, My children, on the earth a few at a time. And every hour you spend in this hell-on-earth with the assholes, you're going to be building up credits for the Big Party. It's gonna take about six thousand years, but by then we'll have all the credits we'll need for our party. And then I'll come, and we'll harvest the earth—basically, we'll remove all the assholes—and clear the dance floor for our thousand-year party.'

"Christ told His children, 'I know life is fucking crazy, but I'm here to tell you there's a purpose behind it. We're working for the Kingdom of God. And the way we do that is we just put in our time here. And every hour you put in here is building up credit for the Big Party. That's the promise. That's the covenant. It's going to be crazy down there for a while, but in the end, through Elijah, I will come.' "

The way Dan sees it, "Since we're all here in hell-on-earth, where the devil and his children run everything that is organized, it makes sense that the children of the devil would trick us into worshiping their asshole god. But before the God of love makes the scene, it will be important somehow to help His children—the children of love—have their eyes opened to who this cool fucker is who will be coming to befriend them on the day known in the Bible as the 'Great and Dreadful Day of the Lord' (great for His children; dreadful for the assholes)—which is also known in the parable of the wheat and tares as 'the harvest.'*

"It is prophesied that the 'Great and Dreadful Day' will be when Christ sends His angels like reapers to gather out of His kingdom all those who are not His and kill them; and that's in part what I was foreshadowing," Dan explains, "when I took the lives of Brenda and Erica. I know that might sound a little gory or something, but it feels like the right interpretation to me. I don't think the angels in this prophesy are beings with wings that fly down from heaven, but more like what Joseph and Brigham called 'avenging angels': men already living here on earth who will just be taking care of their Father's business like I was, once they learn who their Father is and have been properly instructed."

Dan believes that God has designated him, as Elijah, to tell the righteous "who their Father is" at the proper moment, and thereby kick off the thousand-year reign of the Kingdom of God. "I'm sure I will be the one who will identify Christ when He returns," he says. According to Dan, a year or two after he was incarcerated, he "had this experience. . . . I didn't know what it meant at the time. I was just pacing in my cell. It was the middle of the day. And I heard a voice. It was completely different from the revelations that were given through the School of the Prophets. I was pacing and I heard this voice tell me, 'Write this down: The moon will shine from noon until nine.' . . . That was all I heard. And over the years I thought, 'What the hell does this mean?' And finally it came together and made sense. I recently figured it out, just in the last year or so: the sign of Christ will be that the moon will

---

* This biblical allegory, more commonly known as the parable of the weeds ("tare" is a synonym for a noxious weed that infests fields of grain), appears in Matthew 13:24. It tells how one night when everyone was sleeping, Satan sowed weeds through the wheat fields of the Kingdom of Heaven. Jesus instructed his followers to let the weeds grow with the wheat "until the harvest. At that time I will tell the harvesters: 'First collect the weeds and tie them in bundles to be burned; then gather the wheat and bring it into my barn.' " Dan Lafferty, it bears mentioning, is by no means the only zealot enamored of this parable. Brian David Mitchell, the Mormon Fundamentalist who abducted fourteen-year-old Elizabeth Smart in 2002, cited it in his tract, *The Book of Immanuel David Isaiah*: ". . . there has been corruption and perversion in the priesthood. For Satan doth creep in unawares and doth sow tares among the wheat. . . ."

shine in the sky from noon until nine at night. How that will happen, I don't know. But when it happens I'm sure it won't be mistaken for anything else."

By applying his singular logic to the matter, Dan has also figured out why Ron tried to strangle him with a towel back in 1984: it was because the devil had revealed to Ron that Dan was Elijah and had been assigned to let the world know when Jesus had returned. Dan surmises that the devil actually told Ron about Dan's crucial assignment long before God got around to telling Dan about it.

"At some point," Dan explains, "I believe Ron was instructed that it was important to kill me. The basic reason for it was his father"—the devil—"was trying to prevent the unpreventable." The devil had been given the world for six thousand years, but those six thousand years are just about over, Dan says, so "it should come as no surprise that the devil wouldn't want to give up control when his time is up." And the way the devil hopes to extend his reign is to have Ron kill Dan/Elijah, and thus prevent him from announcing Christ's return. "I feel confident," Dan declares, "that this is what was behind Ron's attempts to take my life. Because the Bible says that if Elijah doesn't fulfill his calling, Christ can't return."

Dan says that he should have recognized that Ron was one of Satan's minions back in the spring and summer of 1984, when he and Ron were driving across the West in Ron's Impala, because—contrary to the determination of the experts who testified for the state in Ron's 1996 retrial—his brother was "showing signs of schizophrenia. . . . As we were traveling together and getting to know each other, it was a fairly common phenomenon for Ron to kind of space out and be gone somewhere mentally. I suspect that at such times he was probably listening to voices." And those voices, Dan speculates, were instructions from the devil.

Dan is sure, moreover, that Ron remains determined to murder him and is patiently waiting for an opportunity to do so: "I'm confident that he is still hearing the voices telling him to kill me." Dan is aware of everything churned out by the prison rumor mill. And the buzz from death row, he says, is that "Ron is in very good shape and has been working out like a boxer getting ready for a title fight." Dan takes it for granted that Ron hopes to have one more chance to find himself in Dan's company, and when that opportunity presents itself, "he wants to be ready to take care of business."

For his part, Dan doesn't think God will let Ron kill him. In fact, he is encouraged by Ron's new training regimen, seeing it as an indication that the End Times are imminent: Dan believes the Prince of Darkness must sense that "it's almost time to start the harvest," spurring him to whip Ron into good enough shape to make one final desperate attempt on Dan's life, and thereby prevent the arrival of the Great and Dreadful Day. Because Satan knows that if Dan is allowed to live, there will be no stopping Christ's return, and "the devil and all his brothers and sisters will be killed with much 'wailing and gnashing of teeth.' "

Until that rapturous moment, however, when "the moon will shine from noon until nine" and Dan can shout from the rooftops that Christ has returned, he bides his time within the grim chambers of the prison's maximum-security unit, where he has thus far spent half of his adult life. But what if the moon doesn't shine from noon until nine? What if killing Brenda and Erica Lafferty wasn't actually part of God's plan but was merely a crime of such staggering cruelty that it is beyond forgiveness? What if, in short, Dan got it all wrong? Has it occurred to him that he may in fact have a great deal in common with another fundamentalist of fanatical conviction, Osama bin Laden?

"I've asked myself that," Dan concedes. "Could I be there? Is that what I'm like? And the answer is no. Because Osama bin Laden is an asshole, a child of the devil. I believe his real motivation isn't a quest for honesty and justice, which maybe were his motivations in his earlier life. Now he's motivated by greed and profit and power."

What about Osama's underlings, the holy warriors who sacrificed their lives for Allah by flying jumbo jets into the World Trade Center? Surely their faith and conviction were every bit as powerful as Dan's. Does he think the sincerity of their belief justified the act? And if not, how can Dan know that what he did isn't every bit as misguided as what bin Laden's followers did on September 11, despite the obvious sincerity of his own faith?

As he pauses to consider this possibility, there comes a moment when a shadow of doubt seems to flicker across his mien. But only for an instant, and then it's gone. "I have to admit, the terrorists were following their prophet," Dan says. "They were willing to do essentially what I did. I see the parallel. But the difference between those guys and me is, they were following a false prophet, and I'm not.

"I believe I'm a good person," Dan insists. "I've never done anything intentionally wrong. I never have. At times when I've started to wonder if maybe what I did was a terrible mistake, I've looked back and asked myself, 'What would I have done differently? Did I feel God's hand guiding me on the twenty-fourth of July 1984?' And then I remember very clearly, 'Yes, I was guided by the hand of God.' So I know I did the right thing. Christ says, 'If you want to know if something is true, believe. And I'll help you know the truth.' And that's what he did with me.

"I'm sure God knows I love Him. It's my belief that everything will work out, and there will be a happy ending to this whole strange experience. I've just had too many little glimpses through the thin fabric of this reality to believe otherwise. Even when I have tried not to believe, I can't."

Serene in the knowledge that he has led a righteous life, Dan Lafferty is confident that he won't be festering here in maximum security much longer. He is sure that "any day now" he will hear the blare of the trumpet heralding the Last Days, whereupon he will be released from this hell of strip searches and prison food and razor wire to assume his rightful place in the Kingdom of God.

TWENTY-FIVE

THE AMERICAN RELIGION

Accounts of Mormons and the Mormon Church . . . tend toward one of two extremes. On the one hand, accounts of Mormonism from the church's founding by Joseph Smith in the 1820s have emphasized the sensational, the lurid, the scandalous, the heretical and the titillating, for the reason that, well, there is much in Mormon history, culture, and doctrine that is sensational, lurid, scandalous, heretical and titillating, as measured against mainstream American culture then and now. . . .

On the other hand, other accounts of Mormons—accounts of the people rather than the articles of their strange faith—have often emphasized the cheerful virtue, the upright and yet often relaxed, pragmatic goodness of its adherents, their ability to hold together families and raise decent children and provide the consolations of community in the confusing modern world more successfully than many others. These accounts often pass over in discreet silence the sometimes embarrassing tenets of faith that, especially if one were Mormon, might have been thought an inestimably important part of making that moral success possible. If opponents of Mormonism have often asked, "Can't we stop the Mormons from being Mormon?", ostensible admirers of Mormons as people have often asked, at least by implication, "Can't we have Mormons—but without Mormonism?"

KENNETH ANDERSON,
"A PECULIAR PEOPLE: THE MYSTICAL AND PRAGMATIC APPEAL OF MORMONISM,"
LOS ANGELES TIMES, NOVEMBER 28, 1999

A genuine first-hand religious experience . . . is bound to be a hetero-doxy to its witnesses, the prophet appearing as a mere lonely madman. If his doctrine prove contagious enough to spread to any others, it becomes a definite and labeled heresy. But if it then still prove contagious enough to triumph over persecution, it becomes itself an orthodoxy; and when a religion has become an orthodoxy, its day of inwardness is over: the spring is dry; the faithful live at second hand exclusively and stone the prophets in their turn. The new church, in spite of whatever human goodness it may foster, can be henceforth counted on as a staunch ally in every attempt to stifle the spontaneous spirit, and to stop all later bubblings of the fountain from which, in purer days, it drew its own supply of inspiration.

WILLIAM JAMES,
THE VARIETIES OF RELIGIOUS EXPERIENCE

Most Mormon Fundamentalists share Dan Lafferty's confidence that Armageddon is imminent. In Colorado City the new prophet, Warren Jeffs, is absolutely sure of it. Although the prophecy of his father, Uncle Rulon, that the world would be swept clean in a hurricane of fire by the year 2000 did not come to pass, the events of September 11, 2001, have renewed Warren's optimism.

In public statements Warren has condemned the bloody work of Islamic terrorists, but he preaches to the faithful in Bountiful and Colorado City that the attacks on New York and Washington were a magnificent portent and a cause for great hope. Excitedly, he tells his followers that the eruption of terrorism against the United States is an unmistakable sign that the End Times are indeed at hand, and very soon now God's chosen people will be lifted up to experience Eternal Glory. Up in Canada, dozens of photos of the jets exploding into the World Trade Center, clipped from magazines, have been mounted in the halls of the Bountiful school, lest any of the students doubt that the Last Days are upon us.

As for the mainline LDS Church, it has always maintained that "the

hour is nigh," and that there will be plagues and desolations before the
Second Coming of Christ. Church authorities in Salt Lake have, for a
long time now, urged all Mormons to store a year's worth of food and
survival supplies to prepare for this period of privation. But beyond
quoting scripture predicting that the world will end seven thousand
years after it was created, LDS leaders are circumspect about exactly
when the Apocalypse will occur.

In the meantime, the church has more than sixty thousand missionaries roaming the globe at any given moment, converting new members
at an astounding rate. The respected sociologist Rodney Stark raised
eyebrows in 1984 by predicting that there would be 265 million Mormons on the planet by A.D. 2080. After reassessing his calculations in
1998 to reflect more recent growth rates, Stark revised his prediction
upward; now he believes that the LDS Church will have close to three
hundred million members by the final decades of this century.

If the expansion of the LDS faith continues at its current pace,
within sixty years governing the United States will become "impossible
without Mormon cooperation," according to the eminent scholar Harold
Bloom, Sterling Professor of the Humanities at Yale University—and an
unabashed admirer of Joseph Smith and the Mormons. In 1992, in his
influential book *The American Religion*, Bloom wrote:

> Two aspects of the Saints' vision seem starkly central to me; no other
> American religious movement is so ambitious, and no rival even re-
> motely approaches the spiritual audacity that drives endlessly toward
> accomplishing a titanic design. The Mormons fully intend to convert
> the nation and the world, to go from some ten million souls to six
> billion.

Later in the same book, Bloom made a bold prediction about what the
LDS leadership will do when it gains sufficient political leverage:

> And who can believe that the Mormons ever would have turned away
> from the practice of Celestial Marriage, if it were not for federal pres-
> sure? . . . I cheerfully do prophesy that some day, not too far on in the

twenty-first century, the Mormons will have enough political and financial power to sanction polygamy again. Without it, in some form or other, the complete vision of Joseph Smith never can be fulfilled.

If Bloom's forecast is alarming, it also seems far-fetched. The LDS Church of the twenty-first century is very different from the church of the nineteenth century. As LDS historian Dale Morgan wrote in a letter to Juanita Brooks in 1945, "it was Joseph's personal magnetism that bound people to him originally," but after his church was up and running, the religion "acquired an almost, independent existence. It acquired a dignity from the lives of its converts; it became a social force energizing the lives of innumerable people swept up in its course."

The Mormons have gained so much by abandoning polygamy that it is hard to imagine LDS authorities ever bringing it back by design. Mormondom's path is set less these days by theologians and wild-eyed prophets than by businessmen and publicists. The LDS Church has annual revenues estimated at more than $6 billion, and it is currently the largest employer in the state of Utah. For the better part of a century now, the church has been trending slowly but relentlessly toward the humdrum normality of middle America.

But the mainstreaming of the Mormon Church has a distinctly ironic component. To whatever extent the LDS religion moves beyond the most problematic facets of Joseph Smith's theology and succeeds at becoming less and less peculiar, fundamentalists are bound to pull more and more converts from the Mormon Church's own swelling ranks. Communities like Colorado City and Bountiful will continue to win adherents from among the most fervent Saints, because there will always be Mormons who yearn to recapture the spirit and all-consuming passion of the founding prophet's vision—Mormons like Pamela Coronado.

At the moment Coronado, in her early forties, wearing faded bib overalls, is stripping wallpaper from the front room of a run-down old farmhouse the Prophet Onias recently acquired. Tall and graceful, with piercing blue eyes that project great self-assurance from beneath a nimbus of blond curls, Pamela and her husband, David Coronado, became followers of Onias at the beginning of 1984, just after the School of the Prophets was established in Utah County. "We met Bob Crossfield— Onias—when we went to one of their meetings," Pamela remembers. "We came because we'd come across *The Book of Onias* at a used-book store and had read Bob's revelations. Right away we both thought, 'These sound like the revelations of Joseph Smith! This is just like *The Doctrine and Covenants*!' We were very impressed."

David Coronado was so impressed, in fact, that he wrote to the Philosophical Library, the vanity press that printed the book for Onias, to find out how to contact the author-prophet. "They told David that Bob had just moved his base of operations to the Provo area, right where we lived," Pamela says. "So we went to a meeting. It was at the Lafferty family home in Provo, and we met Bob there, and the Laffertys. That's how we came into the Work."

Pamela had been raised in Provo, in a traditional Mormon family. "My dad was one of the first people to buy shares in the Dream Mine," she announces proudly, although her parents were in no sense funda- mentalists. In 1978, when she turned twenty-one, Pamela was called on a mission to France, and it was her experience as a missionary, she says, "that made me start questioning the direction the church was going. Every day I'd be out there bearing testimony of the truth of *The Book of Mormon* and Joseph Smith, which was fine, but whenever it came time to bear testimony of the prophet as 'the Lord's only true and living prophet,' I had a real tough time saying what I was supposed to say. I just didn't believe in him, or where he was taking the church." At the time, the LDS president and prophet was Spencer W. Kimball, who had just sent shock waves throughout Mormondom by radically revising church doctrine to allow men with black skin to enter the priesthood.

At the conclusion of her mission, Pamela returned to Provo and took a job teaching at the Missionary Training Center, where she met David Coronado; they were married eight months later. David, it turned out, had been born in Colonia LeBaron, in Mexico, and was a member of the infamous LeBaron clan. During the height of Ervil LeBaron's killing binge, one of Ervil's crazed followers had actually fired a gun at David's mother, endeavoring to end her life, which had prompted her to emigrate to the United States with David and his eight siblings in order to escape the bloodshed.

Although troubled by the violence in his heritage, when David reached adulthood he came to believe that the fundamentalist version of Mormonism was the true path to God. After he married Pamela—whose doubts about the mainstream church had only been growing since her mission—she came to share his fundamentalist perspective wholeheartedly. When they met the Prophet Onias in 1984, they were more than ready to join "the Work."

Six months later, though, Dan Lafferty murdered Brenda and Erica Lafferty, and the Coronados' world was upended. "When the Lafferty thing happened it scared everybody around here," Pamela says. "It was so shocking. Because we were associated with the Lafferty family, people thought we had to be evil. We got excommunicated. For a while there, my family was afraid for our lives."

But neither the horror of the Lafferty murders nor the harassment and persecution that followed eroded the Coronados' faith in Onias and the Work. Both David and Pamela are convinced that opening the LDS priesthood to blacks was a terrible apostasy. And both believe completely in the principle of plural marriage—even though they have not yet engaged in polygamy themselves. "We've considered it many times," Pamela says. "There have been many, many women who could have been part of our family—close friends who the whole family felt attracted to, and who felt attracted to the family. But when it came right down to it—well, it just never quite happened. At the time it was just too difficult."

Pamela stops stripping wallpaper, puts down her tools, and goes into the kitchen to prepare lunch for her daughter, Emmylou, and the Prophet Onias. "I could live the Principle more easily now that I'm older," she says brightly. "I've matured a lot. I can see how my children would benefit from the talents of another woman. I'm not saying there wouldn't be difficult times. But I can also imagine how neat it could be."

A frown crosses Pamela's face. It entirely misses the point, she says, to think that joining the Work is mostly about plural marriage, or keep-

ing blacks out of the priesthood, or other matters of doctrine. Such issues, she insists, are only "the superficial reasons" for her belief. She says
the real basis for her faith "is spiritual. It's all about the spirit that exists
in your heart."

Hearing this, the Prophet Onias pipes in. "The LDS Church has
pretty well lost the spirit," he says. "You go and hear them on Sunday, or
you hear the things they say at General Conference, and you realize most
of them feel nothing."

In marked contrast, the spirit burns for Pamela with a white-hot
flame. The energy she draws from it is palpable; one can almost feel the
heat emanating from her skin. "I tell you," Pamela says, pressing her
hands to her chest, beaming, "when you feel that spirit—the real
spirit—there's nothing like it. You're full of fire inside."

And that fire is being spread very effectively to the next generation
of fundamentalists. Pamela's daughter Emmylou, who is on the cusp of
adolescence, lays out the plans for a house she has designed across the
dining room table. "I did it on the Internet, according to the Principle,"
she declares shyly, and then points out the home's numerous special features.

"The exterior is going to be rammed earth or maybe adobe," she explains. "It's eighty-five feet long by seventy-seven feet wide, all on one
floor. This center part here will be open, like a courtyard. Over on this
side is where the children's rooms are—one for the girls, one for the
boys. Plus, there is a nursery for the young ones. The father's room, the
master bedroom, is over here. And these are the mothers' rooms, one
wife here and the other wife there. And the neat thing is, there's space to
add another room here for a third wife."

As she describes the many unique elements she has designed, her enthusiasm builds. By the end of the virtual tour her eyes are gleaming.
This is her dream home, customized for what she imagines to be the perfect life—the life she hopes to live when she grows up.

TWENTY-SIX

CANAAN MOUNTAIN

In the Plateau Country the eye is not merely invited but compelled to notice the large things. From any point of vantage the view is likely to be open not with the twelve- or fifteen-mile radius of the plains, but with a radius that is often fifty and sometimes even seventy-five miles—and that is a long way to look, especially if there is nothing human in sight. The villages are hidden in the canyons and under the cliffs; there is nothing visible but the torn and slashed and windworn beauty of the absolute wasteland. And the beauty is death. Where the grass and trees and bushes are stripped off and the world laid naked you can see the globe being torn down and rebuilt. You can see the death and prognosticate the birth of epochs. You can see the tiny clinging bits of débris that historical time has left. If you are a Mormon waiting for the trump of the Last Days while you labor in building the Kingdom, you can be excused for expecting that those Last Days will come any time now. The world is dead and disintegrating before your eyes.

WALLACE STEGNER,
MORMON COUNTRY

From a tranquil city park at the edge of Colorado City–Hildale, the sheer cliffs of Canaan Mountain erupt heavenward without preamble— a massive scarp of brick-red sandstone streaked with desert varnish,

looming two thousand vertical feet above the fundamentalist stronghold. On top, the flat summit plateau feels like a lost world—an island
in the sky, cut off from civilization, sprouting manzanita and mariposa
lilies, wild roses and yucca, Indian paintbrush and stout ponderosa
pines. "My brother David and I used to sneak up here every chance we
got when we were kids," says DeLoy Bateman. "Seemed like the only
place where the religion couldn't control us."

DeLoy is perched at the edge of this mountaintop, staring down at
the town where he was born and raised. It's the end of July, and the temperature is 104 degrees Fahrenheit in the shade. DeLoy—who seems
oblivious to the withering heat even though he is wearing long polyester
pants, a long-sleeved shirt, and the religion's trademark long underwear—is an apostate from the Fundamentalist Church of Jesus Christ of
Latter Day Saints and has no respect for its new prophet, Warren Jeffs,
but he still resides in this xenophobic community, smack in the middle
of town, and doubts that he'll ever live very far away.

DeLoy no longer practices plural marriage. The second of his two
wives moved out and now lives in St. George; her kids have remained
with DeLoy in Colorado City, and she comes to visit them every week.
"Since I don't believe in what the religion teaches anymore," he explains,
"I just can't justify polygamy." And it isn't merely the fundamentalist
religion that DeLoy has abandoned—he announces that he's done with
religion, period. Unlike most who have rejected the teachings of the
FLDS Church, he didn't convert to mainline Mormonism, or another
branch of Christianity, or some New Age faith. DeLoy has become an
atheist. He no longer believes in God.

It hasn't been an easy transformation. "My whole life, I've had this
need to believe in something," he says. "I've wanted answers to why we
were put here, just like everybody else. The religion provided those answers. And there is so much else that's good about it. The truth is, everything I ever learned came from this religion. It made me what I am. And
I'm proud of what I am. This religion is in my blood. I mean, heck, look
at me."

Holding his arms out from his sides, palms forward, DeLoy looks
down at what he's wearing, and takes stock with a self-deprecating

snort: "Even though I don't believe anymore, I'm still wearing the gar-
ment—the sacred long underwear. I try not to wear it, but I just can't
seem to leave it off, even on hot summer days like this. For some reason
not wearing it just doesn't feel right. I feel naked." He laughs again,
then adds, "That ought to tell you something about the power of this religion."

DeLoy returns his gaze to the orderly grid of homes and fields at the
base of the mountain. "It's hard for outsiders to accept, but there is so
much that's positive about this town. The people that live in those
houses down there, they're *extremely* hardworking. And strong. Yeah, I'm
real attached to Colorado City. . . . I think it's a real good community to
raise a family in." DeLoy says this, and means it, even though he's talked
at length to several of the women in town who've reported being sexually abused as girls and insist that pedophilia is rampant within the
community. "I don't doubt their stories are true," he acknowledges. "I
know for a fact there's men in the priesthood who have slept with their
own daughters, which is horrible. But that kind of thing goes on everywhere, and I actually think there's less of it here than in the outside
world."

In any case, it wasn't the culture's sexual customs or its lifestyle con-
straints that finally induced DeLoy to apostatize. Rather, he says, "It just
got to be where I could no longer ignore that the religion is a lie. It's not
like the prophets that control everybody are intentionally fooling the
people—as far as I can tell Rulon and Warren and Winston and them
sincerely believe the lie themselves. I'm not sure about that, but I think
so. And it's not just their religion that's a lie. I've really come to believe
that all religions are lies. Every single one of 'em.

"Could there be supreme power out there somewhere? Is there a
grand plan behind the big bang, the creation of the universe, the evolution of species? I don't know, I suppose it's possible; I guess I'd like to at
least allow for the possibility in the back of my mind. But common
sense tells me otherwise."

Although DeLoy says that he was "extremely religious" throughout
his youth, he also had a probing, unremittingly curious mind. "Even as
a young boy," he says, "I remember wondering about contradictions be-

tween what the religion taught and scientific truth. But Uncle Roy told us that the way to handle that was just to avoid asking certain kinds of questions. So I trained myself to ignore the contradictions. I got good at not letting myself think about them."

Because DeLoy was smart and the religion needed educators for its school, when he turned eighteen the prophet—his adoptive grandfather, Uncle Roy—sent him to Southern Utah State College, an hour up the road in Cedar City, to become a teacher. "I was sent with him," recalls DeLoy's first wife, Eunice Bateman, who had been commanded by the prophet to marry DeLoy a short while earlier. "Neither of us had ever lived outside of Colorado City. Our second child was born a year after he started school. I felt so different from everyone there—I felt like an outcast. I was homesick for Colorado City the whole time Dee was in college. But I kept pretty busy raising babies and doing his typing and helping with his homework." After getting his degree, DeLoy returned to Colorado City and went to work educating the town's youth.

Despite feeling like a fish out of water when he left his hometown and set up residence in the larger world, DeLoy says, "I loved college. Looking back, I suppose it was the beginning of the end for me. I stayed in the religion for another twenty years, but going to college in Cedar City was when I had my eyes opened. That's where I took my first geology course. Afterward I came home and told Uncle Roy, 'There's a professor over there trying to tell us the earth is four and a half billion years old, but the religion says its only six thousand years old. How can that be?' Which shows you why education is such a problem for the Work. You take someone like me, who was always as stalwart as could be, and then you ship him off to get an education and the guy goes and apostatizes on you. Happens over and over again. And every time it does, it makes the leaders more inclined to keep people from learning."

When DeLoy finally lost his faith and left the UEP, his three oldest kids were married and no longer living at home. These three children have remained in the religion, but he has worked hard to teach the other fourteen kids to think for themselves and to question what the UEP has inculcated. "Sometimes I worry about what would become of the little ones," DeLoy muses, "if something happened to me and the wife—if we died. My older children would take the younger kids into their homes and look after them, but they'd be brought right back into the religion. I think those kids would be happy with that—they'd probably never know the difference. But they'd be stunted. They'd never get to exercise their imaginations."

To help prepare his children for this possibility, and to instill in them a healthy skepticism about religious dogma of all kinds, on December 31, 1999, DeLoy and Eunice loaded their entire brood into two vans (whenever the Bateman family travels anywhere together, at least two large vehicles are required to transport everyone) and made the three-hour drive to Las Vegas in order to ring in the new millennium.

"We took 'em all down to the center of the Las Vegas Strip," he explains, "which is supposedly one of the wickedest places on earth, and the first place God was going to destroy when the clock struck midnight. We went to the New York–New York Casino, and stood outside in the street there with thousands and thousands of other people as the ball dropped and they counted down the seconds to the year 2000. And you know what? The millennium came, and the world didn't end. I think that made quite an impression on the kids." DeLoy laughs hard, shaking his head.

Now that he's no longer a member of the Fundamentalist Church of Jesus Christ of Latter Day Saints, DeLoy is astonished at some of the beliefs the religion instills in its members. "It staggers me," he says, "to look back on the things I used to believe. For example, ever since I was a child we were taught that Negroes were terrible, that they weren't even human. And we had no way to learn otherwise. There were never any blacks in town. They were entirely foreign to us. I never even seen a Negro until I was practically an adult, when I saw one on a trip down to St. George. I remember staring at him for just as long as I could stare— I'd never encountered such a creature. It was like he was some kind of strange animal to me.

"That's an awful thing to believe, I know. I feel guilty about it now. But it's the way I was brought up from day one, and when you're brought up to believe something like that, it's not easy to overcome it. Just the other night, when I went to bed I turned on the TV for a minute, and Oprah happened to be on. And I found myself immediately changing the channel—just because she was black. I knew even as I was doing it that it was wrong, but that's what the religion taught me to think, and it's surprisingly hard to shake something that's so deeply ingrained. What's really sad is, children in the religion are still being taught those same exact things today." Indeed, the FLDS church continues to teach that interracial marriage is a sin so great that "the penalty, under the law of God is death on the spot."*

"It's amazing how gullible people are," DeLoy continues. "But you have to remember what a huge comfort the religion is. It provides all the answers. It makes life simple. Nothing makes you feel better than doing what the prophet commands you to do. If you have some controversial issue that you're dealing with—let's say you owe a lot of money to somebody, and you don't have the means to pay them—you go in and talk to the prophet, and he might tell you, 'You don't have to pay the money back. The Lord says it's Okay.' And if you just do what the prophet says, all the responsibility for your actions is now totally in his hands. You can refuse to pay the guy, or even kill somebody, or whatever, and feel completely good about it. And that's a real big part of what holds this religion together: it's not having to make those critical decisions that many of us have to make, and be responsible for your decisions."

DeLoy looks out across the epic sweep of desert. In the distance, on the far side of the Arizona Strip, the dreamy silhouettes of Mount Dellenbaugh and Mount Trumbull hover in midair, suspended above a quivering sheen of mirage. "If you want to know the truth," he says, squinting against the glare, "I think people within the religion—people who live here in Colorado City—are probably happier, on the whole, than people on the outside." He looks down at the red sand, scowls, and nudges a rock with the toe of one shoe. "But some things in life are more important than being happy. Like being free to think for yourself."

---

* A horror of miscegenation is something Mormon Fundamentalists have in common with their Mormon brethren: even after LDS President Spencer W. Kimball's 1978 revelation reversing the church doctrine that banned blacks from the priesthood, official LDS policy has continued to strongly admonish white Saints not to marry blacks. Make no mistake: the modern Mormon church may now be in the American mainstream, but it usually hugs the extreme right edge of the flow.

There were no formerly heroic times, and there was no formerly pure generation. There is no one here but us chickens, and so it has always been: A people busy and powerful, knowledgeable, ambivalent, important, fearful, and self-aware; a people who scheme, promote, deceive, and conquer; who pray for their loved ones, and long to flee misery and skip death. It is a weakening and discoloring idea, that rustic people knew God personally once upon a time—or even knew selflessness or courage or literature—but that it is too late for us. In fact, the absolute is available to everyone in every age. There never was a more holy age than ours, and never a less.

ANNIE DILLARD,
FOR THE TIME BEING

The genesis for this book was a desire to grasp the nature of religious belief. Because I've spent most of my life in the West, in the happy company of Latter-day Saints, I decided to narrow my subject to a more manageable scope by examining belief more or less exclusively through the lens of Mormonism. I grew up with Mormons in Corvallis, Oregon, which had (and has) a robust LDS community. Saints were my childhood friends and playmates, my teachers, my athletic coaches. I envied what seemed to be the unfluctuating certainty of the faith professed so enthusiastically by my closest Mormon pals; but I was often baffled by it. I've sought to comprehend the formidable power of such belief ever since.

I was irresistibly drawn to write about Latter-day Saints not only because I already knew something about their theology, and admired much about their culture, but also because of the utterly unique circumstances in which their religion was born: the Mormon Church was founded a mere 173 years ago, in a literate society, in the age of the printing press. As a consequence, the creation of what became a worldwide faith was abundantly documented in firsthand accounts. Thanks to the Mormons, we have been given an unprecedented opportunity to appreciate—in astonishing detail—how an important religion came to be.

I must confess that the book you are now reading isn't the book I set out to write. As originally conceived, it was going to focus on the uneasy, highly charged relationship between the LDS Church and its past. I'd even come up with a title: *History and Belief.* I intended to explore the inner trials of spiritual thinkers who "walk in the shadows of faith," as Pierre Teilhard de Chardin described it. How does a critical mind reconcile scientific and historical truth with religious doctrine? How does one sustain belief when confronted with facts that appear to refute it? I was fascinated by the paradoxes that reside at the intersection of doubt and faith, and I had a high regard for congenital skeptics, like Teilhard, who somehow emerged from the fray with their belief intact.

The research, however, kept pulling me onto a slightly different heading, and after fighting it for many months, I decided to surrender to this unplanned course and see where it might take me. The upshot, for better or worse, is that I wrote *Under the Banner of Heaven* instead of *History and Belief.* Who knows, maybe someday I will yet complete the latter.

I spent approximately a year writing this book, and more than three years doing the research on which the writing is based. I traveled many thousands of miles to visit the Saints' most sacred sites and to interview dozens of individual Mormons, Fundamentalist Mormons, and apostate Mormons face-to-face (I interviewed others over the telephone). Some of these people asked me to protect their privacy, and I have done so by giving them pseudonyms in these pages.

In the case of Dan Lafferty, I visited him in November 2001 at Point of the Mountain, in the maximum-security unit of the Utah State Prison. After my initial interview, which lasted the better part of an afternoon, he answered countless follow-up questions, with unsettling candor, by writing me many long, detailed letters. Additionally, I reviewed thousands of pages of transcripts from the three trials and numerous hearings that ultimately determined the guilt of Dan and his brother Ron.

In an essay titled "The Empire of Clean," Timothy Egan, a reporter for the *New York Times,* observed,

In the Beehive State of Utah, nearly every town, church, and family of any standing keeps a record, a daily diary of the Mormon Dream. Typically, it is a ledger of life on two levels—one long on struggle and triumph, the story of the creation of Zion in the American West, the other more spiritual but no less detailed. They know in Orderville exactly who was hungry in 1912 and who committed adultery in 1956, but they also know whether somebody's ancestor from the fifteenth century has been given a valid passport to eternal life. Every wagon train drama, every horrific entry from the epic, killing mistake of the handcart migration, every basketball championship over the Indian kids in Carbon County, is written down, somewhere. No state has more keepers of history, or better archives, honeycombed in climate-controlled vaults, than Utah. . . . Mormons have made a workaday craftsmanship of keeping the past alive. There is a record, the Saints like to say, of everything.

I availed myself of this rich history by draining my bank account in bookstores near and far. I also made several visits to the archives of the Utah State Historical Society in Salt Lake City, and the Harold B. Lee Library at Brigham Young University, in Provo. During my reading, I was struck by the impact three writers, in particular, have made on the interpretation of Mormon history: Fawn Brodie, the author of *No Man*

Knows My History; Juanita Brooks, the author of *The Mountain Meadows Massacre;* and D. Michael Quinn, the author of *Early Mormonism and the Magic World View, The Mormon Hierarchy: Origins of Power,* and *The Mormon Hierarchy: Extensions of Power.*

Each of these historians was born into the Mormon Church, and their faith (or loss thereof, in Brodie's case) informed and enhanced their scholarship, which is distinguished by its courageous, unflinching honesty. Brodie died in 1981, and Brooks in 1989, but Quinn, currently fifty-eight years old, is still a productive scholar at the height of his intellectual powers. Quinn's writing lacks the eloquence of Brodie's and the unembellished narrative force of Brooks's, and as a consequence his books have not been widely read by the general public. The influence of his prodigious work, however, has been huge among Mormon historians. And no writer since Fawn Brodie has provoked such intense condemnation from the LDS General Authorities.

Quinn studied as an undergraduate at BYU, went on to receive a doctorate from Yale, and then returned to BYU as an inspired professor of history. He first aroused the ire of LDS leaders in 1981, when he presented a now-famous lecture to the BYU Student History Association. Titled "On Being a Mormon Historian," it was a response to a recent attack on those academics, like Quinn, who dared to publish work that was critical of the church's official, extensively expurgated version of Mormon history. "The tragic reality," he declared in his lecture, "is that there have been occasions when Church leaders, teachers, and writers have not told the truth they knew about difficulties of the Mormon past, but have offered to the Saints instead a mixture of platitudes, half-truths, omissions, and plausible denials."

Quinn argued, "A so-called 'faith-promoting' Church history which conceals controversies and difficulties of the Mormon past actually undermines the faith of Latter-day Saints who eventually learn about the problems from other sources. One of the most painful demonstrations of that fact has been the continued spread of unauthorized polygamy among the Latter-day Saints during the last seventy-five years, despite the concerted efforts of Church leaders to stop it." Quinn pointed out that after officially renouncing the doctrine of plural marriage in 1890, the highest leaders in fact continued to sanction polygamy, covertly, for many years. And this casuistry, he insisted, has driven many Mormons into the embrace of fundamentalism.

"The central argument of the enemies of the LDS Church," Quinn said, "is historical, and if we seek to build the Kingdom of God by ignoring or denying the problem areas of our past, we are leaving the Saints unprotected. As one who has received death threats from anti-Mormons because they perceive me as an enemy historian, it is discouraging to be regarded as subversive by men I sustain as prophets, seers, and revelators."

The text of Quinn's lecture, which resonated strongly among Mormon intellectuals, was printed on the front page of an underground student newspaper, infuriating the LDS General Authorities in Salt Lake City and sparking a raging controversy that made the pages of *Newsweek* magazine. It was the beginning of Quinn's fall from grace in the church he loved. By 1988 he was pressured into resigning his tenured professorship at BYU. And in 1993, following a highly publicized hearing by an LDS "disciplinary council," he became one of six prominent Mormon scholars who were excommunicated from the LDS Church for apostasy. "The church wanted to send a very public message to dissidents," Quinn says. "Their goal was intimidation, to silence dissent."

Banishment from the church came as a harsh blow. "Even if you have all kinds of objections to church policies," he explains, "when you're a believing Mormon, to be excommunicated is like a form of death. It's like attending your own funeral. You feel the loss of that sense of community. I miss it deeply."

Quinn's standing in the LDS Church was not helped by the fact that in the mid-1980s he revealed that he is gay; the Mormon General Authorities continue to make the church a very difficult place for homosexuals. Despite Mormonism's entrenched homophobia, and Quinn's unsparing, clear-eyed assessment of Mormonism's faults, his faith in the religion of Joseph Smith remains undiminished. "I'm a radical believer," he says, "but I'm still a believer." He seems to be one of those rare spiritual thinkers, as Annie Dillard puts it, who possess "a sort of anaerobic capacity to batten and thrive on paradox."

"At a very early age," Quinn acknowledges, "I developed what I call 'a complex testimony.' Instead of a black/white view of Mormonism, I have an Old Testament sort of faith. The writers of the Old Testament presented the prophets as very human vessels, warts and all. Yet God still chose them to be His leaders on earth. That's how I see Mormonism: It is not a perfect church. It has huge flaws, in both the institution and the people who lead it. They are only human. And I have no trouble accepting that. It's all part of my faith.

"On the very first page of *The Book of Mormon*, Joseph Smith wrote that if it contained mistakes or faults, 'it be the mistakes of men.' And this same thing is stated in various ways throughout the text that follows—that errors in this sacred book are possible, even likely. I have always believed that Mormonism was the one true church, but I don't think it has ever been infallible. And I certainly don't believe it has a monopoly on the truth."

One of the events that led to Dr. Quinn's excommunication was the publication, in 1987, of *Early Mormonism and the Magic World View*, a fascinating, exhaustively researched examination of Joseph Smith's involvement in mysticism and the occult. In the preface to a revised 1998 edition of the book, Quinn astutely observed that "many academics feel embarrassed for a scholar who even briefly acknowledges belief in the metaphysical." He argued, nevertheless, that authors had an intellectual and ethical responsibility "to state one's own frame of reference when writing about the metaphysical"—which he proceeded to do, succinctly describing his Mormon faith. And regarding that faith, he wrote, "I make no apologies to secular humanists or religious polemicists."

I happen to find Quinn's argument compelling. He's convinced me that those who write about religion owe it to their readers to come clean about their own theological frame of reference. So here's mine:

I don't know what God is, or what God had in mind when the universe was set in motion. In fact, I don't know if God even exists, although I confess that I sometimes find myself praying in times of great fear, or despair, or astonishment at a display of unexpected beauty.

There are some ten thousand extant religious sects—each with its own cosmology, each with its own answer for the meaning of life and death. Most assert that the other 9,999 not only have it completely wrong but are instruments of evil, besides. None of the ten thousand has yet persuaded me to make the requisite leap of faith. In the absence of conviction, I've come to terms with the fact that uncertainty is an inescapable corollary of life. An abundance of mystery is simply part of the bargain—which doesn't strike me as something to lament. Accepting the essential inscrutability of existence, in any case, is surely preferable to its opposite: capitulating to the tyranny of intransigent belief.

And if I remain in the dark about our purpose here, and the meaning of eternity, I have nevertheless arrived at an understanding of a few more modest truths: Most of us fear death. Most of us yearn to comprehend how we got here, and why—which is to say, most of us ache to know the love of our creator. And we will no doubt feel that ache, most of us, for as long as we happen to be alive.

JON KRAKAUER
JANUARY 2003

Acknowledgments

This book benefited tremendously from the expert attention it received from numerous individuals at Doubleday Broadway, Anchor-Vintage, and Villard. I am especially grateful to Charlie Conrad, Bill Thomas, Steve Rubin, Alison Presley, Kathy Trager, John Fontana, Caroline Cunningham, Bette Alexander, Suzanne Herz, Michael Palgon, David Drake, Alison Rich, Rachel Pace, Jackie Everly, John Pitts, Claire Roberts, Louise Quayle, Carol Lazare, Laura Welch, Brian McLendon, Marty Asher, LuAnn Walther, Deb Foley, and Jennifer Marshall.

Thanks to John Ware for being such a terrific agent, Bonnie Thompson for her meticulous copyediting, Jeff Ward for the monochrome maps, and Linda Moore for creating the exquisite map of the Arizona Strip printed on the endpapers.

Bill Briggs, Pat Joseph, Carol Krakauer, David Roberts, and Sharon Roberts read the book in manuscript and offered valuable criticism when it was needed most.

I'm grateful to Ruth Fecych, David Rosenthal, Ann Godoff, Mark Bryant, and Scott Moyers for reading an early, partial draft of the manuscript and providing helpful feedback.

This undertaking would have gone nowhere without considerable assistance from DeLoy Bateman, Eunice Bateman, Virginia Bateman, David Bateman, Jim Bateman, Holly Bateman, Ellen Bateman, Fern

Bateman, Diana Bateman, Roger Bateman, Sarah Bateman, Maria Bateman, Kevin Bateman, Randy Bateman, Jason Bateman, Craig Chatwin, D. Michael Quinn, Debbie Palmer, Jolene Palmer, Jay Beswick, Flora Jessop, Lorna Craig, Wesley Larsen, Wynn Isom, Mareena Blackmore, Bernice DeVisser, Gayla Stubbs, Lenora Spencer, Mary Taylor, Robert Crossfield, Barry Crowther, Betty McEntire, LaRae Wright, Debbie Babbitt, Thomas Brunker, Kris C. Leonard, Michael Wims, Creed H. Barker, Nora S. Worthen, Tasha Taylor, and Stan Larsen.

My research was informed by the work of fellow journalists Peggy Fletcher Stack, Carolyn Campbell, Michael Vigh, Greg Burton, Tom Zoellner, Fabian Dawson, Dean E. Murphy, Daniel Woods, Angie Parkinson, Will Bagley, Pauline Arrillaga, Chris Smith, Mike Gorrell, Ann Shields, Kevin Cantera, Holly Mullen, Paul Angerhofer, Geoffrey Fattah, Rebecca Boone, Brandon Griggs, Phil Miller, Brian Maffly, Susan Greene, Suzan Mazur, Julie Cart, Dave Cunningham, Dave Wagner, Dawn House, Hilary Groutage Smith, Robert Matas, Robert Gehrke, Maureen Zent, Tom Gorman, Bob Mims, Tom Wharton, John Llewellyn, John Dougherty, Marianne Funk, Joan Thompson, Lee Davidson, Susan Hightower, Ellen Fagg, Mike Carter, Jennifer Dobner, Pat Reavy, Jerry D. Spangler, Elaine Jarvik, James Thalman, Derek Jensen, Lucinda Dillon, Lee Benson, Ted C. Fishman, Chris Jorgensen, Alf Pratte, Dave Jonsson, Elizabeth Neff, Brooke Adams, Matt Canham, Stephen Hunt, Taylor Syphus, David Kelly, Jeffrey P. Haney, Dennis Wagner, Patty Henetz, Mark Havnes, Bob Bernick, Adam Liptak, Norman Wagner, Tim Fitzpatrick, Maureen Palmer, and Helen Slinger.

For providing inspiration, companionship, and sage counsel I'm indebted to Becky Hall, Neal Beidleman, Chhongba Sherpa, Tom Hornbein, Pete Schoening, Klev Schoening, Harry Kent, Owen Kent, Steve Komito, Jim Detterline, Conrad Anker, Dan Stone, Roger Schimmel, Beth Bennett, Greg Child, Renée Globis, Roger Briggs, Colin Grissom, Kitty Calhoun, Jay Smith, Bart Miller, Roman Dial, Peggy Dial, Steve Rottler, David Trione, Robert Gully, Chris Archer, Rob Raker, Larry Gustafson, Steve Swenson, Jenni Lowe, Gordon Wiltsie, Doug Chabot, Steve Levin, Chris Reveley, Andrew McLean, Liesl Clark, John Armstrong, Dave Hahn, Rob Meyer, Ed Ward, Matt Hale, Chris Gulick,

Chris Wejchert, Mark Fagan, Sheila Cooley, Kate Fagan, Dylan Fagan, Charlotte Fagan, Karin Krakauer, Wendy Krakauer, Sarah Krakauer, Andrew Krakauer, Tim Stewart, Bill Costello, Mel Kohn, Robin Krakauer, Rosalie Stewart, Alison Stewart, Shannon Costello, Maureen Costello, Ari Kohn, Miriam Kohn, Kelsi Krakauer, A. J. Krakauer, Mary Moore, Ralph Moore, David Quammen, Laura Brown, Pamela Brown, Helen Apthorp, Bill Resor, Story Clark, Rick Accomazzo, Gerry Accomazzo, Alex Lowe, Steve McLaughlin, Marty Shapiro, Caroline Carminati, Brian Nuttall, Drew Simon, Walter Kingsbery, Eric Love, Josie Heath, Margaret Katz, Lindsey Delaplaine, Rosemary Haire, Nancy McElwain, Andy Pruitt, and Jeff Stieb.

And special thanks to John Winsor, Bridget Winsor, Harry Winsor, Charlie Winsor, Paul Fuller, Mary Gorman, Amy Beidleman, Nina Beidleman, Reed Beidleman, Kevin Cooney, Annie Maest, Emma Cooney, Mike Pilling, Kerry Kirkpatrick, Charley LaVenture, Sally LaVenture, and Willow LaVenture for the crucial advice and support they provided in Mexico.

The following notes document the most important sources for each chapter, but by no means do they list the source of every quotation and fact. Quotes that appear without citation came from interviews conducted by the author.

Prologue

The quotes attributed to Allen Lafferty were taken from the transcript of Ron Lafferty's 1996 trial. Facts about the murders of Brenda and Erica Lafferty, as well as the arrest and conviction of Ron and Dan Lafferty, came primarily from interviews and correspondence with Dan Lafferty, trial transcripts, and, to a lesser extent, articles published in the *Salt Lake Tribune, Deseret News,* and *Provo Daily Herald.* My main source for the footnote on Shoko Asahara was an article by Kyle B. Olson, "Aum Shinrikyo: Once and Future Threat?" published in the journal *Emerging Infectious Diseases* in July 1999.

One: The City of the Saints

Many of the facts about the modern LDS Church came from *Mormon America: The Power and the Promise* by Richard N. Ostling and Joan K. Ostling and *The Mormon Hierarchy: Extensions of Power* by D. Michael Quinn.

Two: Short Creek

My knowledge of Colorado City–Hildale and the UEP comes from several visits to the community and interviews with numerous members and ex-members of the Fundamentalist Church of Jesus Christ of Latter Day Saints. I also relied on Ben

Bistline's self-published book, *The Polygamists: A History of Colorado City*; *Kidnapped from That Land: The Government Raids on the Short Creek Polygamists* by Martha Sonntag Bradley; and articles in the the *Salt Lake Tribune,* the *Deseret News,* the *Kingman Daily Miner,* the *St. George Spectrum*, and the *Salt Lake City Weekly*. The quote attributed to Apostle Boyd K. Packer about threats faced by the LDS Church was cited in *The Mormon Hierarchy: Extensions of Power*.

Three: Bountiful

Background for this chapter came primarily from interviews with Debbie Palmer, and a single visit to Bountiful. The 1979 quote from Eldon Tanner in *Ensign* magazine was cited in *The Mormon Hierarchy: Extensions of Power*.

Four: Elizabeth and Ruby

Facts about the Elizabeth Smart abduction were drawn from "The Book of Immanuel David Isaiah" by Brian David Mitchell; articles published in the *New York Times,* the *Salt Lake Tribune,* the *Deseret News, Time,* and *Newsweek;* and reports by the Associated Press, ABC News, and NBC News. My sources for the material about Ruby Jessop were Jay Beswick, Flora Jessop, and Lorna Craig.

Five: The Second Great Awakening

My main sources were *No Man Knows My History* by Fawn Brodie; *Early Mormonism and the Magic World View* by D. Michael Quinn; *By the Hand of Mormon* by Terryl L. Givens; *Joseph Smith and the Beginnings of Mormonism* by Richard L. Bushman; and *History of the Church* by Joseph Smith Jr.

Six: Cumorah

My main sources were *The Book of Mormon* and *By the Hand of Mormon*.

Seven: The Still Small Voice

I relied on interviews with Robert Crossfield, Bernard Brady, and Debbie Palmer; *The First Book of Commandments* and *The Second Book of Commandments,* both by Crossfield; and the LDS *Doctrine and Covenants*. Facts about the Dream Mine and its history came primarily from *John H. Koyle's Relief Mine* by Ogden Kraut; and articles in the *Salt Lake Tribune*.

Eight: The Peace Maker

My main sources were Dan Lafferty and *The Peace Maker* by Udney Hay Jacob. Quotes attributed to Matilda Lafferty came from the transcript of Ron Lafferty's 1996 trial.

Nine: Haun's Mill

My main sources were *The 1838 Mormon War in Missouri* by Stephen C. LeSueur; *Mormonism Unveiled; or the Life and Confessions of the Late Mormon Bishop, John D. Lee*, edited by William Bishop; and *No Man Knows My History*. The 1830 review of *The Book of Mormon* in the Rochester *Daily Advertiser* was cited in *No Man Knows My History*, as was the 1838 speech by Joseph Smith in which he compared himself to Muhammad. The corresponding footnote, about parallels between Mormonism and Islam, was based on information from a 1971 article by Arnold H. Green and Lawrence P. Goldup, "Joseph Smith, An American Muhammad? An Essay on the Perils of Historical Analogy," published in *Dialogue: A Journal of Mormon Thought* (quotes attributed to Eduard Meyer and George Arbaugh were cited in this article).

Ten: Nauvoo

My main sources were *Kingdom on the Mississippi Revisited: Nauvoo in Mormon History*, edited by Roger D. Launius and John E. Hallwas; *Cultures in Conflict: A Documentary History of the Mormon War in Illinois* by John E. Hallwas and Roger D. Launius; *Orrin Porter Rockwell: Man of God, Son of Thunder* by Harold Schindler; and *No Man Knows My History*.

Eleven: The Principle

My main sources were *No Man Knows My History*; *In Sacred Loneliness: The Plural Wives of Joseph Smith* by Todd Compton; *Mormon Polygamy: A History* by Richard S. Van Wagoner; *Mormonism Unveiled; or the Life and Confessions of the Late Mormon Bishop, John D. Lee*; and *An Intimate Chronicle: The Journals of William Clayton*, edited by George D. Smith. The quotes from Marinda Johnson were cited in *In Sacred Loneliness*. The quote attributed to Luke Johnson about the attempt to castrate Joseph Smith in Ohio came from the article "History of Luke Johnson," published in the *Deseret News* on May 19, 1858. The excerpt from Lucy Walker's memoirs was cited in *No Man Knows My History*.

Twelve: Carthage

My main sources were *An Intimate Chronicle: The Journals of William Clayton*; *No Man Knows My History*; *Mormon Polygamy: A History*; *Kingdom on the Mississippi Revisited: Nauvoo in Mormon History*; *Cultures in Conflict: A Documentary History of the Mormon War in Illinois*; *Doctrine and Covenants*; and *Among the Mormons: Historic Accounts by Contemporary Observers* by William Mulder and A. Russell Mortensen. The letter from William Clayton describing the dictation of Joseph Smith's revelation on plural marriage was cited in *An Intimate Chronicle*.

Thirteen: The Lafferty Boys

My main source was Dan Lafferty.

Fourteen: Brenda

I relied on interviews with Betty Wright McEntire, LaRae Wright, Penelope Weiss, and Dan Lafferty, and, to a lesser extent, on the transcript of Ron Lafferty's 1996 trial.

Fifteen: The One Mighty and Strong

My main sources were Robert Crossfield, Bernard Brady, Dan Lafferty, Betty Wright McEntire, and Pamela Coronado. I also relied on *The First Book of Commandments, The Second Book of Commandments, The Book of Mormon,* and photocopies of Ron Lafferty's revelations.

Sixteen: Removal

My main sources were Dan Lafferty, Betty Wright McEntire, and LaRae Wright. I also relied on the transcript of Ron Lafferty's 1996 trial. Facts in the footnote about marijuana use among Mormons in the early twentieth century were gleaned from *Prophet of Blood: The Untold Story of Ervil LeBaron and the Lambs of God* by Ben Bradlee Jr. and Dale Van Atta; a 1985 article by D. Michael Quinn, "LDS Church Authority and New Plural Marriages, 1890–1904," published in *Dialogue: A Journal of Mormon Thought*; and articles in the *Salt Lake Tribune*.

Seventeen: Exodus

My main sources were *The Mormon Hierarchy: Origins of Power* by D. Michael Quinn; *Among the Mormons: Historic Accounts by Contemporary Observers*; *Orrin Porter Rockwell: Man of God, Son of Thunder*; *Cultures in Conflict: A Documentary History of the Mormon War in Illinois*; *Blood of the Prophets: Brigham Young and the Massacre at Mountain Meadows* by Will Bagley; *The Year of Decision: 1846* by Bernard DeVoto; and *Mormonism Unveiled; or the Life and Confessions of the Late Mormon Bishop, John D. Lee*. The quote attributed to Illinois congressman John Alexander McLernand decrying polygamy was cited in *Mormon Polygamy: A History*. The quote attributed to Dr. Roberts Bartholow in the corresponding footnote was cited in a 1979 article by Lester E. Bush, Jr., "A Peculiar People: The Physiological Aspects of Mormonism 1850–1975," published in *Dialogue: A Journal of Mormon Thought*.

Eighteen: For Water Will Not Do

My main sources were *Blood of the Prophets: Brigham Young and the Massacre at Mountain Meadows*; *The Mountain Meadows Massacre* by Juanita Brooks; *Mormonism Unveiled; or the Life and Confessions of the Late Mormon Bishop, John D. Lee*; *A Mormon Chronicle: The Diaries of John D. Lee, 1848–1876*, edited by Robert Glass Cleland and Juanita Brooks; *Orrin Porter Rockwell: Man of God, Son of Thunder*; *Forgotten Kingdom: The Mormon Theocracy in the American West, 1847–1896* by David L. Bigler; and *Desert Between the Mountains: Mormons, Miners, Padres, Mountain Men, and the Opening of the Great Basin, 1772–1869* by Michael S. Durham. The vivid descriptions of the attack on the Fancher party attributed to survivors Sarah Frances Baker Mitchell and Nancy Huff were cited in *Blood of the Prophets: Brigham Young and the Massacre at Mountain Meadows*.

Nineteen: Scapegoats

My main sources included those listed for Chapter 18 plus a 1993 article by Wesley P. Larsen, "The 'Letter,' or Were the Powell Men Really Killed by Indians?" published in the journal *Canyon Legacy*; *Colorado River Controversies* by Robert Brewster Stanton; *Beyond the Hundredth Meridian: John Wesley Powell and the Second Opening of the West* by Wallace Stegner; *The Exploration of the Colorado River and Its Canyons* by John Wesley Powell; *Indian Depredations* by Peter Gottfredson; and *The "Tribune" Reports of the Trials of John D. Lee for the Massacre at Mountain Meadows, November 1874–April 1877*, edited by Robert Kent Fielding. I also relied on interviews with Wesley P. Larsen and Wynn Isom. The quote attributed to D. Michael Quinn describing how Union troops trained their guns on Brigham Young's home during their Civil War occupation of Salt Lake City was taken from an interview with Quinn by Ken Verdoia.

Twenty: Under the Banner of Heaven

My main sources were *The Four Hidden Revelations*, a compilation of divine commandments revealed to John Taylor and Wilford Woodruff, published by the Fundamentalist Church of Jesus Christ of Latter Day Saints; *Mormon Polygamy: A History*; and "LDS Church Authority and New Plural Marriages, 1890–1904." The prophecy from John D. Lee about the death of Brigham Young was cited in *Blood of the Prophets: Brigham Young and the Massacre at Mountain Meadows*. The quote attributed to John Taylor (from which the title of this book was drawn) came from an anonymously authored article, "A Den of Treason: That's What John Taylor Made the Assembly Hall Last Sunday," published in the *Salt Lake Daily Tribune* on January 6, 1880.

Twenty-One: Evangeline

My main sources were DeLoy Bateman, Craig Chatwin, Debbie Palmer, Lavina Stubbs, Lenora Spencer, Annie Vandeveer Blackmore, Lena Blackmore, and Evangeline Blackmore. I also relied on *The Blood Covenant* by Rena Chynoweth; and *Prophet of Blood: The Untold Story of Ervil LeBaron and the Lambs of God*.

Twenty-Two: Reno

My main sources were Dan Lafferty, Bernard Brady, and the transcript of Ron Lafferty's 1996 trial.

Twenty-Three: Judgment in Provo

My main source was the transcript of Ron Lafferty's 1996 trial. I also relied on interviews with Betty Wright McEntire, LaRae Wright, Dan Lafferty, Thomas Brunker, Kris C. Leonard, and Michael Wims; and articles in the *Salt Lake Tribune,* the *Deseret News*, and the Provo *Daily Herald*.

Twenty-Four: The Great and Dreadful Day

My main source was Dan Lafferty.

Twenty-Five: The American Religion

I relied on personal visits to Colorado City and Bountiful and on interviews with Pamela Coronado, Emmylou Coronado, Robert Crossfield, DeLoy Bateman, Craig Chatwin, and Debbie Palmer. Rodney Stark's predictions about the growth of the LDS Church were cited in *Mormon America: The Power and the Promise*. The excerpted 1945 letter from Dale Morgan to Juanita Brooks was cited in *Juanita Brooks: Mormon Woman Historian*, by Levi S. Peterson.

Twenty-Six: Canaan Mountain

My source was DeLoy Bateman.

Author's Remarks

Timothy Egan's essay "The Empire of Clean" was published in his book *Lasso the Wind: Away to the New West*. The quotes attributed to D. Michael Quinn were drawn from my interviews with him, and from his 1981 lecture "On Being a Mormon Historian." The quote attributed to Annie Dillard was taken from her book *For the Time Being*.

Bibliography

Altman, Irwin, and Joseph Ginat. *Polygamous Families in Contemporary Society.* Cambridge: Cambridge University Press, 1996.

American Psychiatric Association. *Diagnostic and Statistical Manual of Mental Disorders.* 4th ed. (DSM-IV). Washington, D.C.: American Psychiatric Association, 1994.

Anderson, Kenneth. "The Magic of the Great Salt Lake." *Times Literary Supplement,* March 24, 1995.

———. "A Peculiar People: The Mystical and Pragmatic Appeal of Mormonism." *Los Angeles Times,* November 28, 1999.

Arbaugh, George Bartholomew. *Revelations in Mormonism: Its Character and Changing Forms.* Chicago: University of Chicago Press, 1932.

Armstrong, Karen. *The Battle for God.* New York: Ballantine Books, 2001.

———. *Buddha.* New York: Viking Penguin, 2001.

———. *A History of God: The 4,000-Year Quest of Judaism, Christianity and Islam.* New York: Ballantine Books, 1994.

Arrington, Leonard J. *Adventures of a Church Historian.* Urbana: University of Illinois Press, 1998.

———. *Brigham Young: American Moses.* New York: Alfred A. Knopf, 1984.

Arrington, Leonard J., and Davis Bitton. *The Mormon Experience: A History of the Latter-day Saints.* New York: Alfred A. Knopf, 1979.

Bagley, Will. *Blood of the Prophets: Brigham Young and the Massacre at Mountain Meadows.* Norman: University of Oklahoma Press, 2002.

Bancroft, Hubert Howe. *History of Utah, 1540–1886.* San Francisco: History Company, 1889.

Bayle, Pierre. *Historical and Critical Dictionary: Selections.* Translated, with an introduction and notes, by Richard H. Popkin. Indianapolis: Bobbs-Merrill Company, 1965.

Belshaw, Michael. "The Dunn-Howland Killings: A Reconstruction." *Journal of Arizona History*, vol. 20 (winter 1979).

Bigler, David L. *Forgotten Kingdom: The Mormon Theocracy in the American West, 1847–1896.* Logan: Utah State University Press, 1998.

Bishop, William, ed. *Mormonism Unveiled; or the Life and Confessions of the Late Mormon Bishop, John D. Lee.* Albuquerque: Fierra Blanca Publications, 2001.

Bistline, Benjamin. *The Polygamists: A History of Colorado City.* Colorado City, Ariz.: Benjamin Bistline, 1998.

Bloom, Harold. *The American Religion: The Emergence of the Post-Christian Nation.* New York: Simon & Schuster, 1992.

Bradlee, Ben Jr., and Dale Van Atta. *Prophet of Blood: The Untold Story of Ervil LeBaron and the Lambs of God.* New York: G. P. Putnam's Sons, 1981.

Bradley, Martha Sonntag. *Kidnapped from That Land: The Government Raids on the Short Creek Polygamists.* Salt Lake City: University of Utah Press, 1996.

Bringhurst, Newell G. *Brigham Young and the Expanding American Frontier.* Boston: Little, Brown and Co., 1986.

———. *Fawn McKay Brodie: A Biographer's Life.* Norman: University of Oklahoma Press, 1999.

———. *Saints, Slaves, and Blacks: The Changing Place of Black People Within Mormonism.* Westport: Greenwood Press, 1981.

———, ed. *Reconsidering* No Man Knows My History: *Fawn M. Brodie and Joseph Smith in Retrospect.* Logan: Utah State University Press, 1996.

Brodie, Fawn M. *The Devil Drives: A Life of Sir Richard Burton.* New York: W. W. Norton, 1967.

———. *No Man Knows My History: The Life of Joseph Smith, the Mormon Prophet.* 2nd ed. New York: Alfred A. Knopf, 1995.

Brooke, John L. *The Refiner's Fire: The Making of Mormon Cosmology, 1644–1844.* Cambridge: Cambridge University Press, 1994.

Brooks, Juanita. *Emma Lee.* Logan: Utah State University Press, 1984.

———. *John Doyle Lee: Zealot, Pioneer Builder, Scapegoat.* Logan: Utah State University Press, 1992.

———. *The Mountain Meadows Massacre.* Foreword and afterword by Jan Shipps. Norman: University of Oklahoma Press, 1991.

Burton, Richard F. *The City of the Saints and Across the Rocky Mountains to California.* Edited, with an introduction and notes, by Fawn M. Brodie. New York: Alfred A. Knopf, 1963.

Bush, Lester E. Jr. "A Peculiar People: The Physiological Aspects of Mormonism 1850–1975." *Dialogue: A Journal of Mormon Thought*, vol. 12, no. 3 (fall 1979).

Bushman, Claudia L., ed. *Mormon Sisters: Women in Early Utah.* Logan: Utah State University Press, 1997.

Bushman, Richard L. *Joseph Smith and the Beginnings of Mormonism*. Urbana: University of Illinois Press, 1984.

Campbell, Carolyn. "Fugitive Witness: Tom Green's Ex-wife Defends Her Decision to Let Her Daughter Marry Her Husband." *Salt Lake City Weekly*, February 22, 2001.

Card, Brigham Y., Herbert C. Northcott, John E. Foster, Howard Palmer, and George K. Jarvis, eds. *The Mormon Presence in Canada*. Edmonton: University of Alberta Press, 1990.

Church of Jesus Christ of Latter-day Saints. *"The Book of Mormon," "The Doctrine and Covenants," "The Pearl of Great Price."* One-volume edition. Salt Lake City: Church of Jesus Christ of Latter-day Saints, 1981.

Chynoweth, Rena, with Dean M. Shapiro. *The Blood Covenant*. Austin: Diamond Books, 1990.

Cleland, Robert Glass, and Juanita Brooks, eds. *A Mormon Chronicle: The Diaries of John D. Lee, 1848–1876*. 2 vols. San Marino, Calif.: Huntington Library, 1955.

Compton, Todd. *In Sacred Loneliness: The Plural Wives of Joseph Smith*. Salt Lake City: Signature Books, 1997.

Corbett, Pearson Harris. *Jacob Hamblin: The Peacemaker*. Salt Lake City: Deseret Book Co., 1952.

Crapanzano, Vincent. *Serving the Word: Literalism in America from the Pulpit to the Bench*. New York: New Press, 2000.

Crossfield, Robert (Onias). *The First Book of Commandments*. Salem, Utah: United Order Publications, 1998.

———. *The Second Book of Commandments*. Salem, Utah: United Order Publications, 1999.

Dellenbaugh, Frederick S. *A Canyon Voyage: The Narrative of the Second Powell Expedition down the Green-Colorado River from Wyoming, and the Explorations on Land, in the Years 1871 and 1872*. Tucson: University of Arizona Press, 1996.

"A Den of Treason: That's What John Taylor Made the Assembly Hall Last Sunday." *Salt Lake Daily Tribune*, January 6, 1880.

DeVoto, Bernard. *The Year of Decision: 1846*. Boston: Little, Brown and Co., 1943.

Dewey, Richard Lloyd, ed. *Jacob Hamblin: His Life in His Own Words*. New York: Paramount Books, 1995.

Dillard, Annie. *For the Time Being*. New York: Alfred A. Knopf, 1999.

———. *Holy the Firm*. New York: Harper & Row, 1977.

Dobyns, Henry F., and Robert C. Euler. "The Dunn-Howland Killings: Additional Insights." *Journal of Arizona History*, vol. 21 (spring 1980).

Dolnick, Edward. *Down the Great Unknown: John Wesley Powell's 1869 Journey of Discovery and Tragedy Through the Grand Canyon*. New York: HarperCollins, 2001.

Dougherty, John. "Polygamy in Arizona: The Wages of Sin." *Phoenix New Times*, April 10, 2003.

Durham, Michael S. *Desert Between the Mountains: Mormons, Miners, Padres, Mountain Men, and the Opening of the Great Basin, 1772–1869.* Norman: University of Oklahoma Press, 1999.

Egan, Timothy. *Lasso the Wind: Away to the New West.* New York: Vintage, 1999.

Embry, Jessie L. *Black Saints in a White Church: Contemporary African American Mormons.* Salt Lake City: Signature Books, 1994.

Ferguson, Charles W. *The Confusion of Tongues: A Review of Modern Isms.* Garden City, New York: Doubleday, Doran & Co., 1928.

Fielding, Robert Kent. *The Unsolicited Chronicler: An Account of the Gunnison Massacre, Its Causes and Consequences, Utah Territory, 1847–1859—a Narrative History.* Brookline, Mass.: Paradigm Publications, 1993.

————, ed. *The "Tribune" Reports of the Trials of John D. Lee for the Massacre at Mountain Meadows, November 1874–April 1877.* Higganum, Conn.: Kent's Books, 2000.

Fishman, Ted C. "Unholy Voices?" *Playboy,* vol. 39, no. 11 (November 1992).

Fundamentalist Church of Jesus Christ of Latter Day Saints. *The Four Hidden Revelations.* Salt Lake City: Fundamentalist Church of Jesus Christ of Latter Day Saints, n.d.

Gilmore, Mikal. *Shot in the Heart.* New York: Anchor, 1995.

Givens, Terryl L. *By the Hand of Mormon: The American Scripture That Launched a New World Religion.* New York: Oxford University Press, 2002.

Gottfredson, Peter. *Indian Depredations.* Salt Lake City: 1919.

Green, Arnold H., and Lawrence P. Goldrup. "Joseph Smith, an American Muhammad? An Essay on the Perils of Historical Analogy." *Dialogue: A Journal of Mormon Thought,* vol. 6, no. 1 (spring 1971).

Green, Tom. "Why We Talk to the Media." www.polygamy.com/Mormon/Why-We-Talk-To-The-Media.html.

Greene, Graham. *The End of the Affair.* New York: Viking, 1961.

Gunnison, Lieutenant J. W. *The Mormons, or Latter-Day Saints, in the Valley of the Great Salt Lake: A History of Their Rise and Progress, Peculiar Doctrines, Present Condition, and Prospects, Derived from Personal Observation, During a Residence Among Them.* Philadelphia: Lippincott, 1860. Reprint, Brookline, Mass.: Paradigm Publications, 1993.

Hallwas, John E., and Roger D. Launius, eds. *Cultures in Conflict: A Documentary History of the Mormon War in Illinois.* Logan: Utah State University Press, 1995.

Hardy, B. Carmon. *Solemn Covenant: The Mormon Polygamous Passage.* Urbana: University of Illinois Press, 1992.

Holzapfel, Richard Neitzel, and T. Jeffery Cottle. *Old Mormon Palmyra and New England: Historic Photographs and Guide.* Santa Ana, Calif.: Fieldbrook Productions, 1991.

Jacob, Udney Hay. *An Extract, from a Manuscript Entitled "The Peace Maker," or the*

Doctrines of the Millennium: Being a Treatise on Religion and Jurisprudence. Or a New System of Religion and Politicks. Nauvoo, Ill.: J. Smith, 1842.

James, William. *The Varieties of Religious Experience: A Study in Human Nature, Being the Gifford Lectures on Natural Religion Delivered at Edinburgh in 1901–1902.* New York: Modern Library, 1999.

Jeffs, Rulon. *History of Priesthood Succession in the Dispensation of the Fullness of Times, and Some Challenges to the One Man Rule. Also Includes Personal History of President Rulon Jeffs.* Hildale, Utah: Twin City Courier Press, 1997.

————. *Purity in the New and Everlasting Covenant of Marriage.* Sandy, Utah: President Rulon Jeffs, 1997.

————. *Sermons of President Rulon Jeffs*, Vols. 1–8. Hildale, Utah: Twin City Courier Press, 1996.

————, ed. *Sermons of President LeRoy S. Johnson*, Vols. 1–8. Hildale, Utah: Twin City Courier Press, 1997.

Jenkins, Philip. *Mystics and Messiahs: Cults and New Religions in American History.* New York: Oxford University Press, 2000.

Johnson, Luke. "History of Luke Johnson." *Deseret News*, May 19, 1858.

Kraut, Ogden. *John H. Koyle's Relief Mine.* Salt Lake City: Pioneer Press, 1978.

————. *Polygamy in the Bible.* Salt Lake City: Pioneer Press, 1983.

Larsen, Wesley P. "The 'Letter,' or Were the Powell Men Really Killed by Indians?" *Canyon Legacy*, no. 17 (spring 1993).

Larson, Stan. *Quest for the Gold Plates: Thomas Stuart Ferguson's Archaeological Search for the Book of Mormon.* New York: Oxford University Press, 1991.

Launius, Roger D., and John E. Hallwas, eds. *Kingdom on the Mississippi Revisited: Nauvoo in Mormon History.* Urbana: University of Illinois Press, 1996.

Launius, Roger D., and Linda Thatcher, eds. *Differing Visions: Dissenters in Mormon History.* Urbana: University of Illinois Press, 1994.

LeBaron, Garn Jr. "Mormon Fundamentalism and Violence: A Historical Analysis." www.exmormon.org.violence.html.

LeSueur, Stephen C. *The 1838 Mormon War in Missouri.* Columbia: University of Missouri Press, 1990.

Limerick, Patricia Nelson. *The Legacy of Conquest: The Unbroken Past of the American West.* New York: W. W. Norton, 1988.

Linden, Eugene. *The Future in Plain Sight: The Rise of the "True Believers" and Other Clues to the Coming Instability.* New York: Plume, 2002.

Lindsey, Robert. *A Gathering of Saints: A True Story of Money, Murder and Deceit.* New York: Simon & Schuster, 1988.

Mailer, Norman. *The Executioner's Song.* New York: Vintage, 1998.

Marston, Otis "Dock." "Separation Marks: Notes on the 'Worst Rapid' in the Grand Canyon." *Journal of Arizona History*, vol. 17 (spring 1976).

Menand, Louis. *The Metaphysical Club: A Story of Ideas in America.* New York: Farrar, Straus and Giroux, 2001.

Mitchell, Brian David. "The Book of Immanuel David Isaiah." www.sltrib.com/2003/Mar/03142003/Manifesto/book.pdf.

Mitchell, Sallie [Sarah Frances] Baker. "The Mountain Meadows Massacre—an Episode on the Road to Zion." *American Weekly*, September 1, 1940.

Moore, R. Laurence. *Religious Outsiders and the Making of Americans*. New York: Oxford University Press, 1987.

Morgan, Dale, ed. *Utah Historical Quarterly*, vol. 15 (1947). Special issue dedicated to various firsthand accounts of John Wesley Powell's Colorado River Expedition of 1869.

Mulder, William, and A. Russell Mortensen, eds. *Among the Mormons: Historic Accounts by Contemporary Observers*. Salt Lake City: Western Epics, 1994.

New Mormon Studies CD-ROM: A Comprehensive Resources Library. Salt Lake City: Smith Research Associates, 1998.

Nibley, Preston, ed. *Pioneer Stories*. Salt Lake City: Bookcraft, 1976.

O'Dea, Thomas F. *The Mormons*. Chicago: University of Chicago Press, 1957.

Olson, Kyle B. "Aum Shinrikyo: Once and Future Threat?" *Emerging Infectious Diseases*, vol. 5, no. 4 (July–August 1999).

Ostling, Richard N., and Joan K. Ostling. *Mormon America: The Power and the Promise*. San Francisco: HarperSanFrancisco, 1999.

Pagels, Elaine. *The Gnostic Gospels*. New York: Vintage Books, 1989.

Peterson, Levi S. "A Christian by Yearning: The Personal Spiritual Journey of a 'Backslider.' " *Sunstone*, vol. 12:5, issue 67 (September 1988).

———. *Juanita Brooks: Mormon Woman Historian*. Salt Lake City: University of Utah Press, 1996.

Powell, John Wesley. *The Exploration of the Colorado River and Its Canyons*. New York: Penguin, 1997.

Quinn, D. Michael. *Early Mormonism and the Magic World View*. Rev. and enl. ed. Salt Lake City: Signature Books, 1998.

———. "Jerald and Sandra Tanner's Distorted View of Mormonism: A Response to 'Mormonism—Shadow or Reality?' " www.lds-mormon.com/mo2.shtml.

———. "LDS Church Authority and New Plural Marriages, 1890–1904." *Dialogue: A Journal of Mormon Thought*, vol. 18, no. 1 (spring 1985).

———. *The Mormon Hierarchy: Extensions of Power*. Salt Lake City: Signature Books, 1997.

———. *The Mormon Hierarchy: Origins of Power*. Salt Lake City: Signature Books, 1994.

———. *On Being a Mormon Historian: A Lecture Before the BYU Student History Association, Fall 1981*. Salt Lake City: Utah Lighthouse Ministry, 1982.

———, ed. *The New Mormon History: Revisionist Essays on the Past*. Salt Lake City: Signature Books, 1992.

Reilly, P. T. *Lee's Ferry: From Mormon Crossing to National Park*. Logan: Utah State University Press, 1999.

Remini, Robert V. *Joseph Smith*. New York: Viking Penguin, 2002.

Rusho, W. L. *Lee's Ferry: Desert River Crossing*. Salt Lake City: Tower Productions, 1998.

Russell, Bertrand. *Why I Am Not a Christian, and Other Essays on Religion and Related Subjects*. New York: Touchstone, 1957.

Schindler, Harold. *Orrin Porter Rockwell: Man of God, Son of Thunder*. Salt Lake City: University of Utah Press, 1993.

Shipps, Jan. *Mormonism: The Story of a New Religious Tradition*. Urbana: University of Illinois Press, 1985.

Shipps, Jan, and John W. Welch, eds. *The Journals of William E. McLellin: 1831–1836*. Provo: BYU Studies, 1994.

Sillitoe, Linda, and Allen Roberts. *Salamander: The Story of the Mormon Forgery Murders*. 2nd ed. Salt Lake City: Signature Books, 1989.

Smith, George D., ed. *Faithful History: Essays on Writing Mormon History*. Salt Lake City: Signature Books, 1992.

———, ed. *An Intimate Chronicle: The Journals of William Clayton*. Salt Lake City: Signature Books, 1995.

Smith, Joseph, Jr. *History of the Church*. 7 vols. Salt Lake City: Desert News Press, 1932.

Sobel, Dava. *Galileo's Daughter: A Historical Memoir of Science, Faith, and Love*. New York: Penguin Books, 2000.

Stanton, Robert Brewster. *Colorado River Controversies*. New York: Dodd, Mead & Co., 1932.

Stegner, Wallace. *Beyond the Hundredth Meridian: John Wesley Powell and the Second Opening of the West*. New York: Penguin, 1992.

———. *Mormon Country*. Lincoln: University of Nebraska Press, 1981.

———, ed. *The Letters of Bernard DeVoto*. Garden City, New York: Doubleday, 1975.

Storr, Anthony. *Feet of Clay: Saints, Sinners, and Madmen—A Study of Gurus*. New York: Free Press, 1996.

Tanner, Jerald, and Sandra Tanner, eds. *Joseph Smith and Polygamy*. Salt Lake City: Utah Lighthouse Ministry, n.d.

———, eds. *3,913 Changes in the Book of Mormon: A Photo Reprint of the Original 1830 Edition of The Book of Mormon With the Changes Marked*. Salt Lake City: Utah Lighthouse Ministry, 1996.

Tate, Lucile C. *Boyd K. Packer: A Watchman on the Tower*. Salt Lake City: Bookcraft, 1995.

Taylor, John. *Items on Priesthood, Presented to the Latter-Day Saints*. Salt Lake City: Geo. Q. Cannon & Sons, 1899.

Teilhard de Chardin, Pierre. *Letters from a Traveller*. New York: Harper & Row, 1962.

Thomas, John L. *A Country in the Mind: Wallace Stegner, Bernard DeVoto, History, and the American Land*. New York: Routledge, 2000.

Turley, Richard E. *Victims: The LDS Church and the Mark Hofmann Case*. Urbana: University of Illinois Press, 1992.

Twain, Mark. *Roughing It*. New York: Penguin, 1985.

Updike, John. *Roger's Version*. New York: Alfred A. Knopf, 1987.

Ure, James W. *Leaving the Fold: Candid Conversations with Inactive Mormons*. Salt Lake City: Signature Books, 1999.

Van Wagoner, Richard S. *Mormon Polygamy: A History*. Salt Lake City: Signature Books, 1989.

Verdoia, Ken. "Interview with D. Michael Quinn." *Promontory*. www.kued.org/productions/promontory/interviews/quinn.html.

Waterman, Bryan, and Brian Kagel. *The Lord's University: Freedom and Authority at BYU*. Salt Lake City: Signature Books, 1988.

Waterman, Bryan, ed. *The Prophet Puzzle: Interpretive Essays on Joseph Smith*. Salt Lake City: Signature Books, 1999.

Westergren, Bruce N., ed. *From Historian to Dissident: The Book of John Whitmer*. Salt Lake City: Signature Books, 1995.

Williams, Brooke. *Halflives: Reconciling Work and Wildness*. Washington, D.C.: Island Press, 1999.

Williams, Terry Tempest. *Leap*. New York: Pantheon, 2000.

Wood, James. *The Broken Estate: Essays on Literature and Belief*. New York: Random House, 1999.

Worster, Donald. *A River Running West: The Life of John Wesley Powell*. New York: Oxford University Press, 2001.

Wright, Lawrence. "Lives of the Saints." *New Yorker*, January 21, 2002.

Jon Krakauer is the author of *Eiger Dreams, Into the Wild,* and *Into Thin Air* and is editor of the Modern Library Exploration series.